Contemporary Perspectives on Socialization and Social Development in Early Childhood Education

A volume in
Contemporary Perspectives in Early Childhood Education
Series Editors: Olivia N. Saracho and Bernard Spodek

Contemporary Perspectives in Early Childhood Education

Series Editors:
Olivia N. Saracho, *University of Maryland*,
Bernard Spodek, *University of Illinois*

Contemporary Perspectives on Socialization and Social Development in Early Childhood Education

Edited by

Olivia N. Saracho
and
Bernard Spodek

INFORMATION AGE
PUBLISHING

Charlotte, NC • www.infoagepub.com

Library of Congress Cataloging-in-Publication Data

Contemporary perspectives on socialization and social development
in early childhood education / edited by Bernard Spodek and
Olivia N. Saracho.
    p. cm. – (Contemporary perspectives in early childhood education)
  Includes bibliographical references.
  ISBN 978-1-59311-634-7 (hardcover) – ISBN 978-1-59311-633-0 (pbk.)
  1. Socialization. 2. Early childhood education–Social aspects. 3. Child
development. I. Spodek, Bernard. II. Saracho, Olivia N.
  LC192.4.C66 2007
  303.3'24–dc22

                                                            2007006593

Printed in the United States of America

CONSULTING EDITORS

CONTENTS

EXPLORATIONS IN SOCIAL DEVELOPMENT

The Theory Base

Olivia N. Saracho and Bernard Spodek

Social development refers to the process by which individuals develop the competencies needed to formally conduct themselves in conformity to social expectations. From birth, children have an enormous ability to develop appropriate behavior that has been established based on expected standards of their group. These expectations have existed for decades. For example, more than a half a century ago, Kluckhohn and Murray (1949) point out:

> Beginning in the nursery, the process of socialization continues throughout life. Among other things, what must be learned is: the power to inhibit, or to moderate, the expression of unacceptable needs; the ability to transfer cathexis from a prohibited goal-object to an acceptable substitute; the habitual and automatic use of a large number of approved action patterns (methods, manners, and emotional attitudes); and the ability to adapt to schedules (to do things at the proper time, keep appointments, etc.). It is assumed that, having acquired these abilities, the average person will be capable of establishing satisfactory interpersonal relations within the legal and conventional framework of society. When the child begins to behave in a predictable, expectable manner it is well on the road to being socialized. (p. 25)

Contemporary Perspectives on Socialization and Social Development..., pages ix–xix
Copyright © 2007 by Information Age Publishing

FUNCTIONS OF SOCIAL DEVELOPMENT

Social development allows children to incorporate two reciprocal functions instead of their becoming opposing life paths: *socialization* and *integration*. These functions compliment each other in contributing to the individual's growth and successful social adjustment. In socialization individuals learn to establish and maintain relationships with others, to become accepted by others, to get along with others, and to adapt their behavior to meet society's codes and standards. Integration refers to the functions individuals use to be accepted as members of society. Through their life, children encounter a variety of thrusts toward socialization and integration into society (Damon, 2006).

Socialization is an important process. Emotions, attitudes, interests, and values affect the children's relationships in their social development. Children grow, mature, and develop physical, emotional, and attitudinal behaviors parallel their social functioning and character. The socialization process is composed of three components. These components may be isolated and different, but they function together during the socialization process.

1. *Learn expected social behavior.* Social groups have established appropriate social behavior standards. Children need to know these expected social behaviors.
2. *Assume appropriate social roles.* Social groups have defined expected patterns of appropriate social behavior for each social group including gender, parents, children, teachers, and students.
3. *Develop acceptable social attitudes.* Children are friendly, like others, have favorable attitudes toward others, and enjoy social activities.

Few children have mastered all three components nor have some adults. Those who want social approval, conform to the social group's expectations. Some may conceal inappropriate thoughts and feelings. For example, they might seem interested in a boring conversation, discuss only acceptable topics, and show sympathy when someone they dislike gets hurt.

Children's social development is influenced by a series of group memberships, which begin in the family and continuously expand. A comfortable family environment promotes the development of social skills. When family members are consistent with their values, children discover a harmony between what the parents teach and their behavior. Parents who are accepting during infancy facilitate the children's relationships with their peers.

Slowly children become interested in those individuals around them. They take pleasure in watching other children. When the family has been responsive to them, they expect friendly relationships and enjoy social interactions. At the age of two years, children typically play well with older children. They enjoy watching others, but they still have not learned to play with children their own age. This is a period of parallel play. Children of this age can be together and may exchange toys, but they each play with their own toys.

Mildred Parten (1932) identified a series of stages in children's social play. Three-year-old children were either *unoccupied* (they did not play), *solitary players* (playing alone), or *onlookers* (observing the play of other children). Four-year-old children participated in *parallel play* (playing side-by-side with others), and five-year-olds participated in *associative* or *cooperative play* (playing with other children). She considered parallel play to be a bridge between solitary play and cooperative play, permitting children to adapt to social situations in play. Parten proposed that onlooker and solitary play indicated that children were immature, while cooperative play suggested more maturity. Current studies show that both older and younger children engage in solitary play. In addition, they have identified different levels of participation. For example, Saracho (1999) shows that children's play behaviors consist of

1. *Frequency of play* suggests that children display play behaviors in all of the areas (e.g., sociodramatic play, block play, manipulative play, and physical play).
2. *Communication of ideas* suggests that children communicate ideas in their play.
3. *Socialization levels* suggest that children exhibit several socialization levels (e.g., cooperative play, parallel play, solitary play).

Although some contemporary researchers have challenged Parten's stages of social play, her stages are considered universal and are used by many.

Play helps the children explore and understand role dimensions and interaction patterns, thereby helping them understand their social world and develop a realistic sense of *self*. It assumes an essential socializing role. George Herbert Mead (1934) advocated that children use play to develop their concept of *self* (who they are) by assuming a variety of roles in dramatic play. During play young children encounter a variety of play experiences. Important factors in young children's play include: (a) imitative experiences, (b) communication of ideas, (c) concrete objects, and (d) parallel/associative levels of socialization in young children's social play (Saracho, 2001) as well as play activities in the discussion of ideas, sociodramatic play behaviors, and physical action play. These factors suggest the importance of discussing ideas, engaging in sociodramatic play, and using actions in their play activities and support the patterns in children's play in their cognitive, social, and emotional development (Saracho & Spodek, 1998).

Play promotes young children's understanding of their world and their development of learning constructs (e.g., cognitive, creative, language, social, physical). In addition, several domains are integrated within the socialization process. When children play, they encounter social situations where they collaborate, help, share, and resolve social problems (Saracho, 1986). These social behaviors require children to think, consider their peers' points of view, assess patterns, develop social abilities, and learn to establish rapport with others. These behaviors help young children to become social individuals and to be able to interact with others. When children interact with others, they learn to carry on a conversation, create emotional ties, become a participating member of different groups at home, in the neighborhood, and at school. For example, a newborn is immediately assigned the status of son or daughter in a family. When children enter an early childhood program (e.g., preschool or kindergarten program), they assume a different status in that setting. They need to become acceptable playmates in the classroom and neighborhood. They continue this type of role changes throughout their life. As children become socialized, they discover different expectations in each of these settings as well as at different ages. The children's socialization process becomes more demanding with age, adjusting standards of knowledge, understanding emotion, and performance (Damon, 2006).

Social agents assume the responsibility for children's socialization processes. The primary social agents include the family, school, church, peer groups, and, recently, television. The contribution of these socialization agents differ, although there is some overlap. Nevertheless, they prepare children to become a successful member of the society into which they were born. In addition, the family's social class and ethnic group contribute to the socialization agent's role (Damon, 2006). The purpose of this volume is to present a selection of chapters that reflect current issues relating to children's socialization processes that help them become successful members of their society.

From birth children are unique in their rates of growth and development, including the development of their social awareness and their ability to interact socially. They interpret social events based on their developing life style and environmental experiences. The children's socialization is influenced by several important social forces including the family and its organization, their peer group, and the significant others in their lives. In "Theories of Socialization and Social Development," Olivia Saracho and Bernard Spodek describe the children's socialization forces and the different developmental theories that have influenced our understanding of the socialization process. These include maturationist theory (developed by Arnold Gesell), constructivist theories (developed by such theorists as Jean Piaget, Lev S. Vygotsky, and Jerome Bruner), psychodynamic theories (developed by such theorists as Sigmund Freud, Erik Erikson, Harry Stack Sullivan, and Alfred Adler), and ecological theory (developed by Urie Bronfenbrenner). Each theory provides interpretations of the meaning of the children's social development and describes the different characteristics for each age group in the developmental sequences.

Young children's social competence does not develop as an isolated skill; rather, it is closely tied to cognitive, emotional, and humor development. Children's humor can be both an important means for assessing their social competence and a vehicle through which such competence can be increased. Many other social skills are enhanced, such as the ability to understand humorous incongruity. For example, the ability to understand what others are thinking (Theory of Mind), may be related to what they are feeling (empathy), and how they evaluate what types of discourse are appropriate in various social contexts (metacommunication). These are all aspects of social competence that humor can facilitate in the early childhood years. In her chapter titled, "Humor as a Facilitator of Social Competence in Early Childhood," Doris Bergen explores the meanings humor can have in social contexts, the ways humor develops, the social interactions that foster its development, and its role in helping children deal with bullying and other challenging social interactions. A sense of humor can be a social coping mechanism that is useful throughout life. Its development during the early childhood years can be an important aspect of social competence.

In the next chapter, "Attachment in the Preschool Years: Implications for Social Learning," Gary Creasey and Patricia A. Jarvis suggest that contemporary attachment theory provides an important framework to consider for preschool social learning and behavioral/emotional adjustment. They begin their chapter with an overview of attachment theory and how the operation, structure, and content of attachment functioning undergo important transformations during the preschool years. Next, they discuss the importance of preschool attachment functioning and its relationship to a variety of competencies that may inhibit or facilitate social learning. Theory and research are then presented concerning the role of principal attachment figures in the development and maintenance of attachment functioning in preschoolers. Finally, they offer implications of the emerging work in this field and discuss the relevance of attachment theory and research to the broader educational context.

In "Feeling, Thinking, and Playing: Social and Emotional Learning in Early Childhood," Christopher J. Trentacosta and Carroll E. Izard describe social and emotional learning (SEL) in early childhood education. Their chapter begins by describing SEL in the framework of differential emotions theory. They present emotional knowledge, emotional regulation, and social skills as essential elements of SEL. They discuss important contextual factors in the early childhood education environment that can promote these SEL skills such as pretend play and teacher–child relationships. Trentacosta and Izard discuss studies that examine outcomes of SEL during early childhood, paying special attention to the effects of social skills and emotional competence during the transition to kindergarten and elementary school. They also provide an overview of some prevention and intervention programs for young children that have empirical support. Their chapter concludes with future directions for research in this area as well as new directions for the practical application of SEL in the early childhood classroom.

A full understanding of learning and cognitive development in childhood requires examination of the social context in which this development occurs. In "Cognitive Development in Social Context and Its Implications for Early Childhood Education," Mary Gauvain discusses cognitive development as an emergent property of social experience. The social context of cognitive development provides the core activities through which children are exposed to and learn about thinking. Her chapter describes how the requirements of early human development establish conditions for cognitive development as a social process. Gauvain then discusses the sociocultural approach to cognitive development, which considers the social context as a key component of cognitive development. The contribution of social experience to cognitive development and its relation to young children's experience in educational settings is illustrated with research on the development of attention, memory, and problem solving.

A number of researchers and practitioners have found that self-concept is a major source of intrinsic motivation (e.g., Skaalvik & Skaalvik, 2005). In early childhood education, intrinsic motivation typically takes place in children's play, a fact that underscores its potential for learning (Lillemyr, 2001). The importance of self-concept for intrinsic motivation is one reason why competence is now suggested as a main concept in the field of motivation instead of achievement, not the least because perceptions of competence are closely tied to the concept of competence. Therefore, competence motivation is proposed as the relevant term rather than achievement motivation (Elliot & Dweck, 2005). For some years now it has been argued with increasing strength that social aspects of motivation play a major role in children's learning and academic performance. The chapter by Ole Fredrik Lillemyr titled, "Social Learning through Social Motivation," suggests that for social learning to take place, social motivation is often needed, especially intrinsic motivation. He argues that self-concept constitutes a major source of intrinsic motivation. Intrinsically motivated behaviors are those whose motivation is based in the inherent interest or internal satisfaction of the behaviors per se, rather than being contingent on some sort of reward, praise or external consequence. In early childhood education intrinsic motivation typically takes place in children's play, which underscores its potential for learning, social learning in particular.

Recent motivation theories argue that social aspects of motivation play a major role for children's learning and academic performance. It is fundamental to pursue social goals in early childhood education, for several reasons. While social goals have an importance of their own, social goals also promote learning in general. While the field of motivation has much to offer in this concern, research in the field of early childhood education has paid little attention to the inclusion of motivational components, and the field of motivation seldom has focused early childhood education. An integration of these two fields is suggested in future research, more precisely a social learning through social motivation approach.

In the next chapter, "Social Learning in the Peer Context," Gary W. Ladd appraises what is known about social learning in the peer context during early and middle childhood by examining relevant theory and pertinent empirical evidence. He addresses his aim by considering some of the foundational premises that have guided research on early social learning in the peer context, and by reviewing evidence that addresses three principal questions: (a) "When does peer social learning begin?" (b) "How does social learning occur in the peer context?" and, (c) "What do young children learn from peers"? From the theory and evidence that was assembled for this purpose, he infers that: (a) multiple processes are responsible for children's learning within the peer context, (b) many of these processes are present in children's peer relations even during the earliest stages of child development, and (c) the forms of social learning that occur in peer contexts are associated with many aspects of children's development.

In "Friendships in Very Young Children," Barbara Davis Goldman and Virginia Buysse present evidence of the existence of friendships in typically developing children under three years of age. The existence of such friendships, especially in the second year of life, is finally beginning to be acknowledged more broadly in reviews of the peer interaction and relationship literature, but such acknowledgement is not universal. Though the reported frequency varies, the similarity of the descriptive evidence of early friendships in diverse times, places, and childrearing contexts is striking. Although early friendships are manifest in playful activities and game-like interactions, there is also evidence that these friendships are more than fun and games. They can provide emotional and instrumental support for young children, just as friendships do for more mature individuals. They also can serve as a supportive context for further development. Preschoolers with disabilities (who may be developmentally similar to typically developing toddlers) can also participate in friendships, though those friendships may be less frequent, and most likely to occur in inclusive early care and education programs. Both emergent and developed friendships are possible for the very young, and for some, a meaningful friendship is a central part of their social life.

Much research on bullying has been done on students between the ages of 12–18, and has focused on the individual bully or victim (Olweus, 1993). In the United States, the *Indicators of School Crime and Safety Report* (2005), indicates that the younger the child, the higher his or her chances are for being bullied. Therefore, it is critical that early childhood educators confront the issue of bullying. This analysis adds to the literature in early childhood bullying by identifying, then adapting, the research gap in adolescent bullying research to make it applicable to younger aged children. Vickie E. Lake's chapter, "Confronting Issues of Bullying: Implications for Early Childhood Education," explores the role that peers play in promoting bullying and victimization by either (a) ignoring and supporting the aggressor, or defending themselves from the aggressor, and (b) failing to intervene to stop the victimization because of a lack of verbal scripts and/or social skills training.

The chapter that follows, "The Development of Ethnic Prejudice in Early Childhood: Theories and Research," by Drew Nesdale discusses how researchers have been interested in the development of children's ethnic prejudice for more than 75 years. The author briefly evaluates three of the main theoretical explanations for children's prejudice, including emotional maladjustment, social reflection, and cognitive development. Nesdale concludes that none of the explanations provide a comprehensive account of the development of children's prejudice, encompassing within it all of the available research findings. A new approach to children's ethnic prejudice, social identity development theory (SIDT) (Nesdale, 2004), is outlined and the results of studies using this research paradigm are described. Thus far, SIDT provides a good account of the extant findings, and has received consistent support in more recent research. Drawing on SIDT, it is proposed that interventions designed to reduce ethnic prejudice should emphasize five critical elements, including enhancing children's category awareness, individual differentiation, intercultural contact, and emotional empathy, as well as the development of zero tolerance coalitions involving children, parents, and teachers.

According to the social-learning model, individuals learn new behaviors by observing others and by developing expectations of consequences. Children's food intake and physical activity are influenced by availability and accessibility of opportunities, as well as by their role models—learning through observation of parents, peers, or the media. Moria Golan, in the third chapter titled "Social Learning and Weight-Related Problems," discusses the multiple factors that are related to the high incidence of weight-related problems in early childhood. She identifies the environmental factors that encourage the consumption of greater food energy than is required, as well as those that encourage sedentary behavior, or that discourage physical activity, and affect how dietary intake patterns are established in early childhood. These may ultimately influence the development of obesity. Her chapter discusses the impact of the child's social environment on the etiology and management of weight related problems, which are most relevant in early childhood education.

In "Morality and Gender in Preschool: Children's Moral Contracts," Eva Johansson discusses the children's morality in relation to gender, that is, culturally grounded expectations regarding how to behave towards others "as a girl" or "as a boy" in preschool. Educational research on gender and children's morality is first discussed. This is followed by an analysis of daily interactions between Swedish preschool children in which there is evidence for a moral contract in the manner in which children relate to each other. The manner in which gender impacts on these contracts is also examined. Her analysis suggests that the children, irrespective of gender, defend values such as rights, justice and the wellbeing of others. She shows that children sometimes vary in the strategies that they use to give expression to or defend values. She believes that gender is important as one of several factors, including children's intentions and the meaning that they assign to the interactions in which they are involved. The challenge for teachers is to become aware of the complex understandings that children may hold about morality and use these understandings to analyze and interpret children's moral behaviors and intentions in order to uncover the own stereotypical expectations about young children's capacities to make moral judgments.

Children's social behaviors are developmental and change throughout infancy, the preschool years, and the school years as well as throughout their life. In their social development, children generate behavior that is socially expected of them. They acquire the ability to draw desirable social behaviors and preclude negative ones across a variety of social contexts. Thus, social development is the children's inborn potential to develop social behavior that meets the standards of a group, which makes them socially competent. In the final chapter, "Developmental Perspectives of Social Development," Olivia Saracho and Bernard Spodek discuss social competence, social interactions, and stages of social behaviors, social contexts (e.g., family, neighborhood, community, and school), social interventions, and future perspectives in social development. Perspective researchers in social development may include a variety of results and components, which may lead to redefining the term social development. Its definition may become more broad and incorporate early social skills and competencies in a variety of contexts and social networks to promote academic achievement and reduce the children's risk factors. Interventions can be expanded to promote the children's social development in a variety of contexts, include the children's social networks, focus on multiple indicators of the children's adjustment, and promote their social competence across developmental contexts (Stormashak & Welsh, 2005).

CONCLUDING REMARKS

Social development can be defined and described in a variety of ways, but its importance relates to the social competence and relationships of young children. Developmental changes in peer groups changes the children's loyalty beyond their family to significant others and motivate them to cope with new relationships. Within these new and more complex relationships, they need a variety of social skills. Social development assumes a major role in determining the quality of the children's social relationships. This influence is bidirectional in that relationships with others provides them with opportunities to improve their social competence.

REFERENCES

Damon, W. (2006). Socialization and individualization. In G. Handel (Ed.), *Childhood socialization* (pp. 3–9). New Brunswick: Aldine Transaction.

Elliot, A.J., & Dweck, C. S. (2005). Competence and motivation: Competence as the core of achievement motivation. In A. J. Elliot & C. S. Dweck (Eds.), *Handbook of competence and motivation* (pp. 3–12). New York: Guilford.

Indicators of School Crime and Safety. (2005). National Center of Educational Statistics. U.S. Department of Education. NCES 2006-001.

Kluckhohn, C., & Murray, H. A. (1949). *Personality in nature, society, and culture.* New York: Alfred A. Knopf.

Lillemyr, O. F. (2001) Play and learning in school: A motivational approach. In D. M. McInerney, & S. Van Etten (Eds.), *Research on socio-cultural influences on motivation and learning* (pp. 363–385). Greenwich, CT: Information Age Publishing.

Mead, G. H. (1934). *Mind, self, and society.* Chicago: University of Chicago Press.

Nesdale, D. (2004). Social identity processes and children's ethnic prejudices. In M. Bennett & F. Sani (Eds.), *The development of the social self* (pp. 219–245). East Sussex: Psychology Press.

Olweus, D. (2003). A profile of bullying at school. *Educational Leadership, 6*(6), 12–17.

Prte, M. B. (1932). Social participation among preschool children. *Journal of Abnormal and Social Psychology, 27,* 243–269.

Skaalvik, E. M., & Skaalvik, S. (2005). *Skolen som laeringsarena. Selvoppfatning, motivasjon og laering* [The school as learning arena: Self-concept, motivation and learning]. Oslo: Universitetsforlaget (University Press Ltd).

Saracho, O.N. (1986). Play and young children's learning. In B. Spodek (Ed.), *Today's kindergarten: Exploring the knowledge base, expanding the curriculum* (pp. 91–109). New York: Teachers College Press.

Saracho, O. N. (1999). A factor analysis of preschool children's play strategies and cognitive style. *Educational Psychology, 19*(2), 165–180.

Saracho, O. N. (2001). Factors in three- to five-year-old children's play. *Play and Culture Studies, 3*, 401–416.

Saracho, O. N., & Spodek, B. (1998). Preschool children's cognitive play: A factor analysis. *International Journal of Early Childhood Education, 3*, 67–76.

CHAPTER 1

THEORIES OF SOCIALIZATION AND SOCIAL DEVELOPMENT

Olivia N. Saracho and Bernard Spodek

Right from their moment of birth, children are unique in their rate of growth and development, as well as in their social awareness and ability to interact socially. Characteristics for each age group have been identified, but these are only norms that indicate expected developmental sequences. However, there is a range of individual differences among children.

Newborn infants are aware of their needs and use their activity level to make these needs known. As they mature, they develop other ways to make their needs known. They also become aware of both their physical and social environment. Interactions between mothers and children are important for social development as adequate mothering satisfies children's social and emotional needs.

SOCIALIZATION FORCES

Children's socialization is influenced by several important social forces such as those found in the family, the peer group, and among significant others. Each is discussed separately here.

The Family Context

Children are first influenced by their early exposure at home with their family. Each family reflects an ethnic background, a series of relationships, educational attitude, and a social status. Each family also establishes definite rituals, habits, and attitudes. The family is the child's first and most important socializing agency. An emotional attachment to family is essential in the development of all relationships in life. Within the family environment, children begin to understand and build relationships and interactions among all the family members.

Children's experiences within the family ultimately give them a feeling that the primary group accepts or rejects them. Children may develop an unhealthy personality when they experience feelings of rejection. They may become aggressive, attention-getting, hostile, hyperactive, jealous, or rebellious. If this happens, the children can use one or many attention-getting mechanisms, not all of which are positive. Parents can help children acquire a healthy personality by creating an environment of acceptance through love and encouragement. The family can establish a set of standards and provide security for the emerging child. Children need to have opportunities to assume responsibilities and make choices as early as they can handle these. They may experience the natural consequences of bad choices and learn from them as long as the family provides them with support. If the children are independent from adults and experience the consequences of their behavior, they will ultimately be able to deal with the realities of their social world.

Peer Group Affiliates

Achieving the highest level of social development depends on the children's ability to meet their social needs to have more intense social contacts with friends. As they mature, children make a transition from affiliation with family members to affiliations with peers. Peers assume an increasingly important role in the children's social development. The children's peer groups represent a unique society that helps them make the transition to adult status. Becoming an equal member of the peer group becomes a basic need.

Peer groups are important disciplinary agents who monitor how the children conform to the social expectations of the group. When children interact within peer groups, they experience workshops of human relationships. In these situations, children first encounter children from different backgrounds. They learn to accept, work with, and cooperate with those who possess different opinions and beliefs. They also feel a new kind of security and belonging. The children's transfer of loyalty from the family to the peer group contributes to a later development of loyalty to society. Peers also contribute to the children's self-concept when they provide them with feedback about who they are and the type of behavior that will be accepted or rejected in their peer group.

Originally the peer groups may emerge from the children's immediate neighborhood. As children have contact with the world outside their family, various larger, more remote peer groups appear. At this time, children select their peer group based on their interests and social status needs. The peer groups' contribution is crucial, because it prepares the children to succeed in several give-and-take relationships. If children want to belong to a peer group, they need to conform to the peer group's expectations, follow its standards, maintain its secrets, and meet its expectations.

The Role of Significant Others

Children identify and have contact with many individuals who are important to them. These individuals differ based on the range of the children's experiences. They may be the parents, siblings, older children in the neighborhood, or leaders of a child's group. Initially, children learn social behavior from the family constellation. Later they meet individuals outside their family and encounter a variety of experiences and learn different social behaviors. As others approve, accept, or reject them, children identify and learn different social roles. For example, when children play, they attach specific meaning to their experiences. As the children mature, they usually identify and imitate those individuals who are important to the children. This is another way that children identify and formulate social values and attitudes.

Acculturation Thrusts

Socializing forces (e.g., family, family constellation, peer group, significant others) influence the children's social development. These social forces help them develop their ability to give or receive attention and affection. The similarity in expectations in the family, family constellation, and peer groups can facilitate the children's socialization process. In contrast, different expectations among these socialization forces can create a conflict in values and standards and the socialization process can become unpredictable. In any case, the children's perceptions and experiences are the guiding force in the children's socialization process. Children develop their social behaviors based on their perceptions, beliefs, and convictions.

SOCIALIZATION THEORIES

Several developmental theories have influenced our understanding of the socialization process. These include maturationist theory (developed by Arnold Gesell), constructivist theories (developed by such theorists as Jean Piaget, Lev S. Vygotsky, and Jerome Bruner) and psychodynamic theories (developed by such theorists as Sigmund Freud, Erik Erikson, Harry Stack Sullivan, and Alfred Adler), and ecological theory (developed by Urie Bronfenbrenner). Each theory provides interpretations on the meaning of the children's social development.

Maturationist Theory

Maturation theory suggests that human development is mainly genetically determined with the environment having a minimum influence. Although negative environmental conditions can prevent the emergence of natural developmental patterns, this theory indicates that the patterns continue their course. Thus, children's maturation is an unfolding process. Specific attempts to create desired behaviors before their natural manifestation should be avoided, because such forcing may be detrimental. Children who are coerced to function at a higher level than their natural stage may develop inadequately and may have a negative effect on their sense of worth and self-confidence. Intervention, however, may take place if the children's expected maturation patterns fail to develop. According to Murray Thomas (2004), an intervention can occur if (1) the characteristic is unacceptable, (2) the children's maturational ability allows movement to an advanced stage, and (3) the constituents in the children's environment neglect to "naturally" modify the unaccepted characteristic.

Arnold Gesell (1880–1961) was the psychologist who contributed most to the maturationist view of children's social development. He observed and described in detail infants and children from birth through age ten in different domains, including social development. He generated norms according to ages for these children, which he considered to be representative of their normal development. Gesell posited that forces within the organism that unfold with age determine children's development. He felt that the environment was a less important element in modifying their development. Gesell recognized that children have their own developmental pattern and need to develop at their own pace. He believed that educational environments need to support the children's development, needs, and interests, following the individual children's developmental patterns.

Psychodynamic Theories

Psychodynamic theory focuses on personality, which is a major aspect of children's social development. Although psychoanalysis relates to the adults' personality problems, it helps one understand how childhood experiences contributed to adult personalities. Since it provides important insights concerning childhood, it was added to the study of child development. The theorists that contributed to the children's personality include Sigmund Freud, Erik Erikson, Harry Stack Sullivan, and Alfred Adler.

Sigmund Freud (1856–1939) was the pioneer of psychoanalysis, where patients explore their past history and their present situation. He used a variety of techniques to help patients face their fears and struggles. Freud's theory of development identifies a series of psychosexual stages. Freud considered these stages of psychosexual development to be universal. He believed that they reflect developmental human needs that are embedded in all cultures. Individuals need to successfully evolve through these stages to develop a healthy personality. However, if individuals become fixated at a certain stage, they would have to cope with needs from an earlier developmental period even though they are mature adults, possibly making their behavior seem irrational.

Freud's psychoanalytic theory extensively influenced the thinking of psychologists, psychiatrist, and psychoanalysts. Though he focused on the adults' childhood experiences, his theory stressed the importance of early childhood experiences in the individual's personality development. Freud's contribution to child development has motivated several psychologists and social workers to accept several elements of Freudian theory, even though they might not accept the entire psychoanalytic theory. Freud influenced others throughout Europe and the United States. Other psychoanalysts studied psychoanalytic theory, modified it, and searched for cultural influences. Eric Erikson was one of these psychoanalysts.

Erik Erikson (1902–1994) broadened Freud's thoughts on personality development, altering Freud's psychosexual stages into a set of psychosocial stages, where each stage is associated to the ego's effectiveness initiating its form at birth and continues throughout development (Erikson, 1963). He assumed that individuals evolve throughout their lives through interactions within their social environment. Each of Erikson's stages develops throughout an individual's life (Erikson, 1968) and each has a distinguishing critical conflict related to it. Individuals need to resolve the conflict before proceeding to the next stage.

One major difference between Freud's and Erikson's stages of development is that Freud believed that development terminates by the end of adolescence, whereas Erikson believed that development continues throughout the individuals' life. He based his stages (Table 1.1) on a series

Table 1.1.   Erikson's Stages of Psychosocial Development

Age	Stage	Characteristics
0–1½ years	trust vs. mistrust	Reliance on caregiver, predictability leads to trust in environment, or lack of care leads to basic mistrust.
1½–3 years	autonomy vs. shame and doubt	Environment encourages independence, pride and sense of self-worth, or doubt and lack of self-esteem result from overt-control.
3–6 years	initiative vs. guilt	Ability to learn and to enjoy mastery; or fear of failure and of punishment leads to guilt.
6 years–puberty	industry vs. inferiority	Valuing work, skill, and competence; or feelings of inadequacy and inferiority.
Adolescence	identity vs. role confusion	Development of individuality; or confusion related to self.
Young adulthood	intimacy vs. isolation	Commitment to personal reactions; or withdrawal from others and self-absorption.
Middle age	generativity vs. stagnation	Care of next generation, widening interests; or self-indulgence.
Old age ego	identity vs. despair	Gaining the meaning of one's existence or disappointment with life and fear of death.

From Spodek, B., & Saracho, O. N. (1994). *Right from the start: Teaching children ages three to eight.* Boston: Allyn & Bacon.

of social conflicts in which all individuals need to become successfully proficient to reach maturity (Erikson, 1982). The individuals' culture and historical reference point affects those conflicts.

Harry Stack Sullivan's (1892–1949) stages of development also differed from Freud's. His stages were based on the interpersonal relationships in which individuals experience as they strive for confidence (Sullivan, 1953). These stages are presented in Table 1.2.

Many views on social development are based on Sullivan's (1953) theory of friendship. He suggested that individuals experience different developmental stages where they have precise interpersonal needs and have different kinds of relationships with different needs at each stage. Individuals must acquire the social skills and competencies for successful social interactions within the context of these relationships. Researchers have identified several approaches as they examined different populations, cultural groups, and age groups. The concern for social interest in Sullivan's theory is similar to the development of social interest in Adlerian psychology (Savage, & Nicholl, 2003; Seligman, 2006).

Alfred Adler's (1870–1937) observation that "human beings live in the realm of meanings" reflects the social constructivist view of human behav-

Table 1.2. Sullivan's Stages of Social Development

Age	Stage	Characteristics
Infancy	Empathetic relationship with "mothering" individuals	Infants respond to the significant adults about them. They reflect the parents' mood. For example, an anxious parent may have an anxious, crying infant. Infants are in a state of equilibrium and need their parents' approval. When infants can distinguish between the others and their own bodily limitations, they also develop the need for confidence.
Childhood	Relationship with peers	Children develop the need for playmates, especially their own age group. They have the motor and language skills to move and interact more freely. They also learn that language is a means of communication and become aware about the dimensions of their culture.
Juvenile Era	Determine their own status and identify the self	This stage relates to the children's entry into school and continues through most of their grammar-school years. Children are beginning to separate themselves from other entities and identify the self. They are surrounded by peers and meet significant adults other than their parents. They begin to objectively analyze themselves, becoming internal critics who test their impulses. Since the internal critic reflects the assessments by significant adults, it may be compared to the superego. Attitudes of competition, rivalry, and ultimately a realistic compromise start to emerge.
Preadolescence	Strong interest toward another person	An extremely essential but chronologically condensed interval that psychologically or psychiatrically terminates with the individuals' strong interest for another individual. Thus, the preadolescents make a transition from egocentric achievements and begin to need approval and satisfactions of significant others. They become capable of a more mature love that goes beyond the pursuit of their own security. Their concern for others may be conveyed toward a friend of the same sex with a similar pattern of behavior as their own.
Adolescence	Interest toward a person of the opposite sex	Adolescents transfer their interest from an individual of the same sex to one of the opposite sex. Thus, they need to must come to terms with the sex drive. Society's attitudes toward sex usually forces adolescents to encounter new difficulties in integrating their personality.
Late Adolescence	Personality development	The individual's personality continues to develop into their appropriate relationship.
Adulthood	Intimacy with another person	Individuals establish a love relationship with a significant person. This may be a very intimate relationship with another individual, which becomes their major source of satisfaction in life.

ior. Alfred Adler strongly advocated the importance of understanding individuals within their social context. He believed that everybody has the basic desire and goal to belong and feel important. Adlerian theory has been important in the children's growth and development. Adlerians assume that "a misbehaving child is a discouraged child" and that the most effective strategy in coping with difficult children's behaviors is to help them feel valued, significant, and competent. They are interested in understanding the specific and private beliefs and strategies that each individual produces in childhood. This cognitive schema and personal life style become the individuals' reference for attitudes, behaviors, and one's private view of self, others, and the world. For healing, growth, and change to occur, individuals need to examine their early life experiences, the continuous behavior patterns, and the methods that individuals use to acquire significance and belonging (Savage & Nicholl, 2003; Seligman, 2006).

As articulated by noted Adlerian psychotherapist Henry Stein, the theory and application of Adlerian Psychology have as their lynchpins seven critical ideas. According to Stein (2003), in psychotherapy the progressive development of the feeling of community usually involves the organization of cognitive, affective, and behavioral strategies. Henry T. Stein (2003), of the Alfred Adler Institute of Northwestern Washington, developed the following *Developmental Sequence of The Feeling of Community* (See Table 1.3), which was based on concepts originally developed by Heinz Ansbacher, who was one of the world's leading experts on Adlerian psychology.

Children's personality development begins in infancy. Infants become conscious of inadequacies in everyday tasks as compared to older children and adults. Adler attributed this consciousness to inferiority feelings, where children become aware of their limitations. However, these feelings motivate individuals to strive in a direction where they develop, strive, achieve, and seek for success to compensate for their defeats. According to Adler, individuals sometimes use both reality and fiction to guide their actions, which they believe are true. Therefore, Adler established a final goal: a fictional perception of individuals in which they visualized an idealistic situation of perfection, completion, or overcoming. Individuals strive toward the final goal to overcome their feelings of inferiority. While this final goal symbolizes a subjective, fictional perception of the future; it motivates the individuals toward the future.

Constructivist Theory

Constructivist theory offers a philosophical resolution to the confrontation between rationalism and empiricism. Both of these perspectives provide an understanding of how individuals learn about the world. They

Table 1.3.   Stein's Developmental Sequence of the Feeling of Community

Sequence		Characteristics
Aptitude	**Potential**	The feeling of community is an innate potential that has to be consciously developed by training into skill and ability. It is innately so small that it must benefit from social understanding to develop. After becoming an ability, it may then acquire secondary dynamic characteristics of attitude and motivation.
Ability	**Behavioral**	Behavioral capacities include: making contact with others; relating to others in a useful way; and contributing to the common welfare. The ability to cooperate depends on the degree of the feeling of community.
	Intellectual	Intellectual capacities include: understanding others' point of view and needs; accepting common sense over private logic; recognizing the inter-dependency of people; appreciating the contributions of others; and reasoning with view of immediate and future social consequences.
	Emotional	Emotional capacities include: empathy for others (to see with their eyes, to hear with their ears, to feel with their hearts); feeling connected to others; and the ability to feel and express acceptance, liking, and love for others.
Style of Life	**Attitudinal**	Attitudinal capacities include: feeling at home on the earth; a sense of harmony with the universe; a deep identification with others; a letting go of a preoccupation with self; and a profound feeling of belonging and embeddedness in social evolution.
	Motivational	Motivational capacities include: sustaining an active, creative, and generous interest in the welfare of others; contributing significantly to the community; and making unconditional, ongoing, spontaneous, positive social effort. The feeling of community is not manifest as mere conformity; it implies a constant striving for improvement and correction toward an ideal community for all people. The feeling of community, as a value, can be adopted as the individual's primary meta-motivation. From an Adlerian viewpoint, genuine ethics are a result of a very high level of the feeling of community, and are a reflection of optimal mental health.

(continued)

Table 1.3.   Stein's Developmental Sequence of the Feeling of Community (Cont.)

Sequence		Characteristics
	Influential People and Social Adjustment	
Early Development	**Mother**	The potential for contact and cooperation first develops between the child and mother. These capacities should be extended in ever widening social circles. She may mistakenly limit the child's interest to herself.
	Father	The father has the second chance for making a cooperative connection with the child and spreading it beyond the home. He may be able to enhance what the mother has started, or compensate for what she has been unable to accomplish.
	Siblings	Brothers and sister have the third chance of stimulating a cooperative attitude and extending it to other children.
	Teachers	If the family members have not won the child's cooperation, teachers have the fourth and crucial opportunity to elicit this crucial quality. Many earlier mistakes made in the family can still be corrected in the school.
Later Development	**Friends**	Encouraging and supportive friends offer many opportunities for pursing interests and engaging in activities for mutual benefit. For some people, they may also provide an extended or substitute "family-like" network.
	Love/Sexual Partner	A mentally, emotionally, and physically intimate relationship can deeply enrich the feeling of community, both between the individuals involved, as well as between the couple and society.
	Work Associates	Meaningful work, with cooperative, encouraging, and creative associates, can validate the feeling of having made a valuable individual or team contribution.
	Spiritual Community	A spiritual community or practice may offer a feeling of belonging to a group, and sense of interconnectedness with all of life.
	Therapist	The therapist provides a safe and supportive relationship for the individual to make a trustworthy mental and emotional connection, stimulating the development of a mutually respectful cooperation. This experience must then be extended to others in that individual's life.

Table 1.3. Stein's Developmental Sequence of the Feeling of Community (Cont.)

Sequence		Characteristics
Adjustment	**Normal**	The feeling of community is the Adlerian barometer of mental health. It also provides a positive compensation for the normal inferiority feeling, by generating the knowledge of being genuinely valuable—which originates from contributing to the common welfare.
	Maladjustment	All forms of social failure and psychological disorder reveal a lack of a sufficient feeling of community. Problems are approached or avoided without adequate cooperation, and fictional goals of personal superiority are pursued, yielding imagined triumphs or defeats that have only private meaning and value.

Note: Henry T. Stein claims this Table is based on concepts originally developed by Heinz Ansbacher and that this is a work in progress.

Source: Stein, H. T. (2003). *Developmental Sequence of the Feeling of Community.* San Francisco: Alfred Adler Institute of San Francisco and Northwestern Washington. Retrieved September 24, 2006, from http://ourworld.compuserve.com/homepages/hstein/dev-si.htm.

differ in their source of knowledge; the rationalist uses reason (that is, the mind) whereas the empiricist uses experience. Constructivists believe that individuals create knowledge by acting upon (or thinking about) information they acquire through experience. Children of all ages have some understanding about the world. Their understanding guides them to interpret the information they receive. However, this information may also alter their understanding of the world. This active process continues throughout the individual's life. Several theorists (e.g., Jean Piaget, Lev. S. Vygotsky, and Jerome S. Bruner) developed constructivist views on the children's social and intellectual development.

Jean Piaget (1896–1980) explored how children of different ages resolve reasoning problems, communicate their dreams, make moral judgments, and conduct other mental activities. Piaget found that the children's thought processes develop through a series of stages that can be generalized to children in all cultures. Children find an appropriate way to adapt to their environment. They develop schemas or schemata to make sense of their world. They produce and alter schemes through *assimilation* and *accommodation.* In *assimilation,* children search their repertoire of schemes to solve problems. They analyze the situation to match the pattern of their repertoire of schemes and conform the environmental stimuli to their existing knowledge. Piaget assumes that: "To assimilate an object to a schema means conferring to that object one or several meanings" (Piaget, Jonckheere, & Mandelbrot, 1958, p. 59). Children will use *accommodation* when the pattern in the situations does not match the children's repertoire of schemes. Then they may not assimilate the incident or they may attempt to alter an existing scheme. Piaget (1963) states:

> New objects which present themselves to consciousness do not have their own qualities which can be isolated...they are vague, nebulous, because in assimilable, and thus they create a discomfort from which there emerges sooner or later a new differentiation of the schemas of assimilation. (p. 141)

An instinctual balance, or *equilibrium*, develops between the assimilation and accommodation actions when the children's cognitive patterns evolve and interact with their environment. This *equilibrium* continues until new information initiates the process again. Adjusting to the environment is achieved through the assimilation and accommodation processes; therefore, within the children's biological-mental self the function of *organization* occurs to adequately combine all schemes that have pertinently conformed to each other. Piaget (1963) assumes that

> It is sufficiently well known that every intellectual operation is always related to all the others and that its own elements are controlled by the same law. Every schema is thus coordinated with all the other schemata and itself constitutes a totality with differentiated parts. Every act of intelligence presupposes a system of mutual implications and interconnected meanings. (p. 7)

Many perceive that Piaget's theory is a contrast to the theory of behaviorism. Children's play behavior represents Piaget's idea of *equilibration*. When children play, they assimilate new information and accommodate to their intellectual frameworks. In this process, the children's knowledge systems resemble those of the adults, thus, becoming effective, competent, thinking grown-ups. Piaget identifies four major stages of cognitive development (See Table 1.4), in which children progress in a normal sequence and at their own developmental rate. Experiences and their own maturing abilities prompt this progress.

Piaget's theory suggests that to the degree that young children are intellectually competent, they process information and develop concepts, though in a way that is different from older children and adults. They construct knowledge through appropriate experiences; just talking to them is not enough.

Lev Semenovich Vygotsky (1896–1934) believed that children develop naturally as a result of maturation, while other forms of knowledge come from cultural transmission. Their thinking patterns are developed through their experiences in the culture in which they grow up. In addition, their

Table 1.4.   Piaget's Stages of Intellectual Development

Stage	Characteristics	Age
Sensorimotor	Children develop schemas based on sensory input and bodily motion.	Birth–1½ or 2 years
Preoperational	Children develop language and other symbolic representations. Intuitive thought is not systematic or sustained.	2–7 years
Concrete operational	Children deal with logical processes, can deal with only one form of classification at a time, logical thought requires actual physical objects or events.	7–11 years
Formal operational	Children reason logically; formulate and test hypotheses; think abstract.	11 years +

From Spodek, B., & Saracho, O. N. (1994). *Right from the start: Teaching children ages three to eight.* Boston: Allyn & Bacon.

Table 1.5.   Vygotsky's Stages of Cultural Development

Stage I   Thinking in *unorganized congeries* or heaps. During this period the child puts things in groups (and may assign the group a label) on the basis of what are only chance links in the child's perception.

Stage II   Thinking in *complexes*. Individual objects are united in the child's mind not only by subjective impressions but also by bonds that actually exist among the objects. This is a step away from egocentric thinking and in the direction of objectivity. In a complex, the bonds between components are *concrete* and *factual* to some degree rather than abstract and logical. Five types of complexes succeed one another during this stage of thought.

Stage III   Thinking in *concepts*. On the threshold of this final major stage, we will pause and inspect two paths of thought and development—*synthesizing* and *analyzing*—that have converged to make conceptual thinking possible (Thomas, 2004, pp. 335–336).

advanced modes of thought (conceptual thinking) are verbally transmitted, which makes language essential to assess their thinking ability. That is, if they experience simplistic or "primitive" language, their thinking will be the same. In contrast, if they experience a language environment with varied and complex concepts, their thinking will be divergent and intricate, provided that their initial biological equipment (sense organic, central nervous system) is not handicapped. Vygotsky introduced three stages of cultural development (See Table 1.5), which are divided into substages (Thomas, 2004).

According to Vygotsky, children develop through their *zone of proximal development*, which is at the level they are able to function independently through a support system such as more mature thinkers.

Jerome Bruner's (1915–) primary theoretical framework indicates that learning is an active process in which learners use their present and past knowledge to construct new ideas or concepts. Learners use their cognitive structure to choose and process information and then develop hypotheses and make decisions. Their cognitive structure (i.e., schema, mental models) creates meaning and organization to the individuals' experiences, which helps them to "go beyond the information given."

As a structural theorist, Bruner assumes that information or knowledge is acquired through personal discovery. He shows how thought processes are subdivided into three distinct modes of reasoning. Bruner posits three modes of thought:

1. *Enactive mode.* Individuals use actions to stand for information (e.g., tying a shoe).
2. *Iconic mode.* Individuals use visual images to interpret information (e.g., thinking of someone's face).
3. *Symbolic mode.* Individuals use language.

Bruner proposes that cognition moves from an *enactive* to an *iconic* and finally to a *symbolic* mode of representation (See Table 1.6). Young infants interpret the world *enactively.* Children physically behave the way they think, which justifies the *enactive* mode of representation. Infants who clutch a rattle are communicating the thought that they want the rattle. Usually two- or three-year-olds are at the *iconic* mode. Children manifest an action through a sensory image, which may be visual in nature, auditory, tactile, or kinesthetic (Pylyshun, 2001). In this mode young children can have a mental "image" of a person who is absent, a previously performed

Table 1.6.   Bruner's Stages of Cognitive Development

Age	Stage	Characteristics
Infants	*enactive mode*	Infants interpret the world *enactively.* Children physically behave the way they think, which justifies the *enactive* mode of representation.
		Infants who clutch a rattle are communicating the thought that they want the rattle.
2 or 3 years	*iconic mode*	Children manifest an action through a sensory image, which may be visual in nature, auditory, tactile, or kinesthetic (Pylyshun, 2001). In this mode young children can have a mental "image" of a person who is absent, a previously performed action, or a situation that they have just witnessed.
5 or 6 years	*symbolic mode*	Children try to convey experience. Language assists children to represent their experiences and helps them manipulate and change them.

action, or a situation that they have just witnessed. Five- or six-year-olds are usually at the *symbolic* mode. They try to convey experience. Language assists children to represent their experiences and helps them manipulate and change them. Infants learn language as a tool of thought and action in a combined mode (Bruner, 1983). Knowledge evolves through the same stages as representation in intellectual development, where they understand by doing, visualizing, and representing symbolically.

Later Bruner's (1986, 1990, 1996) theoretical framework included the social and cultural aspects of learning. His theoretical framework is more in common with Vygotskian theory than with Piagetian Theory. Bruner believes that (1) young children need to make sense of the world, (2) mature thinkers need to assume an active role in assisting young children to develop their thinking, (3) learning influences development, and (4) intellectual development occurs within the cultural context of the child (Bruner, 1990).

Ecological Theory

In ecological theory the environment affects the children's lives and their development. This theory considers the whole child is an integrated organism that is affected by environmental elements. Development advances through small, supplementary quantities that sporadically increase to develop the personality through the integration of the children's repertoire of experiences. Since a new stimulus or experience adds a new ingredient to the children's knowledge, new meaningful experiences can modify the existing elements that contribute to the individuals' unique personality (Thomas, 2004). Urie Bronfenbrenner is the main proponent of ecological theory in child development.

Urie Bronfenbrenner (1917–2005) believed that the ecology of human development provides an understanding of how the active, growing human being relates to the environment. He examined the relationship between the children's immediate settings and those settings that are imposed. Bronfenbrenner explored the children's interpretations of their environment. Bronfenbrenner (1979) assumes that

1. The phenomenological (internally interpreted or experienced) environment dominates the real environment in guiding behavior.

2. It is folly to try to understand a child's action solely from the objective qualities of an environment without learning what those qualities mean for the child in that setting.

3. It is important to discover how the objects, people and events in the situation affect the child's motivations, and

4. It is essential to recognize the influence on behavior of "unreal" elements that arise from the child's imagination, fantasy, and idiosyncratic interpretations (pp. 24–25).

Bronfenbrenner's theory has had an impact in social policy. He has provided support to consider the home, school, community, and culture in the children's development.

THEORIES AND SOCIALIZATION

While the developmental theorists' concepts may overlap, they differ in the way that each theory relates to the various development areas. Several theories concentrate on all developmental areas, whereas others focus on only a narrow range of development (e.g., intellectual or socioemotional). They may also differ in their perception concerning the individuals' genetic makeup (nature) or may believe that the children's experiences (nurture) are essential in their development. Theorists, like Gesell, assume that nature influences the individuals' development; whereas a mediocre environment can restrict the individuals' predominant development. He believed that the individuals' environment has a minor influence on their development. Other theorists, like Bruner and Vygotsky, propose that the children's experiences contributes to a major degree to the individual's final development, particularly in relation to their cultural development. Many assume that both theories need to be considered. However, the family is the primary environmental influence, especially in the social context where children are raised. Developmental theories in conjunction with research describe the children's normal and average development, although many of them differ from the average. Norms provide a gauge on what to expect of the children; however, such early assessments must be individually altered for each individual child.

REFERENCES

Bronfenbrenner, U. (1979). *The ecology of human development: Experiments by nature and design.* Cambridge, MA: Harvard University Press.
Bruner, J. (1983). *Child's talk: Learning to use language.* New York: Norton.
Bruner, J. (1986). *Actual minds, possible worlds.* Cambridge, MA: Harvard University Press.
Bruner, J. (1990). *Acts of meaning.* Cambridge, MA: Harvard University Press.
Bruner, J. (1996). *The culture of education.* Cambridge, MA: Harvard University Press.
Erikson, E. (1963). *Childhood and society.* New York: Norton.
Erikson, E. H. (1968). *Identity: Youth and crisis.* New York: Norton.

Erikson, E. (1982). *The life cycle completed: A review.* New York: Norton.

Piaget, J. (1963). *The origins of intelligence in children.* New York: Norton.

Piaget, J., Jonckheere, A., & Mandelbrot, B. (1958). *La lecture de l'experience.* Etudes d'Epistemologie Genetique V. Paris: Presses Universitaires de France.

Pylyshun, Z. (2001). Is the imagery debate over? If so, what was it about? In E. Dupoux (Ed.), *Language, brain and cognitive development: Essays in honor of Jacques Mehler* (pp. 59–83). Cambridge, MA: MIT Press.

Savage, A. M., & Nicholl, S. W. (2003). *Faith, hope, and charity as character traits in Adler's individual psychology.* Lanham, MD: University Press of America.

Seligman, L. (2006). *Theories of counseling and psychotherapy: Systems, strategies, and skills.* Upper Saddle River, NJ: Prentice Hall.

Spodek, B., & Saracho, O. N. (1994). *Right from the start: Teaching children ages three to eight.* Boston: Allyn & Bacon.

Stein, H. T. (2003). *Developmental sequence of the feeling of community.* San Francisco: Alfred Adler Institute of San Francisco and Northwestern Washington. Retrieved September 24, 2006, from http://ourworld.compuserve.com/homepages/hstein/dev-si.htm.

Sullivan, H. S. (1953). *The interpersonal theory of psychiatry.* New York: Norton.

Thomas, R. M. (2004). *Comparing theories of development.* Belmont, CA: Wadsworth.

CHAPTER 2

HUMOR AS A FACILITATOR OF SOCIAL COMPETENCE IN EARLY CHILDHOOD

Doris Bergen

While the promotion of competence in many developmental domains is of concern during early childhood, one of the most important of these is social competence. The ability to gain friendships and bond with peer groups in ways that promote healthy social development is not distributed equally among young children, however. This may be due to child personality factors such as shyness or aggressiveness, to disabilities that hinder social interaction, or to characteristics of family environments that have not promoted social trust or empathy development. The pervasive media reports of horrific tragedies prompted by the bullying of socially isolated children during the late elementary and adolescent years have directed attention to the plight of children who do not seem to have the social skills they need to survive in group environments.

One characteristic that is often minimally present in socially isolated children is their ability to use humor as a way to gain acceptance by peers (Sobstad, 1990). Many studies of adult humor show that a sense of humor can be evidence of general social competence (see Ruch, 1998 for discussion of aspects of adult humor). In regard to children, there is some research that indicates rejected children have a low sense of humor (Williams & Asher, 1988), and that the absence of humor behaviors promotes

Contemporary Perspectives on Socialization and Social Development..., pages 19–38
Copyright © 2007 by Information Age Publishing
All rights of reproduction in any form reserved.

social distance with peers (Sherman, 1985). In contrast, friendship is promoted by the sharing of humor (Foot, 1986), and active social interaction increases humor behaviors (Sobstad, 1990). Thus, it is likely that a lack of appropriate humor behaviors can lead to social isolation (Masten, 1986), at least by elementary age.

A recent study of how elementary school children deal with one type of humor-related behavior, teasing, depending on their interpretation of the situation, provides some insights into the ambiguity that is often inherent in children's humor interactions with peers (Evans, 2002). Teasing is a particularly difficult issue in schools because it is an ambiguous behavior that can elicit reactions that range from laughter responses to teasing or joking back responses to angry physical assault responses to tears and withdrawal responses. Adults often tell children to ignore teasing (Warm, 1997) but this may be an unsuccessful strategy, and humor may be an alternative effective response (Scambler, Harris, & Milch, 1998). The prosocial functions of humor, such as promoting bonding with peers (Terrion & Ashforth, 2002), safely conveying feelings (Graham et al., 1992), and defusing aggression (Tyson, 1998) at least potentially can make the use of humor an effective social strategy in dealing with at least some forms of teasing in childhood. Thus, peer socialization may require helping children learn to interpret various forms of humor and to respond appropriately to the ambiguous messages often conveyed in teasing behavior.

Scambler, Harris, and Milch (1998) had children rate the responses to teasing interactions in videotape examples and found that the children judged hostile and ignoring responses as less effective than humorous responses. Evans (2002) gave children a questionnaire requiring a choice of reactions, such as ignoring teasing or using various forms of humor—self-effacing, self-enhancing, or other-insulting—and found that children's responses to the questions of strategy varied depending on the type of teasing event described. That is, most children distinguished humor-related teasing from totally hostile teasing. An interesting additional finding, however, was that teachers' ratings of students as teasers or teasing targets did not relate to children's ratings, and the researcher suggests that teachers may not be aware of many types of the teasing behaviors present in school settings.

Given that teasing and other humor-related behaviors, such as clowning, are often a social problem in schools and that certain groups of children are more likely to be teased, to clown, or to use humor in hurtful ways, and given that many variations of humor, including teasing, are pervasive in human society, it is important to help children learn how to interpret and use humor in ways that facilitate their social competence rather than in ways that harm others or make them open to being victims of bullying. Many parents and educators are unaware of the research on humor development and do not realize that humor is one of the many domains of development that progresses from infancy to late elementary years. Thus, they may not be cognizant of ways that they can help young children learn how to use humor as a facilitator of social competence. This discussion provides the background on humor development and suggests ways that children's use of humor can be a positive method of promoting social competence.

PERSPECTIVES ON THE SOCIAL SOURCES OF HUMOR DEVELOPMENT

Part of the answer to the puzzle of why some children are adept at using humor and some are not may lie in the social interactions of parents and children in the children's earliest years. Likewise, the emotional tone of educational environments, which may encourage or discourage humor development may contribute to children's development of varied humor strategies. The development of humor has been considered a meaningful indicator of young children's overall development from psychoanalytic, constructivist, and sociological/communication theory perspectives. Each of these perspectives discusses the developmental dimensions of humor and gives insights into how humor facilitates social development in the early childhood years.

Psychoanalytic Perspective on Social-Humor Connections

Freud (1960) was primarily interested in how the joking behavior of adults reflected their unconscious motives, but because he also saw humor as a method of coping with difficult social situations and a way of expressing both meanings and emotions, he discussed how it developed from childhood. He noted three stages, beginning with a stage called "play" (ages 2–3); followed by "jesting" (ages 4–6), and finally true "joking," (beginning at about age 6 or 7 and extending through adulthood). He reserved the term "humor" for its use as a social-emotional coping strategy; that is, as a way to gain perspective on unpleasant, fear inducing, or demanding circumstances (Martin, 1998).

The *play* stage involves repeating and elaborating sounds or unusual actions with objects, thus, "rediscovering the familiar"(p. 157). One of the earliest social examples of the generation of this type of humor (evident in the infant's escalating laughter and elaborations of the activity) is in "peek-a-boo" and other similar reciprocal interaction social games, which are first initiated by parents. These early social humor/play interactions convey to the child that there is pleasure in enhancing the excitement of a social interaction by repeating and elaborating on that social interaction. It does not take long after adults initiate such social games that infants and toddlers become the initiators, attempting to engage the parent or sibling in another round of this humor inducing play. Essential for these social interactions to be understood as humorous by the child is that there must be a sense of social trust already established. If an unknown adult were to initiate a tickling game or peek-a-boo interaction, it would generate fear and crying rather than fun and laughter. During this first stage it is also common to observe toddlers joining in the laughter of others even when they don't know what caused that laughter. This illustrates that they already have learned a "social convention" of laughter behavior, which is another evidence of its early social nature.

Freud saw *jesting* as an originating point for nonsense or "comic" expression, and it is the first evidence of actions that require an audience in order to be funny. Jesting doesn't really intend to convey meaning, but rather it is exaggeration and absurdity; it intends to provoke a social response to the unreasonable behavior. The role of the social partner is to "go along with" the jesting behavior (this behavior is often called "teasing" or "clowning"). For example, the child may call everyone in the family "mom" or put a hat on the dog. Jesting doesn't work if the social partner (adult, sibling, or peer) does not react, either by being "fooled" or by elaborating the jest even further. This stage is very interesting because it requires the child to recognize that all actions do not have to be "real." Usually children who can use jests have had parents who modeled jesting behavior to them, and they began to understand the difference between these two modes of action. For example, the parent may have made deliberate mistakes, such as singing a song with the wrong words or doing some other act of "fooling" so the child learns how to react to this behavior.

In observational studies of toddler's humor expressions, the initiation of jests by parents was a common action (Bergen, 2002). For example, at the dinner table at the end of the meal, a toddler (in high chair) was asked if she wanted another bean and she said "No" in a definite-sounding voice; the parent repeated, "Do you want a bean? "No"(with a big smile). The parent then began a routine asking in a mocking voice about other food possibilities, none of which were present at the dinner table: "Do you want some meat"? The child replied with giggles, "No.".; "Milk?" "No."; "Candy?" "No."; "Cookies?" "No."; "Ice cream?" "No, No."; and as the questions escalated, the laughter also escalated. In a study of children's humor in which parents collected observations, the type of humor situations often described for children of age 2 to 5 were ones in which either the child or parent initiated a jesting (often called teasing by the parent) behavior (Bergen, 1989). By toddler age, parents also reported the "laugh in social situations convention" sometimes results in "false" laughter, a product of imitative behavior.

A recent study comparing the humor development of Down's syndrome and autistic children (chronological age about 4 years; development age range of about 1 to 2 years) found that parents often reported "teasing" their Down's syndrome young children but rarely reported this behavior with their autistic children because "the child would not understand it or would throw a tantrum" (Reddy, Williams, & Vaughan, 2001, p. 231). In regard to child attempts to make others laugh, almost all of the parents of Down's children recorded the child's "clowning" attempts, but very few of the autistic children attempted clowning. Because autistic children often have difficulty interpreting social interactions and connecting socially with others while Down's children are usually seekers of social interactions, these findings are not surprising. Similarly, there was a difference in the amount of joining in the social laughter of others, with Down's children much more likely to laugh socially without understanding the meaning of the humor event. When "false" laughter occurred, it was usually in social situations for the Down's children and in non-social situations for the autistic children.

The stage of most interest to Freud, *joking*, is when humor is used to convey meaning, often emotion-laden meanings. Adults make good use of the "joking facade" (Wolfenstein, 1954), which permits expression of emotion-laden sexual, hostile, or otherwise unacceptable meanings that could not be expressed seriously. Elementary age children begin to be adept at using the "joking facade" and by age 9 to 12, many of their jokes have hostile and/or sexual themes (e.g., insult jokes). Younger children's attempts at joking are crude because they have not yet mastered the facade, which allows the initiator to claim, "it was only a joke" when conveying a hurtful or undesirable idea. The joking facade underlies much teasing behavior of older children, because it can be designed to be hurtful and mean, as well as symbolic (i.e., "just words") while the teasing of younger children is not (Warm, 1997). Warm suggests that changes in cognitive capacity account for the increase in hurtful teasing and that by late adolescence teasing may return to the playful, benign types of teasing, which were described earlier. Children of age 4–8 do make jokes that refer to body parts, body elimination, or other "unacceptable" topics, however. Although adults usually do not approve of this type of humor, it is often considered hilarious by peers and serves to bond the peer group. An example is a group of kindergarteners' repeated laughter at a song phrase, "U is for underwear down in the drier," which they played over and over on the tape recorder (Bergen, 1990).

Play and humor arise at similar times and are closely tied in infancy; however, when pretend play develops, humor begins to diverge from play to become a separate entity (see Bergen, 2006 for an in-depth discussion of this relationship). Psychodynamic theorist Wolfenstein (1954) suggested that about the age of 18 months, pretense becomes differentiated into two strands, which she called "serious" make-believe and "joking" make-believe. In serious make-believe, the real world is simulated, and children try to make their actions resemble the real world as closely as their understanding permits. For example, they will take the role of "Mom" and "cook" dinner. On the other hand, in joking make-believe, children deliberately distort reality with the intention of getting a surprise effect or humorous response. According to Bariaud (1989) incongruities expressed in humorous actions are not "incorrect" but of a "pretend" nature. That is, "there is a certain 'distancing' from the norms of reality, and a combination of being fooled and complicity required from the other" (p. 21). She adds that the purpose of pretense-related joking is "to trigger laughter" (p. 23). Sinclair (1996) suggests that very young children's ability to use "practical deception" in a playful way indicates that they are beginning to have some sense that they are aware others think differently than they do. She comments, "Even very young children show that they are aware of the pretend nature, inappropriateness or falsity of their pretense; otherwise there is no joke. Jokes work because the truth value or sincerity...proffered by the actor is shared by the audience" (p. 165).

Examples of "joking" make-believe in preschool include pretending to "play" piano on a toy cash register, "fighting" a pretend snake, combing another child's hair with a wooden rod, and feeding the "baby" (another child) with exaggerated motions and baby talk (Bergen, 2002). This type of play is always accompanied by much elaborated vocalizations and laughter. Surprisingly, although there has been extensive study of young children's play, it is rare that researchers report evidence of the humor generated in the play experience (Bergen, 2002). By age 4, children who have older siblings or joking parents may also have mastered the social convention of "joke telling," in which they use the form of a joke or riddle without getting the point of the humorous meaning. An almost 4 year old told this knock-knock joke (a favorite early type), "Knock-knock." Mom said "Who's there?" and he said, "T." Mom said, "T-who" and he replied, "Trex dinosaur," with exaggerated laughter. (He has heard about dinosaurs at preschool that week).

Because Freud reserved the word "humor" for situations in which fear, sadness, or anger might be generated, he saw humor as enabling individuals to gain an altered perception of threatening situations, thus reducing the threat. Parents and other adults sometimes use a tactic of exaggerated response to provoke laughter in children when they are in threatening situations. One example, from a kindergarten teacher occurred when a child was on the verge of tears because of tearing a small hole in his drawing paper. Instead of commiserating, the teacher said, "Oh, let's not tell the other kids because they will all want one," and she then made some exaggerated suggested for ways to make the hole bigger. After a startled look, the child began to laugh as the teacher got him another paper to use (Bergen, 1990). Humor is often a way that hospital personnel help assuage young patients' anxiety (Bergen & Gaynard, 1986; Schwekbe & Gryski, 2003). Wolfenstein (1954) suggested that humor also helps children cope with anxieties about their abilities, especially in situations where they have mastered some concept but are not yet confident about their knowledge. Often children enjoy joking about a concept that they have just mastered, as illustrated by Dad and Sean, age 4½, driving home in their car (Bergen, 2004). Dad asked Sean to tell him their house address (to check whether Sean remembered it), but instead of the real address, which he had learned, Sean said, "105 Easy Street." Dad (into the joke) replied, "Are you sure? Tell me again" to which Sean replied, "105 Beasy Street." Dad and Sean engaged in this exchange, with Sean's street names changing each time (all rhyming), amid Sean's laughter. As they finally approached their house, Sean gave the correct name "105 East Street," and Dad said (in a joking manner), "I'm glad you told me or we would never have found our way home." This example shows that humor often serves as an indicator of children's cognitive development as well as their social-emotional development. Thus, the importance of a cognitive connection to humor also has social implications.

Constructivist Perspective on Social-Humor Connections

The constructivist theoretical perspective is based on the recognition that much of humor relies on recognition of cognitive incongruity. As cognitive development occurs, children construct many experientially based concepts, which are built through interactions with the physical world and through "social transmission" from other people. The perspective stresses that, in order for children to find events humorous they must have a knowledge-base that enables them to recognize that there has been an incongruous visual, verbal, or conceptual event, which then elicits a humor response. Some of these incongruous events involve inappropriate juxtaposition or substitution of objects and some involve an unexpected consequence of some behavior, thus rendering the event humorous. More sophisticated incongruity humor involves multiple word meanings and concept incongruity, and thus it is essential for a knowledge base to be present so that the incongruous event is recognized. This ability to recognize incongruity requires many kinds of knowledge, including social knowledge. Even adults have difficulty in recognizing humor if the social group initiating the humor knows concepts that the adult does not; for example, physicists and anthropologists both may use humor that does not seem funny to people who do not have their knowledge base or their social networks.

One of the theorists who studied humor development, McGhee (1979), drew on Piagetian theory (Piaget, 1962), to define four stages of humor based on the ability to both recognize incongruity and to perform incongruous acts. McGhee (2002) subsequently revised these stages by indicating that at first there is laughter without humor and then laughter with the attachment figure (e.g., with peek-a-boo), then the use of objects with different objects (incongruous actions) and misnaming objects and play with words (incongruous language), and finally riddles and jokes (conceptual incongruity and word play with multiple meanings).

Although humor recognition usually begins before production, it is not uncommon to see toddlers deliberately produce incongruity with the social expectation that parents or siblings will respond with laughter. The earliest evidence of incongruity humor is related to these "incongruous actions" (starting about ages 1–2), when children begin to laugh at juxtaposed unrelated objects and perform incongruous actions themselves. Often children's early recognition of incongruous acts come through book reading activities with parents. Many books use "funny" juxtapositions and as parents point these out, children begin to notice and respond to them with laughter. An example of an incongruous action performed by a preschooler occurred when a group of boys were sitting at the table awaiting materials to be used in a project. The first material they got was a square of wax paper, and one of the boys picked up his paper and "kissed" it. Then all the boys began kissing their paper, laughing and looking around to get the teacher's reaction (Bergen, 2002). Although the action was one of incongruity, it required the "audience" in order to be truly funny.

The second type of incongruity humor is "incongruous language" (beginning about age 2), often in the form of sound play, such as chanting nonsense words or repeating a song but changing the lyrics (Bergen, 1998a). For example, one parent reported of her 18-month-old child, "she laughed loudly when I read "Hey, diddle, diddle" and another said her 30-month-old child changed the lyrics of a song from "peanut butter" (in original song) to "tuna butter" and laughed loudly as he repeated this over and over. The social quality of the verbal incongruity stage is also illustrated by a 3 year old when his mother was leaving for the store and she said, "You can come too." He then said, "And Cam (his brother) can come too, and Dad can come too, and Fluffy can come too, and cheese can come too, and bread can come too... (pattern continued, with laughter) (Bergen, 2004). Peer play interactions often involve verbal incongruity as this example illustrates: Two boys had been playing and it was now time for one to go home. The first said, "Goodbye Billy" and the other replied, "Goodbye Silly," and then the goodbyes escalated into a round of incongruous goodbye words (Bergen, 1998b). The evidence that a social setting promotes this type of humor is very clear.

A number of researchers have looked at very early social play that has incongruity elements and have noted that young children progressively used pre-verbal symbols, deliberate finger and body movements, and finally symbolic play to initiate humor with the parent (Hill, 1996). Johnson and Mervis (1997) observed that toddler humor attempts included verbal humor such as mislabeling (incongruent labels), verbal puns, and nonsense word production. McGhee (1979) asserts, "[T]he majority of toddlers' humor is self-generated." Aimard (1992) says that two-year-old humor is often "iconoclastic," and she suggests that it is designed to help children gain control in social interactions.

"Conceptual incongruity" (beginning about age 4), and "word play/multiple meanings" (beginning about age 7) are other evidences of cognitive aspects of humor development. Even though much humor has novel elements, reacting to incongruity is not the same as reacting to novelty because "an incongruous stimulus is *mis*expected...while a novel stimulus is *un*expected." (Pien & Rothbart, 1976, p. 3). That is, while laughter is often elicited when an unexpected stimulus occurs (e.g., when a block structure falls), incongruous humor has an element of planned surprise, in which a certain expectation is changed deliberately in order to make the "audience" laugh. In a study conducted in a preschool setting, Varga (2001) found that some children used hyperbole, which requires understanding of figurative instead of literal meanings. They made outrageously false statements about their abilities (i.e., tall tales), stimulating other children to respond by elaborating on the claims, thus engendering increasing levels of laughter. The "laughter in social situations convention" that was observed with toddlers is also evident in preschool groups in the phenomenon of "group glee" (Masellos 2003; Sherman, 1975), in which an incongruous event may start a few children laughing and the laughter is then taken up by a larger group of children (usually 7–10). Although it started with a humor event, the laughter becomes a social bonding situation.

Through the early childhood years, children gain increasing sophistication in demonstrating the *social forms* of humor interactions. For example, by age 4 or 5, children demonstrate that they know that laughter should follow the telling of a riddle or joke. One interesting behavior that often occurs at about that age is a "pre-riddle" stage (Bernstein, 1986), in which children tell "riddles" that have the form of a riddle but are missing the incongruous element. For example, one child's older sister told the riddle, "Why did the boy salute the refrigerator? Because it was General Electric" (incongruity resolution) and her younger sister then told this riddle: "Why did the boy salute the refrigerator? Because he was hungry" (no incongruity resolution). Nevertheless, the child (and the adults!) also laughed at the younger child's riddle!

An example from Ron (age 4) in interaction with his younger friend Sam (age 2½) shows that sometimes pre-riddles have an element of incongruity but they are still not "true" riddles. Ron asked Sam, "What do ducks drink?" and Sam said, "Water." The older child said, "No, ducks drink orange juice." Sam reiterated, "Ducks drink water" and Ron, laughing, replied, "Ducks drink orange juice." At 2½ Sam is not able to "get" the incongruity of the pre-riddle, which Ron finds hilarious. Even when children can tell a credible riddle, knock-knock joke, or narrative joke, however, younger children rarely can explain why it is funny. They may say their pre-riddle or riddle is funny, "Because when I tell it, my mother laughs." Children's ability to explain the incongruous reasons that made their riddle or joke funny rarely occurs before second grade level (Bergen, 2006). Bowes (1981) found that most early elementary age children tell riddles of only moderate complexity and primarily of the lexical ambiguity type.

Researchers have looked at some issues related to children's ability to understand incongruous humor. For example, Shultz and Horibe (1974) presented examples of humor that resolved the incongruity and examples that did not resolve it (didn't really make sense). They reported that younger children said humor that didn't resolve the incongruity was as funny as humor in which the incongruity was resolved but that older children preferred incongruity resolution humor. Pien and Rothbart (1976), however, did not find a difference in children's appreciation of incongruity resolution humor. Whitt and Prentice (1977) found differences only in the understanding of some types of riddles, so they concluded that they could not demonstrate a clear relationship between humor understanding and cognitive stage.

Researchers who have studied spontaneous humor in school, on playgrounds, and in other non-home settings (e.g., Canzler, 1980; McGhee, 1976, Masten, 1986) have found that, in such settings, boys usually express more humor. Parents typically rate boys and girls similarly on their sense of humor. Teachers, however, rate the sense of humor of boys and girls similarly in early childhood grades but rate boys as having a greater sense of humor at later ages, although there is no difference between boys and girls ratings of themselves (Bergen, 1998a). This is possibly another example of how social settings affect humor expression since older boys have often been allowed to show humor expression in public settings, with girls serving as the "audience." In home observations both girls and boys are experts at generating humor that is appropriate for their age. The major types reported by parents in preschoolers include clowning (making exaggerated movements or vocal sounds designed to make an effect), teasing (using actions or words to provoke another), performing incongruous or fantasy actions in the presence of others, and describing impossible events (Bergen, 1989). Of course, as any early childhood teacher knows, true riddles are the primary humor of children in kindergarten and early elementary years. Children often tell the same riddle over and over to all who will listen and because the audience reaction is a necessary part of the humor social circle, adults usually laugh at the same riddle over and over as well.

Studies of children's understanding of verbal irony and its relationship to teasing have provided insights that may explain how ironic expressions of humor (similar to teasing expressions) affect children's cognitive and social understanding. Teasing is characterized by "intentional provocation and playful off-record markers, which together comment on something relevant to the target" (Kehner, Capps, Kring, Young, & Heerey, 2001, p. 335). Children of 5–6 show recognition that speakers who make ironic comments do not literally believe what they have said; however, children of this age do not find the remarks humorous (Harris & Pexman, 2003). Recently Pexman, Glenwrighht, Krol, & James (2005) studied how children of age 7–10 interpret ironic criticisms and compliments in comparison to literal criticisms and complements, using puppet scenarios in which the puppets were labeled "friends," "strangers," or "enemies." They state, "...irony comprehension involves social and cultural knowledge, in conjunction with particular cognitive skills, such as first and second-order mental state attribution" (p. 260). The older children in their study were more able to find ironic compliments humorous. Because the children typically identified more with the "target" puppet, however, even the older children did not find ironic criticism humorous. The older children were more likely to interpret the ironic criticism as being similar to teasing, however. Although adults consider relationship information in interpreting the humor of irony, the children considered social relationships only in interpreting literal criticism, inferring the speaker attitude for "enemy" criticism most accurately.

SOCIOLOGICAL/COMMUNICATIONS THEORY PERSPECTIVE ON SOCIAL-HUMOR CONNECTIONS

Theorists from this perspective are interested primarily in how adult-child early social interactions communicate shared cultural understandings and identify appropriate frames for social behaviors. When adults interact in playful and humor-eliciting ways with young children, they are giving them communication signals that help children learn what behaviors should be exhibited when social interactions occur in different social "frames." Thus, when adults engage with infants and toddlers in playful ways, they are communicating that there is a "play frame," which signals "This is play" (Bateson, 1956). Children's responses within this frame are expected to be different than those desired in a "serious" frame. Although these theorists primarily have been concerned about play communication, engagement within a play frame is also essential for humor expression. According to Bariaud (1989), "Humor supposes this dual awareness...[that there is]...an intent to amuse" (p. 18). The signals that communicate a humor frame are similar to those that identify a play frame, such as exaggerated facial expressions, higher-pitched voice, intense gaze, and smiles or open mouth (Stern, 1974). By four months of age, infants can distinguish play frames and respond differentially within those frames (Pien & Rothbart, 1980). From this theoretical perspective, it is vitally important that young children have both serious and playful/humorous social interactions so that they will learn to interpret these social-cultural differences and know how to respond appropriately in both types of settings.

Thus, this perspective suggests that human capacity to become socially skilled users of humor depends on learning how to interpret and react to the metacommunication "This is humor" (Bergen, 1998a). One finding from studies of child abuse is that abused children have difficulty engaging in play; it is probably likely that they also may not have learned how to engage appropriately in humor events. It may also be the case that, because there is a wide variation in social interaction patterns even in "good enough" families (see Scarr, 1992 for discussion of such families) that some children learn to be much more comfortable within a "humor frame" than others do. For example, the earlier examples of adult and child initiation of humor illustrate how the responses of the social partner can make a big difference in how often humor is initiated. Children who initiate humor attempts but get angry or puzzled rather than accepting and elaborating responses from adults will probably be less likely to try to express humor-related behaviors. Similarly, parents of children with autism or other cognitive impairments may have a harder time helping their child learn appropriate humor responses since the children's ability to differentiate the "humor frame" from other social situations is poorer.

PROMOTING HUMOR DEVELOPMENT AND SOCIAL COMPETENCE

The issues addressed in the first paragraphs regarding socially isolated and rejected children and their inability to use humor as a facilitating device for gaining friends or general social acceptance is an important one for parents and educators to address. Also, adult intervention to help children know how to deal with "problem behaviors" such as teasing in school or on the playground may need to start in preschool and kindergarten rather than being first addressed at elementary age.

To learn how to use humor as a facilitator of social interaction, children must have experienced such interactions with adult models initially, and later with sibling and peer models. Given this assumption, however, the question of how to help children deal with the double-edged facets of humor (e.g., teasing) is a very important one. Humor development clearly involves the ability to interpret a range of humor expressions (e.g., jesting/ teasing, clowning, using visual and verbal incongruity, pre-riddling, riddling, joking) and to determine appropriate responses to each of those types. If it is the case that the "humor frame" of a culture needs to be understood and that children need to find strength in both the social-emotional and the cognitive aspects of humor, then attention to how humor facilitates social competence in early childhood is essential.

Family Influences on Humor Development

Studies of humor development often describe the quality of family interactions and how adults model humor behaviors (e.g., Bergen, 1998a; Hill, 1996; Johnson & Mervis, 1997; Reddy, Williams, & Vaughn, 2002). These studies all have the bias that agreement to participate in the study may already rule out parents who do not facilitate humor development. However, the studies may still give insights into appropriate ways to promote humor. These studies typically show the parents of young children as active in initiating humor episodes and responsive to their children's early humor attempts. For example, they will play teasing games or use exaggerated voices when pretending with their child. They will pretend not to know the answer to a riddle the child has told many times, still laughing at the "punch" line no matter how inexpertly the riddle is told. Siblings are also prime initiators and models of humor for young children and children often first learn how "to take a joke" from their interactions with siblings. In interviews with school-age children about humor at home, funny things that their animal pets did ("my cat started to eat a pillow"), siblings' actions ("my brother talks like a chipmunk"), and parent humor attempts ("Mom helped us put candles that wouldn't blow out on dad's birthday cake") are often cited (Bergen, 2002).

Thus, a climate of humor acceptance and encouragement in the family is probably very important if children are to understand the "humor-frame" and be able to judge the effects of their humor by observing the social reactions of others. The children discussed earlier, who do not seem to be able to "get" a joke or to use humor as a social facilitator may be children who have not had the opportunity to learn about the "humor frame" in their families. Although no longitudinal research has investigated the influence of family humor interactions on children's long-term social development, it is likely that children who were raised in climates where humor expression was not an important part of the family context may not have the humor-related social skills that could facilitate their social development. For those children, the role of the teacher as a humor promoter may be especially important.

Promoting Humor Development in Educational Settings

In early childhood educational settings, there is great variety in how much teachers promote (or even allow) humor expression. One context that seems to foster expressions of socially promoted humor in preschool and kindergarten classrooms is the time period that was called "free play," an apparently fast disappearing feature of most classrooms. Observational studies typically find many humor examples generated during such play (Bergen, 2002; Klein, 1985; Varga, 2001). Studies of children's humor expression conducted in these social play settings have found that children express a range of humor types, many of which show both their thinking processes and their social skills. Unfortunately, there is wide variation in how teachers encourage or understand children's humor expression. In one study, teachers' assessment of preschool and kindergarten children's humor was not related to the children's own assessment of their humor (Sletta & Sobstad, 1993). Whether teachers promote humor may depend on what types and opportunities for play occur in the classroom. Although humor expression is especially likely in spontaneous free play sessions, art experiences, lunchtime, outdoor playtime, group time, and even computer time can be venues where humor is encouraged. In another study, teachers' ratings of children's cognitive spontaneity and sense of humor were negatively related to the amount of time children spent in functional computer play, rather than in constructive or dramatic computer play (Liang & Johnson, 1999). When preschool and kindergarten teachers collected observations of humor occurring in their preschool and kindergarten classrooms, most reported many examples. However, some teachers had very few examples, and one remarked that she had not realized how little time for humor was included in her class day. Here are a few of the examples, teachers reported (Bergen, 1990). As is evident, these all involve social interactions, either with teacher or peers.

Preschool: A boy and a girl in the playhouse began a series of "Pour coffee on your head; pour coffee on your cheek, etc., laughing after each new remark" (The teacher allowed the children to escalate incongruous actions and language.)

Preschool: Two girls bring "colorform" picture to Ms. M. with pieces in obviously wrong places (lettuce in stove, dog on table, etc.). They keep changing pieces after teacher playfully scolds them for their ridiculous deed. They "fool" the teacher five times before getting the picture correct, all the while giggling and smiling. (The teacher responded to this teasing by being "fooled" over and over.)

Preschool: Ms. K. is reading a story to the children. The funny rhyming names made the children laugh. (The teacher selected a book she knew her children would find funny.)

Preschool: Ms. W. asks, "Do you know any jokes? M. says, "Why did the turtle cross the road?" B. answers, "To get to the other side." M. says, "No, to get to the Shell station...You know, to get a new shell for his back." (A true riddle, with explanation by child; note that the teacher initiated a "joke-telling" session.)

Preschool: In group time Ms. M. initiates a hiding and finding game related to identifying colors. As each color is pulled out of the bag, the children laugh with delight in being able to guess the color. (The teacher used a humor-generating way of teaching.)

Kindergarten: Boys made play-do cookies for Mrs. W. After she "ate" them, they laughed and said, "We tricked you—they had a bomb in them!" (An early example of a "hostile" joke.)

Kindergarten: J. was cutting at free choice time. He made a paper mustache and put it up to his face. (An incongruous action, done for effect on other children.)

Kindergarten: K. says, "Ms. P. I have joke for you. Why did goofy eat a banana? Ms. P.: I don't know, why?" K.: "He thought it was an orange." (laughs) M.: "I have a better one. Why did the chicken cross the road?" K.: To eat an egg with a baby in it. M: No, to eat an orange. (These pre-riddles are expressed with all the social conventions of laughter, but obviously are missing the incongruity resolution/double meanings. The teacher, however, encourages their expression by being responsive.)

Kindergarten: M. says, Ms. P., I don't have a plate. Ms. P.: Oh, no, I guess you can't eat lunch (smiling) M. (laughs) Yes! Ms. P. asks other children, "Should we get M. a plate?" The other children shout, "No, no!" M. says, "You're kidding!" and begins laughing. (This example shows how a child can be teased but understand that it is within a humor frame and thus respond appropriately rather than getting upset.)

Kindergarten: K. and M. are singing, "All I want is a Mouse Mickey, Mickey (repeated three times). M.: "Mickey, Mickey (laughing) K.: "M. Mickey. We can call her M. Mickey." (says M.'s name in phrase). (Another tease but with verbal elaborations.)

In formal educational settings, like the first to third grades, children usually have more humor interactions with peers than with adults. Their humor often seems to be designed to get the teacher's reaction (as they realize adults may not like "absurdity"). Therefore, teachers of older children sometimes take the role of "toning down" humorous play, especially if it was in an "inappropriate" setting or was threatening to become "out of bounds" behavior. Teachers vary in how they handled such humor expression, however. In the instance mentioned earlier when the boys "kissed" the wax paper, the teacher chose to ignore the actions and instead quickly added the other materials and gave directions for the activity. In another example, at lunchtime one child engaged in a series of food-related humor-eliciting acts, making "Yum, yum" and chewing noises very loudly. Everyone at the table was laughing until the teacher told the child, "Don't play with your food!" Adult tolerance of humor expression probably is a major influence in how often it occurs in educational settings and what form it takes in those settings. In one study of how teachers used humor in their classrooms, it was found that middle school teachers reported using humor much more often than did elementary school teachers (Bergen & Jewett, 2000).

PROMOTING HUMOR DEVELOPMENT AS A FACILITATOR OF SOCIAL COMPETENCE

Humor, almost by definition, requires social interaction. For human beings of all ages it often serves as a get-acquainted strategy, as a bonding mechanism, and as a reliever of social tension (Terrion & Ashforth, 2002). The audience for humor differs at various ages, with parents and other caregivers being the first audience for children, and, progressively, siblings, peers, teachers, and people in other settings being involved in the audience role. Usually expression of social humor requires a "safe" environment in which children can take the risk of humor expression. Depending on their socialization in early childhood, as well as their own personalities (e.g., outgoing or shy), children show a wide range of social uses and extensiveness of humor expression. However, almost every kindergarten or first grade child can tell a riddle if asked to do so. Knowing when to interpret an action or a verbal comment as "this is humor" is an important social skill, and often teasing of children who can't "take" the joke may occur in elementary school. Older children, adolescents, and adults will rate a peer who has a "sense of humor" very positively; thus, a sense of humor fosters social acceptance and friendship at all ages. In early childhood, therefore, helping children to learn how to interpret and use humor effectively is an important part of the educators' role. To further humor development, and thus social development, they can do the following:

1. Express appreciation for children's humor attempts, and give them opportunities to extend these attempts.
2. Share one's own humor attempts in the classroom (even if somewhat lame!).
3. Provide social environments that invite humorous rather than serious elaborations of learning tasks (see Struthers, 2003, for some excellent suggestions).
4. Teach about different types of humor, such as riddling, tall tales, irony/teasing, and practice those.
5. Read humorous stories and show humorous videos that give examples of different types of humor and talk about what made them funny.
6. Discuss what is appropriate teasing and what is inappropriate, and empower children to find ways to handle teasing so that it does not become bullying.

In summary, social competence does not develop as an isolated skill; rather, it is closely tied to cognitive, emotional, and humor development. The ability to understand what others are thinking (Theory of Mind), to be in touch with what they are feeling (empathy), and to evaluate what types of discourse is appropriate in various social contexts (metacommunication) are all aspects of social competence that develop through the early childhood years. Children's humor can be both a means for assessing social competence and a vehicle through which such competence can be increased. Moreover, a sense of humor can be a social coping mechanism that is useful throughout life.

REFERENCES

Aimard, P. (1992). Genese de phumour. *Devenir, 4*(3), 27–40.

Bariaud, F. (1989). Age differences in children's humor. *Journal of Children in Contemporary Society, 20*(1–2), 15–45.

Bateson, G. (1956). The message "This is play." In B. Schaffner (Ed.), *Group processes: Transactions of the second conference* (pp. 145–241). New York: Josiah Macy Jr. Foundation.

Bergen, D. (1989). Characteristics of young children's expression of humour in home settings as observed by parents. *International Journal of Educology, 3*(2), 124–135.

Bergen, D. (1990, July). *Young children's humor at home and school: Using parents and teachers as participant observers.* Paper presented at Eighth International Conference on Humor, Sheffield, England.

Bergen, D. (1998a). Development of the sense of humor. In W. Ruch (Ed.), *The sense of humor: Explorations of a personality characteristic* (pp. 329–358). Berlin: Mouton deGruyter.

Bergen, D. (1998b). Play as a context for humor development. In D. P. Fromberg, & D. Bergen (Eds.), *Play from birth to twelve and beyond: Contexts, perspectives, and meanings* (pp. 324–327). New York: Garland Press.

Bergen, D. (2002). Finding the humor in children's play. In J. Rooparine (Ed.), *Conceptual, social-cognitive, and contextual issues in the fields of play (Play and Culture Studies)* (Vol. 4, pp. 209–220). Westport, CT: Ablex.

Bergen, D. (2004). Humor development of gifted and typically developing children: A synthesis of present knowledge. *Revue Quebecoise de Psychologie, 25*(1), 1–21.

Bergen, D. (2006). Play as a context for humor development. In D. F. Fromberg & D. Bergen (Eds.), *Play from birth to twelve: Contexts, perspectives, and meanings* (2nd ed., pp. 141–156). New York: Routledge.

Bergen, D., & Gaynard, L. (1986). *Young children's discovery of humorous incongruity in a hospital setting.* Paper presentation at annual meeting of the Association for the Anthropological Study of Play, Phoenix.

Bergen, D., & Jewett, L. (2000, July). *Teacher facilitation of learning through play and humor in early childhood and elementary/middle school classrooms.* Symposium paper presented at the 16th Biennial Meeting of the International Society for the Study of Behaviour and Development, Beijing, PRC.

Berstein, D. (1986). The development of humor: Implications for assessment and intervention. *Topics in Language Disorders, 6*(4), 65–71.

Bowes, J. (1981). Some cognitive and social correlates of children's fluency in riddle-telling. *Current Psychological Research, 1,* 9–19.

Canzler, L. (1980, April). *Humor and the primary child.* (ERIC Document Reproduction No. ED 191 583)

Evans, V. P. (2002). Coping with teasing: Children's evaluations of humorous responses. *Dissertation Abstracts International: Section B: The Sciences and Engineering, Vol. 63(11-B),* 2003-5566.

Freud, S. (1960). *Jokes and their relation to the unconscious.* New York: Norton.

Foot, H. (1986). Humor and laughter. In O. D. W. Hargie (Ed.), *A handbook of communication skills* (pp. 355–382). London: Croom Helm.

Graham, E. E., Papa, M. J., Brooks, G. P. (1992). Functions of humor in conversation: Conceptualization and measurement. *Western Journal of Communication, 56*(2), 161–183.

Harris, M. & Pexman, P. M. (2003). Children's perceptions of the social functions of verbal irony. *Discourse Processes, 36,* 147–165.

Hill, C. (1996). Ego development, creative humour and play, in a "good enough" mothering experience: An infant observational study. *Australian Journal of Psychotherapy, 15*(1), 82–91.

Johnson, K. E., & Mervis, C. B. (1997). First steps in the emergence of verbal humor: A case study. *Infant Behavior and Development, 20*(2), 187–196.

Keltner, D., Capps, L., Kring, A. M., Young, R. C., & Heerey, E. A. (2001). Just teasing: A conceptual analysis and empirical review. *Psychological Bulletin, 127*(2), 229–248.

Klein, A. (1985). Humor comprehension and humor appreciation of cognitively oriented humor: A study of kindergarten children. *Child Development, 56,* 223–235.

Liang, P. H. & Johnson, J. (1999). Using technology to enhance early literacy through play. *Computers in the Schools, 15*(1), 55–63.

Martin, R. (1998). Approaches to the sense of humor: A historical review. In W. Ruch (Ed.), *The sense of humor: Explorations of a personality characteristic* (pp. 15–60). Berlin: Mouton de Gruyter.

Masselos, G. (2003). "When I play funny it makes me laugh": Implications for early childhood educators in developing humor through play. In D. E. Tytle (Ed.), *Play and educational theory and practice* (pp. 213–222). West Park, CT: Praeger.

Masten, A. S. (1986). Humor and competence in school-aged children. *Child Development, 57,* 461–473.

McGhee, P. (1976). Sex differences in children's humor. *Journal of Communication, 26,* 176–189.

McGhee, P. (1979). *Humor: Its origin and development.* San Francisco: Freeman.

McGhee, P. (2002) *Understanding and promoting the development of children's humor.* Dubuque, IA: Kendall-Hunt.

Pexman, P. M., Glenwright, M., Kroi, A., & James, T. An acquired taste: Children's perceptions of humor and teasing in verbal irony. *Discourse Processes, 40*(3), 259–288.

Piaget, J. (1962). *Play, dreams and imitation in childhood.* New York: Norton.

Pien, D., & Rothbart, M. K. (1976). Incongruity and resolution in children's humor: A reexamination. *Child Development, 47,* 966–971.

Reddy, V., Williams, E., & Vaughan, A. (2002). Sharing humour and laughter in autism and Down's syndrome. *British Journal of Psychology, 93*(2), 219–242.

Ruch, W. (Ed.), (1998). *The sense of humor: Explorations of a personality characteristic* (pp. 329–358). Berlin: Mouton deGruyter.

Scambler, D. J., Harris, M. J., & Milch, R. (1998). Sticks and stones: Evaluations of responses to childhood teasing. *Social Development, 7*(2), 234–249.

Scarr, S. (1992). Developmental theories for the 1990s: Developmental and individual differences. *Child Development, 63,* 1–19.

Schultz, T. R. & Horibe, F. (1974). Development of the appreciation of verbal jokes. *Developmental Psychology, 10,* 13–20.

Schwekbe, S. & Gryski, C. (2003). Gravity and levity–pain and play: The child and the clown in the pediatric health care setting. In A. Klein, (Ed.). *Humor in children's lives: A guidebook for practitioners* (pp. 49–68). Westport, CT: Praeger.

Sherman, L. W. (1975). An ecological study of glee in small groups of preschool children. *Child Development, 46,* 53–61.

Sherman, L. W. (1985, June). *Humor and social distance ratings among elementary school children: Some differential sex and age patterns.* Paper presented at the Fifth International Conference on Humor, Cork, Ireland.

Sinclair, A. (1996). Young children's practical deceptions and their understanding of false belief. *New Ideas in Psychology, 14*(2), 152–173.

Sletta, O. & Sobstad, F. (1993, March). *Social competence and humor in preschool and school-aged children.* Paper presented at 60th Meeting of Society for Research in Child Development, New Orleans.

Sobstad, F. (1990). Preschool children and humor. Trondheim: Skriftserie fra Peda-gogisk institutt, Univeritetet i Trondheim. Rapport nr. 1

Stern, D. N. (1974). Mother and infant at play: The dyadic interaction involving facial, vocal, and gaze behaviors. In M. M. Lewis & L. Rosenblum (Eds.), *The effect of the infant on its caregiver* (pp. 187–213). New York: Wiley.

Struthers, A. (2003). No laughing! Playing with humor in the classroom. In A. J. Klein (Ed.), *Humor in children's lives: A guide for practitioners* (pp. 85–94). Westport, CT: Praeger.

Terrion, J. L., & Ashforth, B. (2002). From 'I' to 'we': The role of putdown humor and identity in the development of a temporary group. *Human Relations, 55*(1), 55–88.

Tyson, P. D. (1998). Physiological arousal, reactive aggression, and the induction of an incompatible relaxation response. *Aggression and Violet Behavior, 3*(2), 143–158.

Varga, D. (2001). Hyperbole and humor in children's language play. *Journal of Research in Childhood Education, 14*(2), 142–146.

Warm, T. R. (1997). The role of teasing in development and vice versa. *Journal of Developmental & Behavioral Pediatrics, 18*(2), 97–181.

Whitt, J. K., & Prentice, N. M. (1977). Cognitive processes in the development of children's enjoyment and comprehension of joking riddles. *Developmental Psychology, 13*(2), 129–136.

Williams, G. A., & Asher, S. R. (1988). *Subclassifying rejected children: Behavioral style and feelings of loneliness.* Paper presented at NATO Advanced Study Institute on Social Competence in Developmental Perspective, Savoy, France.

Wolfenstein, M. (1954). *Children's humor: A psychological analysis.* Glencoe, IL: Free Press.

CHAPTER 3

ATTACHMENT IN THE PRESCHOOL YEARS

Implications for Social Learning

Gary Creasey and Patricia Jarvis

Tommy, 4 years of age, attends a small, home-based day care. His parents use harsh punishment techniques and it is not surprising that this family has had contact with the Department of Children and Family Services. The mother eventually confides to the child-care worker that she and her husband are having serious marital difficulties, and routinely engage in angry arguments in front of their young son. She remarks that she is seriously concerned about Tommy's development—he is destructive, has low self-esteem, possesses a short attention span, and bullies others. However, one day, his mother indicates that his behavior has improved and remarks to the day care provider, "Tommy has done so much better once he started coming to your home." The mother adds that he now gets along better with his siblings, can better regulate his emotions, and is less oppositional.

There are myriad theories that might account for Tommy's improved psychological functioning and social behavior. A family therapist may suggest that Tommy's parents have undergone marital counseling and that the renewed stability has led to less arguing and harsh parenting, which in turn has had an influence on his adjustment. Another explanation supported by learning theories, would be that the instruction Tommy experienced in

Contemporary Perspectives on Socialization and Social Development..., pages 39–57
Copyright © 2007 by Information Age Publishing
All rights of reproduction in any form reserved.

child-care might have made a difference. Tommy's teacher, in response to his behavior problems, may have consistently withdrawn certain privileges that encouraged a change in his thinking and behavior. Still another expert might suggest that simply removing Tommy from a stressful household for a good portion of the day may have had a therapeutic influence in itself.

Which theory is the most correct? Although all of these perspectives are viable, in this chapter, we assert that contemporary attachment theory also provides a useful framework to consider for preschool social learning and behavioral/emotional adjustment. To build this argument, this chapter begins with a brief overview of attachment theory, and how the operation, structure, and content of attachment functioning undergo important transitions during the preschool years. After a brief description pertaining to methodological issues concerning the assessment of attachment, we discuss the importance of preschool attachment functioning and its relationship to a variety of competencies that may inhibit or facilitate social learning. Next, theory and research are presented concerning the role of principal attachment figures in the development and maintenance of attachment functioning in young children. Finally, the implications of the emerging work in this field are offered and our hypothesis about the role of attachment and social learning in preschool. The relevance of attachment theory and research to the educational context is discussed with a special emphasis on ways that attachment functioning may be improved in preschool settings.

ATTACHMENT: THEORETICAL AND CONCEPTUAL ISSUES

Although attachment functioning plays an important role in the preschool years, its origins are during infancy. Early psychoanalytic (Freud, 1957) and learning (Sears, Maccoby, & Levin, 1957) theories asserted that attachment relationships between caregivers and children evolved through primary drive reduction—you feed an infant and the infant associates your presence with food in a pleasurable manner. In contrast, Bowlby (1969/1982) proposed an ethological perspective and stipulated that attachment relationships between infants and caregivers were necessary from a survival standpoint. For instance, one can imagine a time when proximity to caregivers was mandatory for survival and that wandering from one's community would result in almost certain death. The gradual development of close, affectional bonds between infants and caregivers is theorized as one major reason for why our species has become successful (Bowlby, 1988). This premise suggests that if contact between the infant and caregiver is simply allowed then our biology guarantees infant-caregiver attachments. Indeed, this theory would account for why children of abusive parents, in the absence of positive parenting behavior, become attached to their parents (Cassidy, 1999). The latter finding also accounts for why most attachment experts no longer endorse drive reduction or simple learning theories to explain the infant-caregiver bond.

In the spirit of ethological theory, attachment bonds are a phenomenon that should be witnessed across all cultures. Ainsworth provided support for this premise by documenting that classic signs of infant-caregiver attachment (e.g., proximity seeking; stranger distress; separation anxiety) could be witnessed in other societies (Ainsworth, 1967). However, although most infants eventually become attached to primary caregivers, the caregiving environment has been theorized to produce striking differences in the *quality of this attachment*. To better capture this diversity, Ainsworth and colleagues developed the Strange Situation procedure (Ainsworth, Blehar, Waters, & Wall, 1978). In this widely used method, infants are paired with, and separated from, their primary caregiver, as well as a "stranger" over the course of brief observational segments.

During the Strange Situation, infants display a wide assortment of behavior that can be used to assign an attachment category. Ainsworth developed a classification system that identified three *organized* patterns of attachment that can be witnessed in infants across all cultures (Sagi, 1990). *Secure* infants actively explore their environment when not distressed, yet seek comfort and proximity from caregivers when upset. Most importantly, a caregiver can readily comfort these babies. *Avoidant* infants distance themselves from caregivers and rely on themselves (or focus on the environment) for comfort. For example, during times of duress, the child may focus on toys instead of the caregiver. *Anxious*, ambivalent or resistant infants have difficulty with exploration, often angrily seek contact with caregivers during times of duress; yet cannot be comforted (Ainsworth et al., 1978). The latter two classifications are signs of attachment insecurity. Further, in Ainsworth's original classification scheme (secure, avoidant, anxious/resistant), some infants could not be classified. Upon observing such infants, Main and Solomon (1990) concluded such infants did not have an organized attachment system and classified them as *disorganized/disoriented*. Such infants dramatically oscillate between approach and avoidant behavior, and may display bizarre behavior during the Strange Situation, such as initially approaching a caregiver and then backing away as in fear.

Attachment security is considered the modal attachment classification, and most closely linked with healthy development across cultures (Sagi, 1990). Further, and a point that will be elaborated on throughout this chapter, attachment functioning remains important during the preschool years. During this time period, the potential for social learning becomes vast as the child has the opportunity to interact with both existing, and new attachment figures, such as peers and teachers. An insecure child who lacks the confidence to explore, or does so in an incompetent manner, only hinders opportunities for such learning (Sroufe, Egeland, & Carlson, 1999). Having briefly provided a theoretical and conceptual background on the construct of attachment, we next turn to how attachment processes undergo further development in the preschool years.

ATTACHMENT IN THE PRESCHOOL YEARS: CHANGES IN OPERATION, STRUCTURE, AND CONTENT

It is important to delineate how the operation, structure, and content, of attachment processes develop during the preschool years (Cicchetti, Cummings, Greenberg, & Marvin, 1990). Although these changes signify maturity in the preschooler, they also present certain obstacles for assessment and evaluation. First, in terms of operation, consider the conditions necessary to elicit individual differences in attachment. Due to the gradual movement away from dependency, increasingly more stress is needed to activate the attachment system. Thus, observing the child's behavior during a brief separation from a caregiver or in the presence of a strange person may not constitute a legitimate attachment assessment. For this reason, experts that evaluate attachment in preschoolers use more industrious methods to activate the system, such as lengthier separations from caregivers coupled with a demanding task (e.g., Cassidy & Marvin, 1992).

In the spirit of the original Strange Situation classification system, preschoolers can be rated as secure, avoidant, or anxious-resistant (or ambivalent) (Cassidy & Marvin, 1992; Main & Cassidy, 1988). However, the classifications designed for preschoolers show both similarities and differences than those developed for infants. Unlike secure infants, older secure children tend *not* to become distressed when separated from their caregivers, and display relaxed and confident behavior during separations and interactions with strangers. Like anxious-resistant infants, ambivalent children often strongly protest when separated from caregivers, yet might not display the same angry behavior during reunions experienced by their infant counterparts. For instance, ambivalent children may show babyish, immature behavior when reunited with their parent (Main & Cassidy, 1988). Thus, the contextual cues necessary to activate the attachment system in preschoolers are different than for infants and the outward behaviors that secure and insecure children exhibit around caregivers when distressed also undergoes modifications. Most apparently, the behavior of secure children is autonomous, which is different from the dependency normally associated with infancy.

There is another change in attachment functioning that presents certain assessment challenges. Attachment experiences with principal caregivers during infancy and toddlerhood become internalized as internal working models of attachment or *generalized attachment representations (GAR)* (Bowlby 1969/1982; 1988). Generalized attachment representations are conceptualized as "operable" models of self and caregivers, and serve to "regulate, interpret, and predict both the attachment figure's and the self's attachment-related behaviors, thoughts, and feelings" (Bretherton & Munholland, 1999). Thus, the child not only becomes more competent in predicting the availability and potential effectiveness of various caregivers in their environment, but also develops a comprehension regarding their *own viability* as an attachment figure to others. Thus, another reason that attachment is more elusive to assess during preschool is because attachment processes have become more internalized.

To assess such attachment functioning at the cognitive level, experts have developed attachment-related stories with photographs to induce thinking regarding attachment that can be used with older preschoolers (Kaplan, 1987; Jacobsen, Edelstein, & Hofmann, 1994). The preschool child might be shown a series of pictures depicting an adult who is departing on a plane as a child looks on, the child returning home, and the child next opening a package with a toy plane inside. Experts next code the responses into different attachment categories. Secure children provide empathetic/sympathetic responses to such stories, and offer methods to cope with these feelings of distress, such as, "The little girl feels sad because her dad is away, she can go hug her mommy to feel better". In contrast, insecure children may deny any emotional separations has occurred (avoidant), express strong anger during the story (ambivalent) or express extremely fearful or bizarre responses (disorganized), such as "He's going to die in a plane crash" (Jacobsen et al., 1994). Similar methods have been used to tap individual differences in attachment-related thinking in even younger children (age 3), although experts often relay stories to preschoolers using dolls rather than pictures (Bretherton, Ridgeway, & Cassidy, 1990).

Although the "move to representation" in attachment processes makes such functioning more difficult to evaluate, these representations have important implications for social learning. That is, if these representations are used to interpret and predict the affect, thinking, and behavior of potential attachment partners, then the socio-emotional context provided by caregivers plays an important role in the affirmation or rejection of these models. This is an exciting idea, particularly in relevance to insecure preschoolers that witness the attachment-related behavior of emerging attachment figures that may be inconsistent with their generalized attachment representations. We next turn to theory and research that would support the notion that the emergence of generalized attachment representations has important implications for social learning in the preschool years.

ATTACHMENT AND SOCIAL LEARNING IN PRESCHOOL: RELEVANCE TO SELF-FUNCTIONING

The relationship between attachment and social learning in the preschool years can be better understood by considering Bowlby's (1988) perspective regarding the emergence and refinement of generalized attachment representations. As the child develops an understanding regarding the reliability and viability of attachment figures, she begins to develop a complementary view of the *self* as worthy of the treatment that she receives (Cassidy, 1999). Theoretically, children who receive reliable and effective support from caregivers develop the expectancy that they are valued, important, and loved. These expectancies have a major bearing on the development of self-concept and self-esteem; two vital elements of the self-system that emerge during the preschool years.

Further, the major biological function of attachment—at least in terms of protection of children in danger as they learn to protect themselves—remains an important concern in the preschool years (Cicchetti et al., 1990). The child's *awareness* regarding the promptness and effectiveness of caregivers in alleviating distress increases. A consistent and effective caregiving environment during the preschool years reinforces the child's emerging attachment representation of his social world. Although an *effective* caregiving context would seem paramount in reinforcing these attachment models, it is important to underscore that a *stable*, or *consistent* environment is important as well. Such consistency forecasts stability of attachment functioning from infancy through the preschool years (and potentially beyond) (Main, Hesse, & Kaplan, 2005; Waters, Merrick, Treboux, Crowell, & Albersheim, 2000). This stability probably has more to do with consistency in the caregiving environment rather than anything magical about infant attachment functioning. To underscore this point, major changes in the caregiving environment—for the better or worse—predicts instability in attachment ratings over time (Waters et al., 2000).

The development of perspective taking during the preschool years may also play a major role in the development, maintenance, and even alteration of generalized attachment representations. That is, as the child becomes more aware of the goals and motives of an attachment partner (Bowlby, 1969/1982), they may become more aware of *why* they are treated a certain way, and may more readily attend to the reciprocal emotions and behavior of attachment figures (e.g., marital behavior; peer interactions). In a related fashion, preschoolers differ in their perspective taking abilities and attention to the behavior and emotions of others (Selman, 1980). A central question pertains to whether individual differences in generalized attachment representations play a role in such perspective taking, attention abilities, and even recall of interactions with attachment figures.

To illustrate, adults with different attachment styles interpret, process, and react differently to the emotions and behaviors of attachment partners. A secure adult, when engaged in an argument with an attachment figure may interpret and later recall the encounter very differently than a more avoidant or anxious/preoccupied adult (Fenney & Cassidy, 2003). The more avoidant person may not as readily attend to the interaction as a more secure adult, or a more anxious adult may ruminate about the encounter in a more negative fashion. Although it is well known that older children, adolescents, and adults with different attachment stances interpret and react to their attachment worlds differently—this is the whole essence of the generalized attachment representation construct—such research with preschoolers is still emerging. If our premise is correct, then individual differences in the attachment representations of preschoolers has major implications for social learning, in that, two similar-aged preschoolers may interpret the behavior and affect of the same person (e.g., day care teacher) differently.

In summary, with the ontogeny of generalized attachment representations, the preschooler develops an awareness regarding their worthiness as an attachment figure. Because secure children believe they are highly valued, it is not surprising that secure people of all ages develop coherent self-concepts and have better self-esteem than their insecure counterparts (Thompson, 1999). In addition, secure children simply get used to positive outcomes when they are distressed. That is, the secure preschooler repeatedly observes the following pattern: distress → comfort; distress → comfort; distress → comfort. Thus, it is not surprising that the affect regulation of secure preschoolers, children, and adolescents is better than their insecure peers (e.g., Kobak, 1999); these youth have gradually learned that their troubles will be effectively addressed because there is no reason to think otherwise.

In contrast, the insecure child may experience neglect or rejection when distressed, and these differential experiences provide specific learning contexts for insecure preschoolers. The more avoidant child, as a coping mechanism to address feelings of neglect, may gradually learn to minimize their emotions, and develop a somewhat unhealthy self-reliance or overly inflated self-esteem. In contrast, anxious or resistant children, because they are more likely to have their concerns actively rejected by parents (Main et al., 2005), may view themselves as unworthy as an attachment figure and develop a poor self-concept. Thus, the generalized attachment representations of preschoolers have an important role in the development of self, perspective taking, and affect regulation. However, attachment functioning during the preschool years plays a broader role than unilaterally influencing self-development. In the next section, its relevance to the development of emerging attachment-like relationships is considered.

ATTACHMENT AND SOCIAL LEARNING IN PRESCHOOL: RELEVANCE TO EMERGING RELATIONSHIPS

As preschoolers come to understand the predictability and effectiveness of attachment figures, the child develops a complementary view of the self as worthy of the treatment that he or she receives (Cassidy, 1999). In addition, the child begins to understand their role as an attachment figure to others, which has important implications regarding their interactions with potentially new attachment contacts (e.g., peers; teachers). We assert that certain social interactions during the preschool years may reaffirm or conflict with these expectancies, and argue that *attachment security could also influence the very occurrence of these interactions.*

In terms of the latter issue, attachment in the preschool years does not occur in a vacuum, that is, the initial development of attachment occurs during infancy. Thus, even at age 3, the child has three years of attachment experiences with caregivers that have an impact on exploration and personality development (Sroufe, Egeland, Carlson, & Collins, 2005). For example, attachment security in infancy is predictive of autonomy development and exploration in toddlerhood and the early preschool years (Sroufe, 1983). Further, secure children are more persistent and curious, and cope with stress better than their insecure counterparts (Arend, Gove, & Sroufe, 1979). Insecure children, on the other hand, lack such persistence and engage in novel ways of coping with stress and anger. For example, when engaged in difficult learning tasks with their caregivers, more resistant toddlers direct their frustrations towards their adult mentors whereas more avoidant children ignore the mentoring behaviors of their caregivers or exhibit noncompliant behaviors (Sroufe, 1983).

The implications of these outcomes are important for social learning, that is, a secure, independent preschooler that is comfortable with exploration will more readily seek out social affiliations than a preschooler that is more avoidant or anxious. One domain that this competence has a strong bearing on concerns peer involvement. Preschoolers rated as secure during infancy have more friends, are better liked, and engage in more competent interactions with peers than preschoolers classified as insecure (LaFreniere & Sroufe, 1985). Insecure preschoolers may shun peer interactions, or display immature or hostile behavior when interacting with peers (e.g., Lyons-Ruth, Alpern, & Repacholi, 1993; McElwain, Cox, Burchinal, & Macfie, 2003). Further, more avoidant children display less empathy towards their peers, more anxious or resistant children are timid and suffer from peer rejection, and preschoolers rated as disorganized are more hostile and controlling in their peer interactions (Berlin & Cassidy, 1999). Although these findings seem to suggest that certain forms of attachment insecurity might be linked to unique profiles of peer interaction difficulties, this is an area of study that has been somewhat neglected by attachment researchers.

Perhaps most relevant to social learning, the peer play of secure children is extremely competent. For instance, secure preschoolers are fun to play with! They display more positive affect, exhibit better interactions with their peers, and engage in more elaborate play themes than more insecure children. For example, more avoidant children often are restless and inattentive during play bouts; whereas children rated as disorganized are overly intrusive and display annoying behavior when engaged in peer play (Lyons-Ruth & Jacobvitz, 1999). Further, the play themes that secure children engage in during solitary activities are likely to draw attention from other children, who often seem quite willing to join such interesting play. Given the curiosity and exploratory abilities of secure preschoolers, it is not surprising that the solitary play themes of these children are more elaborate than those of insecure preschoolers (Creasey, Jarvis, & Berk, 1998).

In some sense, the finding that secure children exhibit more competent play makes the case that the "rich get richer". That is, the cognitive, social, and emotional implications for peer play during the preschool years are well known; competent play during the preschool years both reflects and promotes cognitive and social competence (Bond, Creasey, & Abrams, 1989; Creasey & Jarvis, 2003; Piaget, 1951), Thus, play competency partly reflects where preschoolers have come from, and partly where they are going. For instance, competent peer play requires good affect regulation; turn taking, overt communication of planned behaviors, and occasional creativity in terms of all parties involved. Thus, play allows children to practice what they have already learned as well as provides opportunities to learn from others. Although some could argue that preschoolers could get the same "lessons" from parents and teachers, play between children contains novel elements almost never witnessed in child–adult play (Eckerman, Whatley, & Kutz, 1975; Rubenstein & Howes, 1976).

Peer interactions provide important opportunities for social learning, and attachment functioning plays a role in the ontogeny of these affiliations. Of course, interactions with other existing attachment figures, such as parents and siblings, as well as potential new social contacts, such as non-relative caregivers and preschool teachers, also play an important role in social learning, and may be partially governed by the child's attachment stance. For example, preschoolers display different levels of motivation when it comes to mastering learning tasks, and show different rates of competency when learning a task alone or with a teaching partner (Slade, 1987).

Further, and central to our present discussion, is the finding that the attachment functioning of the preschooler plays an important role in learning situations. Secure children, perhaps due to their curiosity and initiative, approach learning tasks differently than insecure children. For example, they display better concentration and persistence, are less defiant, engage in more self directed learning, and are less stressed in learning situations when presented tasks that are initially difficult or beyond their developmental level than their insecure counterparts (Grossmann, Grossmann, & Zimmerman, 1999; Pianta & Harbers, 1996; Suess, Grossmann, & Sroufe, 1992). Similarly, and as stated earlier in this review, insecure children are more likely to become frustrated, restless, and engage in off-task behavior (Suess et al., 1992). Furthermore, these teaching interactions, beyond their importance for cognitive development, have important implications for social learning.

For instance, a child who cannot sit still during story time or is perceived as overly needy when presented relatively easy learning tasks might actually influence subsequent interactions in a negative manner with both parents and preschool teachers. Thus, the child's attachment stance may very well influence the impressions of these adults. For example, more avoidant children—who are prone to indifference, lack motivation, and exhibit peer hostility—are more likely to be targets of teacher anger. In contrast, teachers often perceive anxious-ambivalent children as overly needy during learning tasks (Pianta, Nimetz, & Bennett, 1997). Thus, like interactions with peers, these examples represent a strong case for why attachment functioning in preschoolers has major importance for social learning. In this case, the child's attachment functioning has an important role in shaping the expectancies and behavior of emerging members of their support network (e.g., preschool teachers).

CAN ATTACHMENT FUNCTIONING UNDERGO CHANGE IN PRESCHOOL?

A case has been made that the attachment functioning of the preschooler has important implications for social behavior, learning, and development. We have so far painted the secure or insecure child as a major contributor to his or her own development. For instance, due to their generalized attachment representations, secure and insecure preschoolers wear different lens regarding their social worlds. The way they attend to, interpret, and react to social interactions is already quite different. Further, attachment functioning influences the way that others treat them.

Given these findings, and the rather consistent result that attachment functioning remains stable across the preschool years (Main et al., 2005), it comes as no surprise that major reviews have been devoted to illuminating attachment-based interventions involving infants and young children (e.g., Lieberman & Zeanah, 1999). However, such reviews are often more accessible to professionals that work in practice settings (e.g., psychotherapists), and may not be readily applicable to those of us that work in educational settings. Thus, is there anything that we, as educators, can do to alter the attachment stances of insecure children and maintain those held by more secure preschoolers?

The vignette portraying Tommy in the chapter introduction provides a good example of how generalized attachment representations can undergo modification. Bowlby (1988) himself speculated that while generalized attachment representations are subject to modification given changes in the caregiving environment or events that have a direct impact on the attachment system. Indeed, as stated earlier, major changes in the child's environment have been associated with changes in attachment security over time (Waters et al., 2000).

There are at least two major directions for educational intervention that may have an influence on the attachment functioning of preschoolers. The first pertains to intervention at the level of the parent–child relationship. For example, it has been theorized that the link between the parent's and child's attachment functioning is best explained by parent sensitivity (DeWolff & van IJzendoorn, 1997). That is, a parent that possesses considerable attachment insecurity may exhibit problematic caregiving behaviors, such as neglect or rejection, that in turn may directly contribute to the child's attachment functioning. Thus, in terms of intervention angles, one could possibly attempt to alter the parent's attachment representations, their parenting behavior, or both.

Unfortunately, what might work in theory does not always lend itself well to practice. Although there have been a number of industrious attempts to alter parental sensitivity and patterns of attachment in infants and young children (e.g., Jacobson & Frye, 1991; Lieberman, Weston, & Pawl, 1991; Lyons-Ruth, Connell, Grunebaum, & Botein, 1990), these interventions have mixed outcomes. For instance, some intervention efforts bolster parent sensitivity without an impact on the attachment functioning of the children, whereas other efforts yield improvements in attachment functioning, but have little influence on parent sensitivity (Lieberman & Zeanah, 1999). There may be numerous explanations for these findings, but it should be noted that empirical studies have only documented modest associations between parent attachment functioning, parental sensitivity, and child attachment functioning in the first place. These findings are somewhat inconsistent with Bowlby's notion that the way parents respond to the distress of the child is paramount in predicting the child's attachment status. Although methodological issues concerning the measurement of these constructs could potentially explain the modest links between parent sensitivity and child attachment, it is possible that certain characteristics of the child (e.g., emerging personality), parent (e.g., general emotional functioning), and broader family context (e.g., marital functioning; sibling interactions) mediate or moderate associations between parent sensitivity and child attachment (e.g., Belsky, 1984). Yet, if this premise were true, it would suggest that intervention work conducted in the family context to alter insecure attachment stances of preschoolers would be a very daunting task. Further, one might wonder if certain families with extensive attachment problems, or other difficulties such as marital disharmony, would even volunteer for family-based intervention services.

A second arena for possible intervention work pertains to the preschool context; the vignette provided at the beginning of the chapter suggested that a caring and nurturing child-care context might moderate associations between problematic parenting and child behavior problems. Further there is considerable empirical evidence that the preschool environment has important implications for attachment functioning and social learning. As stated earlier, peer play has important implications for such learning; thus, encouraging children to engage in competent and interesting play bouts could influence attachment, social learning, or both. Of course, such an intervention should consist of more than simply asking children to "play together"; rather, more cooperative or symbolic play might need to be encouraged by the preschool teacher.

Beyond fostering close relationships with peers, it is our opinion that the child's relationship with his or her teacher may be as critical. We suggest that the child's preschool teacher, *in certain cases*, qualifies as an important attachment figure. The idea of multiple attachment to others is not a new one; Bowlby (1969/1982) himself suggested that even infants may form specific attachment relationships with various members of their support network. On the other hand, there is considerable debate regarding who can exactly qualify as a legitimate attachment figure; for some time, attachment experts argued whether even marital couples qualified as true attachment partners in the Bowlby/Ainsworth tradition.

As illustrated earlier, an attachment relationship is one that is persistent and emotionally significant, and true attachment figures are highly invested in protecting the child during times of danger. Thus, it would seem that *certain* child-care providers might meet these criteria; however, the real litmus test for an attachment relationship is the *presence of secure base behavior*. That is, the child should readily seek comfort from attachment figures when distressed, and a secure relationship would be defined as one in which the attachment figure can effectively quell distress in the child. Again, it would seem that certain providers, at least at the preschool level, would meet this requirement and qualify as important attachment figures.

Growing evidence supports this contention. To start, one requirement of an attachment figure pertains to the stability and duration of the relationship (Cassidy, 1999). In the case of preschool child-care providers, identifiable attachment relationships can be observed between children and teachers, but this is more likely to occur in cases where the child has known the teacher for some time. That is, it is more difficult to identify a consistent attachment style between the child and teacher if the teacher is relatively new or unfamiliar (Barnas & Cummings, 1997; Howes, 1999). Further, a very encouraging finding is that the quality of attachment with the teacher is generally secure, *even in cases where the child has an insecure relationship with the parent* (Howes & Ritchie, 1998).

Another sign that such affiliations are attachment relationships is that individual differences in attachment behaviors between preschoolers and teachers resemble those identified between children and parents. That is, some children have more secure relationships with teachers, whereas others appear more avoidant or ambivalent in terms of their attachment stances (Howes & Hamilton, 1992). In the former case, the child readily approaches the teacher during times of distress and receives effective comfort, whereas in the latter cases, the child may not approach the teacher when upset (avoidant), or may approach but cannot be calmed down (anxious-resistant).

These findings suggest that some children develop identifiable attachment relationships with their preschool teachers; thus, the implications for social learning in the preschool years become quite vast. As an example, it is assumed that children, like adults (e.g., Treboux, Crowell, & Waters, 2004), develop *relationship-specific representations* with individual attachment figures. A key issue concerns compatibility of the preschooler's generalized attachment representation with the more specific model of the teacher. For example, the outcomes for generally secure children that develop a secure representation of their preschool teacher would seem clear. That is, this child is used to a stimulating and responsive caregiving environment, and in this case, such expectancies are simply confirmed. Thus, their generalized representations become stronger and more consolidated.

However, what are the outcomes of children that are generally insecure, but have a caring, nurturing teacher? The wish for all developmental experts would be that the child begins to take notice of the teacher's responsiveness, and may begin to alter their generalized representation. However, the true picture of this process is difficult to discern. That is, a general, deep distrust of adults may create very problematic interactions between the child and teacher on the short-term; yet, relationships might begin to improve in the long-term. These improvements could also positively influence peer interactions and lead to more optimal relationships with parents.

On the other hand, perhaps incompatibility of more generalized and relationship-specific representations is much more difficult to resolve. Indeed, studies of dating and marital couples have demonstrated that adults with secure generalized attachment representations that have insecure representations regarding their partner have difficult and lasting problems in their relationships (Creasey, 2002; Treboux et al., 2004). Can the preschool child really reconcile the disparities in these models? Further, how does the *teacher's* generalized attachment representation potentially influence this process? For example, does a teacher with a secure generalized attachment representation persist in helping an avoidant child who does not actively seek his or her help? In a related vein, how does this teacher interact with anxious-resistant children, that is, can the teacher provide effective instruction and support to overly clingy or demanding children? In both cases, the general attachment functioning of the child does not "fit" the teachers' prototype for attachment security. Thus, it is evident that much more research in this arena is needed.

CONCLUSIONS

In this chapter, a case was made that attachment functioning has important implications for social learning during the preschool years. The attachment functioning of preschoolers, both at the cognitive and behavioral levels, appears to influence the manner in which children attend to, interpret, and react to emotional and social information in their growing social worlds. In particular, it was stipulated that children with secure attachment stances are more likely to explore, develop enhanced self-concepts and self-esteem, and exhibit better interactions with potential new attachment figures than more insecure children. Thus, the secure child not only practices what they already have learned, but also may be more open to acquiring new social information based on their curiosity, autonomy and affiliative nature. Further, close relationships with new attachment figures reaffirm their belief that they are valued and important.

Although not every insecure child displays problematic outcomes during the preschool years (Thompson, 1999), it is prudent to posit that such insecure children are at risk for social difficulties. Their potential lack of exploration and autonomy, as well as more problematic relationships with peers and teachers, does little to enhance social learning. Thus, they may be robbed of the social, emotional, and cognitive benefits of social pretend play with peers, and certain teachers may find interactions with these children quite challenging, if not stressful. If anything, such scenarios reinforce the child's expectancies that they are unworthy of affection and attention and their insecurity is reaffirmed.

We would like to think that the positive social environments of certain insecure preschoolers could potentially alter their attachment representations and behavior. However, considerable debate exists if this premise is true, and whether certain social agents—such as peers or teachers—even qualify as attachment figures. Although more research is needed to test these ideas, we remain excited about the potential role of the teacher as an important attachment figure, as well as the preschool context for attachment generalizations to grow and develop. This role may have important implications for social learning at the present, as well as the future. For example, the attachment relationship between the preschooler and teacher may predict adjustment to kindergarten or relationships with future teachers.

In addition, while there are a number of studies that have assessed attachment-like relationships between preschoolers and their teachers, we encourage more work with older children. If anything, these affiliations, if they are attachment relationships, may look very different than the relationships between children and parents, or peers. For instance, an older child or adolescent may develop such a relationship purely at the cognitive level. To illustrate, some older children might develop a secure model of the teacher simply based on the expectancy that the teacher would be available and effective "in case" something problematic were to arise in or out of the classroom environment. It would be interesting to identify both student and teacher variables that forecast such thinking, as well as their impact on the overall learning process in a particular classroom environment. Thus, research specifying the role of attachment in the learning process is needed at all educational levels.

REFERENCES

Ainsworth, M. (1967). *Infancy in Uganda: Infant care and the growth of attachment.* Baltimore: John Hopkins University Press.

Ainsworth, M., Blehar, M., Waters, E., & Wall, S. (1978). *Patterns of attachment: A psychological study of the strange situation.* Hillsdale, NJ: Erlbaum.

Arend, R., Gove, F., & Sroufe, L.A. (1979). Continuity of individual adaptation from infancy to kindergarten: A predictive study of ego-resiliency and curiosity in preschoolers. *Child Development, 50*, 950–959.

Barnas, M., & Cummings, E.M. (1997). Caregiver stability and toddlers' attachment-related behaviors towards caregivers in day care. *Infant Behavior and Development, 17*, 171–177.

Belsky, J. (1984). The determinants of parenting: A process model. *Developmental Psychology, 55*, 83–96.

Berlin, L., & Cassidy, J. (1999). Relations among relationships: Contributions from attachment theory and research. In J. Cassidy & P. Shaver (Eds.), *Handbook of attachment: Theory, research, and clinical applications* (pp. 688–712). New York: Guilford Press.

Bond, L., Creasey, G., & Abrams, C. (1989). Play assessments: Reflecting and promoting cognitive competence. In E. Gibbs & D. Teti (Eds.), *Interdisciplinary assessment of infants* (pp. 113–128). Baltimore, MD: Brookes.

Bowlby, J. (1969/1982). *Attachment and loss: Vol. 1: Attachment* (2nd ed.). New York: Basic.

Bowlby, J. (1988). *A secure base: Clinical applications of attachment theory.* London: Routledge.

Bretherton, I., & Munholland, K. (1999). Internal working models in attachment relationships: A construct revisited. In J. Cassidy & P. Shaver (Eds.), *Handbook of attachment: Theory, research, and clinical applications* (pp. 89–111). New York: Guilford Press.

Bretherton, I., Ridgeway, D., & Cassidy, J. (1990). Assessing internal working models of the attachment relationship: An attachment story completion task for 3-year-olds. In M. Greenberg, D. Cicchetti, & E.M. Cummings (Eds.), *Attachment in the preschool years: Theory, research, and intervention* (pp. 273–308). Chicago: University of Chicago Press.

Cassidy, J. (1999). The nature of the child's ties. In J. Cassidy & P. Shaver (Eds.), *Handbook of attachment: Theory, research, and clinical applications* (pp. 3–20). New York: Guilford Press.

Cassidy, J., & Marvin, R. (1992). *Attachment organization in preschool children: Coding guidelines.* Unpublished manuscript, MacArthur Working Group on Attachment, Seattle, WA.

Cicchetti, D., Cummings, E., Greenberg, M., & Marvin, R. (1990). Attachment beyond infancy: Implications for theory, measurement, and research. In M. Greenberg, D. Cicchetti, & E.M. Cummings (Eds.), *Attachment in the preschool years: Theory, research, and intervention* (pp. 3–49). Chicago: University of Chicago Press.

Creasey, G. (2002). Associations between working models of attachment and conflict management behavior in romantic couples. *Journal of Counseling Psychology, 49.* 365–375.

Creasey, G., & Jarvis, P. (2003). Play in children: An attachment perspective. In O. Satacho & B. Spodek (Eds.), *Contemporary perspectives in early childhood education* (pp. 133–151). Greenwich, CT: Information Age Publishing.

Creasey, G., Jarvis, P., & Berk, L. (1998). Play and social competence. In O. Saracho & B. Spodek (Eds.), *Multiple perspectives on play and early childhood education* (pp. 116–143). New York: SUNY Press.

DeWolff, M., & van IJzendoorn, M. (1997). Sensitivity and attachment: A meta-analysis on parent antecedents of infant attachment. *Child Development, 68,* 571–591.

Eckerman, C., Whatley, J., & Kutz, S. (1975). Growth of social play with peers during the second year of life. *Developmental Psychology, 11,* 42–49.

Fenney, B., & Cassidy, J. (2003). Reconstructive memory related to adolescent-parent conflict interactions: The influence of attachment-related representations on immediate perceptions and changes in perceptions over time. *Journal of Personality and Social Psychology, 85,* 945–955.

Freud, S. (1957). Five lectures on psycho-analysis. In J. Strachey (Eds. And Trans.), *The standard edition of the complete psychological works of Sigmund Freud* (Vol. 11, pp. 3–56). London: Hogarth Press.

Grossmann, K.E., Grossmann, K., & Zimmerman, P. (1999). A wider view of attachment and exploration: Stability and change during the years of immaturity. In

J. Cassidy & P. Shaver (Eds.), *Handbook of attachment: Theory, research, and clinical applications* (pp. 760–786). New York: Guilford Press.

Howes, C. (1999). Attachment relationships in the context of multiple caregivers. In J. Cassidy & P. Shaver (Eds.), *Handbook of attachment: Theory, research, and clinical applications* (pp. 671–687). New York: Guilford Press.

Howes, C., & Hamilton, C. (1992). Children's relationships with caregivers: Mothers and child care teachers. *Child Development, 63*, 859–866.

Howes, C., & Ritchie, S. (1998). Changes in child-teacher relationship in a therapeutic preschool program. *Early education and development, 9*, 411–422.

Jacobsen, R., Edelstein, W., & Hofmann, V. (1994). A longitudinal study of the relation between representations of attachment in childhood and cognitive functioning in childhood and adolescence. *Developmental Psychology, 30*, 11–124.

Jacobson, S., & Frye, K. (1991). Effect of maternal social support on attachment: Experimental evidence. *Child Development, 62*, 572–582.

Kaplan, N. (1987). Individual differences in six-year-olds' thoughts about separation: Predicted from attachment to mother at one year of age. Unpublished doctoral dissertation, University of California—Berkeley.

Kobak, R. (1999). The emotional dynamics of disruptions in attachment relationships: Implications for theory, research, and clinical intervention. In J. Cassidy & P. Shaver (Eds.), *Handbook of attachment: Theory, research, and clinical applications* (pp. 21–43). New York: Guilford Press.

LaFreniere, P., & Sroufe, L.A. (1985). Profiles of peer competence in preschool: Interrelations between measures, influence of social ecology, and relation to attachment history. *Developmental Psychology, 21*, 56–69.

Lieberman, A. F., Weston, D. R., & Pawl, J. H. (1991). Preventative intervention and outcome with anxiously attached dyads. *Child Development, 62*, 199–209.

Lieberman, A., & Zeanah, C. (1999). Contributions of attachment theory to infant-parent psychotherapy and other interventions with infants and young children. In J. Cassidy & P. Shaver (Eds.), *Handbook of attachment: Theory, research, and clinical applications* (pp. 555–574). New York: Guilford Press.

Lyons-Ruth, K., Alpern, L., & Repacholi, B. (1993). Disorganized infant attachment classification and maternal psychosocial problems as predictors of hostile-aggressive behavior in the preschool classroom. *Child Development, 64*, 572–585.

Lyons-Ruth, K., Connell, D., Grunebaum, H., & Botein, S. (1990). Infants at social risk: Maternal depression and family support services as mediators of infant development and security of attachment. *Child Development, 61*, 85–98.

Lyons-Ruth, K., & Jacobvitz, D. (1999). Attachment disorganization: Unresolved loss, relational violence, and lapses in behavioral and attentional strategies. In J. Cassidy & P. Shaver (Eds.), *Handbook of attachment: Theory, research, and clinical applications* (pp. 520–554). New York: Guilford Press.

Main, M., & Cassidy, J. (1988). Categories of response to reunion with the parent at age 6: Predictable from infant attachment classifications and stable over a 1-month-period. *Developmental Psychology, 24*, 415–426.

Main, M., Hesse, E., & Kaplan, N. (2005). Predictability of attachment behavior and representational processes at 1, 6, and 19 years of age: The Berkeley Longitudinal Study. In K.E. Grossmann, K. Grossmann, & E. Waters (Eds.), *Attachment from infancy to adulthood: The major longitudinal studies* (pp. 245–304). New York: Guilford Press.

Main, M., & Solomon, J. (1990). Procedures for identifying infants disorganized/ disoriented during the Ainsworth strange situation. In M. Greenberg, D. Cicchetti, & E. Cummings (Eds.), *Attachment in the preschool years: Theory, research, and intervention* (pp. 121–160). Chicago: University of Chicago Press.

McElwain, N., Cox, M., Burchinal, M., & Macfie, J. (2003). Differentiating among insecure mother-infant attachment classifications: A focus on child-friend interaction and exploration during solitary play at 36 months. *Attachment and Human Development, 5,* 136–154.

Pianta, R., & Harbers, K. (1996). Observing mother and child behavior in a problem-solving situation at school entry: Relations with academic achievement. *Journal of School Psychology, 34,* 307–322.

Pianta, R., Nimetz, S., & Bennett, E. (1997). Mother-child relationships, teacher–child relationships, and school outcomes in preschool and kindergarten. *Early Childhood Research Quarterly, 12,* 263–280.

Piaget, J. (1951). *Play, dreams, and imitation in childhood.* New York: Norton.

Rubenstein, J., & Howes, C. (1976). The effects of peers on toddler interaction with mothers and toys. *Child Development, 47,* 597–605.

Sagi, A. (1990). Attachment theory and research from a cross-cultural perspective. *Human Development, 33,* 10–22.

Sears, R., Maccoby, E., & Levin, H. (1957). *Patterns of child rearing.* Evanston, IL: Row, Peterson.

Selman, R. (1980). *The growth of interpersonal understanding: Developmental and clinical analysis.* New York: Academic Press.

Slade, A. (1987). Quality of attachment and early symbolic play. *Developmental Psychology, 23,* 78–85.

Sroufe, L. (1983). Infant-caregiver attachment and patterns of adaptation in preschool: The roots of maladaption and competence. In M. Perlmutter (Ed.), *Minnesota Symposia on Child Psychology: Vol 16. Development and Policy concerning children with special needs* (pp. 41–83). Hillsdale, NJ: Erlbaum.

Sroufe, L.A., Egeland, B., Carlson, E., & Collins, W. (2005). Placing early attachment experiences in developmental context: The Minnesota Longitudinal Study. In K.E. Grossmann, K. Grossmann, & E. Waters (Eds.), *Attachment from infancy to adulthood: The major longitudinal studies* (pp. 245–304). New York: Guilford Press.

Suess, G., Grossmann, K.E., & Sroufe, L.A. (1992). Effects of infant attachment to mother and father on quality of adaptation in preschool: From dyadic to individual organization of self. *International Journal of Behavioral Development, 15,* 43–65.

Thompson, R. (1999). Early attachment and later development. . In J. Cassidy & P. Shaver (Eds.), *Handbook of attachment: Theory, research, and clinical applications* (pp. 265–286). New York: Guilford Press.

Treboux, D., Crowell, J., Waters, E. (2004). When "New" Meets "Old": Configurations of adult attachment representations and their implications for marital functioning. *Developmental Psychology, 40,* 295–314.

Waters, E., Merrick, S., Treboux, D., Crowell, J., & Albersheim, L. (2000). Attachment security in infancy and early adulthood: A twenty-year longitudinal study. *Child Development, 71,* 684–689.

CHAPTER 4

FEELING, THINKING, AND PLAYING

Social and Emotional Learning in Early Childhood

Christopher J. Trentacosta and Carroll E. Izard

Cody, Brianna, and Dylan are gathered around the sand table during free play time in their preschool classroom. Cody is carefully playing with one of the sand toys when Brianna reaches over and grabs it out of Cody's hands. Cody immediately reacts by reaching out to hit Brianna and yells out "that's mine!" After she gets hit, the toy falls out of her hand, she starts to cry, and Dylan moves closer to hug and comfort her. A nearby teacher hears the commotion and comes over to the sand table. Dylan tells the teacher that Cody hit Brianna. The teacher asks Cody to apologize. Cody responds by saying "she took the toy from me!" and starts yelling and gesturing as if he plans to hit Brianna or the teacher. It takes Brianna nearly a minute to stop crying, and Cody ends up sitting in the time out chair for three minutes due to his temper tantrum.

The scene described above is a relatively typical exchange in an early childhood classroom, particularly a classroom serving children from high-risk or disadvantaged backgrounds. The behaviors described in the scene can be viewed as a series of behavior problems, but an equally helpful way to view

Contemporary Perspectives on Socialization and Social Development..., pages 59–77
Copyright © 2007 by Information Age Publishing

this exchange is within the context of early childhood social and emotional learning. These children, while of roughly the same chronological age, demonstrate varying degrees of emotional and social maturity. As is typical of preschool-aged children, for the most part they have not yet mastered the ability to manage their emotions. Also, their proficiency with rudimentary social skills is limited. However, the preschool play context described above provides a unique venue for these children to learn these skills and abilities so that they can adapt to the challenges that they will face as they leave preschool and enter kindergarten, elementary school, and beyond.

This chapter is intended to describe social and emotional learning (SEL) in early childhood education. First, we discuss the essential elements of SEL in the framework of differential emotions theory. Secondly, we describe the important contextual factors in the early childhood education environment that can promote these SEL skills. Next, we outline some of the important research on outcomes of SEL during early childhood, paying special attention to the effects of social skills and emotion competence during the transition to kindergarten and elementary school. Also, we provide an overview of some of the many prevention and intervention programs for young children that have empirical support. Finally, we provide future directions for research in this area as well as new directions for the practical application of SEL in the early childhood classroom.

THEORETICAL FRAMEWORK: DIFFERENTIAL EMOTIONS THEORY

Our entire discussion of SEL in the early childhood classroom is guided by differential emotions theory (DET) (Izard, 1991) and related basic and prevention research (e.g., Izard et al., 2001; Izard, Trentacosta, King, & Mostow, 2004). According to DET, emotions are inherently adaptive and motivational. Learning to understand, manage, and utilize one's emotions to promote social adaptation and prosocial behavior is a challenge across the lifespan and particularly in early childhood. DET attempts to explain and predict cognition and behavior as well as passage of developmental milestones in terms of discrete emotions, patterns of emotions, and the interactions among emotion, cognition, and action or overt behavior. Conceptualization of each of these aspects of causal processes is influenced by the fundamental psychological principles that recognize the moderating effects of individual differences, family, and culture on each of the foregoing processes. Nevertheless, DET emphasizes the proposition that emotions drive cognition and action.

DET provides a framework for understanding the normative development of emotions and related abilities with implications for the development of psychopathology. DET and the related research have allowed us to more clearly pinpoint the specific emotion skills and behaviors that emerge in early childhood and the ways in which these skills promote social competence and later adaptation. As the above description suggests, DET emphasizes emotion and emotion-related systems as key motivators of early childhood development. Thus, DET is unique from many other psychosocial developmental theories. However, there are important similarities between DET and other developmental theories such as Erikson's (1964) psychosocial theory of development.

Erikson posits a number of universal emotional conflicts—autonomy vs. shame and doubt in toddlerhood, initiative vs. guilt in early childhood, industry vs. inferiority in middle childhood, and identity vs. confusion in adolescence. Erikson argues that individuals must resolve each of these inevitable conflicts to pass the developmental milestones on the way to integrity and wisdom in old age. DET also recognizes that emotion-related issues emerge in the course of development and that some are more likely that others in a given age period. However, it does not see all those on Erikson's list as inevitable. For example, empirical data suggests that boys are more likely than girls to fail to deal effectively with the anger associated with strivings for self-control/autonomy and that that boys' failure to resolve this conflict may lead to fairly stable traits of anger perception bias, anger proneness, and aggressive behavior. If early aggressive behavior does not subside over time and becomes characteristic of a toddler, it will likely remain a stable characteristic of caregiver-infant interactions (Keenan & Shaw, 1994), appear in peer interactions during ages 2–5 years (Cummings, Iannotti, & Zahn-Waxler, 1989), and characterize children with externalizing problems or conduct disorder in middle childhood (Keenan, 2000; NICHD Early Child Care Research Network, 2004; O'Leary, Slep, & Reid, 1999).

While DET has some similarities with developmental stage theories such as Erikson's theory, similarities with cultural or contextual theories such as Bronfenbrenner's (1979) ecological perspective are less apparent. DET recognizes that emotion motivation is affected by person factors (e.g., sex, intelligence, temperament) and contextual factors (e.g., family structure, emotional climate within the family and neighborhood, cultural differences) that help determine the shape, direction, and intensity of the behavior. Studies of emotion-related abilities are not uncommon in diverse samples such as samples of ethnic minority and low-income children (see Raver, 2004), and the prevention research based on DET described below was carried out in a range of Head Start centers. Also, researchers have begun to examine cultural influences on the understanding, experience, and expression of emotion in childhood (e.g., Cole, Bruschi, & Tamang, 2002).

Nonetheless, DET provides less guidance on contextual factors and ecological variables, particularly mesosystems and macrosystems (see Bronfenbrenner & Morris, 2006) such as larger communities, political environments, and changes in these environments over time, as predictors and moderators of emotion development. Furthermore, like numerous other normative developmental theories, DET runs the risk of inappropriately applying our understanding of children's emotions and the development of emotion as a universal, scientifically validated truth (see Cannella, 1997). Those who translate DET and related research into interventions without considering feedback on the program from parents and teachers in the culture/community where the work will be done run the risk of inappropriately labeling certain emotion-related behaviors as "normal" and others as "abnormal." With these cautions in mind, we turn to a discussion of SEL elements based on DET and related research.

ESSENTIAL ELEMENTS OF SEL

SEL is a construct that has been used to describe a wide variety of behaviors, skills, and abilities including adaptive decision-making, self-awareness, and appreciation of diversity (Denham & Weissberg, 2006). In order to maintain a focused discussion of SEL skills, it is important to select a limited set of essential elements that encompass this wide range of specific skills, behaviors, and abilities. Based on DET and related research with young children, we consider three essential elements of SEL: emotion knowledge, emotion regulation, and social skills.

Emotion Knowledge

In the vignette presented above, Dylan's behavior indicates that he possessed adequate emotion knowledge in this situation. His hugging and comforting behavior toward Brianna shows that he understood her tears to be an indicator of sadness. Our implicit understanding of sadness tells us that this emotion often calls for comforting from a caring peer or adult. As this example shows, emotion knowledge is the ability to recognize and understand others' as well as one's own emotions.

Emotion knowledge begins to develop from birth. Soon after birth, infants begin to perceive and recognize the emotions, as shown by their preference for smiles conveyed by a caregiver (Messinger, 2002). In the toddler and preschool years, children first begin to distinguish happy from non-happy expressions (Denham, 1998; Izard, 1971). Then, children begin to distinguish between basic negative emotions such as sadness, anger, and fear. They also begin to learn the situational and behavioral cues that tend to elicit specific emotions. Thus, by the time most children begin elementary school, they are able to begin grasping more complex emotions and the display rules that often govern the expression of emotion (Garner, 1996; Terwogt, Koops, Oosterhoff, & Olthof, 1986).

This development of emotion understanding requires intersystem connections between children's emotion systems and their cognitive and action systems (Izard, Trentacosta, King, Morgan, & Diaz, in press). Thus, emotion knowledge overlaps somewhat with children's temperament and their verbal ability. Children who experience frequent negative emotions often have more difficulty understanding emotions, and children who have less verbal ability often lag behind other children in their recognition and labeling of basic emotions.

Furthermore, early experience affects the development of intersystem connections that foster accurate emotion knowledge. For example, maltreatment has been shown to influence the manner in which children process emotions, particularly anger (e.g., Pollak, Cicchetti, Klorman, & Brumaghim, 1997). From a social information-processing perspective, maladaptive processing of emotions will negatively impact later processing stages such as intent attribution, solution generation, and goal selection in challenging situations (Crick & Dodge, 1994; Lemerise & Arsenio, 2000). Also, patterns of emotion processing and emotion knowledge that may be adaptive in harsh environments may be detrimental in more normative environments that require accurate emotion knowledge. Thus, a child who is sensitized to anger cues in an abusive home may be especially at risk for difficulty when faced with more normative expression of anger and a wide range of other emotions in the preschool classroom.

Emotion Regulation

Themes of emotion regulation, particularly dysregulation of emotion, are present in the above vignette. Brianna's initial impulsive grab for Cody's toy would often be conceptualized as impulsivity but can also be considered poor regulation of the emotion of interest. Brianna becomes uncontrollably interested in obtaining the toy. Cody's immediate reaction to hit Brianna and subsequent temper tantrum are examples of poor anger regulation, and Brianna's tendency to cry uncontrollably is an example of poor regulation of sadness.

Emotion regulation is a complex construct and there have been many attempts to adequately and comprehensively define it (see Cole, Martin, & Dennis, 2004 for a discussion). It is often difficult to separate the activation of an emotion from its regulation (Cole et al., 2004). Similar to our understanding of emotion knowledge, we see emotion regulation as involving the coordination of emotion, cognitive, and action systems (see Izard et al., in press for a more detailed discussion). Thus, emotion dysregulation represents a failure to coordinate interactions between these systems and may demonstrate a failure by the child to adequately and adaptively utilize emotion motivation to meet personal or social goals.

Emotion regulation first develops in tandem with a caregiver. However, even at a very young age, children have rudimentary self-regulatory skills such as the use of gaze aversion when presented with a disturbing stimulus (Izard, Hembree, & Huebner, 1987). In preschool, children more regularly self regulate their emotions, first by self-soothing and then by efforts to actively utilize the social environment to cope with stressful situations (Eisenberg & Spinrad, 2004). The capacity to adaptively regulate emotions, particularly the use of cognitive approaches to manage distressing emotions, continues to develop into childhood, adolescence, and adulthood (Stansbury & Sigman, 2000).

As with emotion knowledge, the development of emotion regulation is impacted by temperament/emotionality, cognitive ability, and the child's environment. Stressful environments can be especially harmful for the development of emotion regulation, particularly when the stressful environment includes inadequate or abusive caregiving (Smith & Walden, 1999). Children from harsh environments or environments characterized by low maternal warmth often are not prepared for the structure of early childhood education and the self-regulatory expectations inherent in many of these settings. However, due to the numerous affectively laden challenges the child will face in the classroom on a daily basis, the early childhood education setting is also an ideal environment for the child to begin to master rudimentary self-regulatory skills.

Social Skills

In the vignette, Dylan's comforting and hugging are examples of positive social behaviors. Furthermore, by asking Cody to apologize to Brianna, the teacher is hoping that Cody can demonstrate his own sympathetic responses and social skills. In general, the initial interaction between Cody and Brianna shows a breakdown of sharing, a key social skill in early childhood settings. The vignette also shows that failures of emotion regulation often lead to the breakdown of social skills, even if the child possesses adequate social skills in less emotionally-charged situations.

As these examples from the vignette suggest, social skills encompass a multi-faceted set of behaviors. Rose-Krasnor (1997) describes social skills as the foundation of an even broader construct called social competence. We see social skills as an essential element of social and emotion learning during early childhood because adequate social skills set the stage for other aspects of social competence to emerge during middle childhood. In particular, adequate social skills promote the development of healthy social relationships and peer acceptance in elementary school (Mostow, Izard, Fine, & Trentacosta, 2002).

Social skills, which in addition to sharing, helping, and comforting, include cooperation, assertion, social problem solving, and various other forms of prosocial behavior, often reflect adequate *emotion utilization*. Emotion utilization includes the ability to harness the motivation from discrete emotion experiences to promote adaptive, prosocial behavior (see Izard et al., in press for a more thorough discussion). Although it is difficult to study on-line emotion utilization, it is often indicated by behaviors such as sharing, helping, or comforting. For example, in the vignette, Dylan is able to utilize his empathy for Brianna to comfort her. It would be difficult to adequately measure Dylan's actual level of internal empathy, but the comforting behavior is a tangible manifestation of his ability to utilize his feelings as motivation to accomplish a prosocial goal.

The use of social skills in emotionally challenging situations likely reflects adequate emotion knowledge and emotion regulation in addition to demonstrating a proper social skill. For example, when an early childhood educator tells a child to "use your words" to express herself, the educator is not only teaching a valuable social skill but is also encouraging the child to effectively understand and manage her feelings.

EARLY CHILDHOOD PREDICTORS OF SEL SKILLS

Many of the earliest predictors of SEL skills such as temperament, cognitive ability, and family influence were described in some detail in the preceding section. There are additional predictors that are especially relevant within the early childhood learning environment. We discuss two of these predictors, social pretend play and teacher–child relationships, below.

Social Pretend Play

The emergence of emotion competence and social skills closely parallels the emergence of play in early childhood. Beginning early in the toddler years, children begin to engage in reciprocal forms of play with their peers (Howes, 1987). During this same period, children also begin to take on pretend roles when engaged in solitary play. The capacity for social play and the ability to engage in pretend play tend to merge during the 2nd year of life when children take on pretend social roles when participating in interactions with their peers (Howes, 1987).

Howes (1987) suggests that as children enter preschool, they begin to acquire knowledge of the behavioral attributes and characteristics of children within their peer group. This acquisition of knowledge overlaps with our descriptions of both emotion knowledge and social skills, and recent empirical research supports the link between the capacity for pretend play and these aspects of SEL. For example, Youngblade and Dunn (1995) showed that involvement in pretend play with a sibling at age 33 months correlated with children's emotion situation knowledge at age 40 months. Similarly, preschool-aged children that had more involvement in pretend play with their peers had higher levels of emotion understanding and, amongst girls, better emotion regulation skills (Lindsey & Colwell, 2003).

Interestingly, in the peer play study described above, other forms of play such as physical play did not significantly predict of measures of emotion competence (Lindsey & Colwell, 2003). Therefore, it appears that social pretend play has a specific benefit in promoting emotion competence. As a result, early childhood educators may want to make special efforts to increase social pretend play in their classrooms as a way to promote children's social and emotional learning.

Teacher–Child Relationships

Because many young children spend much of their time in childcare settings, it is important to consider the quality of children's relationships with their teachers when examining predictors of competence in early childhood. For young children, teachers' functions are not unlike parents' roles. Specifically, teachers provide support both emotionally and physically by feeding the child, helping her sleep, comforting her when she cries and by performing numerous child care duties (Howes & Hamilton, 1992). As such, theoretical conceptions of teacher–child relationships are based largely in attachment theory and emphasize emotional bonding and support as important aspects of relationships between teachers and their students (Pianta, 1999). Empirical research supports this theoretical perspective and suggests that teacher–child relationships can take many forms, ranging from warmth and closeness to dependency and conflict (Pianta, 1994). In terms of DET, these characteristics of secure attachment are seen as reflecting positive emotion expression and the sharing of feelings and intentions through effective communication.

In longitudinal research spanning from the toddler through preschool years, security between children and their teachers predicted numerous social behaviors (Howes, Hamilton, & Matheson, 1994). Children who had more secure relationships with their child care teachers showed more prosocial behavior and less aggressive and withdrawn behavior, and they engaged in more social and pretend play. Similarly, in the NICHD Study of Early Child Care, a broad index of positive caregiving by childcare teachers across the first three years of life was related to positive play with peers in the childcare context (NICHD Early Child Care Research Network, 2001). Although not explicitly examined in either study, children's emotion regulation and social skills are likely reflected in fewer behavior problems and higher levels of prosocial behavior. Children who had positive relationships with their teachers likely had more opportunities to receive help and support from their teachers to learn to manage their emotions and acquire positive social skills. Most importantly, the quality of early childhood teacher–child relationships not only impacted concurrent functioning but, in another recent study, also predicted the child's social competence and level of behavior problems in early elementary school (Howes, 2000).

SEL SKILLS AND SCHOOL OUTCOMES

Now that we have considered the essential elements of SEL and some of the key predictors within the early childhood education environment, it is important to also examine how SEL skills impact children's functioning in middle childhood. Outcomes in middle childhood are especially important to examine because early elementary school is often considered a "critical period" for children's school adjustment and later academic performance (Alexander, Entwisle, & Kabani, 2001). Peer acceptance and academic achievement have special significance during this developmental period and both are consistent predictors of important behavioral and cognitive outcomes into later childhood, adolescence, and adulthood.

Peer Acceptance

Although normatively developing children have the capacity to engage in play with their peers and form friendships across the toddler and preschool years (Howes, 1987), it is not until middle childhood that most children form lasting friendships with peers. Acceptance by peers is especially important in the school context because comfort with peers facilitates positive adaptation to the academic context whereas rejection by peers often leads to aggressive and antisocial behavior that can result in school dropout (Cairns, Cairns, & Neckerman, 1989; Coie & Dodge, 1988; Trentacosta & Shaw, 2007; Wentzel, 1994). Thus, identifying early childhood predictors of positive peer relationships can help educators and mental health professionals target specific areas for prevention and remediation for children at risk for social failure.

Not surprisingly, the essential elements of SEL are some of the most consistent predictors of peer acceptance (e.g., Arsenio, Cooperman, & Lover, 2000). In a longitudinal model of emotional competence and social competence in preschool and kindergarten, emotion regulation in preschool predicted concurrent social competence, and emotion knowledge predicted social competence in kindergarten (Denham, et al., 2003). This study considered social competence as a broad construct consisting of both peer ratings of likeability as well teacher ratings of broader social competence. A similar study conducted in early elementary school specifically examined peer acceptance as the outcome (Mostow et al., 2002). Emotion knowledge was significantly correlated with peer acceptance, and social skills mediated the relation between emotion knowledge and peer acceptance at school (Mostow et al., 2002). These studies suggest that appropriate understanding and regulation of emotion facilitates adaptive social behavior that promotes likeability and acceptance by peers (Izard, 2002). Alternately, when young children lack the ability to effectively understand and manage their emotions and engage in appropriate social behavior, they are often placed at risk for peer rejection and later psychopathology (e.g., Trentacosta & Shaw, 2007).

Academic Achievement

Early academic achievement contributes a substantial portion of the variance in children's later academic performance and likelihood of school drop out (Entwisle & Alexander, 1998). Therefore, examining early childhood predictors of children's kindergarten and early elementary school academic performance is essential to promote optimal achievement and close achievement gaps. Until recently, research has largely neglected social and emotional predictors of academic achievement, but recent basic research and the efforts of the Collaborative for Academic, Social, and Emotional Learning (CASEL) have highlighted the roles that emotional and social predictors can play in enhancing academic performance.

In a longitudinal study, Head Start children were given measures of emotion knowledge at age 5, and their teachers completed a measure of their academic competence in third grade (Izard et al., 2001). Emotion knowledge significantly predicted later academic competence, and, somewhat surprisingly, emotion knowledge mediated the relation between verbal ability and academic competence. In a separate sample of primarily low-income children, emotion knowledge in kindergarten directly predicted academic achievement in first grade (Trentacosta & Izard, in press).

However, the effect of emotion regulation on academic achievement was indirect through the effect of emotion regulation on children's attention to academic tasks. Similarly, another study showed that behavioral regulation mediated the relation between emotion regulation in preschool and their academic achievement in kindergarten (Howse, Calkins, Anastopoulos, Keane, & Shelton, 2003). It appears that children who can manage their emotions demonstrate higher academic achievement because they can better control their behavior and attention in the classroom.

The role of social skills in children's academic achievement has also been examined. McClelland and colleagues (McClelland, Morrison, & Holmes, 2000) suggest that there are a set of work-related social skills that are especially important for academic achievement. Work-related skills include following directions, listening, taking turns, and cooperating (Cooper & Farran, 1988). Work-related skills predicted concurrent academic achievement in a sample of kindergarten children (McClelland et al., 2000). Even more strikingly, these skills predicted academic outcomes at the end of second grade after controlling for kindergarten achievement and a number of additional control variables (McClelland et al., 2000). Also of importance, work-related skills were more consistently related to academic outcomes than more interpersonal forms of social skills (McClelland et al., 2000). Considered with the findings linking emotion regulation, attention, and achievement (Trentacosta & Izard, in press), these findings suggest that SEL skills may predict academic outcomes because SEL skills promote maturity and independence in the classroom.

PREVENTION PROGRAMS TARGETING SEL SKILLS

Numerous well-established school-based prevention programs for preschool children include content related to SEL skills. Many, if not most, of these programs are adaptations of elementary school programs, and their primary aim is usually to reduce behavior problems. We review some of the most well established of these programs below and detail our own prevention program for children in Head Start, the Emotions Course.

One of the most well established early childhood programs is the I Can Problem Solve (ICPS) program developed by Myrna Shure (Spivack & Shure, 1989). This program is largely based on a cognitive–behavioral problem solving approach, but it does include significant content pertaining to recognition of discrete emotions. ICPS has support as an effective program for promoting problem-solving abilities and reducing behavior problems in preschool children (Denham & Almeida, 1987). Less is known about how well ICPS can promote the specific SEL skills that we have outlined above, and, in general, ICPS focuses less on specific "on-line" emotion regulation strategies and use of social skills than other programs.

The Promoting Alternative THinking Strategies (PATHS) program was originally developed for deaf children and has been adapted for regular education elementary school children (Greenberg, Kusche, Cook, & Quamma, 1995). This program stems from a relatively eclectic framework including cognitive–behavioral, attachment, and emotion perspectives, and it has been shown to be effective at increasing emotion understanding and reducing behavior problems in a sample of elementary school children (Greenberg et al., 1995). An adaptation of PATHS for Head Start showed similar positive effects (Domitrovich, Cortes, & Greenberg, 2002). The Head Start version of PATHS includes the "Turtle Technique" where children are encouraged to act like turtles when they become mad or upset. By pulling their arms close, closing their eyes, and putting their heads down, children are encouraged to let their muscles relax and focus on their feelings in order to determine the best way to respond (Denham & Burton, 1986).

The Second Step program follows a similar framework as PATHS and is widely utilized as a violence prevention program in elementary schools. Second Step is described as a program based in social learning theory, and it focuses primarily on empathy, problem solving, and anger management (Frey, Hirschstein, & Guzzo, 2000). As with PATHS, Second Step has been adapted for preschool and kindergarten children. The preschool and kindergarten version has shown positive effects on children's knowledge of program content and reduction of behavior problems based on observational measures (McMahon, Washburn, Felix, Yakin, & Childrey, 2000).

Another program, Carolyn Webster-Stratton's Incredible Years program, was originally developed as a treatment program for conduct-disordered children and demonstrated efficacy with this population (e.g., Webster-Stratton, 1990). This program was adapted for the Head Start population to include both parent and teacher components. The components are based on a combination of social learning and attachment theories and, as a result, emphasize both positive behavior management and adult-child bonding in order to reduce behavior problems and enhance social competence. Children receiving the multi-component Head Start version of the Incredible Years program demonstrated decreased conduct problems at school following the program (Webster-Stratton, Reid, & Hammond, 2001). Compared to the other programs presented above, the Incredible Years program includes a substantial parent component, and, if their parents attended six or more of the parenting sessions, children also demonstrated reduced conduct problems at home (Webster-Stratton et al., 2001).

Our own program, the Emotions Course (EC), shares some content with each of the programs described above. However, EC is firmly grounded in

DET and emphasizes the unique and adaptive motivational properties of discrete emotions and how these properties can promote social competence. As discussed above, programs from more eclectic backgrounds have shown substantial positive effects. However, these programs are unable to provide theory-driven explanations of behavior change (Coie, et al., 1993; Robins, 1992). EC allows us to test theories of emotional development and their relations between emotions and the development of psychopathology. Furthermore, this approach can promote further refinement of emotion theory and inform future basic and applied research on emotions (Izard, Fine, Mostow, Trentacosta, & Campbell, 2002).

The content of EC includes 22 lessons for use by Head Start teachers. The lessons focus primarily on four emotions (happiness, sadness, anger, and fear), but the program also includes some content related to interest and contempt. Lesson content includes puppet vignettes, emotion games, storybooks that include emotion content, and instruction in techniques for the regulation and utilization of emotion. Many of the lessons connect emotion-related abilities to social skills. For example, there is lesson content about helping a friend who is sad or scared. Teachers are encouraged to generalize the abilities and skills taught in the lessons throughout the school day.

One key component of the program, the Hold Tight technique, is taught as an anger management strategy and illustrates the general theoretical principles of EC. In Hold Tight, children are taught four steps: hug yourself or hold tight to a pillow, take three deep breaths, use your words, and play fair. This approach emphasizes the unique motivational qualities of anger. Specifically, children are taught appropriate assertion of anger rather than unregulated aggression. Furthermore, the final step, "play fair" emphasizes the essential connection between effective emotion regulation and utilization and positive social skills. By working with EC staff, teachers are shown how to encourage the use of the Hold Tight technique throughout the day as children become angry.

A pilot implementation of EC with a sample of rural Head Start children showed that the program increased children's emotion knowledge and decreased their expression of negative emotion, but this pilot implementation did not produce changes in children's social competence (Izard et al., 2004). During an implementation of EC in the same Head Start programs the following year, teachers had gained more experience with the program. Also, EC staff visited and consulted with teachers on a regular basis. An evaluation of this implementation showed similar increases in emotion knowledge and emotion regulation, and children receiving EC also demonstrated fewer internalizing and externalizing behavior problems following the program (Izard, King, Trentacosta, & Laurenceau, 2006). Taken together, our results suggest that, with minimal training, teachers can implement a prevention program that is firmly grounded in emotion theory. Furthermore, following increased practice with the program and with a small amount of consultation by project staff, a program such as EC can bring about significant reductions in problem behavior. Unfortunately, our initial EC evaluations did not have the resources to include a substantial parent component. In an ongoing trial in an urban Head Start system, it is proving difficult to engage parents in the prevention program even with increased resources.

FUTURE DIRECTIONS FOR EARLY CHILDHOOD SEL RESEARCH

There are a few important avenues for future basic research on SEL skills. First, research described above suggests that pretend play predicts children's SEL skills. The way in which social pretend play translates into SEL skills deserves more extensive examination. More fine-grained analyses of children's behavior while engaged in pretend play can inform our understanding of the specific aspects of this form of play that best predict SEL skills. For example, the use of pretend play roles may be most predictive of emotion competence when the exchanges are characterized by emotional themes, providing the participants with an opportunity to express emotion either verbally or nonverbally. Also, the study of peer pretend play described above was based on an observation of play behaviors in a structured setting (Lindsey & Colwell, 2003). Future research would benefit from naturalistic observations of social pretend play in the classroom as it relates to children's SEL skills.

Future research should also thoroughly examine teacher behaviors and general classroom characteristics as they relate to children's SEL skills. Discourse about emotion is one important teacher behavior that deserves further attention. Emotion discourse has received extensive attention in early parenting research (e.g., Dunn, Brown & Beardsall, 1991), but a recent examination of child care teacher behavior showed that only $\frac{1}{3}$ of teachers used books as a means to discuss emotions (Ahn, 2005). Further research is needed to determine the extent to which emotion discourse, both in structured activities such as book readings and during less structured time, impacts the development of children's SEL skills. General characteristics of the classroom environment should also be examined in relation to SEL skills. For example, the availability of materials that promote pretend play and books with emotional themes may enhance children's SEL skills, particularly in classrooms with sensitive, responsive, and well-trained teachers. Determining which classroom activities and materials are most beneficial for the development of children's SEL skills is a worthwhile goal for future research.

In terms of prevention research, it is clear that a number of programs with SEL content can enhance children's SEL skills and reduce behavior problems. However, most of these programs tend to rely heavily on lessons or structured activities that are intended to be delivered during circle time or other structured time throughout the day. More focus on evaluating the techniques that teachers can use during less structured playtime is needed. For example, "Turtle" and "Hold Tight" are optimally useful only if teachers spend considerable time helping children apply these techniques throughout the day whenever the child experiences intense and potentially dysregulated emotion. Therefore, an evaluation of teachers' implementation of these techniques across the day may be more important than quality of implementation during circle time or children's rote knowledge of the techniques. Overall, the balance between prevention programming during structured time and less structured activities should be empirically examined. Children may actually need very little instructional time to learn SEL skills if these skills are consistently generalized throughout the day.

IMPLICATIONS FOR EARLY CHILDHOOD EDUCATORS

The broad range of evidence suggests that emotion knowledge, emotion regulation, and social skills are essential SEL skills for teachers and other professionals to emphasize in their work with young children. Explicit instruction in these skills is certainly important, and the prevention programs described above provide the materials and structure for teaching children these skills. As such, early childhood educators should utilize these programs during their structured time with children. Of as much, if not greater, importance, early childhood classrooms would benefit from efforts to generalize the prevention techniques throughout the day. In their interactions with children and with other adults in the classroom, teachers should use the language of emotions and appropriate social expression. Young children also need relatively unstructured time to interact with their peers and gain competence with emotion regulation on-line as they confront challenging situations. Finally, because teachers' relationships with children are vitally important to the development of SEL skills and prosocial behavior, early childhood educators should make efforts to form positive bonds with even the most challenging children. Positive emotion expression and effective emotion communication will facilitate strong social bonds and social support systems. Clearly, this task will be most difficult in classrooms where many of the children are from socio-economically disadvantaged families or families characterized by high levels of parenting stress and conflict. Yet, it is these children who may benefit the most from a supportive, caring relationship with their teacher.

REFERENCES

Ahn, H. J. (2005). Teachers' discussions of emotion in child care centers. *Early Childhood Education Journal, 32,* 237–242.

Alexander, K. L., Entwisle, D. R., & Kabbani, N. S. (2001). The dropout process in life course perspective: Early risk factors at home and school. *Teachers College Record, 103,* 760–822.

Arsenio, W. F., Cooperman, S., & Lover, A. (2000). Affective predictors of pre-schoolers' aggression and peer acceptance: Direct and indirect effects. *Developmental Psychology, 36,* 438–448.

Bronfenbrenner, U. (1979). Context of child rearing: Problems and prospects. *American Psychologist, 34,* 844–850.

Bronfenbrenner, U., & Morris, P. A. (2006). The bioecological model of human development. In W. Damon & R. M. Lerner (Eds.), *Handbook of child psychology,* (6th ed., pp. 793–828). New York: John Wiley & Sons, Inc.

Cairns, R. B., Cairns, B. D., & Neckerman, H. J. (1989). Early school dropout: Configurations and determinants. *Child Development, 60,* 1437–1452.

Cannella, G. S. (1997). *Deconstructing early childhood education: Social justice and revolution.* New York: Peter Lang.

Coie, J. D., & Dodge, K. A. (1988). Multiple sources of data on social behavior and social status in the school: A cross-age comparison. *Child Development, 59,* 815–829.

Coie, J. D., Watt, N. F., West, S. G., Hawkins, J. D., Asarnow, J. R., Markman, H. J., et al. (1993). The science of prevention: A conceptual framework and some directions for a national research program. *American Psychologist, 48,* 1013–1022.

Cole, P. M., Bruschi, C. J., & Tamang, B. L. (2002). Cultural differences in children's emotional reactions to difficult situations. *Child Development, 73,* 983–996.

Cole, P. M., Martin, S. E., & Dennis, T. A. (2004). Emotion regulation as a scientific construct: Methodological challenges and directions for child development research. *Child Development, 75,* 317–333.

Cooper, D. H., & Farran, D. C. (1988). Behavioral risk factors in kindergarten. *Early Childhood Research Quarterly, 3,* 1–19.

Crick, N. R., & Dodge, K. A. (1994). A review and reformulation of social information-processing mechanisms in children's social adjustment. *Psychological Bulletin, 115,* 74–101.

Cummings, E. M., Iannotti, R. J., & Zahn-Waxler, C. (1989). Aggression between peers in early childhood: Individual continuity and developmental change. *Child Development, 60,* 887–895.

Denham, S. A. (1998). *Emotional development in young children.* New York: Guilford Press.

Denham, S. A., & Almeida, M. C. (1987). Children's social problem-solving skills, behavioral adjustment, and interventions: A meta-analysis evaluating theory and practice. *Journal of Applied Developmental Psychology, 8*, 391–409.

Denham, S. A., Blair, K. A., DeMulder, E., Levitas, J., Sawyer, K., Auerbach-Major, S., & Queenan, P. (2003). Preschool emotional competence: Pathway to social competence. *Child Development, 74*, 238–256.

Denham, S. A., & Burton, R. A. (1986). A social-emotional intervention for at-risk 4-year-olds. *Journal of School Psychology, 34*, 225–245.

Denham, S., & Weissberg, R. (2006). Social-emotional learning in early childhood: What we know and where to go from here. In E. Chesebrough, P. King, T. P. Gullotta, & M. Bloom (Eds.), *A blueprint for the promotion of prosocial behavior in early childhood* (pp. 13–50). New York: Springer.

Domitrovich, C. E., Cortes, R., & Greenberg, M. T. (2002). *PATHS: Promoting social and emotional competence in young children.* Paper presented at the Society for Prevention Research, Seattle, WA.

Dunn, J., Brown, J., & Beardsall, L. (1991). Family talks about feelings and children's later understanding of others' emotions. *Developmental Psychology, 27*, 448–455.

Eisenberg, N., & Spinrad, T. L. (2004). Emotion-related regulation: Sharpening the definition. *Child Development, 75*, 334–339.

Entwisle, D. R., & Alexander, K. L. (1998). Facilitating the transition to first grade: The nature of transition and research on factors affecting it. *Elementary School Journal, 98*, 351–364.

Erikson, E. H. (1964). *Childhood and society.* New York: W. W. Norton & Co.

Frey, K. S., Hirschstein, M. K., & Guzzo, B. A. (2000). Second step: Preventing aggression by promoting social competence. *Journal of Emotional and Behavioral Disorders, 8*, 102–112.

Garner, P. W. (1996). The relations of emotional role taking, affective/moral attributions, and emotional display rule knowledge to low-income school-age children's social competence. *Journal of Applied Developmental Psychology, 17*, 19–36.

Greenberg, M. T., Kusche, C. A., Cook, E. T., & Quamma, J. P. (1995). Promoting emotional competence in school-aged children: The effects of the PATHS curriculum. *Development and Psychopathology, 7*, 117–136.

Howes, C. (1987). Social competence with peers in young children: Developmental sequences. *Developmental Review, 7*, 252–272.

Howes, C. (2000). Social-emotional classroom climate in child care, child-teacher relationships and children's second grade peer relations. *Social Development, 9*, 191–204.

Howes, C., & Hamilton, C. E. (1992). Children's relationships with caregivers: Mothers and child care teachers. *Child Development, 63*, 859–866.

Howes, C., Hamilton, C. E., & Matheson, C. C. (1994). Children's relationships with peers: Differential associations with aspects of the teacher–child relationship. *Child Development, 65*, 253–263.

Howse, R. B., Calkins, S. D., Anastopoulos, A. D., Keane, S. P., & Shelton, T. L. (2003). Regulatory contributors to children's kindergarten achievement. *Early Education and Development, 14*, 101–119.

Izard, C. E. (1971). *The face of emotion.* New York: Appleton-Century-Crofts.

Izard, C. E. (1991). *The psychology of emotions.* New York: Plenum Press.

Izard, C. E. (2002). Translating emotion theory and research into preventive interventions. *Psychological Bulletin, 128,* 796–824.

Izard, C. E., Fine, S. E., Mostow, A., Trentacosta, C., & Campbell, J. (2002). Emotion processes in normal and abnormal development and preventive intervention. *Development and Psychopathology, 14,* 761–787.

Izard, C. E., Fine, S., Schultz, D., Mostow, A., Ackerman, B., & Youngstrom, E. (2001). Emotion knowledge as a predictor of social behavior and academic competence in children at risk. *Psychological Science, 12,* 18–23.

Izard, C. E., Hembree, E. A., & Huebner, R. R. (1987). Infants' emotion expressions to acute pain: Developmental change and stability of individual differences. *Developmental Psychology, 23,* 105–113.

Izard, C. E., King, K. A., Trentacosta, C. J., & Laurenceau, J. P. (2006). *Accelerating the development of emotion competence in Head Start children.* Manuscript submitted for publication.

Izard, C., Trentacosta, C., King, K., Morgan, J., & Diaz, M. (in press). Emotions, emotionality, and intelligence in the development of adaptive behavior. In M. Zeidner (Ed.) *Science of Emotional Intelligence: Knowns and Unknowns.*

Izard, C. E., Trentacosta, C. J., King, K. A & Mostow, A. J., (2004). An emotion-based prevention program for head start children. *Early Education and Development, 15,* 407–422.

Keenan, K. (2000). Emotion dysregulation as a risk factor for child psychopathology. *Clinical Psychology: Science & Practice, 7,* 418–434.

Keenan, K., & Shaw, D. S. (1994). The development of aggression in toddlers: A study of low-income families. *Journal of Abnormal Child Psychology, 22,* 53–77.

Lemerise, E. A., & Arsenio, W. F. (2000). An integrated model of emotion processes and cognition in social information processing. *Child Development, 71,* 107–118.

Lindsey, E. W., & Colwell, M. J. (2003). Preschoolers' emotional competence: Links to pretend and physical play. *Child Study Journal, 33,* 39–52.

McClelland, M. M., Morrison, F. J., & Holmes, D. L. (2000). Children at risk for early academic problems: The role of learning-related social skills. *Early Childhood Research Quarterly, 15,* 307–329.

McMahon, S. D., Washburn, J., Felix, E. D., Yakin, J., & Childrey, G. (2000). Violence prevention: Program effects on urban preschool and kindergarten children. *Applied & Preventive Psychology, 9,* 271–281.

Messinger, D. S. (2002). Positive and negative infant facial expressions and emotions. *Current Directions in Psychological Science, 11,* 1–6.

Mostow, A. J., Izard, C. E., Fine, S. E., & Trentacosta, C. J. (2002). Modeling the emotional, cognitive, and behavioral predictors of peer acceptance. *Child Development, 73,* 1775–1787.

NICHD Early Child Care Research Network. (2001). Child care and children's peer interaction at 24 and 36 months: The NICHD Study of Early Child Care. *Child Development, 72,* 1478–1500.

NICHD Early Child Care Research Network. (2004). Affect dysregulation in the mother–child relationship in the toddler years: Antecedents and consequences. *Development & Psychopathology, 16,* 43–68.

O'Leary, S. G., Slep, A. M. S., & Reid, M. J. (1999). A longitudinal study of mothers' overreactive discipline and toddlers' externalizing behavior. *Journal of Abnormal Child Psychology, 27*, 331–341.

Pianta, R. C. (1994). Patterns of relationships between children and kindergarten teachers. *Journal of School Psychology, 32*, 15–31.

Pianta, R. C. (1999). *Enhancing relationships between children and teachers*. Washington, DC: American Psychological Association.

Pollak, S., Cicchetti, D., Klorman, R., & Brumaghim, J. (1997). Cognitive brain event-related potentials and emotion processing in maltreated children. *Child Development, 68*, 773–787.

Raver, C. C. (2004). Placing emotional self-regulation in sociocultural and socioeconomic contexts. *Child Development, 75*, 346–353.

Robins, L. N. (1992). The role of prevention experiments in discovering causes of children's antisocial behavior. In J. McCord & R. E. Tremblay (Eds.), *Preventing antisocial behavior: Interventions from birth through adolescence* (pp. 3–18). New York: Guilford Press.

Rose-Krasnor, L. (1997). The nature of social competence: A theoretical review. *Social Development, 6*, 111–135.

Smith, M., & Walden, T. (1999). Understanding feelings and coping with emotional situations: A comparison of maltreated and nonmaltreated preschoolers. *Social Development, 8*, 93–116.

Spivack, G., & Shure, M. (1989). Interpersonal cognitive problem solving (ICPS): A competence-building primary prevention program. In J. Kelly (Ed.), *Eighty years in the field of prevention: Lela Rowland Prevention Award recipients* (pp. 151–178). New York: Haworth Press.

Stansbury, K., & Sigman, M. (2000). Responses of preschoolers in two frustrating episodes: Emergence of complex strategies for emotion regulation. *Journal of Genetic Psychology, 161*, 182–202.

Terwogt, M. M., Koops, W., Oosterhoff, T., & Olthof, T. (1986). Development in processing of multiple emotional situations. *Journal of General Psychology, 113*, 109–119.

Trentacosta, C. J., & Izard, C. E. (in press). *Kindergarten children's emotion competence as a predictor of their academic competence in first grade*. Manuscript submitted for publication.

Trentacosta, C. J., & Shaw, D. S. (2007). *Emotion, dysregulation, and the development of anti-social behavior in adolescent boys*. (submitted for publication).

Webster-Stratton, C. (1990). Enhancing the effectiveness of self-administered videotaped parent training for families with conduct-problem children. *Journal of Abnormal Child Psychology, 18*, 479–492.

Webster-Stratton, C., Reid, M. J., & Hammond, M. (2001). Preventing conduct problems, promoting social competence: A parent and teacher training partnership in Head Start. *Journal of Clinical Child Psychology, 30*, 283–302.

Wentzel, K. R. (1994). Relations of social goal pursuit to social acceptance, classroom behavior, and perceived social support. *Journal of Educational Psychology, 86*, 173–182.

Youngblade, L. M., & Dunn, J. (1995). Individual differences in young children's pretend play with mother and sibling: Links to relationships and understanding of other people's feelings and beliefs. *Child Development, 66*, 1472–1492.

CHAPTER 5

COGNITIVE DEVELOPMENT IN SOCIAL CONTEXT

Implications for Early Childhood Education

Mary Gauvain

Human beings are born with an extraordinary ability to learn. This ability is fundamental to the dramatic changes in children's understanding of and engagement with the world during infancy and childhood. Research on cognitive development seeks to describe these changes and much of this research has focused on how children think or solve problems on their own. Although this research has provided extensive information about age-related cognitive abilities, it has provided less insight into two other important and related aspects of cognitive development: how cognitive change occurs and how children think when they are with other people.

Children spend much of their time playing and working alongside other people. These experiences provide children with many and varied opportunities for learning that affect the nature and course of cognitive development. The social world provides children with knowledge about the world along with direction and support in the development of skills that are used to guide intelligent action. In other words, cognitive development is socially constituted, both in terms of *what* children think about and *how* children learn to use cognitive abilities to carry out goal-directed actions.

Contemporary Perspectives on Socialization and Social Development..., pages 79–97
Copyright © 2007 by Information Age Publishing
79

This chapter discusses cognitive development as an emergent property of social experience. It begins with discussion of the social foundations of human learning from the vantage of evolutionary psychology. The chapter then turns to a theoretical perspective, the sociocultural approach, which considers cognitive development as a social process. The contribution of this approach to understanding cognitive development in early childhood is illustrated with research in attention, memory, and problem solving. Each of these cognitive processes is essential to learning in informal settings and in more formal arrangements, like school. Finally, some implications of sociocultural research for early childhood education are raised. Despite the promise of this perspective for educational practice, current applications of these findings to the complex demands of the classroom are limited.

THE SOCIAL FOUNDATIONS OF COGNITIVE DEVELOPMENT

Early development is a period of extensive learning that is facilitated by two properties of the brain at the time of birth: immaturity and responsiveness to environmental input (Halfon, Shulman, & Hochstein, 2001). Because the brain is immature there is much room for development; the responsiveness of the brain indicates that development will reflect the experiences children have as the brain matures. Even though much of what young children need to learn is common across social and historical circumstances, such as how objects work and other properties and relations in the world, most learning is specialized to the unique circumstances of growth. Domain-general cognitive processes, such as attention, memory, and problem solving, are adapted to problems at hand (Bjorklund & Pellegrini, 2002). For this type of learning to occur in an effective and efficient way, learners need to capitalize on available resources and one critical resource is found in the social context.

Certain species-level characteristics, specifically the immaturity of the infant brain, the vast learning potential of the organism, and the long period of dependence on mature members, ensure that infants and children will have extensive contact with, and therefore opportunities to learn from, people who already know much of what a child needs to learn and who are invested in the child physically and emotionally (Bjorklund & Pelligrini, 2002). Over development, more experienced and knowledgeable partners facilitate children's learning and development through the support, guidance, modeling, and other forms of assistance they provide. Learning in social situations with more experienced partners is not simply a process of transmitting knowledge and skills to the less experienced partner. It is a socially constructed process and even young infants play an active role in learning in social context, as evident in the socially related biases of the human neonate toward patterns in human faces, speech, and social interaction (Gauvain, 2001). From the vantage of evolutionary psychology, cognitive development is inseparable from the social context in which it occurs.

The social context is a particularly fertile source for cognitive development. It includes information about unique social aspects of the developmental context as well as information about culturally valued skills—the type of skills children need to obtain competence in their community. Because learning in social context involves people who are in sustained relationships with one another and invested in the formal and informal social arrangements in which learning occurs, it has the potential to reap substantial benefits for cognitive development. Sustained social relationships and practices provide children with repeated opportunities for learning, which are especially valuable for learning complex cognitive skills. They also tend to involve people with emotional ties, which can facilitate motivation and other arousal states that enhance learning. Finally, social situations often involve people of different developmental statuses, which increases the likelihood that social learning processes that build upon differential expertise, such as modeling, scaffolding, and guided participation (Rogoff, 1998), will occur. Thus, the complexity inherent in sustained social learning arrangements provides children with a vast and diverse range of opportunities for cognitive development. The next section describes a theoretical perspective that builds on these assumptions and considers social and cognitive experiences as mutual processes of human development.

A SOCIOCULTURAL APPROACH TO COGNITIVE DEVELOPMENT

Over the course of development, children need to develop the knowledge and skills that will enable them to function competently as mature and contributing members of their community. To accomplish this goal, learning must be tailored to the types of problems and demands that children encounter in their everyday lives. Fortunately, children do not need to learn all this information on their own; knowledge and cognitive skills are passed onto children through the many social experiences they have every day.

A sociocultural approach to cognitive development contends that (a) children's learning is adapted to the context in which development occurs and (b) children learn how to function in this context through social experiences (Rogoff, 1998). When children engage in a cognitive activity that is new or challenging to them, more experienced individuals often provide assistance of one form or another. Children may be given the opportunity to observe more experienced individuals carry out the activity, allowed or encouraged to participate in the activity in some rudimentary or guided fashion, or offered instruction. More experienced partners play instrumental roles by orchestrating children's involvement, assisting children as they engage in and learn about the activity, and pulling back on their assistance as the child gains competence. Through social experiences like these, children gradually learn to solve problems on their own. Children play an active role in this process as their developing capabilities and their interests and needs set the stage and establish the boundaries of their involvement.

Much of sociocultural research has been informed by the theoretical formulations of Vygotsky (1978). For Vygotsky, innate cognitive capabilities and elementary mental functions, (e.g., basic attention and involuntary memory), are transformed into higher cognitive functions, (e.g., voluntary attention, intentional remembering, and logical and abstract reasoning). Interactions with other people and with the tools and activities of the culture, including language, literacy, and other symbol systems, are instrumental to this development. For instance, the elementary form of memory, which is similar to perception and largely composed of images and impressions of events, is an unintentional and direct mapping of features of the environment. As children develop, they learn to use psychological tools and activities, like language and literacy, to elaborate and extend this basic memory function into a more deliberate and explicit form. Children do not need to devise the psychological tools and activities that support higher mental functions; they already exist in the culture. However, children do need to learn about these tools and activities and how to use or participate in them effectively to support or mediate cognitive processes (Wertsch, 1985). Children learn this information through the assistance of people in their culture who are experienced in the psychological tools and activities that support thinking. Some of this learning is informal, emerging from the everyday experiences and interactions children have, and some of this learning occurs in more formal societal settings, such as school.

Both formal and informal arrangements of learning involve tools and activities that reflect the broader cultural context. Therefore, as children learn to use tools and activities to support intelligent action, their thinking becomes increasingly aligned with the culture. However, differences can exist between the cultural experiences children have in informal learning situations, such as the family and neighborhood, and the cultural processes embedded in formal learning situations. These differences, which are greater for some cultural communities than others, can lead to tensions between home-based learning experiences and learning at school.

To describe how children learn about psychological tools, Vygotsky introduced the concept of the *zone of proximal development* (ZPD), defined as the difference between a child's "actual developmental level as determined by independent problem solving" and his or her "potential development as determined through problem solving under adult guidance or in collaboration with more capable peers" (Vygotsky, 1978, p. 86). During social interaction targeted to the ZPD, children engage in more advanced cognitive activities than they could undertake alone. The zone or region of sensitivity to learning is defined initially by the child's existing knowledge or competence in an area of intellectual growth. Over the course of an interaction, assistance that is sensitive to a child's learning needs alters the child's level of competence or ZPD.

The construct of scaffolding has been used to describe one way that knowledge is transferred from a more to less experienced partner (Wood, Bruner, & Ross, 1976). In scaffolding, the assistance provided by the more experienced partner is contingent on the learner's needs and includes many techniques that support learning, such as breaking down an activity into component parts to make it more understandable and accessible to a child, modeling new strategies for solving a problem, encouraging and supporting the child's involvement in increasingly complex aspects of the activity, and taking on more difficult task parts so that the learner can concentrate on more accessible components. By carefully monitoring the child's progress, the more experienced partner continually adjusts the task to fit with the child's needs. As the child's skill increases, the more experienced partner reduces support so that eventually the child will be able to execute the task in a skilled fashion independent of the partner's help. In addition to scaffolded interactions, children learn much as they participate alongside more experienced partners in activities that are not intended to instruct but nonetheless impart understanding and skill to the child (Rogoff, 1998) and as they engage in systematic observations of skilled performance (Lave & Wenger, 1991).

The next section discusses the development of attention, memory, and problem solving in relation to the social context. Each of these processes contributes in a direct and significant way to the acquisition and use of knowledge and skills that are critical to children's learning throughout development, including successful adjustment to and achievement in school.

THE SOCIAL CONTEXT OF THE DEVELOPMENT OF ATTENTION

Attention involves directing limited cognitive resources toward specific information in the environment. Attention is critical to knowledge acquisition and skill development and it can be voluntary or involuntary. Voluntary attention, which is the active use of cognitive skills to reach a personal goal, is critical to learning. It develops rapidly over the first years of life and this development is greatly affected by social experience. Involuntary attention, such as when a person looks in the direction of a sudden loud noise, is not under conscious control and is less sensitive to social input. This discussion concentrates on the development of voluntary attention.

In the first two years of life there are enormous changes in children's control of attention and in the strategic use of attention to accomplish goal-directed action. The rapid development of attention over this period reflects changes in the brain (Ruff & Rothbart, 1996) and social interaction also plays a formative role in this development. Social processes that contribute to the development and refinement of attention early in life are intersubjectivity, joint attention, and social referencing.

Intersubjectivity

For children to engage with other people in shared, goal-directed activities, which is part of any collaborative or social learning situation, they must first learn to attend in a meaningful way to other social beings. The process of mutual understanding between interactive partners, or intersubjectivity (Rommetveit, 1985), is critical for effective communication and for learning in social context. Intersubjectivity involves the coordination of the attention of social partners to one another. Although adults assume much of the responsibility for establishing intersubjectivity with young infants, children still play an active role. As early as one-month of age, infants behave differently when they interact with their mothers as compared to objects (Trevarthen, 1980). Young infants actively respond to overtures from social partners by participating in mutual eye gaze and employing attention behaviors, such as body orientation and head turning, to communicate their interest in the interaction to their partner. Adults support these efforts by attending to and monitoring the infant's behaviors and coordinating their own behaviors with those of the infant. Research suggests that the development of intersubjectivity and the skills it entails emerge from social experience. When infants are very young, they appear to engage in interactions that involve intersubjectivity with little understanding of the process or their role in it. However, over time, their participation becomes more explicit and intentional, and by the end of the first year, the social partners have extended this ability to objects of joint or mutual attention.

Joint Attention

In joint attention, social partners focus on a common reference, which may be an object, person, or event (Adamson & Bakeman, 1991). Between

9 and 12 months, infants learn to look reliably toward the place where adults are looking and use active means to direct an adult's attention to features of the environment (Carpenter, Nagall, & Tomasello, 1998). Joint attention is a social-cognitive process in which three things occur: the social partners know that they are attending to something in common, they monitor each other's attention to the target of mutual interest, and they coordinate their individual efforts during the interaction using their mutual attention as a guide (Tomasello, 1995). Joint attention helps children learn about the world around them, such as what objects and events are important. It informs infants that other people can be helpful for learning about the world, which is an initial step in understanding that other people act intentionally, a chief component of social cognition (Tomasello, 1995). Joint attention contributes to the development of referential communication skills by helping children label objects, events and people in ways conventional in their language (Bruner, 1975). It also helps infants and adults share experiences with one another, which has consequences for social, emotional, and cognitive development. Late in the first year, this process is elaborated on as infants seek emotional information from other people and then use this information to organize their own emotional responses to objects and events.

Social Referencing

The process by which an individual looks to someone else for information about how to respond to, think about, or feel about an object, another person, or an event is called social referencing (Campos & Stenberg, 1981). Social referencing appears late in the first year and, though it involves joint attention, it includes an additional step. Before acting upon or reacting to an object or event, the infant looks at another person, assesses the person's reaction, and then uses this information to organize his or her subsequent behavior. The process is not imitative; the infant does not reproduce the behavior of the partner but uses this information to construct his or her own behavioral response. For instance, if a mother expresses happiness toward an object, the baby may explore it more closely; if a mother expresses fear, the infant may move away from the object (Klinnert, 1984). Social referencing relies on a number of cognitive skills. The infant needs to attend to new information in the environment, including changes in the partner's voice and face. The infant also needs to understand the partner's emotional message and the specific referent of this message as well as be able to use this information to guide action. Infants attend carefully to these types of messages and they influence how infants explore and learn about the world (Adamson & Bakeman, 1991).

Although intersubjectivity, joint attention, and social referencing appear in infancy, they continue to play important roles in learning throughout life. For example, mothers and their 4–5- and 6–7-year-old children used joint attention when they constructed a toy from multiple pieces using a pictorial, step-by-step plan (de la Ossa & Gauvain, 2001). Individual and group variations in the development of these abilities have been identified and these differences may have implications for learning later in childhood. For instance, social attention processes rely on the sensitivity of the partner to the child's interests and needs as well as the availability of social skills. Research has demonstrated that maternal depression may lead to difficulties for young children in establishing intersubjectivity with their mothers (Cohn & Tronick, 1983); that children with social difficulties, such as autism, have trouble participating in interactions that rely on social attention skills such as shared eye gaze, coordinated affective expressions, and mutual duration of attention (Sigman & Kasari, 1995); and that when the emotional message provided by an adult is ambiguous, children ignore this information and seek a less familiar source for social referencing (Klinnert, Emde, Butterfield, & Campos, 1986). Cultural variations have also been found in young children's attention skills or preferences, suggesting that the cultural context of development contributes to this development. For example, Chavajay and Rogoff (1999) found differences in the allocation of attention to objects and events by Guatemalan Mayan and U.S. middle-class mothers and their 12- to 24-month-old children. Mayan children and mothers were more likely to attend to several events simultaneously whereas U.S. children and mothers usually attended to one object or event at a time.

Implications for Early Childhood Education

Attention is a critical stepping-stone for learning and attention skills have enormous implications for children's success in the classroom. The educational community has expended much effort identifying and helping children with serious attention-related difficulties, such as attention deficit/hyperactivity disorder (ADHD) (Campbell, 2000). Although severe attention problems need specialized treatment, attention problems of a less severe or more task specific nature may be ameliorated by social practices in the classroom that help direct and keep students' attention focused on relevant aspects of a learning activity. The teacher, an older or more experienced child, or a classmate who is more skilled at regulating attention can provide this assistance. Explicit attention regulating strategies related to the processes of intersubjectivity and joint attention can be encouraged, such as asking students to keep their eyes on the teacher or peer when new information or instructions are given or clearly directing children to focus their attention on objects or object features that are important to learning. Because behaviors alone do not indicate if a child is attending mentally, after the child engages in an activity it is important to monitor the child's attention throughout the activity. Vygotsky (1978) emphasize the importance of language in cognitive development, which can be used to foster or support children's attention, for example, asking questions that direct children toward the aspects of the activity that are important to learning. Emotional support for attention, the type of support sought in social referencing, is also important to learning. This support may be especially important in the early school years, particularly when children work on new or challenging material. Learning and motivation are facilitated when children know that what they are learning has value and interest to other people (Pintrich & Schunk, 2002).

Although it is established that attention-related problems can place children at risk for academic failure, there is no single explanation or remedy for the attention-related difficulties or differences that children exhibit. Social-economic factors, such as poverty and poor nutrition, are associated with poorer attention in the classroom. Disruptions in family interactions stemming from parent or child characteristics can affect the attention skills children have when they enter school. Cultural practices may influence the development or expression of social behaviors related to attention, such as mutual eye gaze, and these can affect children's adjustment to the learning environment and expectations of the classroom. Research has clearly demonstrated that social interaction processes are intricately linked to the development and use of attention in early childhood. Better understanding of these interaction processes may help educators identify and assist children with attention behaviors that interfere with the many types of social learning situations that are vital to academic success.

THE SOCIAL CONTEXT OF THE DEVELOPMENT
OF EVENT MEMORY

Memory includes all the concepts, categories, skills, and understanding a person has acquired. There are several different types of memory. Event or episodic memory includes memories of important experiences, especially events that have happened to an individual, referred to as autobiographical memory. Other types of memory that are not event based, such as concepts, skills, and categories, are referred to as semantic memories. Both event and semantic memories are affected by social experience. Because much of the research on the social context of memory development in early childhood concentrates on event memory, this is the focus of our discussion. Research on social contributions to semantic memory development is largely concerned with memory strategies, like rehearsal and organization. Such strategies are particularly salient during middle childhood because they help children learn and remember complex material.

Event memory emerges shortly after the second birthday when children are capable of reflecting on their own ideas or representations. Over the preschool years, the rapid explosion of language supports the development of event memory as children engage in conversations about the past and as events unfold. These early conversations influence the content of children's event memories as well as the development of techniques for organizing and retrieving these memories.

Discussions of past events are a frequent topic of conversation among young children and their parents. In one study these conversations occurred between five and seven times an hour (Fivush, Haden, & Reese, 1996). When parents and children discuss the past, parents communicate what events are worth remembering (Snow, 1990). The structure of event memory interactions and the way in which adults draw children into these conversations are important features of this process. When children are very young, parents provide significant guidance or scaffolding for children's participation. Such social remembering typically begins when the adult evokes the child's memory of an event. Once the child acknowledges remembering the event, the adult guides the child into a more elaborate, and often emotionally laden, recollection of it. Initially, these discussions are mostly one-sided, with the parent assuming much of the responsibility for reminiscing. With time, as language and social skills develop, children participate more and by 3 years of age, children's contributions are substantial (Hamond & Fivush, 1991).

Because events include a number of actions and a temporal sequence, event memory is aided by the use of a narrative structure. A narrative contains a unique sequence of events that involve human beings as characters (Bruner, 1986). It can be about a real or an imaginary event and it includes information about the intentionality of the actors and the cause and evaluation of the event. Research indicates that the narrative form is useful for organizing event knowledge in children's memory and for helping children retrieve this information and communicate it to others (Engel, 1995). Differences across families in the nature of these conversations and in the use of a narrative style have been observed. Mothers who use an elaborative style encourage the child's involvement in these conversations and build up the event information in a story-like or narrative form. Other mothers offer a more repetitive and pared down description of the event. Children whose mothers use an elaborative style benefit more from memory discussions in terms of language development, memory, and conversational skills than do children whose mothers use a more repetitive style (Reese & Fivush, 1993).

Conversations about the past, especially those using a narrative structure, aid in the development of event memory for several reasons. They are highly motivating; they are often about the children themselves and involve people who are familiar and meaningful to children. These conversations are frequent, especially in some cultural contexts, and, consequently, children have much practice with this type of talk and remembering. These conversations are socially dynamic; they change as the participants add information and rework each other's contributions (Ochs, Taylor, Rudolph, & Smith, 1992). Thus, children are involved in them in meaningful ways and their contributions help shape the focus, content, and direction of the conversation. However, much of the research on this topic has included middle-class families, principally of European American background. Research indicates that these conversations differ from those of adults and children from other cultural backgrounds. In Japan, conversations by mothers and children about past events, and the child's subsequent memory of these events, are quite brief, include little embellishment, and reflect cultural values of self-presentation (Minami & McCabe, 1995). Event conversations and narratives of African American adults and children in the rural southeastern United States include explicit efforts to get and sustain the attention of the listener, such as nonverbal gestures, exaggeration, and distinct stylistic features like poems (Heath, 1983).

Implications for Early Childhood Education

Research has showed that parents who interact with preschoolers in ways that facilitate the development of event memory have children who do better when they enter school than do children without these experiences (Sigel, 2000). Parental practices of discourse in these conversations, especially a more elaborative style, provide children with encouragement and support for the development of skills that benefit children when they enter school, such as language, reflection, negotiation, and the narrative structure. Variation in these practices across families and cultural groups suggests that children may enter school with different skills, especially the skills that are intricately tied to this memory development like the narrative form. Research is lacking on how individual and cultural variations relate to children's adjustment to and experience in school. Furthermore, little is known about the relation between the skills that children develop from social experiences related to event memory and other school activities, such as literacy and other areas that may rely on or benefit from experience with the narrative form.

What is clear is that children enter school with different backgrounds in social practices related to event memory and that these experiences may have consequences for children's success in school. If these social practices reflect individual variation that stem from or reflect parent education or parenting style, interventions in the preschool years or on school entry, such as storytelling, may help bridge children's experiences at home and school. However, when these differences are rooted in cultural values and beliefs, the issue is quite different. Cultural differences in adult–child memory conversations that may have consequences for children's adjustment to and success in school include practices of turn-taking, storytelling, and the role and appropriateness of questioning or negotiating knowledge. What research has revealed is that when the practices and foci of event memories and narratives at home are aligned with school practices and expectations, the transition to school is easier for children than when they are not so aligned (Heath, 1983).

Research has also demonstrated that cultural practices related to event memory can be used effectively in the classroom to support children's learning. In the Kamehameha Early Education Program, or KEEP, in Hawaii (Tharp & Gallimore, 1988), the Native Hawaiian tradition of storytelling was used to develop the classroom practice of "talk-story," an approach to literacy instruction in which the teacher and students jointly produce narratives about the focus of the day's lessons. The KEEP teacher's instructional repertoire includes the techniques of modeling, questioning, and feedback, all of which are related to the zone of proximal development (Vygotsky, 1978) and scaffolding (Wood et al., 1976). This approach emphasizes social participation, story creation, and comprehension, and its use has been related to improvements in the standardized reading scores of Native Hawaiian children. However, this type of culturally based intervention may be easier to implement and lead to more success in a classroom that contains a fairly homogenous cultural group, as was the case in KEEP.

THE SOCIAL CONTEXT OF THE DEVELOPMENT
OF PROBLEM-SOLVING SKILLS

Problem solving involves identifying a goal and carrying out the means to reach this goal. It is a higher-level cognitive skill, relying on many capabilities including attention, perception, memory, concepts, and symbolic processes like language or mathematics. A key aspect of problem solving is overcoming obstacles that interfere with reaching a goal. Due to the complexity and vast array of problems humans confront, these skills develop over a long period of time. Rudimentary abilities are evident in infancy, for example 8-month-olds will deliberately grab a cloth to pull it closer to play with the toy resting on it (Willatts, 1990). As children get older, they encode more features of a problem, allocate attention more effectively during encoding and problem solving, and acquire and use strategies that enhance problem solution.

Early research on adult–child problem solving involving preschoolers demonstrated that social experience supports the development of problem solving skills. Wood and Middleton (1975) studied mothers' instructions as their 3- and 4-year-old children constructed a pyramid of interlocking wooden blocks. The mothers carefully monitored the child's progress, adjusted the task to make it accessible to the child, and provided assistance when needed. The mothers used several techniques to promote learning: they modeled individual steps used to solve the problem, encouraged the child to place the blocks in their correct positions, segmented the task into steps that were more easily understood and managed by the child, and, as the child's skill increased, reduced the amount of support provided. Children of mothers who had higher rates of contingent response to the children's learning needs, and not just higher rates of instruction, performed better on a solitary posttest on a similar problem following the interaction. This research indicates that contingent support during joint problem solving can promote the development of problem solving skills.

Social assistance continues to benefit children as they get older and learn to solve more complex problems. However, the contribution of social interaction depends on age-related changes in children's problem-solving abilities. Whereas preschool children often benefit from help in understanding problems and how to follow rules and manipulate the materials, school-age children benefit from information about strategies (Gauvain, 2001). This difference was demonstrated in a study in which 4–5- and 7–8-year-old children and their mothers worked on a problem-solving task that involved planning a series of errands in a model grocery store (Gauvain, 1992). Mothers who worked with the younger children tended to concentrate on establishing joint understanding of the task. While they worked on the task with their children, these mothers talked mostly about task structure, such as the rules and materials. Mothers who worked with older children tended to emphasize strategies, such as how to search the layout of the store visually and use this information to plan out an efficient route for getting all the items. On the solitary posttest, older children who had been taught a visual search strategy by their mothers planned more effectively than same-age children whose mothers did not teach them this strategy. This result suggests that this type of instruction supported the development of planning skills among the older children. However, when mothers emphasized strategic information with younger children, it was not beneficial. Because younger children are still developing a basic understanding of planning, strategic information was too advanced for their current understanding. This does not mean that social interaction does not benefit younger children on complex problem-solving tasks. When younger children received more explanation about task structure, they participated more in the task, which can facilitate learning (Vandermaas-Peeler, Way, & Umpleby, 2003). These patterns are consistent with Vygotsky's (1978) view that that during joint cognitive activity, more experienced partners may provide opportunities for children's learning and development. However, this research extends this view by showing that what children learn from these transactions reflects their developmental status.

Implications for Early Childhood Education

Children's experiences solving problems with supportive partners before they enter school can ease the transition to school. Neitzel and Stright (2003) found that the cognitive support that mothers provided for children's learning before they entered kindergarten was related to children's self-evaluation or metacognitive awareness of their thinking and performance, monitoring of progress on class work, and seeking help when needed. These findings suggest that children's social learning experiences at home contribute in positive ways to children's adjustment to school. Adult–child problem solving before children enter school can also provide children with introduction to and experience with the types of problems that are the focus of school learning, such as mathematics (Saxe, Guberman, & Gearhart, 1987), and with social skills that are important to learning in social context, such as how to coordinate behaviors during collaboration (Gauvain, 2001). Children who do not have these skills, for example, aggressive children, have difficulty engaging in and benefiting from collaborative learning activities (Lochman & Dodge, 1994).

For collaborative problem solving to be effective, the situation must be sensitive to the needs of the learner. This goal is difficult to accomplish in large group settings, like the classroom, and this difficulty is compounded when children have different presenting skills, backgrounds, and interests. Key ingredients of collaborative problem solving in relation to learning and cognitive development are the availability of appropriate support to help learners engage in an activity in a meaningful way, the gradual withdrawal of these supports as the child's competence increases, and instruction in and provision of tools that support learning (Bransford, Brown, & Cocking, 1999).

CONCLUSIONS

Opportunities for learning and cognitive development in social context are plentiful and they emerge in both informal everyday situations and more formal settings, like school. Social experiences contribute to cognitive development in many ways. They provide children with instruction in the valued practices of their community, opportunities to observe more experienced people as models for future action, introduction to and practice with activities that foster the development of particular cognitive skills, and experience using the material and symbolic tools that support intelligent action. By describing the social nature of children's learning in three specific areas of cognitive development, voluntary attention, event memory, and problem solving, this chapter attempted to show how ignoring the social aspects of this learning obscures understanding of the development of these cognitive processes. The development and expression of cognitive abilities such as these cannot be understood separately from the social environment that gives them form, meaning, and direction. A sociocultural approach provides a way of conceptualizing and examining how social experience, of various sorts, and cultural tools, like literacy and numerical systems, are integrated with learning and cognitive development. Emphasis on the social context of cognitive development advances theory in psychological development and may be especially helpful for linking research on cognitive development with educational practice and, more broadly, with the cultural foundations of children's learning.

A sociocultural approach assumes that children learn and develop cognitive skills through the opportunities provided in the situations in which learning occurs (Cole, 2005). Consistent with the ideas of Vygotsky (1978), this approach contends that effective learning opportunities build on the present capabilities of the child and provide social support and encouragement for the further development of these capabilities. Over the last 15 years educational programs that draw on Vygotskian and sociocultural views have increased (Hyson, Copple, & Jones, 2006). In these programs more knowledgeable people, especially teachers, play critical roles in arranging and supporting children's learning using techniques like scaffolding, collaboration, and the provision of tools that support learning and thinking. These approaches have been successful in demonstration programs. Implementing them more broadly and in diverse cultural and social contexts remains a challenge (Blumenfeld, Marx, & Harris, 2006).

A sociocultural approach also implies that the opportunities for learning and cognitive development that are available to children in the home before children enter school are critical to academic adjustment and success. Many studies support this view by showing that particular types of social experiences before children enter school relate to academic adjustment and performance (Hyson et al., 2006). Verbal experiences, especially interactions with adults that encourage active participation by the child, appear particularly helpful. This suggests that supporting the development of language, communication, and social interaction skills is important for preparing children to participate in and benefit from the social learning opportunities in the classroom.

Many other types of resources and experiences at home, such as shared book reading, also help prepare children for school. These types of learning-related practices and experiences vary across home environments, however. Their presence is related to many factors including a family's economic situation, cultural background, and parental education. Preschool programs based on a social approach to cognitive development may be useful in mediating variations that reflect the availability of resources and support for children's learning at home (Hyson et al., 2006). A different type of challenge is present in variations that stem from cultural differences in values, practices, and beliefs, especially those related to communication patterns, parent–child interaction, and children's learning and socialization. Understanding these differences and crafting ways to enhance educational opportunities for all children that recognize and respect cultural patterns are goals of the 21st century. The design and implementation of early education programs based on sociocultural approaches to cognitive development may be especially helpful in this effort.

Integrating educational practice with ideas about cognitive development derived from a sociocultural approach should, in some ways, be easy. This approach draws inspiration from Vygotsky (1978) who considered the ability of children to learn from social experience to be a fundamental characteristic of human beings. However, difficulties arise when one attempts to fit a social view of cognitive development with much of the current research and theory and with the contemporary realities of the classroom. Both developmental and educational research that concentrate on individual performance are ill suited to examining learning as a socially dynamic process. Although efforts to adapt sociocultural ideas to classroom practice have yielded positive outcomes (Bransford et al., 1999), defining and generating cognitive developmental research that can best inform educational practice also remain as a challenge. For instance, there are few systematic descriptions of cognitive development in specific domains that incorporate in a central way the social basis of the development and expression of these abilities and skills. There is also limited understanding of how social experience before children enter school supports the development of cognitive abilities that are important in the classroom. It is also unclear how to calibrate or scale up the social learning processes that have been identified in controlled laboratory research to the demands and complexity of the classroom environment (Blumenfeld et al., 2006). Finally, the adaptation of these ideas to classrooms with diverse populations of students presents a unique set of difficulties. Classrooms today are diverse along many dimensions: ethnic ancestry, social class, social interactional experience, learning abilities, and language. Language skills are central in a sociocultural approach to cognitive development. These skills serve as the medium of information exchange and as a way of organizing and representing knowledge in the head. Ensuring that children have the language skills to access the social learning experiences of the classroom is vital, especially for English language learners and language minority students who are at high risk of academic failure. Parents also play an important role both before and after children enter school (Weiss, Kreider, Lopez, & Chatman, 2005). Determining and supporting effective means for parents to be involved in children's education is imperative.

REFERENCES

Adamson, L. B., & Bakeman, R. (1991). The development of shared attention during infancy. In R. Vasta (Ed.), *Annals of child development* (Vol. 8, pp. 1–41). London: Kingsley.

Bjorklund, D. F., & Pelligrini, A. D. (2002). *The origins of human nature: Evolutionary developmental psychology.* Washington, DC: American Psychological Association.

Blumenfeld, P. D., Marx, R. W., & Harris, C. J. (2006). Learning environments. In W. Damon & R. M. Lerner (Series Eds.) & K. A. Renninger & I. E. Sigel (Vol. Eds.), *Child psychology in practice: Vol. 4, Handbook of child psychology* (6th ed., pp. 279–342). New York: Wiley.

Bransford, J., Brown, A. L., & Cocking, R. R. (1999). *How people learn: Brain, mind, experience and school.* Washington, DC: National Academy Press.

Bruner, J. (1975). The ontogenesis of speech acts. *Journal of Child Language, 1,* 1–19.

Bruner, J. (1986). *Actual minds, possible worlds.* Cambridge, MA: Harvard University Press.

Campbell, S. B. (2000). Developmental perspectives on attention deficit disorder. In A. Sameroff, M. Lewis, & S. Miller (Eds.), *Handbook of child psychopathology* (2nd ed., pp. 383–401). New York: Plenum.

Campos, J. J., & Stenberg, C. R. (1981). Perception, appraisal, and emotion: The onset of social referencing. In M. E. Lamb & L. R. Sherrod (Eds.), *Infant social cognition: Empirical and theoretical considerations* (pp. 273–314). Hillsdale, NJ: Erlbaum.

Carpenter, M., Nagall, K., & Tomasello, M. (1998). Social cognition, joint attention, and communicative competence from 9 to 15 months of age. *Monographs of the Society for Research in Child Development, 63* (Serial No. 255). Chicago: University of Chicago Press.

Chavajay, P., & Rogoff, B. (1999). Cultural variation in management of attention by children and their caregivers. *Child Development, 35,* 1079–1090.

Cohn, J. F., & Tronick, E. Z. (1983). Three-month-old infants' reaction to simulated maternal depression. *Child Development, 54,* 185–193.

Cole, M. (2005). Culture in development. In M. H. Bornstein & M. E. Lamb (Eds.), *Developmental science: An advanced textbook* (pp. 45–101). Mahwah, NJ; Erlbaum.

de la Ossa, J., & Gauvain, M. (2001). Joint attention by mothers and children while using plans. *International Journal of Behavioral Development, 25,* 176–183.

Engel, S. (1995). *The stories children tell: Making sense of the narratives of childhood*. New York: Freeman.

Fivush, R., Haden, C., & Reese, E. (1996). Remembering, recounting, and reminiscing: The development of autobiographical memory in social context. In D. C. Rubin (Ed.), *Remembering our past: Studies in autobiographical memory* (pp. 341–359). Cambridge: Cambridge University Press.

Gauvain, M. (1992). Social influences on planning in advance and during action. *International Journal of Behavioral Development, 15,* 377–398.

Gauvain, M. (2001). *The social context of cognitive development*. New York: Guilford.

Halfon, N., Shulman, E., & Hochstein, M. (2001). Brain development in early childhood. UCLA Center for Healthier Children, Families and Communities Policy Research Center, *Policy Brief, No. 13,* 1–4.

Hamond, N. R., & Fivush, R. (1991). Memories of Mickey Mouse: Young children recount their trip to Disneyworld. *Cognitive Development, 6,* 433–448.

Heath, S. B. (1983). *Ways with words: Language, life, and work in communities and classrooms*. Cambridge, UK: Cambridge University Press.

Hyson, M., Copple, C., & Jones, J. (2006). Early childhood development and education. In W. Damon &. R. M. Lerner (Series Eds.) & K. A. Renninger & I. E. Sigel (Vol. Eds.), *Child psychology in practice: Vol. 4, Handbook of child psychology* (6th ed., pp. 3–47). New York: Wiley.

Klinnert, M. D. (1984). The regulation of infant behavior by maternal facial expression. *Infant Behavior and Development, 7,* 447–465.

Klinnert, M. D., Emde, R. N., Butterfield, P., & Campos, J. J. (1986). Social referencing: The infant's use of emotional signals from a friendly adult with mother present. *Developmental Psychology, 22,* 427–434.

Lave, J., & Wenger, E. (1991). *Situated learning: Legitimate peripheral participation*. Cambridge, UK: Cambridge University Press.

Lochman, J. E., & Dodge, K. A. (1994). Social-cognitive processes of severely violent, moderately aggressive, and nonaggressive boys. *Journal of Consulting and Clinical Psychology, 62,* 366–374.

Minami, M., & McCabe, A. (1995). Rice balls and bear hunts: Japanese and North American family narrative patterns. *Journal of Child Language, 22,* 423–446.

Neitzel, C., & Stright, A. D. (2003). Mothers' scaffolding of children's problem solving: Establishing a foundation of academic self-regulatory competence. *Journal of Family Psychology, 17,* 147–159.

Ochs, E., Taylor, C., Rudolph, D., & Smith, R. (1992). Storytelling as a theory-building activity. *Discourse Processes, 15,* 37–72.

Pintrich, P. R., & Schunk, D. H. (2002). *Motivation in education: Theory, research, and applications* (2nd ed.). Upper Saddle River, NJ: Merrill/Prentice Hall.

Reese, E., & Fivush, R. (1993). Parental styles of talking about the past. *Developmental Psychology, 29,* 596–606.

Rogoff, B. (1998). Cognition as a collaborative process. In W. Damon (Series Ed.) & D. Kuhn & R. S. Siegler (Vol. Eds.), *Cognition, perception and language: Vol. 2, Handbook of child psychology* (5th ed., pp. 679–744). New York: Wiley.

Rommetveit, R. (1985). Language acquisition as increasing linguistic structuring of experience and symbolic behavior control. In J. V. Wertsch (Ed.), *Culture, com-*

munication, and cognition: Vygotskian perspectives (pp. 183–204). Cambridge, UK: Cambridge University Press.

Ruff, H. A., & Rothbart, M. K. (1996). *Attention in early development: Themes and variations.* Oxford, UK: Oxford University Press.

Saxe, G. B., Guberman, S. R., & Gearhart, M. (1987). Social processes in early number development. *Monographs of the Society for Research in Child Development, 52* (2, Serial No. 216), 3–162.

Sigel, I. E. (2000). Educating the young thinker model from research to practice: A case study of program development, or the place of theory and research in the development of educational programs. In J. L. Roopnarine & J. E. Johnson (Eds.), *Approaches to early childhood education* (3rd ed., pp. 315–340). Columbus, OH: Merrill/Macmillan.

Sigman, M., & Kasari, C. (1995). Joint attention across contexts in normal and autistic children. In C. Moore & P. J. Dunham (Eds.), *Joint attention: Its origins and role in development* (pp. 189–203). Hillsdale, NJ: Erlbaum.

Snow, C.E. (1990). Building memories: The ontogeny of autobiography. In D. Cicchetti & M. Beeghly (Eds.), *The self in transition: Infancy to childhood* (pp. 213–242). Chicago: University of Chicago Press.

Tharp. R., & Gallimore, R. (1988). *Rousing minds to life: Teaching, learning, and schooling in social context.* Cambridge, UK: Cambridge University Press.

Tomasello, M. (1995). Joint attention as social cognition. In C. Moore & P. H. Dunham (Eds.), *Joint attention: Its origins and role in development* (pp. 103–130). Hillsdale, NJ: Erlbaum.

Trevarthen, C. (1980). The foundations of intersubjectivity: Development of interpersonal and cooperative understanding in infants. In D. R. Olson (Ed.), *The social foundations of language and thought* (pp. 316–342). New York: Norton.

Vandermaas-Peeler, M., Way, E., & Umpleby, J. (2003). Parental guidance in a cooking activity with preschoolers. *Journal of Applied Developmental Psychology, 24,* 75–89.

Vygotsky, L. S. (1978). *Mind in society.* Cambridge, MA: Harvard University Press.

Weiss, H. B., Kreider, H., Lopez, M. E., & Chatman, C. M. (2005). *Preparing educators to involve families: From theory to practice.* Thousand Oaks, CA: Sage.

Wertsch, J. V. (1985). *Vygotsky and the social formation of mind.* Cambridge, MA: Harvard University Press.

Willatts, P. (1990). Development of problem solving strategies in infants. In D. F. Bjorklund (Ed.), *Children's strategies* (pp. 23–66). Hillsdale, NJ: Erlbaum.

Wood, D. J., Bruner, J. S., & Ross, G. (1976). The role of tutoring in problem solving. *Journal of Child Psychology and Psychiatry, 17,* 89–100.

Wood, D. J., & Middleton, D. (1975). A study of assisted problem solving. *British Journal of Psychology, 66,* 181–191.

CHAPTER 6

SOCIAL LEARNING THROUGH SOCIAL MOTIVATION

Ole Fredrik Lillemyr

INTRODUCTION

A number of researchers and practitioners have found that self-concept is a major source of intrinsic motivation (Csikszentmihalyi, 1985; Deci & Ryan, 1985; Skaalvik & Skaalvik, 2005). This is not as evident in early childhood education, since motivation research has been limited in this field (Maehr & Meyer, 1997). Intrinsically motivated behaviors are those whose motivation is based in the inherent interest or internal satisfaction of the behaviors *per se*, rather than being contingent on some sort of reward, praise or external consequence (Ryan & Deci, 2002). People who are intrinsically motivated are characterized by what is called true (non-contingent) self-esteem (Deci & Ryan, 1994, 1995). Research has documented that making learning more fun (intrinsically motivated) generates a desire to be taught and increases learning and retention as well as subsequent interest in the subject matter (Lepper & Cordova, 1992; Covington, 1998). This kind of motivation is of tremendous importance to individuals' learning, including social learning, both in school and elsewhere. In the field of early childhood education, it is significant to note that intrinsic motivation typically takes place in *children's play*, a fact that underscore its potential for learning

Contemporary Perspectives on Socialization and Social Development..., pages 99–131
Copyright © 2007 by Information Age Publishing

(Lillemyr, 2001). The importance of self-concept for intrinsic motivation is one reason why *competence* is now suggested as a main concept in the field of motivation instead of achievement, not the least because perceptions of competence are closely tied to the concept of competence. Therefore, competence motivation is proposed as the relevant term rather than achievement motivation (Elliot & Dweck, 2005).

For some years now it has been argued with increasing strength that *social aspects* of motivation play a major role in children's learning and academic performance. Accordingly, social motivation is important to social and academic learning. In particular this can be observed among young children (Juvonen & Wentzel, 1996; Wentzel, 2005). It is documented that children's social competence with peers is positively related to academic accomplishments throughout the school years (Wentzel, 2003). Furthermore, it has also been found that what happens during the first year of school has an essential effect on children's participation and performances later in school. Equally, the way in which young children perceive themselves socially in early school years, strongly influences how they see themselves academically. This had not always been at the forefront of research. It has been found that even first grade students have differentiated perceptions of competence in various kinds of activities (Eccles, Wigfield, Harold, & Blumenfeld, 1993). Patrick and Townsend (1995) found among school starters in New Zealand (5-year olds) that the strongest factor in explaining intrinsic motivation was their perception of social competence, and their sense of social competence was a strong contributor to their perception of academic competence. This means that students who feel good about themselves with regard to having friends (age-mates) in school also think highly about themselves with regard to academic competence, which in turn can promote their intrinsic motivation for school activities. So, acquiring social skills will stimulate social learning, as well as promote school motivation. Several studies indicate that this is particularly important during the transition period (preschool–school), even if children's social and academic development are intertwined during all their educational lives, and it appears that social goal-setting contributes heavily to children's school adjustment. The reason for this seems to be that social goals and social relationships function as significant motivators for children in the process of school adjustment, which can influence their participation and performances in class (Lillemyr et al., 1998; Birch & Ladd, 1996; Wentzel, 1996, 2002).

Therefore, the social self-concept is considered a major antecedent of social motivation, and social motivation is fundamental to the social learning of young children in early childhood education institutions, as well as playing a major role in their learning in general. As it has been found that the early childhood years constitute a sensitive period for social development and self-concept development, several recent research studies have focused on how aspects of social setting and social context can influence children's capacities for learning and achievement, when learning is considered in a broad sense of the word (Ladd, 1999; Ladd, Buhs, & Seid, 2000; Schoenfeld, 1999; Lillemyr, 2003).

Kathryn R. Wentzel (1996) has characterized the importance of social motivation to social and academic learning in school, as follows:

> The social worlds of children are a pervasive and influential part of their lives at school. Each day in class, children work to maintain and establish interpersonal relationships, they strive to develop social identities and a sense of belongingness, they observe and model social skills and standards for performance displayed by others, and they are rewarded for behaving in ways that are valued by teachers and peers. We also know that children who display socially competent behavior in elementary school are more likely to excel academically throughout their middle and high school years than those who do not. (p. 1)

As Wentzel (1996) points out, research has paid little attention to the possibility that children's social development is related to classroom motivation, school adjustment and performances.

RELEVANT CONCEPTS

Early childhood education and care (ECEC) encompasses children from 0 to 8 years of age. It is imperative to state that the pedagogy of the young children in nursery and preschool must be seen in close relation to the pedagogy of the youngest students in primary school, as children need continuity and coherence in their educational lives. The Organization for Economic Co-operation and Development (OECD) defines early childhood education and care as " programmes and provision for children from birth to compulsory school age" (OECD home page). However, early childhood education and care often includes the first three years of primary school as well (Klugman, 1990; Wasserman, 1990; Wood & Attfield, 1996; Lillemyr, Fagerli, & Søbstad, 2001). The demand for a common educational platform and continuity between daycare, preschool, and school is of much concern in recent reforms in many countries (see Broström, 1999; Dockett & Fleer, 1999; Lillemyr, 2002).

Play

Children's play is considered a major component of early childhood education. Several perspectives on play have been put forward. Levy (1978) discussed three dimensions as fundamental to our understanding of children's play: intrinsic motivation, suspension of reality, and internal locus of control. Pellegrini (1991) defined play along three dimensions: play as disposition, play as context, and play as observable behavior. Since a definition of play is hard to come up with, we typically end up with multidimensional understandings of play (Dockett & Fleer, 1999). Some have even conceived play as an important element in the quality of life as such (Huizinga, 1955). For this reason it has become more common to delineate dimensions for the understanding of play or a set of attitudes towards play, in coherence with the expression of "homo ludens" (Huizinga, 1955). From this background a holistic perspective on play has been attempted (Lillemyr, 2004):

- intrinsic motivation
- children's suspension of reality
- internal base of control
- play as social interactions, or communication at different levels

Along these lines scholars in the field draw attention to two main characteristics of play: the unique value of play (in itself) for children, and learning through play. One aspect that often seems to complicate the understanding of play is the gender focus. Sometimes gender differences are directed by societal factors and/or teachers; at other times boys and girls themselves are in charge of gender differences and similarities. Interestingly, there seem to be clear differences in application and attitudes towards play among male and female preschool teachers (Sandberg & Samuelsson, 2005).

Learning

In the field of early childhood education it is meaningful to claim that the relation between play and learning is significant. Nevertheless, the concept of learning is considered the crux of the matter or the number 1 task in school. However, over the years learning has been defined in a number of ways, depending on the underlying theory (Skinner, 1938; Tolman, 1948; Bandura, 1977; Piaget, 1954, 1970; Vygotsky, 1978). I have (Lillemyr, 2003) argued for a concept of learning in a broad perspective, in correspondence with others' suggestions (Bjørgen, 1997; Schoenfeld, 1999).

The understanding of learning in a broad perspective can be related to five main points (Lillemyr, 2003):

- Learning is internal processes caused by training/experiences, providing increased capacity to comprehend, experience, feel, reflect and act
- Learning includes the acquisition of knowledge and skills, as well as applications (as in experimentation and creativity)
- Learning comprises individual processes, but is also influenced by social competence, feelings of relatedness, and socio-cultural aspects
- Learning affects personality, and vice-versa. Learning affects the whole child
- Learning changes the child's competence, and hence its sense of competence (p. 59)

Based on these components, an argument can be made for a new, broader concept of learning in day-care institutions and schools alike. Accordingly, it is necessary to get rid of the old-fashion concept of school learning. In this broad concept of learning, social learning is included and plays an active role.

Social Competence

Social competence has been developing from the concept of competence, first applied in the field of motivation by White (1959) in the term *competence motivation*, launched as a new understanding of motivation as a socio-psychological concept. According to White, all human beings have an urge toward (a desire for) competence, based upon their need for competence. Competence motivation was later elaborated and extended by Harter in her developmental perspective on how senses of competence or feelings of competence developed from childhood to adulthood. Interactions with significant others were considered important in this development as well as meeting challenges of optimal levels of difficulty. Urdan and Turner (2005) argue that competence motivation involves a concern with mastery, where the motive is to develop, attain or demonstrate competence. Wentzel (2005) define *social competence* as the achievement of context-specific social goals that result in positive outcomes not only for the self but also for others. Then it appears important to ask which goals result in positive relationships with peers at preschool and school? More recently, social competence has continued to grow into a major objective for preschools, in many cases in schools as well. In Norway the Framework Plan (1996) for day-care institutions maintains that the main objective *basic competence* is including social competence as a major ingredient. *Social competence* is said to constitute the child's ability to participate in play and interact with others in a positive manner. This is taken further in Framework Plan of 2006 (Framework Plan, 2006), integrating social competence in the concepts care and inclusion. For comprehensive schools the Norwegian Core Curriculum (1997, p. 30) considers educating the social human being as an important component in educating students as integrated human beings. Harter defines social competence or sense of competence as the child's perceptions of popularity with peers imbedded in statements like "some kids find it hard to make friends" (Harter, 1982). In order for social learning to take place, social competence is considered a prerequisite, but social learning contributes primarily to achieving social competence. In this concern it is important to notice the growing interest in focusing on the gender challenges within social learning, even if these aspects appear to be handled differently in preschool and school (Odelfors, 1996; Nielsen, 2000; Bratterud, Emilsen, & Lillemyr, 2006).

To summarize, the concepts presented here, which should encapsulate target endeavors in early years' education today, all are closely related to social learning in schools in Western countries. Even so, the priority given to social learning is not always obvious and social learning is given different levels of priority in different countries. A school-based example illustrates the complex and important relations which exists between self-concept, social motivation, social learning and learning in general:

> In October, two first grade[1] teachers (male and female) arranged a learning session with their classes in the following way. They took their classes (22 and 25 students respectively) on an excursion to a medium-sized Norwegian farm, in the neighborhood of the primary school. The two classes were quite familiar with each other from joint projects and play sessions in school hours and after-school programs since they started at school, and the teachers encouraged the students' self confidence during the first weeks in particular. The excursion was exploratory in nature, allowing small groups of students to look at different places on the farm. They were allowed to choose co-operative companions freely, across the two classes. The process of making groups was observed and encouraged by the teachers. Students who did not seem to end up in a group were guided to a group by the teachers. This resulted in most cases in groups of either boys or girls, but sometimes both sexes. Some groups had members from both classes. At first the student groups were followed around by the farmer and his wife, who told them about the main elements of farming. Later the small groups walked around by themselves, collecting more information. However, they were free to ask questions to either the farmer and his wife or the teachers. During the day, the teachers observed their students and found that most groups functioned well socially, whereas a few did not, typically because students did not seem to like each other very much, and/or disagreed about what to do and what they actually learned. Typically these groups had been put together with the help of the teachers, because their classmates did not choose them. In these cases the

teachers had to assist during the day. So, students' motivation varied, primarily because of social aspects. Accordingly, social motivation was crucial.

Back at school the following day the two teachers decided to let pairs of students do a drawing and writing project using the school library to look for more information as well as elaborating on their experiences from the excursion. Students were allowed to choose with whom they wanted to work. During these activities, the teachers observed the students and tried not to interfere too much, since major objectives were involvement in the team farming as well as social learning. In addition to the drawing and writing project the male teacher decided to let students dramatize "life on the farm" in a self-regulated play session, to document their experiences. This he did to enhance students' social motivation still more. Students in this class were divided into two large groups, with one student as group leader. During the play session the teacher did not interfere, but simply made observations on how groups functioned socially. The female teacher did not give her students this assignment.

After a month with a variety of experiences in the classroom working with this theme in addition to other themes, the two teachers gave the students a test about life on a farm.

Then the two teachers met to share experiences, based upon the test and observations of activities. The teachers found that the test results in the two classes were quite similar. Compared to the teachers' impression of the students' abilities in class, this was not a surprise. However, the male teacher also felt he had observed improved social learning in his class, which affected their academic participation. Students took initiatives and seemed to thrive and function socially even better than before. When the two teachers tried to compare how students were functioning in the class as well as in groups, several more students in the male teacher's class had become autonomous and self-regulated in their learning, and in general more students participated actively in class discussions and showed positive attitudes towards class mates. In this class, most students interacted positively towards the teacher and took responsibility to follow up assignments. The female teacher's opinion was that these tendencies were not identified to such a degree in her class. So she decided to give her students a play session with dramatization as part of the next project in the spring term.

From this example it can be seen that social learning in classrooms can result in an improved classroom climate and increased well-being, as well as easing the process of collaboration, even if it does not necessarily improve student achievements in the short run. However, the example did not shed light on what the effects might be in a slightly longer perspective. As we shall see from the research review below, the elements of social competence and social learning during early childhood education are highly relevant to learning in a lifelong perspective.

WHAT CAN BE LEARNED FROM MOTIVATION THEORY AND RESEARCH?

The theory of personal investment, as a conception of intrinsic motivation, was first presented by Maehr (1984), and then launched as a theoretical framework for school and work settings alike by Maehr and Braskamp (1986). They emphasized people's feelings of meaningfulness with regard to actions in a situation, and argued that the extent of meaning tends to increase the interest for self-investment in the situation. The amount of meaning is seen as depending primarily on three basic elements:

- Personal incentives (task-orientation, performance- or ego-orientation, social-orientation or extrinsic-orientation);
- The nature of selfhood (one's definition of self or sense of self: identity, self-reliance, sense of competence); and
- Perceived options (behavioral alternatives related to choice) Maehr and Braskamp (1986).

This is a goal-theory perspective primarily focusing on the difference between task-orientation and performance-orientation among children or adults. It must be emphasized that the social context, affiliation aspects, perception of option (choice), and the sense of goal-directedness are strongly emphasized. This theory, and its focus on task orientation, was the point of departure in a research study where they set out to transform the culture of schools. The aim was to transform schools into a task-oriented perspective, as opposed to a performance-oriented perspective. Results disclosed that the schools actually succeeded in raising their average student achievements substantially (Maehr & Midgley, 1996). Later this goal theory perspective was extended to the field of socio-cultural research, examining how motivational goals, self-concept, and sense of self predict academic achievement. In any case, the theory has proved useful in contributing to the explanation of how self-concept and motivation influence academic achievement among socio-cultural groups, and how schools are actually working with deep learning strategies, based upon motivation (McInerney, Roche, McInerney, & Marsh, 1997; Watkins, McInerney, Lee, Akande, & Regmi, 2002; McInerney, 2003). A pertinent question aiming at the overall philosophy of the school seems to be: is the school fostering performance goals or encouraging task goals? Maybe both are emphasized, but which one represents the main emphasis? Based upon this framework, research into the influence of motivation on socio-cultural groups and their interest in school learning indicates significant gender differences as well as variations between the socio-cultural groups from two continents (Lillemyr, McInerney, & Søbstad, 2005).

Deci and Ryan (1985, 1991, 2000) are the architects of several theories relevant to intrinsic motivation, most importantly the theory of self-determination (Ryan & Deci, 2002; Reeve, Deci, & Ryan, 2004). Their point of departure is a broad sense of the concept of learning, comprising both cognitive and affective dimensions, as well as social interactions. In their opinion learning is most strongly promoted in contexts where the individual has independent choices and where feelings of competence and affiliation are supported. They find effective learning primarily takes place in settings with optimal challenges and when significant others support autonomy. The primary idea in their theory of self-determination is that the behavior develops from one's sense of self, when the person is "autonomous" or "self-determined," meaning that the person has an internal perceived locus of causality, as deCharms (1968) would have put it. It follows from this that intrinsically motivated behavior promotes development of the self and a stronger sense of a true self worth. Accordingly, they conceive the self as an important and active human agency. They maintain (Deci & Ryan, 1995): "...the term *human agency* refers to those motivated behaviors that emanate from one's integrated self. To be agentic is thus to be self-determined" (p. 35). What characterizes intrinsic motivation in their opinion is:

- Behavior without any kind of extrinsic reward
- Involvement in activities through genuine interest
- Activities which are optimally challenging
- Behavior or activities based on psychological needs

In particular, Deci and Ryan consider it is fundamental to satisfy three main psychological needs in order to obtain intrinsic motivation:

- The need for autonomy (feeling of self-determination)
- The need for competence (feeling competent or effective)
- The need for relatedness (feelings of belonging/sense of affiliation)

For this reason *a true self* develops as one acts volitionally (autonomously), experiences an inner sense of competence, and is loved (feelings of belonging). This actually means feeling good about being the person one is, instead of meeting external standards to obtain extrinsic rewards. With this background, Deci and Ryan (1991) suggested three methodic principles (dimensions) for promoting intrinsic motivation, in an educational context or indeed any other kind of context:

- Support autonomy
- Structure
- Involvement

To support autonomy means providing choices, minimizing pressure to perform in specified ways, encouraging initiatives, and, not least being responsive, listening and demonstrating belief in the child, recognizing his or her competence. Structure primarily has to do with the clearness of the behavior-outcome contingencies, as in intentions, expectations, and provision of feedback according to objectives and intentions. The idea of a clear structure is to enhance the person's sense of control over outcomes. Involvement describes the degree to which significant others are interested in a child and devote time and energy in their relationship to the child. Strong involvement tells the child something about being worthy in a family, a group or educational setting. These principles have been applied with success, confirming the theory in several studies (cf. Deci & Ryan, 2002).

The three principles can also be applied in making assessments or evaluations of a context. "Social contexts that are autonomy supportive, that provide moderate structure, and that contain involved others are optimal for encouraging self-determined engagement and promoting development, because they facilitate the target person's expression and satisfaction of his or her basic psychological needs" (Deci & Ryan, 1991, p. 246).

Optimal challenge, the role of significant others and freedom to choose are three characteristics of the theory of self-determination presented by Deci and Ryan. Since it is not always possible to have intrinsic motivation, extrinsic motivation is relevant as well. According to Deci and Ryan extrinsic motivation should be as self-contingent as possible. They explain this by reference to the process of internalization, described as a continuum from extrinsically regulated behavior (external rewards) at the one end of the continuum, to self-determined or integrated regulation, at the other end of the continuum. Typically, in the latter kind of extrinsic motivation the person has a strong feeling of relatedness, because he or she identifies with values and ideas of a significant other or a group. To ensure an extrinsic motivation that is self-determined, he or she will have to feel competent and autonomous in their behavior. Several research studies have confirmed the theory (Ryan & Deci, 2002). Interestingly, Covington and Dray (2001) found that in the process of coming to care about learning in school, satisfying the psychological needs of affiliation, autonomy and competence undoubtedly play a central role for students, even if personal worth derived from the ability to compete successfully with others also has some influence. All factors were found to promote students' capacity for intrinsic involvement. In general, studies have indicated that students further along the continuum of extrinsic motivation (integrated regulation) cope more actively and display positive effects in school and have a higher self-worth. They argue "self-determination is the key to successful adaptation in multiple domains, including periods of transition in children's lives" (p. 167). They consider the provision of autonomy support, structure, and involvement "as social-contextual 'nutriments'" helping children to move toward more autonomous regulation of tasks.

Wentzel (1991) started out with an interest in the relation between social competence and academic achievement in classrooms and how aspects of social competence at school could influence the students' performances. Later Wentzel (1996) refers to the growing body of evidence that the social world of children is of high importance, and states that the social aspects should not be omitted when examining and understanding children's successes and failures at school. She states that the ability and will to help, share, cooperate, and comply with rules and role expectations are critical to the development of positive social relationships within peer groups. Based upon these ideas she outlined elements of a theory of social motivation, including the acquisition of social competence as a primary concern.

More recently it was found in studies in secondary schools in Norway that a substantial amount (70%) of socially competent students thrives at school, even if they are bored by most of the learning activities. However, only 12% of the students state that their teachers provide them with challenges (Dale, Wærness, & Lindvig, 2005). In secondary schools it appears that there are two different worlds, the student world that is mainly a social one, and the world of the teacher that is primarily about learning and achievements. A considerable number of the students who seem to lack social competence and self-confidence, displays maladjustment (Nordahl, 2000). Results such as these pave the way for research studies into the perspective of self-concept and motivation. Suffice it here to mention that Sørlie (1998) in her study of middle-school children in Norway claim that self-concept, social competence and focus on subject matter constitute what she calls the "triangle of education." She considers the learning of social skills and development of social competence as a necessary ingredient for attempts to enhance learning and prevent behavior problems in school. Emphasis on subject matter competencies alone did not appear to suffice.

From this perspective it is no surprise that Wentzel and others have focused their research on how students' social competence or popularity with peers might relate to academic accomplishments (Wentzel, 2005). She conceives of social competence as comprising a balance between the achievement of positive results for the self and adherence to context-specific expectations of behavior in an educational setting. This then leads to the acquisition of social goals for the student, as well as social integration within the group. This subsequently means achieving personal goals as well as meeting others' expectations. From this it should be clear that meeting social standards affects both the personal sense of self and the social self specifically. Social goals of concern for social competence are, for Wentzel (2005) the ones such as "establishing personal relationships with teachers and peers, gaining approval from others, or behaving cooperatively and responsibly with classmates" (p. 281). Of course it is also possible to evaluate social competence in relation to failure to meet social standards, such as peer rejection, lacking control of anger, etc. Then, social competence is defined as the achievement of context-specific social goals that result in positive outcomes for self and others (loc. cit.). In several research studies the examination of social competence has been studied by identifying popularity with peers, or peer group approval and acceptance. In some studies, students who are often rejected or disliked students have been studied. These students tend to be less compliant, less self-assured, less sociable, and more disruptive (Ladd, Birch, & Buhs, 1999; Buhs & Ladd, 2001). By contrast, popular students are found to be more cooperative, helpful, sociable, better leaders, and more self-assertive (cf. Wentzel & Asher, 1995). Wentzel (2005) points out that the relevance of school context for understanding social competence with peers is reflected in consistent findings relating social acceptance to success in school performances and rejected status to academic difficulties. Wentzel and her co-researchers (Wentzel, Barry, & Caldwell, 2004) have documented that socio-metric status and friendship influence both motivation and school adjustment. She (Wentzel, 2005) concludes, however, that we still know all too little about peer groups and the peer culture influencing school learning, and the picture is not made easier by the growing amount of research showing that there are tendencies towards significant gender differences in relation to social competence and social learning as well. She suggests multiple models to explain the tendency toward a positive relation between positive peer relationships and high academic outcomes. Based on this, it is necessary to be far more aware of how social competence (motivation) and social learning develop in early childhood, because of their important long-term effects. I do not feel that we as researchers are yet fully aware of the consequences of this.

As seen in the theories and research outlined above, social aspects of motivation are prominent and strongly emphasized to enhance learning. Even if little research has been focused on early years' education the social motivation theory perspective is undoubtedly highly relevant to learning in early childhood education, as evidenced in textbooks demonstrating practical implications (Stipek, 2002; Brophy, 2004).

FROM MOTIVATION TO LEARNING— SELECTED RESEARCH STUDIES

At first sight, the amount of research focusing social learning and social competence in the field of early childhood appears somewhat sparse, particularly with regard to research into children in preschools. It is better, although still somewhat sparse, in the case of research into the early grades of primary school. Furthermore, few studies have a motivation theory approach. Nevertheless, several of them touch on the phenomenon of motivation. With this background, I will present a selection of studies in the following pages, which all share a relevance to the perspective of social learning through social motivation.

Based upon their research Smilansky and Shefatya (1990) have claimed that children's attainment of socio-dramatic skills in play during early childhood education, promote their social and cognitive abilities. In this regard teachers' interventions on children's dramatic play during preschool were found to be effective, particularly in terms of the make believe elements in play. They found that this affected positively the children's development of cognitive, creative and socio-emotional abilities, which later turned out to be of fundamental value to their learning in school. Actually results from several studies are pointing out that there is a close connection between young children's play and their cognitive style, and these will in the next run be of help for the children when they attempt to understand the world, including their social world (Saracho, 2003). It has been found that some children are more field and others—independent, while others are field and others—dependent. It can be outlined from this research that aspects of communication, socialization and imitation, all so important to children's social learning, often are attained during different types of social play in early childhood, for example through playing roles (Hellendoorn, van der Kooj, & Sutton-Smith, 1994). This means that the social learning is influenced by social motivation, as intrinsic motivation and the social aspect are major elements of play.

Lamer (1997) was only one focusing the importance of social competence for all children. She developed a practical method of promoting children's self-concept and social competence as well as other pro-social abilities. She has come up with the following as essential aspects of social competence: empathy and role-taking, pro-social behavior, self control, self-assertion, and lastly, play, joy and humor. These five elements she considers to constitute a framework for ECEC staff for promoting social competence and social learning in practice, for which reason the model has been applied in several Norwegian preschools and primary schools. The achievement of goals, such as social abilities and social competence as a means to promote learning in school, has been focused on by several others (cf. Sletta, 1983; Wasserman, 1990; Broström, 1998; Dockett & Fleer, 1999).

Many researchers underline the importance of play and humor for different kinds of learning, social learning as well as academic. In preschools, Søbstad (1990, 1995) found that play and humor often take place in children's communicative activities. He argues that the parathelic[2] state typical for children's way of behaving in play and humor often accompany their activities of learning and social interaction. He sees humor as important for children's development of self and regards a playful attitude to be an antecedent for humor. He examined expressions of humor among pre-school children and found their humor to be influenced by experiences in the local environment. He differentiated humor in the following catego-ries: lingual humor, incongruent and absurd humor, aggressive humor, taboo humor, and societal humor. Søbstad (1999) claimed the parathelic state is a common trait typical for creative activities, humor, and play. In this respect the ability to decentrate[3] or see things from another person's perspective and see oneself in relation to others, appears to be fundamen-tal. In all cases a "here and now" or "flow" state, is characteristic (Csikszent-mihalyi, 1985). When children produce or generate humor Søbstad claims the following traits to be typical: a humor signal, transformations, sense of liberation, certain feelings for the context, strong interest, and autonomy. He considers humor to be intrinsically motivated and encourages ECEC staff to be aware of the positive value of humor in children's development, particularly as it interacts with and promotes social learning.

Løkken (1996) argued that it is important to focus on children's play, in order to get to know more about children's social development and every-day life in preschool, as this tells a lot about their social learning. While they are playing, children (aged 1 or 2 years) clearly communicate with each other, and obviously derive pleasure from being together. The tod-dlers show this in different ways, not always orally, but often by using their bodies (Merleau-Ponty, 1962). The communication is often deep between two or more children, and can be seen as a kind of physical as well as social interaction. Løkken stated that freedom, spontaneity and joy are momen-tous characteristics of play. Spontaneity often conveys into different kinds of creative activities, and therefore will have consequences for cognitive development. However, all three factors will influence social learning, directly or indirectly. These results were derived from analyses of observa-tions of groups of children (Løkken, 1989). Clearly, it can be seen that even 1–2 year old children can have pleasure and satisfaction from each other's company, and hence stimulate each other's social learning and well being. Later, in a more thorough study on "toddlers," Løkken attempted to find the *social style* of the toddler. She refers to several studies that found that bodily or physical play at this age is one of the richest aspects of play in terms of variation and social meaning. In her own study Løkken drew upon the theory of Merleau-Ponty (Løkken, 2000a, 2000b) and found that the characteristic toddler's social style (Løkken, 2000c) seemed to be based on bodily communication. The toddler's way of being during social play (Løkken, 2000d) can be regarded as the child's struggle to understand itself and others in the world. The characteristics of social style as a phenomenological concept were summarized as follows:

- The child as subject (the significance of the body)
- The construction of meaning
- Playfulness
- Inter-subjectivity (social relations)
- Humor and greetings

She concluded that toddlers are social persons, a fact that preschool teachers need to take into account in their work.

Lindahl carried out a study in Sweden, videotaping 10 1-year-olds during their first three months in preschool with the intention to document their learning. The focus of the study was on infants' everyday experiences and spontaneous learning. First she wanted to study children's experiences in social relations. Analyses were inspired by a phenomenological research approach. Her results supported the ideas of Daniel Stern (1985) about the child as an active individual developing its different interpersonal selves in interaction with the social environment. Lindahl found that the subjects (10 children) were approaching the surrounding world in various ways. Some of them were a lot more active in seeking social company than others. All children developed a competence in feelings or affection, even if sense of well-being, and the warm relations between child and adult influenced the social learning as well. She found that conscious elaboration by the child could suddenly provide new insight. In many cases their motor development and/or social relationships could assist their achievement of knowledge. This, and many other studies, has resulted in a new approach to our understanding of the infant and our attitudes toward young children in general (Sommer, 1997; Samuelsson & Carlsson, 2003). However, it is characteristic that the social setting, sense of feeling, and intellectual development all integrate to influence learning. At this age, learning for the child is often primarily motivated by the intent to master challenges in their surroundings. Surely, social relationships and conditions of affiliation and attachment must all contribute strongly to motivate learning.

A study on quality characteristics of preschools began in 2001 in five municipalities (Søbstad, 2004; Kvistad & Søbstad, 2005). The project was intended to describe, develop, evaluate, and document quality in five preschools from five municipalities of mid-Norway (one in a city). In this study, quality in preschool was defined as follows:

> Preschool quality means children's, parents', and staff's beliefs and experiences about the preschool and to what extent the preschool satisfies educational and societal criteria of what a good preschool is. (Søbstad, 2002, p. 17)

In this definition of quality, two perspectives are outlined: experienced quality and criteria quality. In developmental projects each preschool was encouraged to take its own point of departure in order to raise quality, according to its plan for the year. In this study information was collected from children, parents, and staff. In order to evaluate quality, different scales have been developed and various definitions of quality have been attempted (Sheridan, 2001; OECD Report, 2001). Such scales were not applied in this study, but in definitions they were taken as points of departure. It turned out that the staff in the participating preschools was primarily concerned with social interaction, play, and evaluation and documentation of their work. Certain presuppositions were found to be characteristic of quality in Norway compared to what has been reported from preschools in other countries: more out-door activities, fathers more visible in preschool, less weight on language and intellectual and school-like activities, more emphasis on play and social interaction, and more interaction with the local society. Thus, these were hypotheses to be examined. Data from children and staff also focused on bullying and harassments among children, in order to obtain a foundation for developing suitable means to decrease bullying tendencies (Midtsand, Monstad, & Søbstad, 2004).

The results indicated that these groups of children, parents, and staff were largely satisfied with their preschool. In general, children thrived, were satisfied with the variety and priority of activities, and seemed to emphasize strongly that they had good friends to play with. In general all participants in the preschool context characterized the social environment from good to excellent. This was seen as the experienced quality. Results (Kvistad & Søbstad, 2005) indicated that for parents the most frequently identified arguments for their children's attendance in preschool were: gets to play with other kids (97%), learn to relate to others (81%), have fun with other kids and adults (79%). Typically, all these aspects are social in nature. In general, the analyses of the different kinds of data more or less disclosed a similar picture in all participating preschools. The preschool environments were characterized by the following:

- An environment with positive social interactions, happiness and humor
- Play is important and emphasized
- Not too much emphasis on activities preparing children for school
- A stimulating out-door environment close to the preschool
- Frequent tours to forests, fiords, etc.
- Frequent contact and cooperation with parents
- The staff were responsive and listened to the children

It was found that the content of the preschools was characterized by play and social interaction combined with providing children with feelings of safety and good care. To achieve this, a certain amount of stability in the staff was necessary, and good cooperation between parents and preschool and preschool and school was required.

Despite this positive picture, they still found 11% of the children (among the 3 to 5s) were experiencing bullying every day or more than once a week (Midtsand, Monstad, & Søbstad, 2004). It was found that 35% of the children experienced physical harassments and more than 50% were often or occasionally excluded in play. These figures are high, and therefore raise concern, for which reason remedial means were developed to prevent bullying. This illustrates the fact that we often consider a preschool to be of good quality, even if there are some underlying negative elements that are not easily discovered at first. In this regard, identifying friendship relations is important, as research tells us that children with friends are less inclined to be bullied and have stronger resistance to bullying, compared to friendless children (Olweus, 2001; Ladd & Kochenderfer-Ladd, 2002). In developing measures to prevent bullying, training children in social skills is seen as significant (Buhs & Ladd, 2001).

Summing up, this study found certain staff characteristics would enhance quality (Kvistad & Søbstad, 2005, p. 198):

- Emphasizing joy and humor in child–child and child–adult interactions (happiness, parathelic situations)
- Helping children establish and care for healthy friendships (facilitating friendship development, decentration, social interaction)
- Being aware of the adult's role-modeling function for children (cf. equity, recognition, inclusion)
- Being respectful and protective towards children's play (cf. support, involvement, self-worth)
- Being a stimulator for, and an observant and encouraging initiator of children's play (observation, respect, promotion, encouragement)

However, as Kvistad and Søbstad maintain, for the quality work to be meaningful in the preschool, evaluations continually need to be made according to changes in society. Furthermore, questions concerning quality have to be set up at all levels, the municipality, the county municipality and nationally (Kvistad & Søbstad, 2005). As we have seen, the emphasis on social competence and the elements of motivation to enhance social learning were rather obvious in this study. Many of the characteristics documented in this study, were also found in an Icelandic study, from children's perspectives: good relationship with other children, be able to choose what to do, and have opportunities for play (Einarsdottir, 2005).

In a longitudinal case study Eide and Winger (1996) focused on the development of identity during children's lives at the transition between preschool and school, when they were 6 years and 8 years old, respectively. Based on the results, they regarded focus on children as participants and interactive actors in the context to be fundamental in order to function effectively in society. This indicates that it is significant to emphasize social and affective and relational elements in the classroom during the transition period, as other studies have also demonstrated (cf. Patrick & Townsend, 1995; Broström, 1999). Children's participation in class has important consequences for their self-concept and identity development, and for the achievement of social goals. In early childhood education and during transition in particular, several research studies have indicated these are elements of primary concern (Broström, 1998; Lindahl, 1998; Lillemyr, 2001; Creasy & Jarvis, 2003). To meet the challenge of getting children to participate in class, Eide and Winger (1996) found it necessary to organize curriculum programs that emphasize social-environmental aspects, such as developing a supportive teacher-student relationship, provision of student choice, and promotion of student co-decisions. They find a broad perspective of learning is needed, including social learning as a main ingredient. In particular, they emphasize the necessity for the teacher to take the perspective of the child, and develop the ability to decentrate (cf. Mead, 1969).

A qualitative study of the transition years (Lillemyr et al., 1998; Lillemyr, 2002) focused upon students' competence in major areas, based upon a theoretical framework combining the motivational theories of personal investment and self-determination (Deci & Ryan, 1991; Maehr & Midgley, 1996), a combination that has later been encouraged by others (Urdan, 2000). Interestingly, this study, as well as others (cf. Seljelid, 1994; Henningsen, 1999) showed a tendency for a substantial proportion (17%) of students to worry about starting school, in particular the extent to which they will have friends at school. Results (Lillemyr et al., 1998) indicated a clear tendency of a decline in students' sense of social competence at the age of starting school (among 6- and 7-year-olds), a significant decrease of intrinsic motivation in the same age range, and students' interest in free play was sustained through the first four years of primary (elementary) school. Based on this it is interesting to have a preschool teacher and a schoolteacher working together in the same classroom during grade 1. This is often the case in Norway (two teachers obligatory for classes of more than 18 students). This cooperation often continues during the first four grades of primary school (even if grades 2 to 4 have one teacher per classroom). One main idea behind this kind of arrangement is to ensure a combined and integrated approach to children's social competence and social learning as a platform for academic performances during the first years of school. Research into first grade education in Norway has clearly indicated that the collaboration between the two types of teachers is a relatively successful arrangement (Germeten, 1999, 2002).

Later Bae (2004) based on Schibbye's (1988) theory of dialectical relations (mutual recognition dialogues), carried out an ethnographic study applying videotaped observations of one third of the children in two preschools, encompassing 14 children and two preschool teachers. Bae maintains that the theory perspective of Schibbye is suitable to her research because the focus is clearly on the phenomenological aspects of the relational experience, based upon the principle of equity between the two parties in a child–preschool teacher relation. Firstly, Bae set out to present detailed, descriptive documentation of adult–child dialogues in the preschool context. Secondly, she attempted to obtain knowledge about the characteristics of *recognizing (supportive) adult–child dialogues*, particularly regarding the qualitative and processual aspects, and where the child gets to learn that his or her experiences are respected as valid ones.

She found that complex processes at the micro level characterized the dialogues. She was also struck by the high speed of shifts and changes in the dialogues, even within short interchanges, and a high richness of interactions for one and the same teacher was documented. The educators, in addition to adopting the child's point of view (ability to decentrate) showed a wide repertoire of expressing feelings, reactions and intentions. Furthermore, observing the dialogue from the child's perspective, she demonstrated a variety in interactions towards different children, depending on what the interaction was all about. Bae concludes that, in order to understand the dialogue from the perspective of the child, a focus on the micro-level seems necessary.

Bae refers to the fact that dialogues between 1- and 2-year-olds are widely documented (Løkken, 2000a; Sandvik, 2001). In her study, however, Bae describes characteristics in 4-, 5-, and 6-year olds individual dialogue abilities from interactions with preschool teachers. She illustrated how the child tried to catch the teacher's attention in verbal and non-verbal ways. She also found that the children adjusted their contributions to the dialogue and synchronized them to the adult's actions and expressions (Bae, 2004, p. 220). A tendency in this study seems to be how the *individual* child stands out as a dialogue partner rather than being documented within group means, as has most often been the case in earlier studies.

Bae advocates that the recognition in dialogues between teacher and child has to be understood as a process phenomenon, almost like a processual flow, where reciprocity in the interaction is typical. In her study she found the recognition from the teacher's point of view to be characterized (and expressed) by:

- Focused attention
- The will to listen
- An interest in understanding
- A well-meant interpretation
- Tolerance
- Willingness to wait for the child's reaction
- Receptive ability
- Flexible role distribution

Bae considers these traits to be empirical documentations of the teacher's recognizing (supportive) ways when developing the relationship. Building a sound, recognizing relationship is fundamental to the development of the child's self-esteem, and will influence the child's experiences of self and others, which is fundamental for all kinds of learning.

Further, Bae found that the social ecology within which the dialogues are embedded is characterized by multidimensionality, simultaneity, and unpredictability. She found that four relationship themes occurred repeatedly in adult–child interactions:

- Conversation
- Practical cooperation
- Play/humor
- Setting limits

Three kinds of interaction were found: mutual interest and humor, changing dialogical processes, and troublesome interactions. Generalizations were not possible from this study. However, the concept of mutual (reciprocal) recognition proved fruitful as a theoretical means for differentiating between dialogues as valid or not valid regarding children's experiences. The study also contributed to identifying relational modes that mediate recognition between children and preschool teachers. Interestingly, Bae found play and humor interchanges contain an important potential for the development of recognition. For this to happen, preschool teachers need to be observant of the meta-communicative signals provided by the child.

It is then important to ask: What kinds of information about the children do preschools and primary schools need to exchange in the transition years? Bø, Thorsen, Løge, and Omdal (2004) consider the school start to be one of the most dramatic and fundamental transitions a child can experience in its life, for which reason they argue that teachers and parents should be cautious *not to stigmatize* children in this sensitive period of time. They maintain it often can be observed that a new constellation of friends and social relations might make a significant difference for a child. They emphasize that all children in preschool and school deserve the best possible opportunities in relation to their potential. The theoretical framework of this study was Bronfenbrenner's developmental ecological model, in particular his thinking of the *meso* level. They applied questionnaires to parents, preschool teachers and preschool head teachers, and schoolteachers and other school personnel, in two waves (2002 and 2003). According to their overall results, exchange of information concerning children's *social competence* (e.g., social motivation) now obviously seems to have top priority. Information about children's development, abilities and knowledge is still important as well, but has a lower priority. They define social competence as: children's social functioning, how they interact with others (children and adults), and children's lingual competence (even if this element contains cognitive aspects as well).

According to the results, the schools in this study were primarily interested in getting information from parents and preschools about children's social functioning and special needs, how they function with language, and in social interactions. Parents and preschools agreed about the type of information that is important to give to schools: information about children's special needs, and social competence. Next, parents emphasize information about children's expectations regarding starting school, which preschools did not. Information about children's interests was ranked higher by preschools, than by parents. However, in general parents and preschool staff agreed to a large degree (over all rank correlation .65). The correlation between school staff and preschool staff on what information the school needs from the preschool was even higher (rank correlation .91). The authors were cautious in interpreting the results, as the answer percentage was somewhat low, especially among preschool staff (29), in schools it was higher (60). Still, the extent of agreement across the informant groups was perhaps the most interesting aspect of this study, in addition to the high priority of social competence.

In a study of early childhood education, Grolnick (1990) examined how it might be advantageous to target children's motivational resources from a social and affective approach in order to enhance adjustment to school and improve learning among children with special needs. She pointed out that often focus on motivation in early childhood has included intellectual and cognitive elements, rather than social and affective ones. She found that social and affective components of motivation are assumed to be stronger, not least in the long term. In particular this seems to be the case for elements based in children's attitudes towards self and others and attitudes towards challenges they meet in the preschool context and elsewhere. She reminds us that such objectives were quite common in Head Start programs some years ago. In her opinion, these are primarily objectives that to a greater degree encompass the whole child, compared to targeting cognitive objectives and academic achievements alone. Applying a developed model, she identified specific "inner affective resources" in the child that appeared to facilitate learning in school. She presented three kinds of school-related inner resources based upon the motivation theory of Deci and Ryan (1985):

- Perceived competence (sense of competence)
- Perceived control (understanding of what controls what is happening)
- Self-regulation of learning (motivation orientation toward one's values)

She then referred to factors in the learning environment (the classroom) that facilitate these above-mentioned resources. These factors have been found by several researchers to be important in the transition to school (Entwisle et al., 1987; Patrick & Townsend, 1995). These authors all find that social and affective status probably shapes cognitive status more than the other way around. In Grolnick's (1990) opinion an affective approach to objectives in early childhood education should have consequences for teaching, cooperation between parents and school, and the policy in this area. In conclusion Grolnick stated in her report: "It is hoped that it will spark increased dialogue between researchers in motivation and those in early childhood education" (p. 270).

However, it should not be forgotten that much social learning of children takes place through play, even in school, mostly as social play. Bennett, Wood, and Rogers (1996) examined nine reception teachers' thinking (theories) about play in their practice and found that teachers' theories of play were eclectic, but still shared common ground. Teachers' general teaching orientation revealed that play was one of their priorities, and was incorporated in their practice in various ways. A predominant concern was found with free play or role play, but it turned out that the teachers actually structured children's play to a certain degree, because their intentions for play needed to be educationally worthwhile in curriculum areas, notably literacy, as well as social and language development. The emphasis on the social learning aspect in a learning through play perspective can also be realized by the dilemmas pointed out by the teachers in this study with regard to children's play: choice and ownership, independence, discovery learning, the teachers' intentions versus children's intentions, and not least assessment. Reading between the lines in the researchers' discussion of results, it is possible to recognize that a balance between social and cognitive goals in learning through play is a major dilemma. Among the recommendations the researchers provide are "making time for quality interactions . . . , teaching children the requisite skills and strategies for becoming independent, making choices and decisions" (p. 130).

An interesting study recently carried out in Australia examined parents' and teachers' views on what makes a successful transition to school for the children (Dockett & Perry, 2004). The teachers mostly emphasized the children's adjustment to the school context and their feelings about being at school. Characteristically, less emphasis was attributed to goals related to knowledge. However, parents in this study focused more on knowledge, in addition to taking care of children's dispositions.

Perhaps the strongest arguments from recent research for the relevance of social competence and social goals to social learning and academic achievements in early grades have been derived from the research by Ladd and his co-researchers. For several years they have studied how young children's peer relationships and social competence, from Kindergarten turn out to function as fundamental antecedents for school adjustment (Ladd, 1999; Ladd, Birch, & Buhs, 1999; Buhs & Ladd, 2001; Ladd, Herald, & Andrews, 2006). These have been child × environment studies of school adjustment and longitudinal studies of the relation between social learning, classroom participation and school performances. Their primary research focus has been on understanding children's early experiences with peers and how their social competence develops, to examining how these factors are linked to current and later indicators of children's health, learning and development, and adjustment (Ladd, Herald, & Andrews, 2006). They find that different people influence the socialization of children, and accordingly influence their development of peer relationships and social competence: parents, teachers, family milieu, local environments, and child-care and preschool environments. Parents influence their child's peer relations and social competence through indirect influences, attachment, parent–child relationship, parent discipline style, initiating playgroups, etc. Contextual antecedents are effective in this concern as well, such as neighborhoods, community settings, childcare and preschools, and early school environments. It has been indicated that friendship relations that children are building during child-care tend to last for a considerable amount of time. These early-developed friendships in many cases turned out to support subsequent development during demanding transition periods (Ladd, 1990). Likewise, the existence of local playgrounds can be important arenas for peer interaction and development of peer relationships. Importantly, Ladd et al. state that the meaning of social competence varies according to culture, which could of course be said about most concepts, as socio-cultural research on motivation and learning has told us (e.g., McInerney & Van Etten, 2002).

Ladd et al. (2006) refer to the consequences of teacher–child relationships that will influence the development of peer relations, social competence, and school adjustment. Furthermore, in order to better understand the acceptance or rejection of becoming a member of a peer group, the processes and antecedents for entering a peer group has been examined, in addition to research on intervention programs to enhance positive peer group relations (cf. Ladd, 2005). These include social skills training and developing measures to prevent negative social relations. They conclude that the relationships children develop with peers cannot be obtained with others. The development of relationships with peers now start earlier than ever, because of the strong institutionalization of childhood. Research has shown that the social capabilities of children develop far earlier than was previously thought (cf. Merleau-Ponty, 1962; Trewarthen, 1979; Stern, 1985). As Ladd et al. (2006) state, research in preschool and school clearly illustrates the importance of children's behavior in determining their status among peers. In particular these findings disclose that children who succeed in developing positive peer relations did so because they managed interactions and gained respect for their interests from their playmates. However, the role of the adult as a socializing agent and significant other similarly influenced the forming of peer relationships. Parent–child relations and the parents' role as mediators influence children's peer competence more than is usually realized, and likewise for the teacher–child relationship. Even so, there is still much to be learned about how teacher–child relationships and child–peers relationships are associated and influence each other reciprocally. It gets particularly complicated when research strategies attempt to focus on peer–peer relations, adult–child relations and variation in social contexts at the same time. However, we need to keep in mind that these processes start early, tend to have a broad perspective, and an on-going influence on school adjustment and performances. They documented that young children who are accepted by their peers form friendships which have positive supportive effects for their participation and learning: they are less likely to be victimized by age-mates and have fewer problems adjusting to school (Ladd, Birch, & Buhs, 1999; Buhs & Ladd, 2001).

From these studies it can be seen that recommendations for practice clearly need to involve social motivation. Based upon studies from different countries, we seem to be left with the following important dilemma: Should the achievement of social goals and social competence be first priorities in early childhood education and particularly during the transition years, as a foundation for developing comprehension, understanding, creativity, and reflection; to promote learning in a broad perspective? As argued in the first sections of this chapter, learning in a broad perspective certainly include social learning as a main ingredient.

CONCLUSIONS

As illustrated in the presented case and theory and research presented above, a high level of social self-concept and a certain level of social competence seem to be necessary for children to feel secure enough to be self-confident, active, creative and autonomous in an educational setting. Motivation theories and research clearly emphasize social motivation to be important to an effective and thriving educational environment, particularly when focusing learning in a broad perspective. These indications are obvious for example in the motivation theories of Deci and Ryan (2002) and Wentzel (2005). The promotion of social skills and social competence is obtained in favorable social settings regarding parental involvement, sound peer relationships, mutual recognition in child-teacher dialogues, and contextual antecedents that positively influence the social learning process, and directly or indirectly affect learning in general.

It has been found that play and humor are strongly related to social learning. In early childhood education communication with each other and development of social competence are important, even for toddlers. Research on preschool quality has documented that social goals are strongly represented in parents' arguments for their children's attendance. It is found that certain staff characteristics promote children's well-being and social learning, and accordingly enhance quality in preschool environments. The practical implications of this are for preschool teachers to take social motivation into account to promote social learning, as well as learning in general. In particular, the social perspective of mutual recognition in a child–preschool teacher-dialogue has been found to be of great importance for children's development and performances in a lifelong perspective. In dialogues with children teachers have to support autonomy and recognize the child's own experience as valid. How is this taken care of during the transition to school? It is sometimes unclear how and if the school takes into account children's social competence in their first grade programs. Several research studies document that a substantial proportion of children worries whether they are going to make friends at school, and many studies indicate a significant effect of social competence on children's participation and performances (learning) later in school, for example, school adjustment (cf. Ladd, 2005). This indicates social motivation is crucial at the school start. We have seen that preschools and schools agree about what information schools should get from preschools: Exchange of information about social competence seems to have top priority. However, more research is needed to obtain information about what characteristics of social competence or social motivation should be focused.

We have seen a growing tendency to emphasize social goals in recent reforms in early childhood education. However, application of the motivational values and principles upon which the social goals are grounded do vary, and the prioritization of social learning in primary schools sometimes appears to decrease. In early childhood education today the social goals appears to be a *high priority*. However, achieving social goals has important practical consequences into social motivation, like satisfying the need of self-determination, the need of social competence and the need of affiliation. For this reason theories of motivation have to be taken into account, to obtain the development of democratic attitudes and social learning in general. However, it is a fact indicated in several research studies that when social goals are obtained, attaining other academic goals would follow.

Based upon the selection of research studies presented and discussed in this chapter, I find that a social learning through social motivation approach would be advantageous to the field of early childhood education. I suspect the consequences of such a change in the research approach will affect the practical implications of research in the future.

NOTES

1. First grade of primary school in Norway compares to Kindergarten in US schools, for example, students aged around 6, normally starting in late August every year.
2. Apter (1982) uses parathelic condition to mean a situation characterized by a here-and-now attitude where one wants to enjoy the moment as much as possible, as in play. Compare Csikszentmihalyi's (1985) concept of "flow." In a thelic situation, however, the individual is goal-oriented and acts to achieve certain goals.
3. To be able to decentrate means the ability to see things from another (or from another person's) point of view.

REFERENCES

Bae, B. (2004). *Dialoger mellom førskolelærer og barn—en beskrivende og fortolkende studie* [Dialogues between preschool teacher and children—a descriptive and interpretive study]. Dissertation Dr. Philos. Oslo: The University of Oslo. Published by The Oslo University College: Report no 25/04.

Bandura, A. L. (1977). *Social learning theory.* Englewood Cliffs, NJ: Prentice-Hall.

Bennett, N., Wood, L., & Rogers, S. (1996). *Teaching through play teachers' thinking and classroom practice.* Buckingham, UK: Open University Press.

Birch, S. H., & Ladd, G. W. (1996). Interpersonal relationships in the school environment and children's early school adjustment: The role of teachers and peers. In J. Juvonen & K.R. Wentzel (Eds.), *Social motivation: Understanding children's school adjustment* (pp. 199–225). New York: Cambridge University Press.

Bjørgen, I. (1997) Ansvar for egen læring [Responsibility for own learning]. In a Norwegian anthology: *Learning in Play and Social Interaction.* Report from a national conference in Trondheim, Norway Trondheim: *The Queen Maud's College Publications,* 1997, no. 1: 14–45.

Bratterud, Å., Emilsen, K., & Lillemyr, O. F. (2006). *Menn og omsorg i familie og profesjon* [Men and care in family and profession]. Bergen, Norway: Fagbokforlaget.

Brophy, J. (2004). *Motivating students to learn* (2nd ed.). Mahwah, NJ: Erlbaum.

Broström, S. (1998). *Social Kompetance og samvær—vi er venner ik'?* [Social competence and being together—We are friends, aren't we?]. Copenhagen: Systime Forlag.

Broström, S. (1999). *En god skolestart—fælles ansvar og fælles udvikling* [A good school start—Common responsibility and common development]. Copenhagen: Systime Forlag.

Buhs, E. S., & Ladd, G. W. (2001). Peer rejection as an antecedent of young children's school adjustment: An examination of mediating processes. *Developmental Psychology, 37,* 550–560.

Bø, I., Thorsen, A. A., Løge, I. K., & Omdal, H. (2004). Overgangen fra barnehage til skole [The Transition from Preschool to School]. *Bedre skole [Better schools], 4,* 80–87.

Core Curriculum. (1997). The Core Curriculum for Primary, Secondary and Adult Education in Norway) Oslo, Norway: Ministry of Education, Research and Church Affairs.

Covington, M. V. (1998). *The will to learn a guide for motivating young people.* Cambridge, UK: Cambridge University Press.

Covington, M. V., & Dray, E. (2001). The developmental course of achievement motivation: A need-based approach. In A. Wigfield & J. S. Eccles (Eds.), *Development of Achievement Motivation* (pp. 33–56). New York: Academic Press.

Creasy, G., & Jarvis, P. (2003). Play in children: An attachment perspective. In O. N. Saracho & B. Spodek (Eds.), *Contemporary perspectives on play in early childhood education* (pp. 53–73). Greenwich, CT: Information Age Publishing.

Csikszentmihalyi, M. (1985). Emergent motivation and the evolution of the self. In D. A. Kleiber & M. L. Maehr (Eds.), *Motivation and Adulthood, 14,* 93–120.

Dale, E. L., Wærness, J. I., & Lindvig, Y. (2005). *Tilpasset og differensiert opplæring i lys av Kunnskapsløftet* [Adapted and differentiated learning based upon the New Curriculum Guidelines of 2005, called "Extended knowledge"]. Oslo: The Learning Lab.

deCharms, R. (1968). (In collaboration with others) *Enhancing motivation: Change in the classroom.* New York: Irvington Publishers.

Deci, E. L., & Ryan, R. M. (1985). *Intrinsic motivation and self-determination in human behavior.* New York: Plenum Press.

Deci, E. L., & Ryan, R. M. (1991). A motivational approach to self: Integration in personality. In I. R. Dienstbier (Ed.), *Nebraska symposium on motivation: Perspectives on motivation* (Vol. 38, pp. 237–288). Lincoln, NE: University of Nebraska Press.

Deci, E. L., & Ryan, R. M. (1994). Promoting self-determined education. *Scandinavian Journal of Educational Research, 38*(1), 3–14.

Deci, E. L., & Ryan, R. M. (1995). Human autonomy: The basis for true self-esteem. In M. H. Kernis (Ed.), *Efficacy, agency, and self-esteem* (pp. 31–49). New York: Plenum Press.

Deci, E. L., & Ryan, R. M. (2000). The "what" and "why" of goal pursuits: Human needs and the self-determination of behavior. *Psychological Inquiry, 11,* 227–268.

Deci, E. L., & Ryan, R. M. (2002). (Eds.). *Handbook of self-determination research.* Rochester, NY: University of Rochester Press.

Dockett, S., & Fleer, M. (1999). *Play and pedagogy in early childhood: Bending the rules.* Marrickville, NSW: Harcourt Brace.

Dockett, S., & Perry, B. (2004). What makes a successful transition to school? Views of Australian parents and teachers. *International Journal of Early Years Education,12*(3), 217–230.

Eide, B., & Winger, N. (1996). *Kompetente barn og kvalifiserte pedagoger i den nye småskolen* [Competent children and qualified teachers in the new primary school]. Oslo: Cappelen Academic Publications.

Eccles, J., Wigfield, A., Harold, R. D., & Blumenfeld, P. (1993). Age and gender differences in children's self- and task-perceptions during elementary school. *Child Development, 64*, 830–847.

Einarsdottir, J. (2005). Quality of early childhood education from children's perspectives. Paper presented at the annual meeting of the American Educational Research Association in Montréal, April 2005.

Elliot, A. J., & Dweck, C. S. (2005). Competence and motivation: Competence as the core of achievement motivation. In A. J. Elliot & C. S. Dweck (Eds.), *Handbook of competence and motivation* (pp. 3–12). New York: Guilford Press.

Entwisle, D. R. et al. (1987). The emergent academic self-image of first graders: Its response to social structure. *Child Development, 58*, 1190–1206.

Framework Plan (1996). *The framework plan for day care institutions: A brief presentation* (English ed.) Oslo: The Ministry of Children and Family Affairs.

Framework Plan (2006). *Rammeplan for barnehagens innhold og oppgaver* [The framework plan for the content and tasks of kindergartens]. Oslo: The Ministry of Education and Research.

Germeten, S. (1999). *Evaluering av Reform 97: "På vei mot ny grunnskole i Oslo"* [The Evaluation of Reform 97: "Heading towards a new obligatory education in Oslo"]. Report I: Results from a questionnaire Fall 1998. Oslo: Oslo College Publications.

Germeten, S. (2002). *Grenser for undervisning? Frihet og kontroll i 6-åringenes klasserom.* [Are there limitations to teaching? Freedom and control in 6 year olds' classrooms] Dissertation Dr. Polit. Stockholm: Stockholm Institute of Education.

Grolnick, W. S. (1990). Targeting children's motivational resources in early childhood education. *Educational Policy, 4*, 267–282.

Harter, S. (1982). The perceived competence scale for children *Child Development, 53,* 87–97.

Hellendoorn, J., van der Kooij, R., & Sutton-Smith, B. (1994). *Play and intervention.* Albany, NY: State University of New York Press.

Henningsen, G. (1999). *La lek være lek! En undersøkelse om lek i 1. klasse fra et barneperspektiv.* [Let play be play! An examination of play from a child's perspective]. Oslo: Oslo University College

Huizinga, J. (1955). *Homo Ludens: A study of the play element in culture.* London: Beacon Press.

Juvonen, J., & Wentzel, K. R. (1996). (Eds.). *Social motivation: Understanding children's school adjustment.* New York: Cambridge University Press.

Klugman, E. (1990). Early childhood moves into the public schools: Mix or meld. In E. Klugman & S. Smilansky (Eds.), *Children's play and learning: Perspectives and policy implications.* New York: Teacher's College Press.

Kvistad, K., & Søbstad, F. (2005). *Kvalitetsarbeid i barnehagen* [Work of quality in pre-school]. Oslo: Cappelen Academic Publishers.

Ladd, G. W. (1990). Having friends, keeping friends, making friends, and being liked by peers in the classroom: Predictors of children's early school adjustment? *Child Development, 61,* 1081–1100.

Ladd, G. W. (1999). Peer relationships and social competence during early and middle childhood, *Annual Review of Psychology, 50,* 333–359.

Ladd, G. W. (2005). *Children's peer relationships and social competence: A century of progress.* New Haven, CT: Yale University Press.

Ladd, G. W., Birch, S. H., & Buhs, E. (1999). Children's social and scholastic lives in kindergarten: Related spheres of influence? *Child Development, 70,* 1373–1400.

Ladd, G. W., Buhs, E., & Seid, M. (2000). Children's initial sentiments about kindergarten: Is school liking an antecedent of early classroom participation and achievement? *Merill-Palmer Quarterly, 46,* 255–279.

Ladd, G. W., & Kochenderfer-Ladd, B. J. (2002). Identifying victims of peer aggression from early to middle childhood: Analysis of cross-informant data concordance, estimation of relational adjustments, prevalence of victimization, and characteristics of identified victims. *Psychological Assessments, 14,* 74–96.

Ladd, G. W., Herald, S. L., & Andrews, R. K. (2006). Young children's peer relations and social competence. In B. Spodek & O. N. Saracho (Eds.), *Handbook of research on the education of young children* (2nd. ed., pp. 23–54). Mahwah, NJ: Erlbaum.

Lamer, K. (1997). *Du og jeg og vi to! Om å fremme barns sosiale kompetanse Teoriboka* ["You and me, and the two of us!" About promoting children's social competence theory book]. Oslo: Universitetsforlaget.

Lepper, M. R., & Cordova, D. I. (1992). A desire to be taught: Instructional consequences of intrinsic motivation. *Motivation and Emotion, 16,* 187–208.

Levy, J. (1978). *Play behavior.* New York: Wiley.

Lillemyr, O. F. (2001). Play and learning in school: A motivational approach. In D. M. McInerney, & S. Van Etten (Eds.), *Research on socio-cultural influences on motivation and learning* (pp. 363–385). Greenwich, CT: Information Age Publishing.

Lillemyr, O.F. (2002). "Reform '97" in Norway: A new perspective on motivation and learning? *Nordic Educational Research, 22,* 38–52.

Lillemyr, O. F. (2003). Play in school—The teacher's role. Reforms and recent research. In O. N. Saracho & B. Spodek (Eds.), *Contemporary perspectives on play in early childhood education* (pp. 53–73). Greenwich, CT: Information Age Publishing.

Lillemyr, O. F. (2004). *Lek—opplevelse—læring, i barnehage og skole* [Play—experience—learning, in preschool and school]. Oslo: Universitetsforlaget

Lillemyr, O. F., Bergstrøm, S., Eggen, A., Skevik, S., Støp, K., & Voll, A.L.S. (1998). *Overgangen barnehage—småskole: Et forsknings- og utviklingsprosjekt i Nord-Trøndelag* [The Preschool—School Transition: A research and development project in North Troendelag]. Report to the Ministry of Education, Research and Church Affairs. Steinkjer: North Troendelag Research Institute.

Lillemyr, O. F., Fagerli, O., & Søbstad, F. (2001). *A global perspective on early childhood care and education: A proposed model.* Paris: Monograph no 17/2001, UNESCO.

Lillemyr, O. F., McInerney, D., & Søbstad, F. (2005). *A socio-cultural perspective on play and learning: Report from a primary school comparative study of students 8 to 10 year old in Australia and Norway.* Trondheim, Norway: The Queen Maud's College Publications.

Lindahl, M. (1998). *Lärande småbarn* [Learning preschoolers]. Lund, Sweden: Studentlitteratur (Student Literature).

Løkken, G. (1989). *ATTI! Om flirekonserter og små barns gruppeglede I barnehagen* [Funny! On glee concerts and toddlers' group glee in day care institutions]. Trondheim: Graduate dissertation at Queen Maud's College/University of Trondheim.

Løkken, G. (1996). *Når små barn møtes* [When young children meet]. Oslo: Cappelen Akademisk Forlag.

Løkken, G. (2000a). *Toddler peer culture The social style of one and two year old body-subject in everyday interaction.* Dissertation of Dr. Polit. Trondheim, Norway: The Norwegian University of Science and Technology.

Løkken, G. (2000b). Using Merleau-Pontyan phenomenology to understand the toddler Toddler interactions in child day-care. *Nordic Educational Research, 1/00,* 13–23.

Løkken, G. (2000c). Tracing the social style of toddler peers. *Scandinavian Journal of Educational Research, 44*(2), 163–176.

Løkken, G. (2000d). The playful quality of the toddling "style". *International Journal of Qualitative Studies in Education, 5,* 531–542.

Maehr, M. L. (1984). Meaning and motivation: Toward a theory of personal investment. In R. Ames & C. Ames (Eds.), *Research on Motivation in Education, volume 1: Student Motivation* (pp. 115–144). New York: Academic Press.

Maehr, M. L., & Braskamp, L. (1986). *The motivation factor: A theory of personal investment.* Lexington, MA: Lexington Books.

Maehr, M. L., & Midgley, C. (1996). *Transforming school cultures.* Boulder, CO: Westview Press.

Maehr, M. L., & Meyer, H. A. (1997). Understanding motivation and schooling: Where we've been, where we are, and where we need to go. *Educational Psychology Review, 9,* 371–409.

Maehr, M. L., & McInerney, D. M. (2004). Motivation as personal investment. In D. M. McInerney & S. Van Etten (Eds.), *Big theories revisited* (Vol. 4, pp. 61–90). Greenwich, CT: Information Age Publishing.

McInerney, D. M. (2003). Motivational goals, self-concept and sense of self—What predicts academic achievement? In H. W. Marsh, R. G. Craven, & D. M. McInerney (Eds.), *International advances in self research: Speaking to the future* (pp. 315–346). Greenwich, CT: Information Age Publishing.

McInerney, D. M., Roche, L. A., McInerney, V., & Marsh, H. W. (1997). Cultural perspectives on school motivation: The relevance and application of goal theory. *American Educational Research Journal, 34*(1), 207–236.

McInerney, D. M., & Van Etten, S. (2002). (Eds.) *Socio-cultural influences on motivation and learning.* Greenwich, CT: Information Age Publishing.

Mead, G. H. (1969). *Mind, self, and society.* Chicago: University of Chicago Press.

Merleau-Ponty, M. (1962). *Phenomenology of perception* (English ed). London: Routledge and Kegan Paul.

Midtsand, M., Monstad, B., & Søbstad, F. (2004). *Tiltak mot mobbing starter i barne-hagen* [Remedial means towards bullying starts in preschool]. Trondheim, Norway: Queen Maud's College Publications, report no 2/04.

Nielsen, H. B. (2000). *Inn i klasserommet* [Into the classroom]. In G. Imsen (Ed.), *Likestilling i grunnskolen* [Equality in comprehensive school]. Oslo: Gyldendal.

Nordahl, T. (2000). *En skole—to verdener: Et teoretisk og empirisk arbeid om problematferd og mistilpasning i et elev- og lærerperspektiv* [One school—two worlds: A theoretical and empirical examination of problem behavior and maladjustment in a student and teacher perspective]. Dissertation Dr. Philos. University of Oslo. Oslo: Report from Norwegian Institute for Research on Growing up, Welfare and Aging.

OECD Report (2001). *Starting strong early childhood education and care.* Paris: OECD

Odelfors, B. (1996). *Att göra sig hörd och sedd. Om vilkåren för flickor och pojkars kommunikation på daghem* [To be heard and seen: About the conditions for the communication of girls and boys in a day care center]. Dissertaion Dr. Phil. Stockholm, Sweden: University of Stockholm.

Olweus, D. (2001). Peer harassment: A critical analysis and some important issues. In J. Juvonen & S. Graham (Eds.) *Peer Harassment in School* (pp. 3–20). New York: Guilford Press.

Patrick, H., & Townsend, M. A. R. (1995). The influence of perceived social competence on school: Beginners' emergent academic intrinsic motivation. Paper presented at the annual meeting of American Educational Research Association, April 1995, San Francisco, CA. Ann Arbor, MI: School of Education, Educational Studies Program.

Pellegrini, A. (1991). *Applied child study: A developmental approach.* Hillsdale, NJ: Erlbaum.

Piaget, J. (1954). *The construction of reality in the child.* New York: Basic Books.

Piaget, J. (1970). *The science of education and the psychology of the child.* New York: Orion Press.

Reeve, J., Deci, E. L., & Ryan, R. M. (2004). Self-determination theory: A dialectical framework for understanding socio-cultural influences on student motivation. In D. M. McInerney & S. Van Etten (Eds.), *Big theories revisited* (pp. 31–60). Greenwich, CT: Information Age Publishing.

Ryan, R. M., & Deci, E. L. (2002). Overview of self-determination theory: An organismic dialectical perspective. In E. L. Deci & R. M. Ryan (Eds.), *Handbook of self-determination research* (pp. 3–29). Rochester, NY: University of Rochester Press.

Samuelsson, I. P., & Carlsson, M. A. (2003). *Det lekande lärande barnet i en utvecklingspedagogisk teori* [The playing learning child in a developmental educational theory]. Stockholm, Sweden: Liber.

Sandberg, A., & Samuelsson, I. P. (2005). An interview study of gender differences in preschool teachers' attitudes toward children's play. *Early Childhood Education Journal, 32,* 297–305.

Sandvik, N. (2001). *Småbarnas bidrag til barnehagens sosiale miljø* [Infants' contributions to the preschool's social environment]. *Barn* [The child], 2, 21–42.

Saracho, O. N. (2003). Young children's play and cognitive style. In O. N. Saracho & B. Spodek (Eds.), *Contemporary perspectives on play in early childhood education* (pp. 75–96). Greenwich, CT: Information Age Publishing.

Schibbye, A. -L. L. (1988). *Familien. Tvang og mulighet: om samspill og behandling* [The family, force and opportunity: About interaction and treatment]. Oslo: Universitetsforlaget.

Schoenfeld, A. H. (1999). Looking toward the 21st century: Challenges of educational theory and practice. *Educational Researcher, 28*(7), 4–14.

Seljelid, T. (Ed.). (1994). *Med iver og lyst. Beskrivelse og vurdering av et prosjekt om motivasjon i skolen* [With interest and involvement Description and evaluation of a project on motivation in school]. Hamar, Norway: Kapére Forlag.

Sheridan, S. (2001). Pedagogical quality in preschool: An issue of perspectives. Göteborg: Acta Universitatis Gothoburgensis.

Skinner, B. F. (1938). *The behavior of organisms.* New York: Appleton-Century-Crofts.

Smilansky, S., & Shefatya, L. (1990). Facilitating play: A medium for promoting cognitive, socio-emotional and academic development in young children. Silver Springs, MD: Psychosocial & Educational Publications.

Sommer, D. (1997). *Barndomspsykologi Utvikling i en forandret verden* [Psychology of childhood development in a changed world]. Oslo, Norway: Universitetsforlaget.

Stern, D. (1985). *The interpersonal world of the infant.* New York: Basic Books.

Skaalvik, E. M., & Skaalvik, S. (2005). *Skolen som læringsarena: Selvoppfatning, motivasjon og læring* [The school as a learning arena: Self-concept, motivation and learning]. Oslo: Universitetsforlaget.

Sletta, O. (1983). *Sosiale bytteforhold ved samspill i skoleklasser* [Social exchange relations in interactions in the classroom]. Dissertation Dr. Philos. Trondheim, Norway: University of Trondheim.

Stipek, D. J. (2002). *Motivation to learn: Integrating theory and practice,* 3rd ed. Boston: Allyn & Bacon.

Søbstad, F. (1990). *Førskolebarn og humor* [Preschool children and humor]. Trondheim: Dissertation of Dr. Polit. Trondheim, Norway: University of Trondheim.

Søbstad, F. (1995). *Humor i pedagogisk arbeid* [Humor in educational work]. Oslo: Tano AS.

Søbstad, F. (1999). *Humor i lekfamilien* [Humor in the play family]. In S. Kibsgaard & A. Wostryck (Eds.), *Mens leken er god* [While play is good]. Oslo: Tano Aschehoug.

Søbstad, F. (2002). *Jaktstart på kjennetegn ved den gode barnehagen. Første rapport fra prosjektet 'Den norske barnehagekvaliteten'* [Starting hunting for characteristics of the good day care center (preschool). First report on the project 'The Quality of the Norwegian Day Care Centre']. Trondheim: Queen Maud's College Publications, no. 2/02.

Søbstad, F. (2004). *Mot stadig nye mål... Tredje rapport fra prosjektet "Den norske barnehagekvalitetet"* ["Towards even further aims..." Third report on the project 'The Norwegian day care centre quality']. Trondheim: Queen Maud's University College Publications, report 1/04.

Sørlie, M. -A. (1998). *Mestring og tilkortkomming i skolen Fokus på elevers skolefaglige kompetanse, sosiale kompetanse og selvoppfatning* [Mastery and shortcoming in school focus on subject matter competence, social competence, and self-concept]. Oslo: Report from the Norwegian Institute for Research on Growing up, Welfare and Aging.

Trewarthen, C. (1979). Communication and cooperation in early infancy. In I. M. Bullowa (Ed.), *Before speech: The beginnings of human communication* (pp. 321–346). London: Cambridge University Press.

Tolman, E. C. (1948). Cognitive maps in rats and men. *Psychological Review, 55,* 189–208.

Urdan, T. C. (2000). The intersection of self-determination and achievement goal theories: Do we need to have goals? Paper presented at the annual meeting of The American Educational Research Association, New Orleans, LA.

Urdan, T. C., & Turner, J.C. (2005). Competence motivation in the classroom. In A. J. Elliot & C. S. Dweck (Eds.), *Handbook of competence and motivation* (pp. 297–317). New York: Guilford Press.

Vygotsky, L. S. (1978). *Mind and society: The development of higher mental processes.* Cambridge, MA: Harvard University Press.

Wasserman, S. (1990). *Serious players in the primary classroom: Empowering children through active learning experience.* New York: Teachers' College Press.

Watkins, D., McInerney, D. M., Lee, C., Akande, A., & Regmi, M. (2002). Motivation and learning strategies: A cross-cultural perspective. In D. M. McInerney & S. Van Etten (Eds.), *Research on socio-cultural influences on motivation and learning* (Vol. 2, pp. 329–343). Greenwich, CT: Information Age Publishing.

Wentzel, K. R. (1991). Relations between social competence and academic achievement in early adolescence. *Child Development, 62,* 1066–1078.

Wentzel, K. R. (1996). Social goals and social relationships as motivators of school adjustment. In J. Juvonen & K. R. Wentzel (Eds.), *Social motivation: Understanding children's school adjustment* (pp. 226–247). New York: Cambridge University Press.

Wentzel, K. R. (2002). The contribution of social goal setting to children's school adjustment. In A. Wigfield & J. Eccles (Eds.), *Development of achievement motivation,* (pp. 221–246). New York: Academic Press.

Wentzel, K. R. (2003). School adjustment. In W. Reynolds & G. Miller (Eds.), *Handbook of psychology: Vol. 7., Educational psychology* (pp. 235–258). New York: Wiley.

Wentzel, K. R. (2005). Peer relationships, motivation, and academic performance at school. In A. J. Elliot & C. S. Dweck (Eds.), *Handbook of competence and motivation* (pp. 279–296). New York: Guilford Press.

Wentzel, K. R., & Asher, S. R. (1995). Academic lives of neglected, rejected, popular, and controversial children. *Child Development, 66,* 754–763.

Wentzel, K. R., Barry, C., & Caldwell, K. (2004). Friendships in middle school: Influences on motivation and school adjustment. *Journal of Educational Psychology, 96,* 195–203,

White, R. W. (1959). Motivation reconsidered: The concept of competence. *Psychological Review, 66,* 297–333.

Wood, E., & Attfield, J. (1996). *Play, learning and the early childhood curriculum.* London: Paul Chapman.

CHAPTER 7

SOCIAL LEARNING IN THE PEER CONTEXT[1]

Gary W. Ladd

Persons who are about the same age and who mature on similar timetables are called peers or agemates. During early childhood, peers who grow up together often have similar interests, develop similar skills, and have similar experiences. It is not surprising, therefore, that children tend to see peers as attractive play partners and companions and, as they grow older, often prefer their company to that of siblings and parents.

For most young children, sustained contact with peers begins when they enter some form of childcare or preschool environment. Typically, childcare settings contain more children than caregivers and such arrangements make it likely that toddlers and preschoolers will spend more time interacting with peers than with adults. Peers, therefore, become children's everyday companions for many of the activities and experiences that occur during the early years of their development.

Because peers mature on similar timetables, develop similar interests and skills, and spend increasing amounts of time with each other during the early childhood years, it has been theorized that children learn different things from agemates than they are likely to acquire from other socializers, such as parents, siblings, and teachers (see Furman & Robbins, 1985; Hartup, 1979). This premise can be seen as part of a larger "social learning hypothesis" that depicts peers as important and influential socializing agents, and that attributes the bulk of peer influence to the interactions

Contemporary Perspectives on Socialization and Social Development..., pages 133–164
Copyright © 2007 by Information Age Publishing
133

that children have with peers and the experiences they are afforded in peer relationships (see Ladd, 2005).

Exploring this hypothesis, and how researchers have used it to gain an understanding of children's social learning in the peer context, is the primary aim of this article. Accordingly, the sections that follow are organized to accomplish the following two objectives: First, I consider some the assumptions and premises that underlie the "social learning hypothesis". This hypothesis has guided much of what has been learned from research on children's social learning in the peer context and so it is instructive to consider its origins and central premises. Second, I identify three questions that have been emphasized within social learning theories, and consider what researchers have discovered about children's social learning in the peer context by investigating these questions empirically. For purposes of this review, these questions are phrased as follows: (1) "*When* does peer social learning begin?" (2) "*How* does social learning occur in the peer context?" and, (3) "*What* do young children learn from peers"?

THE SOCIAL LEARNING HYPOTHESIS

The origins of this perspective can be traced back to a cadre of investigators (e.g., Miller & Dollard, 1941; Bandura, Ross, & Ross, 1963; Mischel, 1973) who, over the course of several decades, expanded some of the tenets of traditional learning theories (e.g., Skinner, 1953; Thorndike, 1931). These investigators—who would come to be known as "social learning theorists"—questioned the notion that, for learning to occur, a child's behavior *must* be followed by a "response" (a consequence). That is, learning had been thought to occur in "trials" where a child performed a behavior, received a response, and thus "learned" from the nature of the response (e.g., discovered that the behavior resulted in rewards, punishments, etc.). To the contrary, social learning theorists argued that "no trial" learning was also possible—that is, they asserted that a child could learn simply by watching what others did (i.e., by observing what others did, and by watching the consequences of other's actions). This view implied that social learning entailed more than just the process of emitting behavior and experiencing its consequences. Rather, it characterized the learning process as one in which children acquire, interpret, preserve, and utilize social information—not just information about the consequences of their actions, but also information about others (e.g., peers, peers' behaviors, and the antecedents and consequences of peers' behaviors) and many aspects of the contexts in which social interactions occur. These and other such theoretical contributions expanded investigator's conceptions of social learning processes, or the means through which children learn from others.

Not only did social learning theorists propose alternate or competing theoretical premises, but they and their collaborators also gathered a wealth of data that tended to substantiate their hypotheses. Ultimately, the ideas, principles, and findings that resulted from this line of investigation came to be known as "social learning theory" (see Bandura, 1977). Peer relations researchers adopted several premises from social learning theory because they provided useful explanatory frames for investigating how children learn from agemates and are socialized by their interactions and relationships with peers. Hindsight suggests that, of the various social learning premises that were introduced and pursued from the 1970s to present, three were particularly influential, or responsible for creating important empirical breakthroughs or advances. These premises—which are interpreted here as three components of the "social learning hypothesis" (see Dodge, 1986; Ladd & Mize, 1983)—can be described as follows:

- Peer interactions and relationships provide children with social information.
  - As children interact and participate in relationships with age-mates, they acquire information about: (a) themselves and their behavior, (b) peers, peer behavior, and peer relationships, and (c) the situations and contexts in which social interactions and relationships are conducted.
- Children "process" the information they acquire from peer interactions and relationships
  - Children actively process (e.g., sort out, interpret, form conclusion about) the information they obtain from peer interactions and relationships, and store it for future use.
- Children utilize the information they acquire from peer interactions and relationships
  - Children use the information they have obtained from peer interactions and relationships to guide their future behavior toward peers; they apply it to their peer interactions and relationships
  - When children act on previously acquired information, the results of their actions provide new information that may serve as an impetus to: (a) retain or revise their prior conceptions, (b) maintain or change their existing behaviors.

Considered next are the links between these premises and the evidence that researchers have acquired about children's learning in the peer context. Consideration of these links is accomplished in three subsequent sections, the first of which is devoted to evidence that reflects on the question of "when" children begin to learn from peers. In two subsequent sections, attention is focused on the questions of "how" children learn from peers, and "what" children learn from peers. Finally, an evaluation is made of the types of inferences that appear to be supported by available theory and evidence.

WHEN DOES PEER SOCIAL LEARNING BEGIN?

It appears that children begin to learn from peers soon after birth. Although it was once believed that infants and toddlers were relatively asocial in the company of agemates, the results of studies conducted during the latter half of the twentieth century made it apparent that very young children were interested in peers, sociable among agemates, and capable of forming rudimentary peer relationships (see Ladd, 2005). In particular, these findings showed that babies became interested in peers during the first few weeks of life and, by their third month, made rudimentary social gestures toward agemates. By 6 months, infants directed smiles and vocalizations toward peers (Vincze, 1971), and by their first birthdays, they were able to simultaneously direct more than one behavior toward a peer (e.g., smiling and gesturing at the same time), and engage in synchronized sequences of interaction (Vandell, Wilson, & Buchanan, 1980; Hay, Pedersen, & Nash, 1982).

After infancy, evidence indicated that social learning among peers accelerated and broadened into new forms. Studies of toddlers' peer interactions revealed that their interactions were longer and more complex in quality than those of infants. Further, in contrast to infants, toddlers used more elaborate ways of eliciting peers' attention and participation, such as combining multiple gestures into a single overture (Bronson, 1981; Brownell, 1986). These sustained interactions were possible, investigators concluded, because young toddlers had developed the mental and motoric skills to respond to their partners in coordinated and predictable ways.

Investigators also found that toddlers were more sophisticated than infants at responding to peers' social signals. For example, in a study of 18- and 24-month olds in a laboratory play setting, researchers discovered that older toddlers were more likely to imitate or reciprocate a peer's overtures (Eckerman & Stein, 1982). This way of responding to peers represented an important milestone in children's social learning because reciprocal imitation was considered to be an important perquisite for more advanced forms of play, such as early imitative "games" and mutually coordinated exchanges (Eckerman & Stein, 1990). Another way that toddlers' interaction skills became more sophisticated was that they tended to initiate interactions while agemates were watching, thereby increasing the probability that peers would notice their behavior and respond accordingly (Eckerman & Stein, 1982, 1990). Further, between the ages two and three, young children began to exhibit the capacity to adjust their behaviors to complement those of their peer partners (Ross & Lollis, 1989). This skill was significant because a children's competence at adapting to a partner's actions is an essential requirement for forming and maintaining relationships with peers.

HOW DO YOUNG CHILDREN LEARN FROM PEERS?

This question has been an impetus for research designed to elucidate specific social learning processes—that is, the means by which children learn from peers in social contexts. To acquire information about how children learn from peers, investigators have tended to study specific learning principles or mechanisms that have been abstracted from social learning theory and its modern-day derivatives (e.g., social information processing, social skill learning metatheories). As we shall see, several lines of investigation have yielded important clues about the nature and form of early social learning in peer contexts.

Children Learn from Peers' Responses to Their Behaviors

Insight into how children learn from peers has been advanced by research on the behavioral principle of *shaping* and, in particular, the premise that children's social learning is affected by the types of responses they receive from peers. This tenet, which originated within traditional learning theories (e.g., operant conditioning paradigms, etc.), held that children acquire specific social behaviors because these actions elicit rewards from socializers, such as peers. Investigators who embraced this perspective postulated that the repertoire of interpersonal behaviors that children acquire as they mature develops from a history of participating in "natural communities of reinforcement" (Baer & Wolfe, 1970)—that is, contexts in which peers shape children's behavior by rewarding some actions and by punishing or ignoring others.

Much of the research conducted on shaping as a social learning process was undertaken during past decades (i.e., during the 1960s–1980s). Researchers began by examining how adults' reactions to children's social behaviors affected children's interactions with peers. In one study, a team of investigators found that they could increase the amount of time that a preschool girl interacted with peers by making teacher attention contingent on the girl's successive approximations to peer interaction (Allen, Hart, Buell, Harris, & Wolfe, 1964). This was accomplished by having teachers change the contingencies for the administration of attention so that the girl first received attention when she looked at peers, then when she approached peers, and finally only when she interacted with peers. Other applications of this principle were researched as well. For example, investigators found that adult-administered shaping strategies could be used to increase positive behaviors (e.g., cooperation) in characteristically aggressive or oppositional children (Brown & Elliot, 1965; Hart, Reynolds, Baer, Brawley, & Harris, 1968).

Eventually, studies were undertaken to determine whether the reactions that children received from peers affected their social learning and behavior. Findings from these investigations indicated that it was not uncommon for young children reward and punish each other's behaviors. Lamb, Esterbrooks, and Holden (1980), for example, found that whereas preschoolers made approving gestures toward peers who played in gender-consistent ways, they often punished peers who played in gender atypical ways. Investigators also attempted to experimentally manipulate peer shaping by teaching classmates how to reward each other for engaging in specific types of behaviors. Although the results of these studies were not always conclusive, there was some evidence to suggest that peer reinforcement brought about changes in children's social interactions and behaviors (see Strain, 1985).

Children Learn by Watching Peers

The premise that children learn by watching peers was first tested in research on children's observational learning. Early studies of peer "modeling" indicated that after children had observed a peers' behavior they often imitated it. Moreover, evidence indicated that children tended to imitate many types of peer behaviors, including both positive (e.g., prosocial acts; see Cooke & Apolloni, 1976) and negative actions (e.g., aggression; see Bandura, Ross, & Ross, 1963).

One of the ways that researchers sought to determine whether modeling was an important social learning process in early peer contexts was by conducting experimental interventions in which children were encouraged to acquire new social behaviors simply by watching peers demonstrate or perform them. Results from early studies suggested that preschoolers who were isolated from their classmates could became more social after watching a film of agemates approach and engage peers in social interaction (O'Connor, 1969, 1972). In these studies, isolates watched a 23-minute film in which a narrator directed children's attention to the positive attributes and outcomes of the modeled behaviors. After watching the film, socially isolated preschoolers interacted with classmates at a significantly higher rate than did children assigned to a no-film control group. However, attempts to replicate these effects were not always successful. Some investigators found that modeling programs increased preschoolers' social interactions (Evers & Schwartz, 1973; Jakibchuk & Smeriglio, 1976), but others failed to find such effects (e.g., Gottman, 1977). Moreover, in many cases, the changes that were observed in children's behaviors did not persist over time, or generalize across social situations (for a review, see Ladd & Mize, 1983).

Studies by other researchers began to elucidate some of the mechanisms involved in observational learning and delineate the types of models that children were prone to imitate. Findings from this research revealed that the types of models that children were most likely to emulate included persons of the same age and gender (e.g., same-sex peers), dominant members of their peer group, and children who were rewarded rather than punished for their actions (for a review, see Perry & Bussey, 1984).

Children Learn by "Processing" Information Obtained from Peer Interactions

Contemporary social information processing theorists (e.g., Dodge, 1986; Crick & Dodge, 1994) have argued that, in addition to imitating peers' behaviors, children engage in many other types of social learning operations that affect their understanding of peers and their actions toward peers. For example, these investigators contend that, as children approach peer situations, they engage in a range of mental processes including: (1) gathering, focusing on, encoding, and interpreting observable peer behaviors, and (2) constructing possible responses to behaviors that peers have directed toward them. To be specific, Dodge and colleagues proposed that children's responses to peer social overtures could be seen as the end product of a series of mental activities that he termed "social information processing steps"(SIP) (Dodge, 1986; Crick & Dodge, 1994). It was hypothesized that children first perceive, encode, and interpret incoming social information (encoding and representation processes), and depending on the results of these steps (e.g., how they interpret the information), they then search for and evaluate possible behavioral responses (response search and decision processes). After evaluating possible responses and their likely outcomes, children decide on a response and enact it (response decision and enactment processes). In later reformulations of SIP models, these basic premises were revised and elaborated, and additional social cognitive constructs and intervening variables were considered (e.g., children's goals; emotions, etc.; see Crick & Dodge, 1994).

Although most of the research conducted to evaluate these premises was undertaken with grade school or older children, the findings offer a unique perspective on how children learn about peers and respond to agemates in social contexts. For example, several studies have shown that when children are given ambiguous information about a hypothetical peer's actions, they often make different attributions about the peer's intentions (e.g., Dodge, 1980; Steinberg & Dodge, 1983). Results from these studies showed that whereas some children were inclined to see peers' motives as hostile, others tended to perceive peers' motives as benign. More importantly, the interpretation children made (whether they the peer's motive as hostile or not) was found to be predictive of their actual behavior toward peers. To illustrate, investigators found that children who saw peers' motives as hostile were more likely to act aggressively toward playmates. It was also discovered that certain types of children tended to have stronger interpretational biases. The tendency to interpret peers' motives as hostile, for example, was found to be more prevalent among children who relied on aggression as an angry, defensive response to peer provocations (Crick & Dodge, 1996). Others demonstrated that it was possible to induce changes in aggressive boys' intent attributions, and that improvements in this aspect of interpretational processing were associated with reductions in their aggressive behavior (Hudley and Graham, 1993).

Also investigated was the hypothesis that after processing social information about peer situations, children generate, mentally review, and select possible responses from those that they have available in memory. To study this social information-processing step, some researchers presented children with specific peer dilemmas (for example, videos in which a child is described as wanting to play with a peer's toy) and asked them to enumerate potential approaches or "solutions" to the problem(s). Some investigators found that the *quantity* of responses generated was linked with indicators of social competence such as children's popularity with peers (e.g., Richard and Dodge, 1982), but others failed to find such linkages (for example, Krasnor & Rubin, 1981). Investigators also studied the *quality* of children's solutions to peer dilemmas by comparing individual's responses to those suggested by most peers. Comparisons of aggressive and nonaggressive children showed that, although the groups did not differ in the overall number of responses generated, aggressive children suggested a higher proportion of aggressive solutions for peer dilemmas than did nonaggressive children (Dodge, 1986). From these findings, and elaborations that emerged from subsequent investigations (e.g., see Burks, Laird, Dodge, Pettit, & Bates, 1999; Dodge et al., 2003), it was inferred that children with social difficulties have fewer appropriate or competent responses at their disposal when they are contemplating how to react to peer situations.

Children Learn by Inventing, Practicing, and Revising the Ways they Interact with Peers

It has also been proposed that children's learning in the peer context results from their desire to participate in this context, and their efforts to adapt themselves (e.g., change their behavior, thinking, etc.) in ways that make it likely that they will succeed at goals they define for themselves in this context. Researcher's efforts to study this kind of learning process have been guided by theories of social skill learning and behavior change (e.g., see Ladd & Mize, 1983). Within such frameworks, it has been argued that: (a) children's desire to engage in peer interactions is driven by the goals that they invent for themselves and their interaction partners and, (b) once children formulate a goal, they engage in behaviors they think will bring about the realization of that goal, and (c) children constantly monitor and adjust and refine their behaviors, in light of the consequences they produce, to become effective at attaining their goals, to maintain their effectiveness at attaining goals, and to circumvent factors that interfere with the attainment of their goals (see Ladd & Crick, 1989). In other words, as children survey peer situations, they invent a goal for themselves and/or their partners (e.g., to show off versus to avoid looking stupid; to "win" a game vs. to have "fun" with one's companions) and then choose a course of action (e.g., a behavioral strategy) that is designed to accomplish that goal. Next, they embark on that course of action and, as events play out, they monitor or assess its results (e.g., determine whether it has brought them closer to or further from the goal; decide what to do about unforeseen consequences) and adjust their behaviors accordingly (devise and deploy revised, subsequent courses of action). Because children's initial behavioral strategies may not achieve their goals, and because peer interactions become increasingly complex and difficult to manage as children grow older, children must constantly work to develop and refine their strategies or skills so that they are able to become and remain effective at achieving their social purposes. This dynamic and enduring activity, especially when it is directed toward achieving supportive and enduring relationship ties (e.g., friendship, group peer acceptance), has been referred to by researchers as the process of "skill learning" (acquiring a skill) and "skill development" (adapting, refining, perfecting a skill; Ladd & Mize, 1983; Ladd, Buhs, & Troop, 2002).

It is believed that skill learning and development occurs naturally as children attempt to interact with peers and form relationships with age-mates, and that it may also aided by socializers such as parents and teachers who may encourage children to pursue certain types of goals amongst peers, or teach them specific strategies as a means of accomplishing particular social goals (e.g., recommending behaviors that may help a child make a friend; see Ladd & Pettit, 2002). For example, in research conducted on children's goals (see Renshaw & Asher, 1983), investigators have worked from the hypotheses that: (a) children routinely seek to define an aim or goal for themselves in social situations, (b) children vary in the types of goals they invent, and (c) the types of goals they devise may cause them to act in ways that are more or less skillful or adaptive in peer situations. The evidence gathered thus far tends to substantiate these hypotheses. For example, after asking younger and older grade-school children to describe their goals for several types of peer situations, Renshaw and Asher

(1983) found that the goals of children who were well liked by their peers were more positive and outgoing than those of children who were disliked by their peers. In another study, researchers compared third- through sixth-grade children's goals for game situations with peers and found that, particularly among the younger children in the sample, those who favored relationship goals tended to be more accepted among their classmates (Taylor & Asher, 1984). Thus, it would appear that children differ in the types of goals they invent for peer situations, and that the social purposes they construe for themselves are linked with how well liked they become among peers.

Investigators have also examined the hypothesis that, after children define a goal for peer situations, they devise and embark on a "strategy," or course of action that might enable them to achieve their objective. In one study, investigators examined children's strategies both in the presence of an explicitly defined social goal and in the absence of a social goal (Renshaw & Asher, 1983). In the presence of a social goal, children suggested a smaller range of strategies than they reported in the no-goal condition, suggesting that goals are influential in defining the strategies that children devise. It was also discovered that popular children's strategies were rated as more positive and accommodating toward peers than were those suggested by unpopular children, regardless of the goal condition. In another study, investigators presented preschoolers with simulated peer situations and encouraged them to act out a strategy in response to each situation using puppets and props (Mize & Ladd, 1988). Children also verbalized strategies for theses peer situations so that it was possible to assess both their verbal and "acted-out" strategies. Results showed that children who voiced, and in particular, those who acted out predominately friendly strategies, tended to be more prosocial, less aggressive, and better liked among peers. Similarly, it was discovered that children who tended to respond to peer provocation situations with aggressive, withdrawn, or problem solving strategies had social goals and self-efficacy perceptions that were congruent with their behavioral orientations (Erdley & Asher, 1996). Whereas aggressive responders exhibited hostile goals and higher efficacy for attaining these goals, withdrawn and problem-solving responders manifested prosocial goals and greater confidence in producing such outcomes. Only withdrawn responders tended to endorse avoidant goals such as evading confrontations. Additionally, it has been reported that children's goals and strategies tend to be linked in ways that are associated with their success in friendships. Rose and Asher (1999) found that gradeschoolers who desired to maintain their peer relationships favored negotiation strategies, such as compromise and accommodation, whereas those interested in revenge goals endorsed self-interest and hostile interaction strategies. Children who favored revenge goals had fewer friends and, when they did have a best friend, their partners tended to perceive the relationship as high on conflict and low in positive features.

In addition to the evidence gathered on children's goals and strategy production, much of what has been discovered about early skill learning in the peer context comes from experimental studies in which "coaching" procedures have been used to simulate the processes through which skill learning is thought to occur (i.e., to see whether children actually learn social skills in this manner, and whether skill learning affects children's success in peer relationships). In coaching interventions, children typically participate in a series of peer-play sessions that are designed to simulate, or experimentally induce the natural processes of skill learning and development. In these sessions, children are encouraged to define a social goal (e.g., joining peers in an ongoing play activity), and then asked to perform specific behaviors (skills) that can be used to accomplish that objective among peers. Typically, multiple performance trials are provided in which children are encouraged to practice and apply those skills in real-life peer interactions. As children demonstrate skill mastery, they are also encouraged to devise ways to assess the consequences of their skill performances and devise ways to improve their skills, typically through a graduated series of skill rehearsals and critiques of skill performance.

In most coaching studies, skill learning and development was investigated as a means of helping children overcome social difficulties (see Ladd, Herald, Slutzky, & Andrews, 2004; Ladd, 2005). In one of the first interventions of this type, two unpopular third graders were coached to engage in positive peer interaction using videotaped instructions, role playing, and tasks that emphasized listening skills (Gottman, Gonso, & Schuler, 1976). Compared to unpopular children in an attention control group, the trained children evidenced significant gains in peer acceptance that were maintained over a 9-week interval. In a larger investigation, low-accepted third and fourth graders were coached in four types of social skills, including peer communication, cooperation, participation, and support (Oden & Asher, 1977). Unlike controls, coached children received instruction in the targeted social skills, skill-rehearsal opportunities with peer partners, and feedback about how to improve their skill performance. These children, but not controls, exhibited significant improvements in classroom peer acceptance upon completion of the intervention and 1-year later. Subsequently, coaching was evaluated by measuring changes in children's social skills and peer group acceptance.

In an investigation conducted by Ladd (1981) low-accepted third graders were randomly assigned to coaching, attention control, or no-treatment control conditions, and coached children received instruction, rehearsal, and feedback in specific peer-interaction skills, including asking questions of peers, leading peers, making supportive statements to peers. Children rehearsed the skills in series of sessions that approximated classroom peer contexts and received individualized feedback about their skill performance. Assessments conducted after children had completed the coaching program and in a follow-up 4 weeks later showed that coached children, unlike their counterparts in the control conditions, made significant gains in two of the three trained skills, and in their classroom peer acceptance. Similar results were obtained with procedures that were adapted for use with preschoolers (Mize & Ladd, 1990). Low-accepted preschoolers were randomly assigned to either a coaching or an attention control condition, and those in the coaching group received training in four types of social skills: leading, asking questions, supporting, and making comments to peers. Children were encouraged to learn each skill concept, complete a series of skill rehearsals with individuals and groups of peers, and critique videotapes of their skill rehearsals. Unlike their counterparts in the attention control group, coached preschoolers showed significant gains in two of the trained skills (that is, leading peers, making comments), and most of the children who exhibited skill improvements showed gains in their knowledge of friendly social behaviors. Although increases in children's peer acceptance were not apparent immediately after the intervention, evidence of this effect was found 2 weeks later in a follow-up assessment.

Further studies of coaching indicated that this form of intervention often produced gains in children's social skills or peer acceptance, but there were also exceptions to this pattern of findings (see Ladd, 2005). In some studies, the effects of coaching on children's skills and peer group acceptance were not uniform across social skills or types of children. Further, it was not clearly established that coaching benefited children who were prone toward antisocial behavior. Additionally, some researchers failed to detect post-coaching improvements in children's social skills, peer acceptance, or both (see Hymel & Asher, 1977; Tiffen & Spence, 1986). Thus, although many coaching studies produced results that were consistent with a skill learning or development hypothesis, others yielded equivocal findings or failed to provide corroborating evidence.

WHAT DO YOUNG CHILDREN LEARN FROM PEERS?

In contrast to the prior question, this query has focused researcher's attention on the changes that are hypothesized occur in children as a result of their participation with peers. As will be illustrated in the paragraphs that follow, much has been learned about the ways that peers may affect children's behaviors (e.g., skills), thoughts (e.g., understanding of themselves and others), feelings (emotional states, reactions, etc.), and other aspects of their development.

In the Peer Context, Children learn about Themselves as Persons

Although it has been common for researchers to assert that parent–child interactions and relationships affect children's self perceptions (e.g., self-concept, self-esteem, perceived competence, etc.), there is growing evidence to suggest children's self-appraisals are also influenced by their experiences with peers (see Cillessen & Bellmore, 1999; Egan & Perry, 1998). Much of the research conducted to examine this hypothesis has been guided by the premise that children's beliefs about themselves are shaped by the experiences they have in peer interactions and relationships. Peers' influence on children's sense of self may be particularly important during the late preschool and early elementary school years when children begin to construct theories about the self. Studies conducted with preschool and kindergarten children have shown that children's self-appraisals of their social competence depend, in part, on how much experience they have acquired with peers (Harter & Pike, 1984). It was discovered, for example, that young children in new classrooms did not appraise their social competence as highly as did those who had attended school with the same peers for more than a year.

Much of the evidence that has accrued thus far implies that children's self-appraisals are more positive when they participate in supportive peer relations, but suffer when they are exposed to negative peer interactions or adverse peer relationships. Evidence indicates that children who have a close friend tend to see themselves positively (Berndt & Burgy, 1996; Savin-Williams & Berndt, 1990), and these findings are consistent with the premise that friends affirm each other's positive attributes and downplay their shortcomings (Furman & Robbins, 1985; Ladd, Kochenderfer, & Coleman, 1996). In addition, it has been shown that children's self perceptions are related to the processes that occur in their friendships; children who have friendships that contain more positive features, such as closeness and support, tend to report higher levels of self esteem (Berndt, 1996). In contrast, chronically friendless children, and those who have poor quality friendships, appear to be at risk for low self esteem (Ladd & Troop-Gordon, 2003; Parker & Gottman, 1989), perhaps because they are deprived of the affirmation and interpersonal supports offered by friends. Participation in rejecting or abusive peer relations may also foster the development of negative self-perceptions in both younger and older children. It has been proposed, for example, that children who are disliked or rejected by peers may not be able to escape peers' negative sentiments and behavior, or the conclusion that they are unworthy of acceptance and inclusion (Buhs & Ladd, 2001; Ladd & Troop-Gordon, 2003). Consistent with this logic, evidence indicates that peer-rejected children tend to have unfavorable views of themselves and their peer acceptance (e.g., Boivin & Begin, 1989; Ladd & Troop-Gordon, 2003). Likewise, children who are frequently aggressed upon by peers (i.e., victimized children; Perry, Kusel, & Perry, 1988) appear prone to develop low self-esteem and negative self-beliefs (Kochenderfer-Ladd & Ladd, 2001; Perry, Hodges, & Egan, 2001).

In the Peer Context, Children Learn about Peers as Persons

Just as participation in peer relationships may influence children's sense of who they are as persons (Cillessen & Bellmore, 1999), it is conceivable that peer experiences affect the way that children think about agemates. It has been argued, for example, that children form ideas about what peers are like (e.g., "peer theory," such as beliefs about peers' social orientations; see Rabiner, Keane, & MacKinnon-Lewis, 1993), based on the way that peers treat them, respond toward their social overtures, and so on. As with self theory, the late preschool and early elementary school years may be a formative period for the development of peer beliefs. Young children, based on the experiences they have with peers in classrooms, playgrounds, or elsewhere, begin to recognize behaviors and characteristics that are shared by, or typical of agemates (see Ladd & Mars, 1986), and on the basis of these experiences, they may formulate a set of peer beliefs. It has been proposed, for example, that children who are liked and well treated by peers tend to develop positive or prosocial peer beliefs (i.e., the view that agemates, in general, tend to be trustworthy and supportive) whereas those who are disliked and mistreated by peers develop negative or antisocial peer beliefs (the view that agemates, in general, tend to be untrustworthy and hostile toward others; see Rabiner, Keane, & MacKinnon-Lewis, 1993; MacKinnon-Lewis, Rabiner, & Starnes, 1999). Although this hypothesis has not been well researched with preschoolers, MacKinnon-Lewis et al. (1999) found that peer rejection predicted grade-school boys' antisocial beliefs about familiar peers. Moreover, results from a longitudinal study conducted with younger and older children (i.e., kindergarten through fourth-graders; Ladd & Troop-Gordon, 2003) showed that children who were prone to be friendless, and especially those who remained friendless over many years, were more likely to develop the view that peers were untrustworthy and hostile toward others.

In the Peer Context, Children Learn How to Regulate Their Emotions and Overcome Distress

A longstanding premise in the peer relations literature is that agemates provide children with specific emotional resources, such as feelings of security under conditions of threat, or a reduced sense of distress in the face of novel stimuli. In large part, this hypothesis was derived from attachment theory and research conducted on the peer relations children who were orphaned during World War II (Bowlby, 1969; Freud & Dann, 1951). Some of the most convincing support for this premise comes from studies in which researchers placed preschoolers in strange or novel play situations and observed their emotional reactions and behaviors when they were in the presence or absence of peers. Schwarz (1972) had four-year-olds play with a friend, a stranger (an unfamiliar peer), or alone in a novel playroom that contained both familiar and unfamiliar toys. Results showed that children who had a friend present in the playroom were not only happier and less distressed, but also more mobile and interested in unfamiliar toys than were children who played with an unfamiliar peer or alone. Children in the stranger condition were more distressed than those in the friend condition. However, as these children became more experienced with their partners, they too exhibited more positive emotions and exploratory behavior. In contrast, children who played alone did not become significantly more comfortable over time. These findings suggested that children regulate their emotions and adapt better when they are with a friend rather than alone, and that they are even able to draw some comfort from unfamiliar peers.

In a similar study conducted with Russian preschoolers, Ispa (1981) assigned children to one of three conditions and then observed them in an unfamiliar playroom that contained different types of toys. In this study, children were not paired with friends, but rather were placed in a playroom with a familiar peer, an unfamiliar peer, or no peer at all. Compared to children who were paired with familiar peers, those in the unfamiliar peer condition exhibited more negative facial expressions, talked less, and spent more time near the playroom door. Children who did not have a peer present in the playroom were less at ease than their counterparts in the other two conditions. Here again, the results implied that familiar peers were a source of emotional support for young children, and that the effects of this type of support better enabled young children to regulate their emotions under stressful conditions.

Other investigators sought to determine whether familiar peers influenced the quality of young children's play and social interactions. In one such study, 3-year-olds were placed in a laboratory playroom with either a same-sex familiar or a same-sex unfamiliar peer, and observers coded the nature and sophistication of the children's play and social interaction (Doyle, Connolly, & Rivest, 1980). The findings showed that children who were paired with familiar peers played in more sociable ways than did children who were paired with unfamiliar peers, and that girls displayed this pattern more strongly than did boys. Additionally, the quality of children's play, and the skillfulness and success of their social interactions, was more advanced among those who were paired with familiar as compared to unfamiliar peers. Thus, it would appear that familiar peers not only enhance young children's emotional well-being, but also facilitate their social competence.

In the Peer Context, Adverse Experiences Can Endanger Children's Health and Development

There is also evidence to suggest that not all of what children learn in the peer context is beneficial for their behavioral and mental health. Although investigators have undertaken many longitudinal studies to determine whether poor peer relationships are a potential cause of children's health and adjustment problems (see Ladd, 2005), they have only recently begun to examine these linkages with young children (i.e., with samples of preschoolers and grade-schoolers). Thus far, most of this research has been focused on the health consequences of children's experiences with two types of peer relationships: peer group acceptance/rejection and friendship/friendlessness. More recently, investigators have begun to study the consequences of children's participation in bully-victim relations.

Accumulating evidence suggests that early peer rejection experiences are associated with the development of psychological difficulties, including both internalizing (e.g., anxiety, depression, loneliness) and externalizing problems (e.g., misconduct, disruptiveness; see McDougall, Hymel, Vaillancourt, and Mercer, 2001; Ladd, 2003, 2006). For example, Ladd (2006) followed children from age 5 to age 12 and found that, both peer rejection and children's aggressive behavior predicted externaling symptomotology, but that peer rejection was the stronger predictor of externalizing problems during the early rather than later school years. When rejection and children's withdrawn behavior were examined as predictors of internalizing symptomotology, rejection's efficacy as a predictor of internalizing problems was significant in early childhood and then increased progressively thereafter. Another group of investigators followed children from ages 9 through 14 and found that rejected children were more likely than popular children to exhibit externalizing problems such as misconduct, delinquency, and substance abuse (Ollendick, Weist, Borden, & Green, 1990). It was also discovered that children who remained rejected for longer rather than shorter periods of time were more likely to suffer internalizing and externalizing problems (DeRosier, Kupersmidt, & Patterson, 1994; Ladd & Burgess, 2001; Ladd & Troop-Gordon, 2003). Links were also found between peer rejection and loneliness during both early and middle child-hood (Cassidy & Asher, 1992; Crick & Ladd, 1993).

Other investigators have reported that children's participation in friend-ships and the quality of their friendships during childhood are important predictors of both their well-being and their interpersonal and scholastic adjustment. Data from these investigations showed that, not only do chil-dren with close friendships see themselves more positively (Berndt & Burgy, 1996; Savin-Williams & Berndt, 1990), but these children also report greater perceived social support and lesser loneliness (Ladd et al., 1996; Parker & Asher, 1993). In some cases, investigators who studied children's friendships in school contexts assessed multiple features of these relation-ships, such as whether or not children had a close reciprocated friendship in their classroom, the number of mutual friends they had at school, the duration of these relationships, and positive and negative features of their friendships (see Ladd, 1990; Ladd et al., 1996; Parker & Asher, 1993). Find-ings from these studies revealed that children who start kindergarten with previously established friends (for example, friends from preschool) devel-oped more favorable perceptions of school by the second month, and those who maintained these friendships liked school better as the year pro-gressed. Further, kindergartners who made new friends in their classrooms exhibited gains in achievement (Ladd, 1990). In addition, kindergarteners who saw their school friendships as offering higher levels of support and aid tended to perceive their classrooms as supportive interpersonal envi-ronments (Ladd et al., 1996). Conversely, kindergarteners (especially boys) that reported higher levels of conflict within their friendships exhibited lower levels of classroom engagement and participation (Ladd et al., 1996). Similar results were obtained with older children. In a study con-ducted with third- through fifth-graders, results showed that children who thought their friendships lacked supportive features tended to feel more lonely in school (Parker & Asher, 1993). Although friendship seldom has been examined in the context of long-term follow up studies, Bagwell and colleagues (Bagwell, Newcomb, & Bukowski, 1998) identified groups of children who had friends or were friendless in grade 5, and then assessed their adjustment 12 years later during early adulthood. Results showed that, when compared to friendless children, those who had friends in fifth grade were better adjusted in later life on a variety of indicators including trouble with the law, family life, and overall adjustment.

Additional findings suggest that children who are victimized (e.g., harassed, abused) by peers are at risk for developing serious health prob-lems such as anxiety, depression, and suicide (see Perry et al., 2001).

Results have shown that peer harassment and abuse begins at early ages (e.g., is present in kindergarten classrooms; see Kochenderfer & Ladd, 1996) and that victimized children, regardless of their behavioral propensities (passive as well as aggressive victims) are at risk for many types of adjustment problems (Perry et al., 2001; Schwartz, 2000). Early victimization experiences, for example, are associated with feelings of depression that endure over many years. In one long-term follow-up study, it was discovered that boys who were victimized during their school years continued to display depressive symptoms and lower self-esteem at age 23 (Olweus, 1993). Anxiety disorders have also been linked with peer victimization. In several investigations, researchers have reported that victimized children, including passive as well as anxious victims, reported moderate to severe levels of anxiety following bouts of bullying at school (see Perry et al., 2001). Among younger children in particular, peer victimization has been linked with both transient and enduring loneliness. In one study, investigators found that the frequency of children's peer victimization experiences as they entered kindergarten forecasted significant gains in loneliness over the remainder of the school year (Kochenderfer & Ladd, 1996). This study, and others, also showed that increases in children's adjustment difficulties co-occurred with the onset of victimization during the school year, and children who had been victimized over long periods of time had more severe adjustment difficulties than those who had been abused for brief periods (Kochenderfer-Ladd & Wardrop, 2001). Similarly, it was documented that grade-schoolers who experienced increases in victimization over a year developed stronger feelings of loneliness during the same time period (Boivin, Hymel, & Bukowski, 1995).

Gender Segregation in the Peer Context May Cause Children to Learn Unique Ways of Relating to Each Other

There is evidence to suggest that, beginning at early ages, children gravitate toward peers of the same sex for playmates. Descriptive evidence suggests that children prefer same-sex playmates as early as age two, and that girls exhibit this tendency at earlier than boys (Powlishta, Serbin, & Moller, 1993; Serbin, Moller, Gulko, Powlishta, & Colburne, 1994). Once established, it appears that children's tendency to associate with same-sex peers becomes stronger from early to middle childhood. In one study, investigators observed preschoolers' play with peers over a 6-month period and found that, on average, about half or more of their interactions (that is, 50–60 percent) occurred within groups of same-sex peers, and that this pattern of gender segregation was consistent and enduring (Martin & Fabes, 2001).

More importantly, it has been proposed that children's tendency to associate with same-sex peers causes them to learn different ways of relating to each other (Maccoby, 1990, 2002). This hypothesis has been substantiated by a growing corpus of evidence. For example, findings from observational studies indicate that, when preschool boys verbalize prohibitions (demands) during play interactions, peers of both genders tend to comply. However, when girls make such demands, only female playmates are responsive; boys tended to ignore girl's demands. Boys also appear to differ from girls in their tactics for influencing playmates, interaction styles, and preferred modes of play. Although it is typical for young children to seek greater influence over their playmates as they mature, evidence indicates that girls tend to accomplish this through the use of polite requests whereas boys are more reliant on confrontation and direct demands (Serbin, Sprafkin, Elman, & Doyle, 1984). Studies of children's play styles suggest that boys are more likely than girls to compete with each other, engage in one-upmanship, and pursue boisterous group-oriented activities such as rough-and-tumble play (Maccoby, 2002). These findings have been interpreted by some researchers to mean that boys and girls grow up in "separate cultures" (see Maccoby, 2002; Underwood, 2003). A key tenet of this "two cultures" perspective is that boys learn how to interact with each other in different ways than girls do and, therefore, boys and girls form peer relationships for different reasons and develop in different ways as a result of what they learn in these relationships.

These hypotheses have been addressed in longitudinal studies where researchers examine the extent to which children's same-sex play predicts changes in their social *competence* and social *adjustment* at later points in time. In one such study, 4- and 5-year-old's play and interactions with same- and other-sex classroom peers were observed during the fall and spring of a school year, and the amount of time that children spent with same-sex peers was calculated on each occasion (Martin & Fabes, 2001). Results showed that boys' and girls' interactions with same-sex peers increased over the school year, and that boys' play behaviors—but not girls'—became more physically active and emotionally charged. Additionally, as the school year progressed, boys who played proportionately more often with other boys exhibited higher levels of aggression but girls who played primarily with other girls became less aggressive. Other studies were undertaken to examine the possibility that children's propensities to associate with same-sex peers affected their *social adjustment.* Results showed that, among boys who were highly emotionally arousable, the tendency to play among groups of other boys forecasted later behavior problems (Fabes, Shepard, Guthrie, & Martin, 1997). No such linkage was found for girls, even among those who were more arousable relative to other girls. Rather, when excitable girls spent more time among same-sex peers, they were less likely to develop behavior problems. The investigators suggested that the tendency for males to engage in physically active, rough play might make excitable boys less able to control their emotions and refrain from socially inappropriate behaviors.

SUMMARY AND CONCLUSIONS

The purpose of this article was to survey what is known about children's social learning in the peer context during childhood and, particularly, the early childhood years, by examining relevant theory and pertinent empirical evidence. This aim was addressed by considering some of the foundational premises that have guided research on early social learning in the peer context, and by reviewing evidence that addresses three principal questions: (1) "*When* does peer social learning begin?" (2) "*How* does social learning occur in the peer context?" and, (3) "*What* do young children learn from peers"?

Having accomplished this, it may be useful to reflect on available evidence and ask what it teaches us about each of these questions. That is, in view of the research findings assembled to date, what inferences can be drawn about children's social learning in the peer context? Perhaps, as is illustrated in the remaining sections of this article, extant evidence supports three principal conclusions.

1. The Peer Context is a Rich Source of Social Learning, and its Contributions to Children's Development Begin During the Early Years of the Life Cycle

The evidence assembled on the origins of children's peer relations reveals that, although children's peer experience has humble beginnings (e.g., peer interactions are first driven by simple gestures such as smiles), it rapidly becomes a staging area for multiple forms of social learning, including the development of progressively sophisticated, reciprocal, and synchronized forms of peer interaction, many of which become the building blocks of relationships such as friendship (for a more extensive review, see Ladd, 2005). Such a view is consistent with the social learning premise that young children learn and change as a result of their interactions and relationships with peers. Moreover, it would appear that this growth in social learning is accompanied, or made possible by, significant advances in children's understanding of themselves (as actors), of peers (as partners), and of the connections that transpire between these entities (e.g., basic principles of social interaction, response contingencies, etc.). This growth in understanding is illustrated by the fact that, by the second and third years of life, children have learned to do much more than simply imitate an agemate's actions. Rather, by this age, children manifest "authentic" "social skills" (see Eckerman & Stein, 1982)—that is, they have learned how to think in act in ways that enable them to anticipate and negotiate increasingly complex patterns of social interaction and to construct and maintain rudimentary peer relationships. Findings such as these substantiate another basic social learning premise—specifically, that relations with agemates provide children with information about themselves and peers that they subsequently utilize to guide social encounters in the peer context.

2. Multiple Processes are Responsible for Social Learning in the Peer Context

Both old and new theoretical perspectives were brought to bear on the question of *how* social learning occurs in the peer context. Findings from research on shaping implied that this process occurs naturally within the peer context, and that young children learn from the reactions they receive from peers. These discoveries were consistent with the view that, in natural social settings (e.g., preschool classrooms, daycare homes, playgrounds), young children experiment with different behaviors during peer interactions and these behaviors evoke various reactions from peers. Because not all behaviors produce positive peer responses (i.e., rewards; social reinforcement), children learn that some of their actions are more likely to produce favorable consequences than others. In this sense, peers "shape" children's social development by helping them learn which of their behaviors are functional (i.e., have some utility or value) within the peer context. Based on this logic and the available evidence, it would appear that shaping is one of the primary ways that young children learn from peers.

Evidence obtained from research on modeling implies that observation and imitation is another common way that young children learn from peers. Learning via imitation appears particularly prevalent among infants and toddlers, and appears to be one of the principal ways that very young children acquire simple social gestures. Beyond this, imitation appears to serve a communicative function in the social interactions of very young children and, thus, appears to facilitate more complex and coordinated forms of play.

Thus, an important insight that emerged from this research was that young children do imitate agemates, and that imitation is one of the key mechanisms through which very young children build peer interactions, maintain play, and form relationships with agemates.

Another important discovery that emerged from research on modeling was that children become selective about the types of peers they imitate. This finding led investigators to think that, when children observe peers, they are doing more than simply watching a peer and mimicking the peer's behaviors. Imitation, if it were done selectively, would appear to require certain forms of mental activity, such as considering differences in models' behaviors and disparities in peers' reactions to various models. Findings such as these led investigators to think that, as children matured, they became increasingly adept at "processing" the information that was present in their peer interactions and relationships. Consistent with basic social learning premises, it was also surmised that the goal of this activity was to extract information that could be applied within future social encounters.

The research conducted from a social information processing perspective elaborated on this premise, and generated a sizeable body of corroborating evidence (for reviews, see Crick & Dodge, 1994). Findings from this domain of investigation implied that many of the processing steps that are stipulated within social information processing models are proxies for the social cognitive mechanisms that children naturally utilize to abstract meaning from their peer interactions and devise ways of responding to peers' overtures. When viewed from this perspective, children can be seen persons who not only observe their social surroundings (i.e., peers, and the peer context), but who also work (mentally) to make sense of what they see, and make use of this information when responding to their social surroundings. Thus, these findings imply that social learning occurs because children engage in these processes when they are confronted with social tasks (e.g., entering a peer group, finding a friend, etc.)—that is, children learn about themselves, others, and the peer context as they seek to understand their social surroundings, devise ways of responding to peers, etc.

Research that was intended to explain how children acquire and develop social skills also expanded what is known about social learning processes in the peer context. The overall pattern of findings that emerged from these studies underscored the importance of three specific processes that were hypothesized to be an integral part of children's social learning, adaptation, and ultimately, their success in the peer context. These processes were conceptualized as follows: (1) children routinely devise or invent goals for themselves in peer situations, (2) once children have a goal, they choose and enact a behavioral strategy, or a course of action that they think will accomplish their goal, (3) children consider the consequences of their actions, and work to perfect their behavioral strategies so that their actions enable them to achieve their goals more effectively. With some exceptions, findings from correlational studies and from experimental work on coaching suggest that children who engage in these processes as a means of obtaining prosocial goals tend to develop better or higher-quality relations with agemates. The reverse was found for children who were prone to devise and pursue antisocial goals. The coaching results are particularly persuasive in this regard because they were obtained from controlled, experimental manipulations. These findings supported the inference that all three skill learning and development processes (as they were operationalized in coaching programs) were instrumental in bringing about changes in children's social skills and peer relations. Thus, to the extent that these manipulations (i.e., the processes that children engaged in during coaching) are indicative of what children actually do in peer situations, or are encouraged to do by socializers, they serve to illuminate how a particular kind of social learning occurs in the peer context—that is, the process of learning how to perform and perfect social interaction skills.

3. Social Learning in the Peer Context Transforms Children and Affects the Course of Their Development

Not only do multiple avenues of social learning exist within the peer context, but also multiple forms of learning result from children's experiences in this context. As documented here, and in many other reviews of research on children's peer relations, it is increasingly apparent that children learn from peers, and that these learning experiences have lasting consequences for their development. In fact, the prevailing view among contemporary investigators is that peer relationships play a unique role in child development—one that cannot be entirely duplicated by parents or other socialization agents.

What children learn from peers is, in part, determined by how they learn it. Although considered separately in this article, it is likely that the processes and consequences of children's social learning in the peer context are interdependent. Thus, it is important to consider how specific learning processes may be linked with particular learning outcomes. Shaping has been implicated primarily as a determinant of children's behavioral development—that is, as having substantial effects on the way children act toward peers. Whether young children tend to act more or less prosocially or aggressively toward peers, for example, can be seen as resulting from the types of responses they have received for these behaviors. By differentially rewarding children's behaviors (e.g., by reacting to some and ignoring or failing to respond to others), peers raise or lower the likelihood that children will "learn" or repeat certain behaviors. Among older children, peers' reactions may be expressed in words and, thus, affect more than just children's behavior. Words may, for example, ascribe certain characteristics to children (e.g., indicate that they are smart, funny, lazy, fat, etc.) or convey evaluations of children's actions (e.g., accepting vs. rejecting reactions). Peer feedback of this type may teach children about who they are as persons (e.g., affect the development of self concept, self-esteem), and what peers are like as persons (i.e., affect the formation of peer beliefs). It may also inform children about how they fit into peer groups and the reputations they have developed among peers (e.g., becoming an accepted vs.

rejected member of their peer group). Further, such reactions may cause children to feel specific emotions (e.g., attraction, anger toward peers) and affect their emotional development.

Modeling too, is a form of social learning that has been linked primarily with the behavioral development of young children. The crux of this premise is that young children expand their behavioral repertoires by imitating novel acts that they see peers perform. The importance of modeling as a mechanism for expanding children's social behavior has been demonstrated most clearly with very young children. Infants and toddlers, it would appear, learn by mimicking each other's behaviors, and peer interactions appear to be an important staging area for this process. As children become capable of social play, for example, they hear peers make new sounds or vary the way they respond to play overtures. When children imitate these actions, they are essentially experimenting with the same behaviors that peers have "invented" and, by doing this they have introduced "novel" actions into their own behavioral repertoires. In the play example provided here, for example, modeling can be seen as a mechanism that enhances language development and adds behaviors to children's repertoire of play skills.

As children mature, however, it is less clear whether the contributions of modeling alone—that is, social learning that occurs principally through imitation—are as large, or as significant as they appear to be during early childhood. Evidence from experimental research on modeling suggested that older children primarily learn simple rather than complex behaviors by observing peers, and that the primary effect of peer models is to increase or decrease the frequency of behaviors that children already know how to perform (for reviews, see Ladd & Mize, 1983; Ladd, 2005). It seems likely that what children learn by imitating peers varies a function of their age and the developmental level of their peer companions.

The mechanisms specified in social information processing and skill-learning theories also provide important clues about what children learn from peers. Unlike shaping and modeling, which have been implicated in children's behavioral development, these learning processes appear to be more closely associated with children's social cognitive development. For example, there is evidence to suggest that the interpretive processes that children engage in as they attempt to understand peer situations and behaviors affects the types of attributions they make about themselves (e.g., beliefs about the self), peers (e.g., beliefs about peers), and the effectiveness of their own behaviors in peer situations (e.g., beliefs about one's competence, self-efficacy perceptions, etc.). These same processes appear to predict the success with which children devise solutions for social dilemmas (e.g., conflicts with peers), and the extent to which children are knowledgeable about how peers are likely to respond to their own social behaviors.

Likewise, the process that are hypothesized to account for children's social skill learning and development, such as inventing social goals and devising behavioral strategies, have been linked with the development of social problem solving skills, children's awareness and understanding of social norms, and various forms of self-referent thought (e.g., self concept, self esteem, perceived social competence, etc.). Although not well researched, it seems likely that children who engage in processes such as monitoring and evaluating the effects of their behaviors on peers, and adjusting their behavior in light of peers' responses, would be adept at forming relationships with peers, such as friendships (see Ross & Lollis, 1989).

The experiences that children have in the peer context determine what they learn. Beyond what can be inferred from research on social learning processes, research on the nature and quality of children's experiences with agemates adds to what is known about *what* they learn in the peer context. From this type of evidence, it can be inferred that peers make important contributions to several areas of children's development. First, there is evidence to suggest that the experiences children have in friendships and peer group contexts affect the way they think and feel about themselves. Whereas friendships and other positive peer experiences appear to be a source of self-affirmation and esteem, negative peer experiences and relational adversity appear to lower children's appraisals of their worth and competence as persons. For example, peer group rejection, and children's participation in bully-victim relations have been linked with child maladjustment and poor health outcomes across a wide range of ages. Second, there is support for the premise that experience with negative peer interactions and relations (e.g., peer aggression and maltreatment) skews children's perceptions of agemates, leading them to conclude that peers are hostile, untrustworthy, lacking in prosocial characteristics, and so on (Burks et al., 1999; Dodge et al., 2003; Ladd & Troop-Gordon, 2003; Troop-Gordon & Ladd, 2005). Moreover, it has been shown that children who develop biased perceptions of peers—particularly negative peer beliefs—are more likely to develop adjustment problems during childhood (Ladd & Troop-Gordon, 2003). Whether it is the case that positive or rewarding peer experiences lead children to develop more flattering assessments of peers remains to be seen. It might be expected, however, that children who experience rewarding peer relations tend to develop the belief that peers are helpful, friendly, and trustworthy, and it is conceivable that such beliefs might protect or buffer them from dysfunction. Third, children's experiences with peers appear to play an important role in helping them learn how to regulate their emotions. Familiar peers, in particular, appear to provide children with "attachment-like" resources, such as offering the comfort of a "secure base," and the emotional supports that are needed to regulate fear or insecurity. This benefit, it would appear, increases the likelihood that children will engage in exploratory behavior and become more social responsive to their playmates. Because familiar peers elicit higher levels of social responsiveness from children, they also provide a better context for children to learn and develop social interaction skills. The types of peers with whom they interact and form relationships, it appears, also shape children's social development. As has been illustrated, gender segregation is common in young children's peer groups, and it appears that by engaging in interactions primarily with same-sex peers, children learn to behave differently from the ways they might act with cross-sex agemates. Over time, this propensity makes it likely that boys and girls develop distinct interaction patterns, play styles, and behavior patterns. Once developed, these rather distinct ways of relating to others may cause boys and girls to develop different forms of competence and experience different types of adjustment outcomes.

In conclusion, evidence from studies of children's peer interactions and relations offers important insights into how social learning occurs in early peer contexts, and what children learn from these processes. Collectively, these findings suggest that: (a) multiple processes are responsible for children's learning within the peer context, (b) many of these processes are present in children's peer relations even during the earliest stages of child development, and (c) the forms of social learning that occur in peer contexts are associated with many aspects of children's development.

NOTE

1.   Portions of this article were written while the author was supported by a grant from the National Institutes of Health (R01HD-045906) to support the Pathways Project, a long-term longitudinal investigation of children's social/psychological/scholastic adjustment in school contexts. Special appreciation is expressed to all the children, parents, teachers, and principals who made this study possible, and to members of the Pathways Project for assistance with data collection.

REFERENCES

Allen E. K., Hart, B., Buell, J. S., Harris, F. T., & Wolfe, M. M. (1964). Effects of social reinforcement on isolate behavior of a nursery school child. *Child Development, 35,* 511–518.

Baer, D. M., & Wolf, M. M. (1970). The entry into natural communities of reinforcement. In R. Ulrich, T. Stachnik, & J. Mabry (Eds), *Control of human behavior* (Vol. 2, pp. 42–63). Glenview, IL: Scott Foresman.

Bagwell, C. L., Newcomb, A. F., & Bukowski, W. M. (1998). Early adolescent friendship and peer rejection as predictors of adult adjustment. *Child Development, 69*, 140–153.

Bandura, A., Ross, D., & Ross, S. A. (1963). Imitation of film-mediated aggressive models. *Journal of Abnormal and Social Psychology, 66*, 3–11.

Bandura, A. (1977). Toward a unifying theory of behavior change. *Psychological Review, 84*, 191–215.

Berndt, T. J. (1996). Exploring the effects of friendship quality on social development. In W. M. Bukowski, A. F. Newcomb, & W. W. Hartup (Eds.), *The company they keep: Friendship in childhood and adolescence* (pp. 346–365). New York: Cambridge University Press.

Berndt, T. J., & Burgy, L. (1996). Social self-concept. In B. A. Bracken (Ed.), *Handbook of self-concept: Developmental, social, and clinical considerations* (pp. 171–209). New York: Wiley.

Boivin, M., & Begin, G. (1989). Peer status and self-perception among early elementary school children: The case of the rejected children. *Child Development, 60*, 591–596.

Boivin, M., Hymel, S., & Bukowski, W. M. (1995). The roles of social withdrawal, peer rejection, and victimization by peers in predicting loneliness and depressed mood in childhood. *Development and Psychopathology, 7*, 765–785.

Bowlby, J. (1969). *Attachment and loss: Vol. 1. Attachment.* (2nd ed.). New York: Basic Books.

Bronson, W. C. (1981). Toddlers' behavior with agemates: Issues of interaction, cognition, and affect. In L. Lipsitt (Ed.), *Monographs on Infancy, 1* (pp. 1–128). Norwood, NJ: Ablex.

Brown, P., & Elliott, R. (1965). Control of aggression in a nursery school class. *Journal of Experimental Child Psychology, 2*, 103–107.

Brownell, C. A. (1986). Convergent developments: Cognitive-developmental correlates of growth in infant/toddler peer skills. *Child Development, 57*, 275–286.

Buhs, E. S., & Ladd, G. W. (2001). Peer rejection as antecedent of young children's school adjustment: An examination of mediating processes. *Developmental Psychology, 37*, 550–560.

Burks, V. S., Laird, R. D., Dodge, K. A., Pettit, G. S., & Bates, J. E. (1999). Knowledge structures, social information processing, and children's aggressive behavior. *Social Development, 8*, 220–236.

Cassidy, J., & Asher, S. R. (1992). Loneliness and peer relations in young children. *Child Development, 63*, 350–365.

Cillessen, A. H. N., & Bellmore, A. D. (1999). Accuracy of self-perceptions and peer competence in middle childhood. *Merrill-Palmer Quarterly, 45*, 650–676.

Cooke, T., & Apolloni, T (1976). Developing positive social-emotional behaviors: A study of training and generalization effects. *Journal of Applied Behavior Analysis, 9*, 65–78.

Crick, N. R., & Dodge, K. A. (1994). A review and reformulation of social information processing mechanisms in children's social adjustment. *Psychological Bulletin, 115*, 74–101.

Crick, N. R., & Dodge, K. A. (1996). Social information-processing mechanisms in reactive and proactive aggression. *Child Development, 67*, 993–1002.

Crick, N. R., & Ladd, G. W. (1993). Children's perceptions of their peer experiences: Attributions, social anxiety, and social avoidance. *Developmental Psychology, 29,* 244–254.

DeRosier, M. E., Kupersmidt, J. B., & Patterson, C. J. (1994). Children's academic and behavioral adjustment as a function of the chronicity and proximity of peer rejection. *Child Development, 65,* 1799–1813.

Dodge, K. A. (1980). Social cognition and children's aggressive behavior. *Child Development, 51,* 162–170.

Dodge, K. A. (1986). A social information processing model of social competence in children. In M. Perlmutter (Ed.), *The Minnesota symposium on child psychology: Vol. 18* (pp. 77–125). Hillsdale, NJ: Erlbaum.

Dodge, K. A., Lansford, J. E., Burks, V. S., Bates, J. E., Pettit, G. S., Fontaine, R., & Price, J. M. (2003). Peer rejection and social information processing factors in the development of aggressive behavior problems in children. *Child Development, 74,* 374–393.

Doyle, A. B., Connolly, J., & Rivest, L. P. (1980). The effect of playmate familiarity on the social interactions of young children. *Child Development, 51,* 217–223.

Eckerman, C. O., & Stein, M. R. (1982). The toddler's emerging interactive skills. In K. H. Rubin and H. S. Ross (Eds.), *Peer relationships and social skills in childhood* (pp. 41–71). New York: Springer-Verlag.

Eckerman, C. O., & Stein, M. R. (1990). How imitation begets imitation and toddlers' generation of games. *Developmental Psychology, 26,* 370–378.

Egan, S. E., & Perry, D. G. (1998). Does low self-regard invite victimization? *Developmental Psychology, 34,* 299–309.

Erdley, C. A., & Asher, S. R. (1996). Children's social goals and self-efficacy perceptions as influences on their responses to ambiguous provocation. *Child Development, 67,* 1329–1344.

Evers, W., & Schwartz, S. A. (1973). Modifying social withdrawal in preschoolers: The effects of filmed modeling and teacher praise. *Journal of Abnormal Child Psychology, 1,* 248–256.

Fabes, R. A., Shepard, S. A., Guthrie, I. K., & Martin, C. L. (1997). Roles of temperamental arousal and gender-segregated play in young children' social adjustment. *Developmental Psychology, 33,* 693–702.

Freud, A., & Dann, S. (1951). An experiment in group upbringing. In R. Eissler, A. Freud, H. Hartmann, & E. Kris (Eds.), *Psychoanalytic study of the child, Vol. 6* (pp. 127–168). New York: International Univ. Press.

Furman, W., & Robbins, P. (1985). What's the point? Issues in the selection of treatment objectives. In B. Schneider, K. H. Rubin, & J. E. Ledingham (Eds.), *Children's peer relations: Issues in assessment and intervention* (pp. 41–54). New York: Springer-Verlag.

Gottman, J. M. (1977). The effects of a modeling film on social isolation in preschool children. A methodological investigation. *Journal of Abnormal Child Psychology, 5,* 69–78.

Gottman, J. M., Gonso, J., & Schuler, P. (1976). Teaching social skills to isolated children. *Journal of Abnormal Child Psychology, 4,* 179–197.

Hart, B. M., Reynolds, N. J., Baer, D. M., Brawley, E. R., & Harris, F. R. (1968). Effect of contingent and noncontingent social reinforcement on the cooperative play of a preschool child. *Journal of Applied Behavioral Analysis, 1*, 73–76.

Harter, S., & Pike, R. (1984). The pictorial scale of perceived competence and peer acceptance for young children. *Child Development, 55*, 1969–1982.

Hartup, W. W. (1979). The social worlds of childhood. *American Psychologist, 34*, 944–950.

Hay, D. F., Pedersen, J., & Nash, A. (1982). Dyadic interaction in the first year of life. In K. H. Rubin & H. S. Ross (Eds.), *Peer relationships and social skills in childhood* (pp. 11–40). New York: Springer-Verlag.

Hudley, C., & Graham, S. (1993). An attributional intervention to reduce peer-directed aggression among African-American boys. *Child Development, 64*, 124–138.

Hymel, S., & Asher, S. R. (1977). *Assessment and training of isolated children's social skills.* Paper presented at the biennial meeting of the Society for Research in Child Development, New Orleans, April.

Ispa, J. (1981). Peer support among Soviet day care toddlers. *International Journal of Behavioral Development, 4*, 255–269.

Jakibchuk, Z., & Smeriglio, V. L. (1976). The influence of symbolic modeling on the social behavior of preschool children with low levels of social responsiveness. *Child Development, 47*, 838–841.

Kochenderfer, B. J., & Ladd, G. W. (1996). Peer victimization: Cause or consequence of school maladjustment? *Child Development, 67*, 1305–1317.

Kochenderfer-Ladd, B., & Ladd, G. W. (2001). Variations in peer victimization: Relations to children's maladjustment. In J. Juvonen & S. Graham (Eds.), *Peer harassment in school: The plight of the vulnerable and victimized* (pp. 25–48). New York: Guilford Press.

Kochenderfer-Ladd, B., & Wardrop, J. (2001). Chronicity and instability in children's peer victimization experiences as predictors of loneliness and social satisfaction trajectories. *Child Development, 72*, 134–151.

Krasnor, L. R., & Rubin, K. R. (1981). The assessment of social problem solving skills in young children. In T. Merluzzi, C. Glass, & M. Genest (Eds.), *Cognitive assessment* (pp. 452–476). New York: Guilford.

Ladd, G. W. (1981). A social learning method for enhancing children's social interaction and peer acceptance. *Child Development, 52*, 171–178.

Ladd, G. W. (1990). Having friends, keeping friends, making friends, and being liked by peers in the classroom: Predictors of children's early school adjustment? *Child Development, 61*, 1081–1100.

Ladd, G. W. (2003). Probing the adaptive significance of children's behavior and relationships in the school context: A child by environment perspective. In R. Kail (Ed.), *Advances in Child Behavior and Development* (Vol. 31, pp. 43–104). New York: Wiley.

Ladd, G. W. (2005). *Children's peer relationships and social competence: A century of progress.* New Haven: CT: Yale University Press.

Ladd, G. W. (2006). Peer rejection, aggressive or withdrawn behavior, and psychological maladjustment from ages 5 to 12: An examination of four predictive models. *Child Development, 77*, 822–846.

Ladd, G. W., Buhs, E., & Troop, W. (2002). Children's interpersonal skills and relationships in school settings: Adaptive significance and implications for school-based prevention and intervention programs. In P. K. Smith & C. H. Hart (Eds.), *Blackwell's handbook of childhood social development* (pp. 394–415). London: Blackwell.

Ladd, G. W., & Burgess, K. B. (2001). Do relational risks and protective factors moderate the linkages between childhood aggression and early psychological and school adjustment? *Child Development, 72,* 1579–1601.

Ladd, G. W., & Crick, N. R. (1989). Probing the psychological environment: Children's cognitions, perceptions, and feelings in the peer culture. In C. Ames & M. Maehr (Eds.), *Advances in motivation and achievement* (pp. 1–44). London: JAI Press.

Ladd, G. W., Herald, S., Slutzky, C., & Andrews, K. (2004). Preventive interventions for peer group rejection. In L. Rapp-Paglicci, C. N., Dulmus, & J. S. Wodarski (Eds.), *Handbook of prevention interventions for children and adolescents* (pp. 15–48). New York: Wiley.

Ladd, G. W., Kochenderfer, B. J., & Coleman, C. C. (1996). Friendship quality as a predictor of young children's early school adjustment. *Child Development, 67,* 1103–1118.

Ladd, G. W., & Mars, K. T. (1986). Reliability and validity of preschoolers' perceptions of peer behavior. *Journal of Clinical Child Psychology, 15,* 16–25.

Ladd, G. W., & Mize, J. (1983). A cognitive-social learning model of social-skill training. *Psychological Review, 90,* 127–157.

Ladd, G. W., & Pettit, G. S. (2002). Parents and children's peer relationships. In M. Bornstein (Ed.), *Handbook of parenting: Vol. 5: Practical issues in parenting* (2nd ed., pp. 377–409). Hillsdale, NJ: Erlbaum.

Ladd, G. W., & Troop-Gordon, W. (2003). The role of chronic peer adversity in the development of children's psychological adjustment problems. *Child Development, 74,* 1325–1348.

Lamb, M. E., Easterbrooks, M. A., & Holden, G. W. (1980). Reinforcement and punishment among preschoolers: Characteristics, effects, and correlates. *Child Development, 51,* 1230–1236.

Maccoby, E. E. (1990). Gender and relationships. *American Psychologist, 45,* 513–520.

Maccoby, E. E. (2002). Gender and group process: A developmental perspective. Current Directions in *Psychological Science, 11,* 54–58.

MacKinnon-Lewis, C., Rabiner, D., and Starnes, R. (1999). Predicting boys' social acceptance and aggression: The role of mother–child interactions and boys' beliefs about peers. *Developmental Psychology, 35,* 632–639.

Martin, C. L., & Fabes, R. A. (2001). The stability and consequences of young children's same-sex peer interactions. *Developmental Psychology, 37,* 431–446.

McDougall, P., Hymel, S., Vaillancourt, T., & Mercer, L. (2001). The consequences of childhood peer rejection. In M. R. Leary (Ed.), *Interpersonal rejection* (pp. 213–247). Oxford, UK: Oxford University Press.

Miller, N. E., & Dollard, J. (1941). *Social learning and imitation.* New Haven: Yale University Press.

Mize, J., & Ladd, G. W. (1988). Predicting preschoolers' peer behavior and status from their interpersonal strategies: A comparison of verbal and enactive responses to hypothetical social dilemmas. *Developmental Psychology, 24,* 782–788.

Mize, J., & Ladd, G. W. (1990). A cognitive-social learning approach to social skill training with low-status preschool children. *Developmental Psychology, 26,* 388–397.

Mischel, W. (1973). Toward a cognitive social learning reconceptualization of personality. *Psychological Review, 80,* 252–283.

O'Connor, R. D. (1969). Modification of social withdrawal through symbolic modeling. *Journal of Applied Behavior Analysis, 2,* 15–22.

O'Connor, R. D. (1972). Relative efficacy of modeling, shaping, and the combined procedures for modification of social withdrawal. *Journal of Abnormal Psychology, 79,* 327–334.

Oden, S., & Asher, S. R. (1977). Coaching children in social skills for friendship making. *Child Development, 48,* 495–506.

Ollendick, T. H., Green R. W., Weist, M. D., & Oswald, D. P. (1990). The predictive validity of teacher nominations: A five-year follow-up of at risk youth. *Journal of Abnormal Child Psychology, 18,* 699–713.

Olweus, D. (1993). Victimization by peers: Antecedents and long-term outcomes. In K. H. Rubin & J. B. Asendorf (Eds.), *Social withdrawal, inhibition, and shyness in childhood* (pp. 315–342). Hillsdale, NJ: Erlbaum.

Parker J. G., & Asher, S. R. (1993). Friendship and friendship quality in middle childhood: Links with peer group acceptance and feelings of loneliness and social dissatisfaction. *Developmental Psychology, 29,* 611–621.

Parker, J. G., & Gottman, J. M. (1989). Social and emotional development in a relational context: Friendship interaction from early childhood to adolescence. In T. J. Berndt & G. W. Ladd (Eds.), *Peer relationships in child development* (pp. 95–131). New York: Wiley.

Perry, D. G., & Bussey, K. (1984). *Social development.* Englewood Cliffs, NJ: Prentice-Hall.

Perry, D. G., Hodges, E. V., & Egan, S. (2001). Determinants of chronic victimization by peers: A review and new model of family influence. In J. Juvonen & S. Graham (Eds.), *Peer harassment in school: The plight of the vulnerable and victimized* (pp. 73–104). NY: Guilford Press.

Perry, D. G., Kusel, S. J., & Perry, L. C. (1988). Victims of peer aggression. *Developmental Psychology, 24,* 807–814.

Powlishta, K. K., Serbin, L. A., and Moller, L. C. (1993). The stability of individual differences in gender typing: Implications for understanding sex segregation. *Sex Roles, 29,* 723–737.

Rabiner, D. L., Keane, S. P., & MacKinnon-Lewis, C. (1993). Children's beliefs about familiar and unfamiliar peers in relation to their sociometric status. *Developmental Psychology, 29,* 236–243.

Renshaw, P. D., & Asher, S. R. (1983). Children's goals and strategies for social interaction. *Merrill-Palmer Quarterly, 29,* 353–374.

Richard, B.A., & Dodge, K.A. (1982). Social maladjustment and problem solving in school-aged children. *Journal of Consulting and Clinical Psychology, 50,* 226–233.

Rose, A. J., & Asher, S. R. (1999). Children's goals and strategies in response to conflicts within a friendship. *Developmental Psychology, 35,* 69–79.

Ross, H. S., & Lollis, S. P. (1989). A social relations analysis of toddler peer relationships. *Child Development, 60,* 1082–1091.

Savin-Williams, R. C., & Berndt, T. J. (1990). Friendship and peer relations. In S. S. Feldman & G. R. Elliott (Eds.), *At the threshold: The developing adolescent* (pp. 277–307). Cambridge, MA: Harvard Press.

Schwartz, D. (2000). Subtypes of victims and aggressors in children's peer groups. *Journal of Abnormal Child Psychology, 28,* 181–192.

Schwarz, J. C. (1972). Effects of peer familiarity on the behavior of preschoolers in a novel situation. *Journal of Personality and Social Psychology, 24,* 276–284.

Serbin, L. A., Moller, L. C., Gulko, J., Powlishta, K. K., & Colburne, K. A. (1994). The emergence of gender segregation in toddler play groups. *New Directions for Child Development, 65,* 7–17.

Serbin, L. A., Sprakfkin, C., Elman, M., & Doyle, A. (1984). The early development of sex differentiated patterns of social influence. *Canadian Journal of Social Science, 14,* 350–363.

Skinner, B. F. (1953). *Science and human behavior.* New York: Macmillan.

Steinberg, M. D., & Dodge, K. A. (1983). Attributional bias in aggressive adolescent boys and girls. *Journal of Social and Clinical Psychology, 1,* 312–321.

Strain, P. S. (1985). Programmatic research on peers as intervention agents for socially isolated classmates. In B. H. Schneider, K. H. Rubin, & J. E. Ledingham (Eds.), *Children's peer relations: Issues in assessment and intervention* (pp. 193–206). New York: Springer-Verlag.

Taylor, A. R., & Asher, S. R. (1984, April). Children's interpersonal goals in game situations. In G. W. Ladd (Chair), *Are children's interpersonal goals and strategies predictive of their social competence?* Symposium at the American Educational Research Association, New Orleans, LA.

Thorndike, E. L. (1931). *Human learning.* New York: Century.

Tiffen, K., & Spence, S. H. (1986). Responsiveness of isolated versus rejected children to social skills training. *Journal of Child Psychology and Psychiatry and Allied Disciplines, 27,* 343–355.

Troop-Gordon, W., & Ladd, G. W. (2005). Trajectories of peer victimization and perceptions of the self and schoolmates: Precursors to internalizing and externalizing problems. *Child Development, 76,* 1072–1091.

Underwood, M. K. (2003). *Social aggression among girls.* New York: Guilford Press.

Vandell, D. L., Wilson, K. S. and Buchanan, N. R. (1980). Peer interaction in the first year of life: An examination of its structure, content, and sensitivity to toys. *Child Development, 51,* 481–488.

Vincze, M. (1971). The social contacts of infants and young children reared together. *Early Child Development and Care, 1,* 99–109.

CHAPTER 8

FRIENDSHIPS IN VERY YOUNG CHILDREN

Barbara Davis Goldman and Virginia Buysse

INTRODUCTION

In this chapter, we explore the evidence for the existence of friendships in very young children across diverse times, places, and childrearing contexts. Although it is commonly accepted that three- or four-year-old children have friendships (e.g., Corsaro, 1985; Gottman, 1983; Rubin, 1980), there has been much less unanimity about whether young children close to their second birthdays could be friends, not just playmates. For example, in a chapter that reviewed the literature on childhood friendships, Furman (1982) denied the possibility of toddler friendships, stating, "Unlike toddlers, preschool children can be said to have friends" (p. 329). Other scholars are more tentative, and while acknowledging the existence of peer interactions in very young children, they appear to be uncomfortable with the term friendship for this age-group. In a chapter on the behavioral manifestations of children's friendships, Hartup (1989) noted the following:

> Specifying an age when friendships first become visible in social interaction is extremely difficult. Mothers sometimes insist that their infants or toddlers have "best friends"—usually meaning a regular playmate with whom the child acts

Contemporary Perspectives on Socialization and Social Development..., pages 165–192
Copyright © 2007 by Information Age Publishing

harmoniously. This may or may not be semantically appropriate since the babies have not chosen one another from among many different associates.

Sometimes the acceptance is lukewarm: "To the extent that reciprocal interchanges of positive overtures may characterize particular dyads, it may be said that toddlers do have friendships" (Rubin, Bukowski, & Parker, 1998, p. 634). Obviously, those who study early friendships (some of that work is described in this chapter) acknowledge friendships. In her overview of her 20-year research program, Howes (1996) indicated that preferences for particular peers, or differential relationships, can appear prior to the end of the first year, about the time of the transition to toddlerhood, and that early friendships are possible in toddlerhood, before the second birthday. But a growing number of peer researchers, including some who do not study early friendships, embrace the terminology. Though Rubin (1980) indicated that children in general could be friends at two and a half (see page 17) he also repeatedly referred to the 17–20 month old familiar playmates of Rubenstein and Howes (1976) as friends (see pages 23–24) even though they did not use that term themselves. Parker, Rubin, Price, and DeRosier (1995) simply asserted, "The formation of specific friendships begins to be observed during the period from 18 to 36 months" (p. 100). Under a section heading of "Infants and Toddlers' Friendships," Ladd, Herald, and Andrews (2006) stated, "Researchers often document the earliest of friendships with parent and teacher-report data, or observations of children's social interactions" (p. 24). However, others still rely on more conservative terms such as "preferred partner" or "reciprocal relationship" for relationships of children less than 3 years old.

To contribute to the emerging acceptance of the possibility of early friendships, we focus in this chapter on the descriptions of early friendships, so that readers can learn what these early relationships look like. Secondly, we propose that the striking similarity of the descriptive evidence of early friendships between very young children from diverse times, places, and childrearing contexts argues for the universality of at least the possibility of early friendships, given fairly regular access to other children.

Accepting the possibility of friendships in very young children has implications for helping parents and early educators notice, and nourish, such relationships, but there is another motive: Those who doubt whether typically developing two-year-olds could be friends also might question whether such relationships are possible for three-, four-, or five-year-old children with disabilities who may be developmentally young, that is, on par with typically developing toddlers. Demonstrating that friendships are possible with the developmentally very young across time, place and context opens the door for the possibility of friendships in young children with disabilities; some empirical evidence for the existence of those friendships in this population also is included.

As noted above, some of the literature on early peer interactions among typically developing children that documents friendships in the very young is beginning to be acknowledged in recent reviews of the peer interaction and relationship literature that focus on older children. Studies that are less well known are combined here with the more commonly cited references on early friendship to provide strong evidence of friendships in the very young. The studies selected are illustrative; there is no intention to be exhaustive. For the most part, the cited work is descriptive in nature, and only some of the studies had friendship as the focus. In some cases, we, rather than the authors of the studies, have chosen to designate the relationships described as friendships. And though we cannot yet present "scientific proof" that they work as interventions, we end with some promising practices that may help friendships become even more likely among very young children who are developing typically, and among preschoolers with disabilities (who may be developmentally similar to typical toddlers).

Though rarely viewed as an "intervention," a key requirement for the development of a friendship as an enduring relationship between a specific pair is fairly regular contact with specific peers (who do not have to be exact age-mates) through play-dates, weekly or occasional groups, or child care. Even if friendships do not develop quickly, one of the advantages of regular contact with other young children is its potential for supporting social learning. That learning can take place through observations of peers of approximately the same size and interests, so that what they do is likely to be easily emulated. Continuing contact and shared interests provide the context for learning how to get along with others over time—how to share toys; how to initiate and end interactions; and eventually how to be friends.

The potential of such early interactions and friendships should lead parents and early childhood educators of both typically developing very young children, and those with disabilities, to consider how best to tailor the environment and their own behaviors to nurture these early interactions and relationships. For those especially concerned with the development of young children with disabilities, the promise of inclusion is the enhanced possibility for such relationships, especially between children with and without disabilities. Thus, while friendship can be seen as a culmination of social skill development, early peer interaction and especially friendship are also context for further development.

THE BUILDING BLOCKS OF FRIENDSHIP: EARLY SOCIAL BEHAVIORS AND INTERACTIONS

The Competent Infant (Stone, Smith, & Murphy, 1973) is a massive compilation of more than 200 studies of infants up to the age of 15 months. The section on "The Social Infant" was three hundred pages long, but not a single study with peers was included. The opinion at the time was that peer relations were "virtually nonexistent" (p. 985), despite research to the contrary from the 1930s (see Renshaw, 1981 for information about the hiatus in peer research from the mid 1940s to the 1970s). Starting in the 1970s, there has been a resurgence of interest in peer research which created a significant literature on peer interactions and relationships in children during the first five years of life, and a considerable literature that focused on social behaviors, interactions, and social skills during in the first two to three years. This research can be found in encyclopedic chapters in research handbooks (e.g., Hartup, 1983; Mueller & Vandell, 1979; Parker, Rubin, Price, & DeRosier, 1995; Rubin et al., 1998; Vandell & Mueller, 1980), edited books (e.g., Asher & Gottman, 1981; Foot, Chapman, & Smith, 1980; Mueller & Cooper, 1986; Rubin & Ross, 1982), single-authored books (e.g., Ladd, 2005a) and numerous review articles, chapters, and journal articles describing experimental and descriptive studies. Interested readers are referred to these sources as entry points to the literature on early peer interaction and social skills/competence in toddlers, and the literature on friendship in typically developing preschool and older children and adolescents.

Interest in peers, expressed through a variety of social behaviors, and interactions with age-mates are the building blocks of early peer relationships. Compilations of the early social repertoire, as described by the researchers from the 1930s on, can be found in numerous sources (e.g., Hay, 1985; Ladd, 2005b; Rubin et al., 1998; Vandell & Mueller, 1980; Vandell, Nenide, & Van Winkle, 2006). Some of that information is reviewed here, especially for very young children, though the focus is on friendship.

OVERVIEW OF THE ILLUSTRATIVE STUDIES

Though some of the large-scale or analytic studies are discussed, the focus here is on descriptive or qualitative studies of friendships in very young children (under three) with medium-sized to small samples, in order to share what early friendships might look like. Friendships in one or two such studies could be viewed as anomalous by skeptics, but the similarity of the patterns and themes in this body of work, from studies that are dispersed in the research literature across time (eight decades), place (7 countries), and context (hospital for foundlings, residential nurseries, kibbutzim, child care programs, in-home play-dates, and laboratory-based playgroups), collected by observers with widely varying perspectives and assumptions, argues for the validity and relevance of this evidence.

Since the majority of infants and very young children in western countries did not have extensive experience with peers (group care arrangements were not widely available for infants and toddlers until fairly recently), many of the early studies of infant and toddler sociability and peer interactions brought unacquainted young children together for specific periods (for reviews, see Hartup, 1983; Mueller & Vandell, 1979). However, to answer questions regarding the development of peer interactions and relationships, that is, what very young children did and could do together, given *extensive* early contact in naturally occurring situations, many researchers have sought out environments with built-in access to peers. The literature on children in group care provides much of the information on the onset and development of interest in peers, of early social interactions, and, of special concern here, of early friendships. We start with children in contexts that provide the most extensive contact, and progress toward contexts with less.

WORKING DEFINITION OF EARLY FRIENDSHIP

Every researcher uses a slightly different conceptual or operational definition of friendship, and some have modified those definitions over time. For this review, a working definition should suffice. We view early friendships as reciprocal, predominantly positive relationships between two young children. There are multiple possible signs or dimensions of friendship, but not all are necessary for a specific dyad at all points in time. These signs, dimensions, or characteristics include interest in being near each other (seeking and maintaining proximity), affection for each other, positive affect or mutual enjoyment when interacting, preferences for the other as a target of social overtures, relatively higher responsiveness to each other's social overtures compared to others, and the ability to engage in complex interactions, relative to what they demonstrate with other peers—that is, they appear more competent, or the interactions more organized, or harmonious, than with others. Interactions between friends often include repetition over time of specific themes, or games that may be unique to the dyad. Prosocial behaviors such as sharing, helping, and comforting may also be seen, stemming from their affection for, or attachment to, the friend. In addition, both direct observation and report by others are accepted as valid. For many studies, both kinds of data are present, and concur.

RESEARCH ON PEER RELATIONS
IN RESIDENTIAL FACILITIES

The first set of studies of early interactions, preferred partners, and friendship were conducted in residential facilities that provide maximal contact with a group of peers. Bridges (1933) observed almost daily over a 3-month period 62 Canadian infants and toddlers, ranging in age from three weeks to two years, who resided in a foundling and baby hospital. Most of the day for young infants was spent in individual cribs, but those between nine and twelve months of age were placed in large playpens for a few hours daily. Those between twelve and fifteen months were allowed to play together on the floor for several hours each day, and those over fifteen months spent most of the day in a large room together. Four decades later, Vincze (1971) reported her observations of nine Hungarian infants, from 3 to 16 months of age. Compared to the Canadian setting, this environment was much more supportive, the care giving by adults was more adequate, the youngest children did not spend so much of their days in cribs, and the group was constant. They were observed weekly for over a year. The sequences of peer-oriented behaviors documented by Vincze were similar to those Bridges had observed almost 40 years before in a very different context, but, as might be expected, the behaviors emerged earlier in Vincze's study, where even the young infants spent much time together in a large playpen. Looking at and smiling at peers occurred early, followed by mutual smiling and laughing, especially when the infants were on their sides or could otherwise see each other. Touching, including mutual touching, was frequent; hair and hands were favorites of younger infants, and faces of older ones. Mutual touching often preceded mutual smiling. Body contact or scrambling over each other started once some could crawl. Objects then became part of the interactions at seven months, starting with taking toys from each other's hands, progressing to offering toys, then manipulating the same toys, so that object play was coordinated with social play. At 10 months, games such as peek-a-boo, hide and seek, and chasing each other were observed involving the group.

For a second paper that was published in Hungarian on *common activities* in children aged four months to two-and-a-half years, Vincze (1974) observed essentially the same group of children over a 30-month period, extracting those activities where there was not only action and reaction, but also mutual awareness of the other. In this paper, Vincze described extended bouts of imitation, of *doing the same thing together* that started at eight months and increased rapidly to a high level thereafter. By the toddler period, these game-like interactions were frequent. These interactions in particular were characterized by their creativity and variability (e.g., emitting sputtering noises, scratching something, holding the bars of the playpen and bending the head backwards, waddling after each other with a toy between the legs, racing around the room on hands and knees). These interactions also were characterized by their nonliteral nature, that is, the actions were carried out purely to initiate and maintain interaction. Especially with the more vigorous, noisy activities, other infants would join in the play. For example, five infants were observed stepping into plastic mugs and banging the mugs against the floor while wearing *mug-shoes*. High-amplitude, rhythmic motoric actions were frequently the basis for extended imitation episodes or group games, often accompanied by rhythmic shouting. More traditional games, such as peek-a-boo accompanied by much laughter, also occurred. After 20 months, more ritualized actions were observed, such as climbing along a bench in a certain way, carrying sand and pebbles to the slide from a particular spot in the garden, and so forth.

Both Bridges and Vincze found that *preferences for specific partners* (a defining feature of a dyadic friendship) could emerge around the first birthday, but neither of these researchers focused much attention on these particular peer relationships. Surprisingly, partner preferences seem more common in Bridges' work, but she provided no specifics. In her summary, Bridges (1933) noted that when the children were younger "Any responsive child is accepted as a playmate. But by fourteen months a child begins to show preferences. Two children will often take special interest in each other and will frolic together.... A group of three or more seldom forms" (p. 49).

Vincze's goal was to convey the positive tone of peer contacts in general, in order to counteract the bias in the literature at that time that young children were either uninterested in, or hostile to, one another. The fact that the toddlers shared a common playpen from early on, and then a room, may have contributed to the frequency of *group* activities (in contrast to Bridges). In fact, Vincze (1974) noted that only one definite pair (a friendship) was formed before the children she observed were two years old. In that one instance, one child showed a clear preference for a peer from 10 to 20 months, until the peer left the facility. Their cots had been next to each other. The preference, or "sympathy in his choices" was apparent in the ratio of observed interactions that involved these two, but was also confirmed by the comments of the nurses who cared for them. Vincze commented, "Incidentally, this is in conformity with our earlier experiences according to which friendships are generally not observed at that age, but may nevertheless occur" (p. 8). Thus, though dyads and occasionally groups participated in varied activities (sometimes for as long as 15–20 minutes), extended early contact and participation in these shared, clearly enjoyable activities did not appear to lead directly to the development of many enduring relationships in this environment, at least before age two. At the same time, such relationships, though few in number, did develop and in at least one reported case, endure for many months. The kinds of games, or group activities, these children engaged in are exactly the kinds of activities that one could expect to see in toddler friends, along with additional signs such as mutual preference, affection, and so forth.

In contrast to Bridges and Vincze, Zaslow (1980) intended to explore through interviews with adults and direct observations of children the emergence of *focused relationships* in the very young who had extensive early contact. She concentrated on determining when and how children differentiated among their peers, and when and how they showed "enduring preferences for proximity and interaction" (p. 179) with specific peers. The context was an Israeli kibbutz, a communal settlement in Israel in which the primary responsibility for the care of young children is given to caregivers and teachers. Though there has been considerable variability over time, and among the different kibbutzim movements, the infants in this study lived in a separate children's house, and slept in a room with other infants of similar age. Thus, from the infant's point of view, his life was somewhat like that of a quadruplet. Parents devoted themselves only to playful interaction with their children for several hours each afternoon and on weekends.

Like Bridges and Vincze, Zaslow (1980) also found evidence of specificity, or differentiation of relationships by one year. Infants recognized each other's names, could go to or point to the crib or place at the table of specific infants, and showed excitement by smiling or vocalizing when they happened to see group-mates during their visiting time with families in their apartments. Names of group-mates were among the first 2–3 words spoken. *Focused relationships*, marked by consistent mutual preferences for proximity and extended interaction between pairs, what others might call beginning friendships, also began to emerge about the same time, though they grew in intensity over time. Though she provided observations and brief histories of three focused relationships, Zaslow took care to point out that, even in this supportive environment, not all the toddlers showed enduring preferences for a particular group-mate. Some toddlers never were involved in focused relationships, despite the opportunity; however, approximately one-third of the toddlers whose caregivers were surveyed were reported to have such relationships. It is important to note the intensity of one long-lasting friendship only abated at about two-and-a-half, when the girls' preferred play styles diverged and their families had discouraged visits with each other during family time when those requests had become annoyingly persistent. Additional relationships that were more transient occurred, but parents and teachers clearly distinguished those from focused peer relationships. Qualitative analyses of the descriptions and observations of 11 focused relationships indicated that three factors might have supported the development of focused relationships (toddler friendships) in these young children. First, in 9 of the 11 relationships, the children had slept in the same bedroom since early infancy, thus providing for the special interactions and conversations children have before they go to sleep or when they awake. Second, in 8 of the 11, both children in the relationship were particularly responsive to each other. And finally, in 8 of the 11 there was a supportive relationship between the parents of the friends or between one of the parents and the children.

In an earlier study of children in two kibbutzim which differed in educational philosophy, Faigin (1958) focused on peer relationships in slightly older children, 19–38 months old, in three age groups spanning a range of 5–6 months in each. Her motivation was to discover whether this particular rearing context allowed for interactions and group identification prior to age three, which was the expectation then for western societies. The youngest group, where the children were mostly under two years of age, played games together as a group or as dyads; games involved imitation of various actions, conventional games such as peek-a-boo, and pretending together. This youngest group switched partners from activity to activity, but in the two older groups, which included children around 25–31 months of age, "certain friendships had formed and there were often two or three children who usually played together" (p. 122). Faigin noted that though the intensity of the relationships between these friends was not as strong as between siblings who lived in nuclear families outside the kibbutz, these relationships were "more intense than that of friendships among other Israeli children of this age who play together" (p. 124).

RESEARCH IN PEER RELATIONS IN CHILD CARE SETTINGS

Residential facilities are not the norm, but they are of interest as they provide a model of maximal peer contact. Much more common today are child care programs, full- or half-day, which also provide children with the opportunity for extensive contact, though at a somewhat reduced level as compared to residential facilities. The next set of studies of early interactions, preferred partners, and friendship were conducted in the context of American, Italian, French, and Norwegian child care programs, all providing extensive regular contact with the same group of peers.

Howes' (1983) intended to look for friendships in her study of early relationships in the context of American child care centers, and was among the first to use the term *friendship* to describe these relationships in infants. Friendships were defined conceptually as "an affective tie between two children which has three necessary components: mutual preference, mutual enjoyment, and the ability to engage in skillful interaction" (p. 1042). Friendships were determined by analyzing reports by knowledgeable adults and actual observations of peer behavior; the criteria were designed to apply to infants, toddlers, and preschoolers, so that comparisons could be made across the age groups.

Infants, toddlers, and preschoolers were observed individually for 30 minutes at 8-week intervals during six time periods during the year. Specific dyads were determined to be friends during a particular time period if they met the three criteria, operationalized as follows: *mutual preference* was seen in above-average responsiveness to each other's social overtures—specifically, at least 50% of the dyad's social initiations, aggregated together, led to interaction; there was at least one instance of *skillful, coordinated, complementary interaction* where the partners' actions complemented each other, as in games like run–chase with role reversal; and there were indications of *mutual enjoyment* through at least one positive affective exchange. Because each child was the target for 2, 15-minute observations, there were 60 minutes in each time period every two months in which a specific dyad could meet criteria. The three behavioral criteria were validated by teacher nominations of each child's best and second-best friend. In this study, teachers' personal definitions of friendship in young children coincided with observational data gathered by researchers. All of the pairs identified by teachers were also identified by their observed behaviors; ninety-seven percent of pairs identified behaviorally as friends were also listed as friends by teachers. Of the seven infants (5–14 months at the start; median = 10 months), five were part of 3 friend dyads (of the 21 possible) that were identified during the year. The children would have been between 17–26 months of age at the end of the observation year. It is not clear how old those who were designated "infants" at beginning of the study were at the time of meeting the friendship criteria—they could have been close to or past the one-year-old mark that has been found in the work described earlier. Of course, there is no consensus about exactly when an infant becomes a toddler.

All eight toddlers in Howe's study (16–23 months at entry) also had at least one friend in one of the six observation periods; five had two or more. The pattern was similar for the older children too—all had at least one friend, and most had two or more. At least one toddler was in a friendship dyad with five others. Toddlers and preschoolers had both stable friendships (friends across time periods) as well as temporary, sporadic relationships. Importantly, the interactions of children involved in stable friendships showed the greatest increases in complexity over time, indicating that social skills may develop best within a friendship relationship. An extension of this work (Howes, 1988) focusing on social competence with a much larger group used slightly different criteria. Friends were identified on the basis of mutual preference to remain in close proximity, defined as staying within 3 feet of each other during at least 30% of their combined observations, and sharing positive affect during mutual play. Some of these early friendships were maintained across years, not just months.

Though they were not specifically targeting friendships or specific peer preferences, the observations of Musatti and Panni (1981) are instructive of the ways that young, predominantly preverbal children in frequent contact with each other played together in an Italian day care. In many respects, their observations are reminiscent of the work of Vincze (1974) with children in a Hungarian residential facility. Musatti and Panni observed six young toddlers, 11 to 18 months of age, three times a week for five weeks, with each child the focus for four sessions of 20 minutes each, carefully recording on audiotape an analytical description of the action. The children had been in the same group at the day care center for at least seven months, so were well acquainted. These young toddlers were highly observant of each other, alternating glances to their peers in between focused attention to their own object-centered activities. What the children noticed in almost constant monitoring of what the others were doing was then used to create social overtures, as in imitating what the other child had done earlier while looking at or smiling at the peer, which almost always engaged the peer in subsequent interaction. Other overtures were purely social:

> The children often smile to one another and vocalize. This is not mere ges-tural or vocal imitation, as the tone of voice and the sequencing of the inter-action as well as the fact of being accompanied by direct gazing at the partner, show that they are actually calls and responses, often for the sole purpose of making contact with the partner at a distance, without containing any other message. (p. 13)

Offering objects repeatedly in an apparent attempt to sustain interac-tion, physical contact such as caressing the partner's face or hands while smiling, and bringing one's face in close to the partner's are used the same way, that is, to engage in dyadic interaction.

Vigorous motor activities usually engaged multiple children, with sev-eral simultaneously making drum-like noises on an object, pulling to stand on a handrail, and running back and forth from one side of the room to the other, accompanied by laughing, looking at each other, and vocalizing. The running game was especially sophisticated, in that the children would run, one at a time, from one specific location to another while vocalizing, with each waiting for all the players to arrive at the end point before start-ing again, one at a time, to run back to the starting point. The two oldest toddlers introduced variations on the theme: "During the same play epi-sode, which they communicate to each other by means of glances and calls (loud vocalizing), turning round to ensure that the other child has under-stood the innovation" (p. 21). Although the roles here are not complemen-tary or reciprocal, which Howes required as an index of early social understanding and complexity, these games had their own sets of rules and a quasi-simultaneous, quasi-turn-alternating structure. These group games certainly allowed for playful, enjoyable interaction as a group, using the same interaction structure as would be used by two toddler friends. Of great interest was the notation about the sensitivity of the two oldest (but only 17–18 months) who would "wait patiently for the younger participants to carry out the various play phases, however clumsily, and promptly call them to order when their attention is distracted, even performing certain parts of the play, for example, the ritual shout, for them when they forget to do so" (p. 21). Although friendship, as a dyadic relationship, is the focus of this chapter, interactions such as this that may include multiple young peers, who perhaps are all friends, are of importance too. As with Vincze (1974), these are the kinds of interactions that one might expect to see in toddler friends, as well as groups of friends.

Similar observations were made by researchers studying the sharing of meaning before the onset of verbal language in young French toddlers of a similar age (13–18 months) in group care (Stambak & Verba, 1986). The toddlers had been with a consistent set of peers for at least three months. In contrast to most observational work in day care centers, there was a manipulation—for observational sessions, the regular toys were removed and replaced with empty cardboard boxes and detergent containers. Groups of five to seven were videotaped three times a week. Again, these young toddlers were highly attentive to each other, making social overtures and creating rule-governed, turn-alternating games with complementary roles with the novel materials (though only when the interactions were dyadic). Interactions based on imitation could accommodate more than two at a time. The sequences of interaction that were captured are extensive and complex, and provide rich descriptive information about exactly how young toddlers can construct coherent interaction together. Ingenuity is also seen in the interactions of a group of Norwegian toddlers described by Lokken (2000a, 2000b). These two reports also provide inspiring illustrations of early peer interaction as the toddlers participate with great enjoyment in the kinds of vigorous motoric activities described by Musatti and Panni (1981), and demonstrate the creativity of the Hungarian (Vincze, 1974) and French toddlers (Stambak & Verba, 1986) in developing the kinds of games that only children can think of.

Lokken (2000b) also noted that it was striking that so many researchers with diverse theoretical stances, observing in different countries, report almost identical interactions among toddlers. What is also striking is that so many of these interactions are well-coordinated, harmonious, and creative, using the affordances of big and small toys, furniture, open spaces, walls, and developing gross motor skills, to form dyadic and group interactions. The social skills involved in repeated actions, imitating with and without variations on the theme, alternating turns or acting in synchrony, and signaling playful intent are apparent and universal. While there are few indications of the frequency of occurrence of these skillful interactions, these sources are highly recommended for their descriptive detail, which allows the interested reader to learn what to look for either when studying early peer interactions and friendships or attempting to foster such development.

In a longitudinal study of a slightly older group of American toddlers, Whaley and Rubenstein (1994) analyzed an extensive set of videotaped, naturally occurring interactions in a mixed-age classroom over a 10-month period. The five children in the study ranged from 22 to 32 months at the start, and had been attending the program for varying durations, from 9 months to 2 years. Four friendship pairs were identified from observational and field note data, using extremely rigorous criteria. To be labeled as friends, a toddler dyad had to interact consistently with each other whenever they had the opportunity over a period of time (minimum 5 days) and mutually prefer to be together, seen when both partners chose the other over any other child when the opportunity arose. All nine informants (three members of the research team, two research assistants who transcribed the videotapes, and all four teachers in the setting) identified these four pairs of children; additional dyads were also identified, but not by all nine informants.

Interactions between these four pairs of children from a random sample of videotapes across several days revealed key dimensions of friendship. Most frequent was *similarity* that was created by imitation. Toddler friends imitated each other, often for extended periods, and with careful attention to exactly duplicating the partner's actions. In this way, these toddler friends created a "we-ness" or synchrony in their behaviors. Just as more verbal preschoolers remind each other of their similar interests and reassure each other about their relationship, these toddlers told each other, behaviorally, "we're friends, right?" These dyads also developed *ritual behaviors*, which were more elaborated sequences that involved specific behaviors and objects that were repeated over days in their play. These themed interactions (forts, house, monsters, shopping carts) appeared to be natural extensions of the similarity dimension, but went well beyond imitation, and appeared to solidify the relationship. *Intimacy* was seen when the dyad separated themselves from others, either by going off together or by excluding or ignoring others who attempt to join. This particular behavior was critical in distinguishing friendships from other, less intense relationships. Additional dimensions are discussed in a later section on prosocial interactions; the multiple examples of the interactions included in this work provide a primer on observable dimensions, or behavioral markers, of early friendship.

Of the four friendships that met the rigorous criteria at some period over the 10-month study, one boy was involved in two of the friendships, and one girl was involved in three. Re-pairings apparently occurred after their friends had graduated out of the class and grieving for the missed friend subsided. It is also worth noting that the teaching staff did not directly facilitate the development of these friendships, but rather, allowed them to happen, which included allowing the dyads to 1) interact with each other for extended periods (over 30 minutes) without interruption, 2) exclude others without interference, and 3) engage in vigorous physical activity of the type often curtailed by teachers elsewhere (e.g., running, throwing balls, building forts).

RESEARCH ON PEER RELATIONS IN EXPERIMENTER-CREATED GROUPS AND DYADS

Rather than use naturally occurring groups, some researchers have created their own peer groups and dyads to provide extensive contact and study the phenomenon of the development of friendship. Vandell and Mueller (1980) reported the exploration of multiple behavioral criteria for friendship in their extensive study of six American toddler boys who met daily for six months each weekday morning, so these toddlers were as familiar with each other as many in the day care studies. Data from 30 minutes of videotaped observations per child at 16, 19, and 22 months were analyzed to determine who interacted with whom, who initiated interactions, what behaviors were used, and whether interactions met specific stringent criteria for game-like interactions. Various criteria were used separately and in combination to identify friendships, in either in the context of the entire group, or when the toddlers were paired in dyads. When using the criterion of showing a mutual preference for each other, that is, each initiating with each other more than with anyone else in the playgroup, only one dyad of the 15 possible combinations of the six boys was determined to have a friendship in the group context, and only at the last time-point, at 22 months. In contrast, this same pair was determined to be friends at all three time-points when the researchers used a predominance of positive affect as a criterion. The third possible friendship index used Goldman and Ross's (1978) criteria of infant games (mutual engagement, turn alternation, non-literality, and repetition). Goldman and Ross had observed 28 examples of imitative, complementary, and reciprocal games in 24 dyads of previously unacquainted 12-, 18-, and 24-month-olds who met only once in a laboratory setting, so it was plausible that well-acquainted toddlers would also engage in such interactions in a familiar setting. However, games were observed in Vandell and Mueller's group of familiar toddlers only at the last time point, at 22 months, involving only the single dyad identified with the other two indices.

The same six boys had also been videotaped separately in each of the 15 possible dyadic combinations, so the researchers could explore whether a difference in group size might produce a different outcome. In the dyadic setting, reciprocated preferences were present at all three time points, involving three different partners with one boy, one at each time period. The boy in all three of these friendships was also involved in the friendship identified in the group context. A similar pattern occurred for positive affect and games. The dyadic context seemed to allow for more differentiated, sophisticated social behaviors to be demonstrated earlier than did the larger group context. Once again, not all these typically developing toddlers developed friendships according to the criteria studied, but one exceptional toddler had many. They were manifested primarily in the dyadic setting.

Drawing on the members of a naturally occurring group, Camaioni, Baumgartner and Perucchini (1991) created ten same-aged dyads, two at each of 12, 18, 24, 30, and 36 months, composed of Italian children who were in the same peer group in day care for at least six months. Each dyad participated twice. The dyad was taken to a separate room in the center, and a teacher was present to comfort or protect them, as needed, but otherwise was not involved. The approximately 30-minute sessions were videotaped. A coding system focused on imitative and complementary interactions and conventional social games was developed and used to score the tapes. Imitative and complementary interactions were fairly brief, on average, and complementary interactions were more frequent in the older dyads. Across age, games increased in frequency, and length; marked individual differences across the dyads were noted, especially for the number of games, their variety, the frequency of specific preferred games, and the presence of idiosyncratic games that only one dyad played. Only one of the 12-month and 18-month dyads played any games, but the older toddlers at 24 and 30 months played many. Though the focus was on age-related changes in the kinds of interactions demonstrated by toddlers across the second and third year, of special note is the finding that though these children were selected only because their birth dates were within two weeks of each other, six of the 10 dyads of familiar children manifested the kinds of game-playing patterns expected of toddler friends, that is, playing a preferred game multiple times (2–11) across the two sessions, and playing idiosyncratic games that the dyad created and then repeated 2–6 times. From the article, there is no way to know whether these six dyads were already friends (they were already well acquainted) or whether the dyadic situation, separate from the group, allowed them to manifest their social skills as was true for the toddler boys observed by Vandell and Mueller (1980) and the previously unacquainted children of Goldman and Ross (1978).

RESEARCH ON PEER RELATIONS WITH LIMITED CONTACT BETWEEN PEERS

Extensively reducing the frequency of contact brings us to home-reared toddlers who meet occasionally with a specific playmate, arranged by the parents. Though a large proportion of typically developing home-reared infants and toddlers may have regular contact with peers (e.g., Hartup, 1983), it can be difficult to determine whether these familiar playmates are actually friends. However, it would appear that many of the familiar home-reared toddler playmates observed by Rubenstein and Howes (1976) could be considered to be friends, even if they could not demonstrate their preferences by choosing one from many in a group of peers. Though the toddlers observed by Rubenstein and Howes did not spend anywhere near as much time together as did the infants and toddlers reported earlier in this chapter, the interactions between these home-reared *regular playmates* were noticeably similar to those of toddlers from very different environmental contexts that afforded extensive experience with peers. This is all the more compelling given that observation time for each of the eight dyads was limited to a single visit of about an hour. As part of a larger study comparing interactions with mother versus peer, eight toddlers, from 17 to 20 months, were observed with their *regular playmate*. These toddlers had been together at each other's home for the previous 4 to 20 months, meeting about two to three times a week. All were firstborn, with no other experience with peers beyond occasional contact with neighbors. The target toddlers spent on average 50% of their time in social interaction with the toddler we will call their friend—talking, exchanging toys, and playing together, which included games such as chase and peek-a-boo, climbing, sliding and swinging together, and pretend play with toy telephones. They also created novel activities, such as each jumping off a stool, alternating turns and vocalizing, taking turns jumping off of a step 20 times, wearing pots as hats, and bouncing on the bed together. Most likely, the one-to-one context, the common interests and sensorimotor skill levels, and the generally supportive familiar environment facilitated the development of interaction skills and a relationship. And within that relationship, the target toddlers interacted with the objects in the same environment in more mature and creative ways than they did without the peer. Again, early relationships (friendships) are the result of development, and appear to promote further development.

Certainly the dyad involving Mueller's toddler son, whose interactions are described in detail and formed the basis for his stage-like theory of the development of early peer interaction that was then tested in the larger peer group (Mueller & Lucas, 1975; Vandell & Mueller, 1980), would appear to meet the criteria frequently used to determine friendship. Referred to variously as Larry and Bernie or Loren and Robert, they were both firstborn, 2 months apart in age, and started playing together at each other's home two days a week when 12 and 10 months old (or 10 and 8, depending on the source). Videotaping of their interactions started when they were 15 and 13 months. Subsequently, they were joined by three other firstborn boys for a playgroup two mornings a week for three months. Though the focus of that work was developing a stage-like developmental progression of peer interaction rather than friendship, Larry and Bernie appeared to interact in the most complex ways during the playgroup sessions, as compared to all the other possible combinations of the five boys, and continued to play together long after the group ended.

NOTEWORTHY COMPONENTS OF FRIENDSHIP INTERACTIONS: GAMES

One pattern noted by all longitudinal observers of early friendship development, and by many peer interaction researchers as well, is the existence of *games*, or rule-governed interactions, in which the children direct their nonverbal actions to each other and wait for the other to take a turn. The clear alternation of turns, the repetition of the sequences, and the existence of role relationships between the turns of the partners (imitative, complementary, or reciprocal) indicate considerable interactive skill even though the partners may not yet be talking to each other (Goldman & Ross, 1978; Ross & Goldman, 1977; Ross, 1982). These structured interactions, or games, also appear to be the way that nonverbal young children create extended interactions together, often with great delight, which function much like fantasy play or conversations do for older preschoolers. Several researchers (e.g., Vandell & Mueller, 1980) used the presence of games as a criterion of a friendship in toddlers.

An organizational variant of the turn-alternation structure, with its act-pause pattern involves acting in unison, either in complementary roles, as in extended bouts of run–chase, or with partners doing the same thing, either at the same time, or with one starting and the other starting immediately after, and continuing in unison. These latter game patterns lend themselves to interactions involving more than two toddlers and have been noted by observers of Norwegian, Italian, and French children in highly supportive early child care programs as described above (e.g., Camaioni, Baumgartner, & Perucchini, 1991; Lokken, 2000a, 2000b; Musatti & Panni, 1981, Stambak & Verba, 1986), and in the earlier work by Vincze (1974). Whether the turns alternate or are in unison, these early games are among the most complex interactions for toddlers, and their repetition within the comfort of a reciprocal dyadic friendship contributes to the continuing development of interaction skills.

NOTEWORTHY COMPONENTS OF FRIENDSHIP INTERACTIONS: PROSOCIAL INTERACTIONS

But early friendship is more than just fun and games. The potential emotional richness of these enjoyable, responsive dyadic relationships can be seen in interactions that go beyond laughter into the more empathic, prosocial realm. In addition to seeing the dimensions of similarity, ritual behaviors, and intimacy in interactions between these young friends described above, Whaley and Rubenstein (1994) also observed three kinds of prosocial behaviors. *Helping*, primarily unsolicited, was seen both in assisting the friend in an ongoing activity and getting an object the partner needed, and in comforting, the more empathic as well as instrumental assistance offered to the friend who was hurt or sad. In s*haring*, the child gave up an object to the other. *Loyalty* was seen when a toddler supported her friend when the friend was in conflict with another child, or a toddler intervened when another child was attempting to take the friend's objects or invade his space.

The particular kind of helping, specifically offering empathic assistance or comforting to a friend who was hurt or sad, has also been observed by others, even for children this young. For example, Howes and Farver (1987) found that almost half of the 43 16- to 33-month-old toddlers responded when peers cried, and of most interest, they were over three times more likely to respond to a friend than a nonfriend, even though they were actually observed interacting more frequently with children designated as nonfriends. In this study, teachers had identified friendship pairs using the criteria of "two children who prefer to play together, who enjoy playing together, and who play skillfully together" (p. 444). Very young children can respond in comforting ways, even with nonfriends, especially in environments that strongly encourage and model that kind of behavior (e.g., Wittmer & Petersen, 1992), but the likelihood is high that emotional and instrumental support by peers occurs in the context of early friendships.

In intensive observations in an Italian child care center of a close-knit group of six toddlers, aged 11–18 months, who had been attending the same center for at least 7 months prior to the first observations (described above), Musatti and Panni (1981) noted multiple episodes of comforting. The focus here was not on purely dyadic relationships—many of the reported activities involved more than two children. But the toddlers (who were no more than 18 months old) appeared to have multiple relationships that would be called friendships, and the comforting behaviors that were observed appear to have been dyadic, as illustrated in this excerpt:

> Physical contact is particularly used during episodes involving consolation of a partner whose state of discomfort is assumed by the other child. A crying child is observed with extreme gravity by the others and observation sometimes turns into actual consolatory behavior. This kind of behavior can also be displayed by some of the younger children who console the older....In order to console his partner, the child will make a strenuous and persistent endeavor using also communicative means other than actual physical contact. He thus demonstrates both his understanding of the peer's state of

mind and his knowing several ways of cheering him up. The child will use such different behaviors as approaching, squatting before the partner, bringing his face close to the other's and smiling, vocalizing, conversing and lightly tapping various parts of the partner's body, starting to sing a nursery rhyme, sometimes miming in such a way as to arouse laughter (making noises with the mouth, grimacing, falling ostentatiously). Less frequently, objects are offered as consolation. Sometimes, however, the child seeks help from the adult in consoling his peers, by pointing him out and vocalizing with an intense expression on his face. (Musatti & Panni, 1981, p. 18)

FRIENDSHIPS OF YOUNG CHILDREN WITH DISABILITIES

But what about children who are chronologically older, but developmentally young, with disabilities? Do they have friends? Do they help each other? The study of friendship among young children with disabilities has received relatively limited attention in the literature. Much of the research that has been conducted has been influenced by early childhood inclusion—the practice of enrolling children with disabilities in early care and education programs alongside their typically developing peers. Current estimates indicate that more than 50% of preschool children with disabilities are enrolled in some type of inclusive early childhood setting (U.S. Department of Education, 2003). Empirical evidence over the past three decades suggests that children with disabilities benefit socially from placement in inclusive settings as compared to non-inclusive settings, particularly with respect to displaying more positive social interactions and higher levels of social participation with peers (Buysse & Bailey, 1993; Lamorey & Bricker, 1993; Odom & Diamond, 1998).

However, other studies on inclusion have suggested that the road to *friendship* for young children with disabilities may be more perilous. Guralnick's (1999) review of a series of studies focusing on young children with mild disabilities concluded that social separation continues to exist in inclusive programs (particularly for extended social interactions) and that typically developing preschoolers show marked preferences for forming friendships with other typically developing peers. Other studies and reviews of the literature suggest that children with disabilities encounter difficulties during their interactions with peers and are at relatively high risk for peer rejection (Guralnick, Gottman, & Hammond, 1996; Odom & Diamond, 1998; Odom et al., 2002), which does not bode well for friendship formation. But it is important to note that while peer acceptance is an important component of social competence and, in some instances, is a precursor to friendship formation, it is not synonymous with friendship (Asher, Parker, & Walker, 1996). Children can have a friend and generally not be accepted by the group, and vice versa.

One of the challenges in comparing across studies is that there is widespread disagreement about a behavioral criterion for determining friendship status (Guralnick & Groom, 1988; Hinde, Titmus, Easton, & Tamplin, 1980; Price & Ladd, 1986; Roopnarine & Field, 1984). Researchers have selected various social behaviors (e.g., proximity, positive social interactions, positive affect, parallel or cooperative play) in isolation or combination to define friendship in young children and the proportion of time or interactions needed to meet the friendship criteria varies widely across studies. Overly stringent criteria and limited sampling may underestimate the actual prevalence of friendships for children, both those with and without disabilities. While preschoolers with disabilities generally form fewer friendships than do typically developing children (Buysse, Nabors, Skinner, & Keyes, 1997; Guralnick et al., 1996), there is wide variability in the number of children with friends. Field (1984) found that 43% of preschool children with developmental delays formed *close* friends in her study, whereas in Guralnick and Groom's (1988) study, only 7.5% of preschool boys with developmental delays formed *reciprocal* friendships with peers. Buysse (1993) found that 55% of the 58 preschool age children with disabilities had at least one mutual friendship, based on teacher report. Only a few of these friendships involved another child with a disability, that is, these were predominantly inclusive friendships involving one child with and one child without disabilities.

In a more recent sample of 117 preschoolers with disabilities and 198 without, only 29% of the children with disabilities did not have at least one friend (by teacher report) and the number of children with disabilities with two or more friendships (36%) was equal to those with only one (35%). Thus, 71% had at least one teacher-reported friend (Goldman, Buysse, Skinner, & Edgerton, 2005). The same pattern of equivalent percentages for having one or more than one friendship was true for the typically developing children (43% for both), but the percentage without friends was about half (14%) of that for children with disabilities. Buysse, Goldman, and Skinner (2002) examined the number of playmates and friends for children with and without disabilities in two kinds of inclusive preschool classrooms using the *Playmates and Friends Questionnaire* that has undergone updating (Goldman & Buysse, 2005). Overall, the 120 children with disabilities averaged 1.45 friends, and typically developing peers averaged 1.74, but the difference was only significant in the specialized settings, in which the majority of children enrolled had disabilities. Teachers reported an average of 1.4 friends for children with disabilities and 2.0 friends for their typically developing peers. In the inclusive child care programs (in which the majority of children enrolled were typically developing), teachers reported an average of 1.6 friends for children with disabilities and 1.7 friends for their typically developing peers.

In identifying friendships, parent and teacher report may be quite useful either instead of or in addition to using observational criteria. Parents and teachers have the advantage of more extensive knowledge than most researchers can obtain, and parents in particular know about friendships outside the classroom. In the Buysse (1993) study, while teachers reported mutual friends in 55%, parents reported that 79% had mutual friends. Guralnick (1997) used questionnaires and interviews with mothers to learn about the social networks of four- and five-year old boys who were developmentally delayed (n = 75), had communication disorders, or were developing typically. Of particular interest is that by maternal report, 95% of the young boys with delays had regular playmates, most of whom were developing typically. Most of these regular playmates had met each other outside of preschool, and mothers of all three groups were actively involved in organizing play-dates that allowed these relationships to develop. In addition, 47% had a best friend, and again, the majority of the best friends did not have a disability.

A recent qualitative study (Dietrich, 2005) in two Head Start classrooms is remarkable both for the intensity of the data gathering process, and the frequency of friendships in young children with disabilities. There were two children with disabilities available for study in each class. Using extensive observations and independent teacher report, six friendship pairs involving the four children with disabilities were identified and described. These children scored either a minimum of two standard deviations below average overall on development assessments, or 1.5 below standard deviations on two subscales. Each of these four children had at least one friendship with a typically developing child, and one child with cerebral palsy had three friendships, two with typically developing children. The interview and observational data indicated that components found in all of the relationships included *mutual interest* in being together, *playing together* and *having fun together,* and *showing affection. Sharing* was a central component in five of the friendships and *helping* each other in four, with *looking out for the other* (protecting), and *providing comfort,* in one each. As an indication of the persistence of the interest in each other manifested by these friends, these children repeatedly sought to be with each other across the day (in center time, free play outside, and in teacher-directed groups).

In general, studies of friendship and acceptance reveal that both are possible for children with disabilities. For example, in the Odom et al. (2002) study, about one-third (22 out of 80) of the children with disabilities were socially rejected by their peers (and this rate was slightly higher than that found for typically developing children), but about one-third (again 22 out of 80) of the children with disabilities were well accepted. And the reasonable assumption that acceptance and rejection would be related to severity of the disability is not always true. Ten children with significant disabilities were the focus of an exploration of how children with disabilities experience peer culture in the context of inclusive preschool environments (Wolfberg, et al., 1999). Overall developmental scores, as age equivalents, were low, and ranged from 22 months to 46 months, with a mean of 33 months for the 8 who were testable; in certain domains, such as social and communication skills, some of the testable children scored comparably to 12- and 14-month-old infants. However, four of the ten were well liked, and were viewed as highly desirable playmates on sociometric ratings, while six were among the least likely to be chosen as playmates. Consistent with their tested abilities, their attempts to join the social world were often similar to those of very young children in many respects, namely watching, following, touching, and imitating peers and playfully grabbing their toys. But they would also share their food, ask to play, and some would talk about their friends. Observational field notes allow the reader to obtain a sense about what is similar, and what may be different, in peer culture and friendship for young children with significant disabilities, through descriptions of the interactions that became evidence of the themes of expressing the desire to participate, experiencing inclusion, and experiencing exclusion.

At least three of these 10 children with significant to severe disabilities had mutual friendships, one with a typically developing child. Those friendships might include adaptations, such as bending down to be on eye-level when talking with a friend in a wheelchair, or sitting behind the friend on the carpet in circle time and on the slide to provide support. But these adaptations were simply to participate in activities the friends liked to do together—the friendships, as positive, mutual relationships, looked no different from those of other preschoolers.

CONCLUSION

Thus, by the time they are two, typically developing children with at least some consistent exposure to peers can have a friend. The same is true for older preschool children with disabilities. What both groups of children actually think about friendship, and what they can say about it, will develop dramatically over time (e.g., Gleason & Hohmann, 2006; Sebane, 2003), and certainly the interactive complexity of their friendships will continue to grow. But the precursors are present for many around 12–18 months, at least some have friendships before two, and more than a few have friendships at two or a little later. For some sociable toddlers, a friendship is a central part of their social life. Given that a friendship between very young peers not only reflects social skill development but also provides an important context for additional cognitive, social and emotional development, early friendship merits support. Following are ways that support may be achieved.

PRACTICAL IMPLICATIONS FOR PARENTS AND EARLY EDUCATORS

1. Though children may have more than one friend, and friendships can develop and thrive in a group context, friendship is dyadic—it is between two children. Time together as a dyad appears to support the development of friendships, and reinforces the togetherness of established and emerging friendships. In the group context, educators should allow the pair some interpersonal *privacy* so they can concentrate on their relationship. This may mean allowing the friendship pair to exclude others at times—this is protective of their interactive space. Parents can arrange dyadic play-dates, as many of the more complex interactions underlying friendship are more likely to occur when there are just two peers.

2. Attraction is unpredictable and elusive, but if there are hints of interest in each other or the same activities, adult facilitation may help a friendship to emerge. Educators can share information with parents about possible emerging friendships that might benefit from dyadic play-dates, outside the group care context, and parents can share information with teachers about peers their child appears to like or talk about.

3. Classrooms or other places housing groups of children can support the togetherness of established friendships and encourage the development of new ones by including small, cozy spaces just big enough for two as well as toys, materials, and playground equipment that need two partners in order to function well.

4. Adults should provide multiple toys and materials, or sets of them, thereby making it easy for children to do the same thing together, as similarity in action is centrally involved in early friendships.

5. Adults can allow noisy, silly, active play in the group, or the dyad, so that the children can have fun and share the closeness that comes from shared laughter. Running around the room, chasing, making noise, playing with large toys or furniture and so forth are perfect contexts for group and dyadic games that can become rituals for friendship dyads.

6. For younger children and those with special educational needs, some adult support may be necessary to actively bring children together, so they can be in close proximity. Parent and educators can act as *matchmakers*, arranging for children who have shown glimmers

of interest in each other, or in similar activities, to be together, both in the group context and separately.

7. Though adults are definitely in the background in the majority of descriptions of activities between young friends, adults can play a more active role. To help new friendships develop in children whose communication skills are just emerging, adults can sensitively join children in their play, help keep the interaction going if necessary, support early pretend play, and interpret children's behaviors to their peers, as necessary.

Thus, with some attention and planning, many young children, including those with developmental disabilities, can find and be friends.

REFERENCES

Asher, S. R., & Gottman, J. M. (Eds.). (1981). *The development of children's friendships.* New York: Cambridge University Press.

Asher, W. R., Parker, J. G., & Walker, D. L. (1996). Distinguishing friendship from acceptance: Implications for intervention and assessment. In W. F. Bukowski, A. F. Newcomb, & W. W. Hartup (Eds.), *The company they keep: Friendship in childhood and adolescence* (pp. 366–405). New York: Cambridge University Press.

Bridges, K. M. B. (1933). A study of social development in early infancy. *Child Development, 4,* 36–49.

Buysse, V. (1993). Friendships of preschoolers with disabilities in community-based child care settings. *Journal of Early Intervention, 17,* 380–395.

Buysse, V., & Bailey, D. B. (1993). Behavioral and developmental outcomes in young children with disabilities in integrated and segregated settings: A review of comparative studies. *Journal of Special Education, 26,* 434–461.

Buysse, V., Goldman, B. D., & Skinner, M. L. (2002). Setting effects on friendship formation among young children with and without disabilities. *Exceptional Children, 68,* 503–517.

Buysse, V., Nabors, L., Skinner, D., & Keyes, L. (1997). Playmate preferences and perceptions of individual differences among typically developing preschoolers. *Early Child Development and Care, 131,* 1–18.

Camaioni, L., Baumgartner, E., & Perucchini, P. (1991). Content and structure in toddlers' social competence with peers from 12 to 36 months of age. *Early Child Development and Care, 67,* 17–27.

Corsaro, W. A. (1985). *Friendship and peer culture in the early years.* Norwood, NJ: Ablex.

Dietrich, S. L. (2005). A look at friendships between preschool-aged children with and without disabilities in two inclusive classrooms. *Journal of Early Childhood Research, 3,* 193–215.

Faigin, H. (1958). Social behavior of young children in the kibbutz. *Journal of Abnormal and Social Psychology, 56,* 117–129.

Foot, H. C., Chapman, A. J., & Smith, J. R. (Eds.) (1980). *Friendship and social relations in children.* Chichester, UK: Wiley.

Field, T. (1984). Play behaviors of handicapped children who have friends. In T. Field, J. L. Roopnarine, & M. Segal (Eds.), *Friendships in normal and handicapped children* (pp. 153–162). Norwood, NJ: Ablex.

Furman, W. (1982). Children's friendships. In T. M. Field, A. Huston, H. C. Quay, L. Troll, & G. E. Finely (Eds.), *Review of human development* (pp. 327–339). New York: Wiley.

Gleason, T. R., & Hohmann, L. M. (2006). Concepts of real and imaginary friends in early childhood. *Social Development, 15,* 128–144.

Goldman, B. D., & Buysse, V. (2005). *Playmates and Friends Questionnaire for Teachers, 3rd Ed.* Chapel Hill: University of North Carolina, FPG Child Development Institute. Unpublished instrument, available from the authors or online at http://www.fpg.unc.edu/~publicationsoffice/pdfs/playmates_friends_rev.pdf.

Goldman, B. D., Buysse, V., Skinner, M., & Edgerton, D. (2005, April). *The differential impact of friendships vs. friends on peer interactions in preschool children with and without disabilities.* Poster presented at the Society for Research in Child Development Conference, Atlanta, GA.

Goldman, B. D., & Ross, H. S. (1978). Social skills in action: An analysis of early peer games. In J. Glick and K. A. Clarke-Stewart (Eds.), *Studies in social and cognitive development: Vol. 1. The development of social understanding* (pp. 177–212). New York: Gardner Press.

Gottman, J. M. (1983). How children become friends. *Monographs of the Society for Research in Child Development, 48* (Serial No. 201).

Guralnick, M. J. (1997). Peer social networks of young boys with developmental delays. *American Journal on Mental Retardation, 101,* 595–612.

Guralnick, M. J. (1999). The nature and meaning of social integration for young children with mild developmental delays in inclusive settings. *Journal of Early Intervention, 22,* 70–86.

Guralnick, M. J., & Groom, J. M. (1988). Friendships of preschool children in mainstreamed playgroups. *Developmental Psychology, 24,* 595–604.

Guralnick, M. J., Gottman, J. M., & Hammond, M. A. (1996). Effects of social setting on the friendship formation of young children differing in developmental status. *Journal of Applied Developmental Psychology, 17,* 625–651.

Hartup, W. W. (1983). Peer relations. In P. H. Mussen (Series Ed.) and E. M. Hetherington (Vol. Ed.), *Handbook of child psychology: Vol.4. Socialization, personality, and social development* (4th ed., pp. 103–196). New York: Wiley.

Hartup, W. W. (1989). Behavioral manifestations of children's friendships. In T. J. Berndt, & G. W. Ladd (Eds.), *Peer relations in child development* (pp. 46–70). New York: Wiley.

Hay, D. F. (1985). Learning to form relationships in infancy: Parallel attainments with parents and peers. *Developmental Review, 5,* 122–161.

Hinde, R. A., Titmus, G., Easton, D., & Tamplin, A. (1980). Friends and enemies: Cognitive bases for preschool children's unilateral and reciprocal relationships. *Child Development, 51,* 1276–1279.

Howes, C. (1983). Patterns of friendship. *Child Development, 54,* 1041–1053.

Howes, C. (1988). Peer interaction of young children. *Monograph of the Society for Research in Child Development, 53*(1, Serial No. 217)

Howes, C. (1996). The earliest friendships. In W. M. Bukowski, A. F. Newcomb, & W. W. Hartup (Eds.), *The company they keep: Friendship in childhood and adolescence* (pp. 66–86). New York: Cambridge University Press.

Howes, C., & Farver, J. (1987). Toddlers' responses to the distress of their peers. *Developmental Psychology, 8,* 441–452.

Ladd, G. W. (2005a). *Children's peer relations and social competence: A century of progress.* New Haven: Yale University Press.

Ladd, G. W. (2005b). The emergence of peer interaction and sociability. In G. W. Ladd, *Children's peer relations and social competence: A century of progress.* New Haven: Yale University Press.

Ladd, G. W., Herald, S. L., & Andrews, R. K. (2006). Young children's peer relationships and social competence. In B. Spodek & O. N. Saracho (Eds.), *Handbook of research on the education of young children* (pp. 23–54). Mahwah, NJ: Erlbaum.

Lamorey, S., & Bricker, D. (1993). Integrated programs: Effects on young children and their parents. In C. A. Peck, S. L. Odom, & D. D. Bricker (Eds.), *Integrating young children with disabilities into community-based programs: Ecological perspectives on research and implementation* (pp. 249–270). Baltimore: Paul H. Brookes.

Lokken, G. (2000a). The playful quality of the toddling "style." *Qualitative Studies in Education, 13,* 531–542.

Lokken, G. (2000b). Tracing the social style of toddler peers. *Scandinavian Journal of Educational Research, 44,* 163–176.

Mueller, E. C., & Cooper, C. R. (Eds.). (1986). *Process and outcome in peer relationships.* Orlando: Academic Press.

Mueller, E., & Lucas, T. (1975). A developmental analysis of peer interaction among toddlers. In M. Lewis & L. A. Rosenblum (Eds.), *The origins of behavior: Friendship and peer relations* (pp. 223–257). New York: Wiley.

Mueller, E., & Vandell, D. (1979). Infant–infant interaction. In J. D Osofsky (Ed.), *Handbook of infant development* (pp. 591–622). New York: Wiley.

Musatti, T., & Panni, S. (1981). Social behavior and interaction among day-care center toddlers. *Early Child Development and Care, 7,* 5–27.

Odom, S. L., & Diamond, K. E. (1998). Inclusion of young children with special needs in early childhood education: The research base. *Early Childhood Research Quarterly, 13,* 3–25.

Odom, S. L., Zercher, C., Marquart, J., Li, S., Sandall, S. R., & Wolfberg, P. (2002). Social relationships of children with disabilities and their peers in inclusive preschool classrooms. In S. L. Odom (Ed.), *Widening the circle: Including children with disabilities in preschool programs* (pp. 61–80). New York: Teachers College Press.

Parker, J. G., Rubin, K. H., Price, J. M., & DeRosier, M. E. (1995). Peer relationships, child development, and adjustment: A developmental psychopathology perspective. In D. Cicchetti & D. Cohen (Eds.), *Developmental psychopathology: Vol. 2: Risk, disorder, and adaptation* (pp. 96–161). New York: Wiley.

Price, J. M., & Ladd, G. W. (1986). Assessment of children's friendships: Implications for social competence and social adjustment. *Advances in Behavioral Assessment of Children and Families, 2,* 121–149.

Roopnarine, J. L., & Field, T. M. (1984). Play interactions of friends and acquaintances in nursery school. In T. M. Field, J. L. Roopnarine, & M. Segal (Eds.), *Friendships in normal and handicapped children* (pp. 89–98). Norwood, NJ: Ablex.

Ross, H. S. (1982). Establishment of social games among toddlers. *Developmental Psychology, 18,* 509–518.

Ross, H. S., & Goldman, B. D. (1977). Establishing new social relations in infancy. In T. Alloway, P. Pliner, & L. Krames, (Eds.), *Advances in the study of communication and affect, Vol. 3: Attachment behavior* (pp. 61–79). New York: Plenum.

Renshaw, P. D. (1981). The roots of peer interaction research: A historical analysis of the 1930s. In S. R. Asher & J. M. Gottman (Eds.), *The development of children's friendships.* New York: Cambridge University Press.

Rubenstein, J., & Howes, C. (1976). The effects of peers on toddler interaction with mother and toys. *Child Development, 47,* 597–605.

Rubin, K. H., Bukowski, W., & Parker, J. G. (1998). Peer interactions, relationships, and groups. In W. Damon (Ed.), *Handbook of child psychology. Vol. 3, Social, Emotional, and Personality Development* (5th ed, pp. 619–700. New York, Wiley.

Rubin, K. H., & Ross, H. S. (Eds.). (1982). *Peer relationships and social skills in childhood.* New York: Springer-Verlag.

Rubin, Z. (1980). *Children's friendships.* Cambridge, MA: Harvard University Press.

Sebane, A. M. (2003). The friendship features of preschool children: Links with prosocial behavior and aggression. *Social Development, 12,* 249–268.

Stambak, M., & Verba, M. (1986). Organization of social play among toddlers: An ecological approach. In E. D. Mueller & C. R. Cooper (Eds.), *Process and outcome in peer relationships* (pp. 229–247). Orlando: Academic Press.

Stone, L. J., Smith, H. T., & Murphy, L. (1973). *The competent infant.* New York: Basic Books.

U.S. Department of Education. (2003). *Twenty-fourth annual report to congress on the implementation of the Individuals with Disabilities Education Act.* Washington, DC: Author. Retrieved April 19, 2005, from http://www.ed.gov/about/reports/annual/osep/2002index.html.

Vandell, D. L., & Mueller, E. C. (1980). Peer play and friendships during the first two years. In H. C. Foot, A. J. Chapman, & J. R. Smith (Eds.), *Friendship and social relations in children* (pp. 191–208). London: Wiley.

Vandell, D. L., Nenide, L., & Van Winkle, S. J. (2006). Peer relationships in early childhood. In K. McCartney & D. Phillips (Eds.), *Blackwell handbook of early childhood development* (pp. 455–470). Malden, MA: Blackwell.

Vincze, M. (1971). The social contacts of infants and young children reared together. *Early Child Development and Care, 1,* 99–109.

Vincze, M. (1974). Patterning of common activities in a group of infants. Unpublished translation of "Az egyuttes tevekenyseg alakulasa egy egyutt nevelkedo csoportban 3 honapos kortol 2½ eves korig." *Pszichologiai Tanulmanyok, 10,* 289–295.

Whaley, K. L., & Rubenstein, T. S. (1994). How toddlers "do" friendship: A descriptive analysis of naturally occurring friendships in a group child care setting. *Journal of Social and Personal Relationships, 11,* 383–400.

Wittmer, D., & Petersen, M. A. (1992, April). Social development and integration: Facilitating the prosocial development of typical and exceptional infants and toddlers in group settings. *Zero to Three, Bulletin of the National Center for Clinical Infant Programs, 12*(4), 14–20.

Wolfberg, P. J., Zercher, C., Lieber, J, Capell, K., Matias, S., Hanson, M. & Odom, S. L. (1999). "Can I play with you?" Peer culture in inclusive preschool programs. *The Journal of the Association for Persons with Severe Handicaps, 24,* 69–84

Zaslow, M. (1980). Relationships among peers in kibbutz toddler groups. *Child Psychiatry and Human Development, 10,* 178–189.

CHAPTER 9

CONFRONTING ISSUES OF BULLYING

Implications for Early Childhood Education

Vickie E. Lake

Once thought of as only a middle or high school problem, there is growing concern that bullying behaviors are now firmly established in early childhood settings. In a study of third graders, 40% of the children reported being a victim of bullying and 14% reported being the bully (Silvernail, Thompsom, Yang, & Kopp, 2000). Kochenderfer and Ladd's (1997) study of kindergartners reported that approximately half of the children experienced some form of victimization. Acts of bullying and victimization have increasingly become areas of concern for childcare centers and elementary schools. "Research to date suggests we can accept as a reasonable generality that any school anticipate bullying occurring, although with varying degrees of severity" (Smith & Brain, 2000, p. 2). The main focus of the past research has been on individual children, either the bully or the victim (Olweus, 1993). However, one of the key challenges for current researchers is to better understand the role peers play in the bully/victim circle of violence.

Contemporary Perspectives on Socialization and Social Development..., pages 193–211
Copyright © 2007 by Information Age Publishing

THEORIES

There are many theories underlying antisocial behavior. Some scholars believe that aggression is the product of biological and/or genetic factors (Mednick, Moffitt, & Stack, 1987). While other theories include links to mental disorders (Hodgins, 1993) and obstetric/perinatal complications (Casaer, de Vries, & Marlowe, 1991). A psychosocial review of the literature reveals a long list of risk factors such as broken homes, single-parent families, teenage parents, family discord, abuse or neglect, coercive parenting, lack of supervision, family criminality, poverty, large family size, delinquent peer groups, poor schooling, and living in a disorganized area (Farrington, 1995; Junger-Tas, 1992; Loeber & Stoughamer-Loeber, 1986). The strongest association is between delinquency and parent criminality, but it is still unclear whether this association is more influenced by genetic or environmental factors (Rowe & Farrington, 1997).

Not only do family issues impact children but difficult children also appear to influence parenting styles in their households. Parents may change their discipline strategies as a result or consequence of having a difficult child (Rutter & Giller, 1983). Until the 1960s it was believed that there was a casual effect of the environment on the child. However, "it is now clear that the finding could mean at least in part, that children who behave in difficult, disruptive, and socially disapproved ways may cause other people to feel rejecting towards them" (Rutter, Giller, & Hagell, 1998, p. 171).

Considering the evidence regarding parenting, there are several divergent viewpoints. First, on parental effects on child behaviors, there is evidence that demonstrates that the quality of the parenting resulted from past experiences before their children were born (Rutter et al., 1998). Second, it is most likely that parents and children affect each other in a give and take environment or bidirectionally (Patterson, 1995). Finally, experiences individuals bring about by their own behavior have critical consequences for them. People choose to continue antisocial behaviors based on reasons that stem from their personality and the social context (Rutter, Silberg, & Simonoff, 1993). The divergent points add depth to the psychosocial literature but do not provide clarity about whether the association is more influenced by genetic or environmental factors.

Rutter et al. (1998) made the connection between antisocial/bullying behaviors and hyperactivity. Young children who are hyperactive or inattentive are more likely to have difficult temperaments, emotional liabilities, relentlessness, short attention spans, negativism, and rough play behavior. They also found that these children had difficulties in classroom peer relationships. Farrington, Loeber, and Van Kammen's (1990) research also support the connection of hyperactivity and antisocial behavior. However, because the behavior originated in early childhood, they believe it will continue into adulthood.

Studies indicate that people who engage in antisocial or bullying behaviors, which then lead to later criminal acts, are different than the regular population (Farrington, 1995; Jessor & Jessor, 1977; Smith, 1995). The retrospective findings reveal: (a) when they were very young, the individuals repeatedly engaged in antisocial behaviors and had trouble getting along with other children, and they were oppositional and disruptive; (b) when young, they were impulsive and sought excitement; (c) in adolescence they had more reading difficulties, more drug abuse, and reported more feelings of misery; and (d) in early adulthood they were often heavy drinkers, unemployed for periods of time, experienced difficulties in relationships, debts, gambling, and violence.

Although there are many theories for aggression, antisocial, and bullying behaviors, among the most heavily researched is the psychosocial theory discussed here. Children affect how others respond to them, some of the "effects that seem to be environmentally mediated actually represent genetic transmission in part, and that some factors are associated with antisocial behavior only because of their indirect connection with proximal causal processes" (Rutter et al., 1998, p. 212). However, it is the children's effect on their peers and vise-versa that is the focus of this chapter. Most bullying research has been conducted on the aggressor or the victim (Olweus, 1993), but has not concentrated on the influences of the peer group on the bully/victim relationship.

BULLYING BEHAVIORS

When educators think about bullying they usually envision a physical bully. However, bullying includes verbal and psychological behaviors such as teasing, taunting, and manipulating social relationships (Banks, 1997; Ericson, 2001). Olweus' (1993) definition of bullying is one of the most widely used: (a) the behavior is aggressive and negative, (b) the behavior is carried out repeatedly, and (c) the behavior occurs in a relationship where there is an imbalance of power between the subjects involved. His definition is further refined to include two subgroups of bullying. The first subgroup, more often used by boys, is called direct bullying and includes overt, physical contact in which the victim is openly attacked. Indirect bullying takes the shape of social isolation, manipulation, and intentional exclusion. Underwood, Galen, and Paquette (2001) disagree with the phrase indirect and use the term social aggression instead because it describes the harmful intentions of the bullying behavior. Whichever term you prefer, girls more often employ this type of social exclusion.

Banks (1997) states that many bullies share a need to feel powerful and in control. Many derive satisfaction from inflicting injury and suffering on others, seem to have little empathy for their victims, and often defend their actions by saying that their victims provoked them in some way. The U.S. government tracks bullying and reports rates and frequencies in the Indicators of School Crime and Safety Report (2005) for students ages 12–18. This document indicates that incidences of reported bullying increased in schools between 1999–2001. The report goes on to conclude that "grade level was inversely related to students' likelihood of being bullied: as grade level increased, students' likelihood of being bullied decreased" (p. 38). Hence, even though children under 12 years of age are not included in the reporting system, the message is clear: the younger you are, the higher your chances are of being bullied.

Aggressive behaviors in children have been found to remain stable over time and lead to more aggression (Huesmann, Eron, Lefkowitz, & Walder, 1984). A study by Olweus (1991) revealed that approximately 60% of boys identified as bullies in elementary school had at least one criminal conviction at age 24. A similar finding demonstrated that a majority of incarcerated males had been labeled as a bully in their school file by age 8 (Garbarino, 1999). And yet there is minimal official bullying identification in the elementary age group and no process for the early childhood group. Reporting, training, and intervention need to begin at the preschool level, because aggression is steady; those who exhibit aggressive behavior in childhood are more likely to exhibit antisocial and aggressive behaviors in adolescents and adulthood (Huesmann et al.)

Adapting Adolescent Literature for Application to Early Childhood Bullying

Olweus (1979) and Loeber and Hay (1997) identified the role that peers play in promoting bullying and victimization as a gap in the research during early adolescence. The authors indicate that peers play a significant role in promoting bullying and victimization by either

- reinforcing the aggressor,
- failing to intervene to stop the victimization, or
- affiliating with students who bully.

These three descriptors are not directly applicable to early childhood due to the differences in developmental levels. However, modifications can be made in the role played by peers in order to make it applicable to younger aged children. Because of the importance of examining this issue thorough research needs to be conducted in the area of early childhood education. The role that peers play in promoting bullying and victimization may be addressed by either:

- ignoring and supporting the aggressor, or defending themselves from the aggressor, and
- failing to intervene to stop the victimization because of a lack of verbal scripts and/or social skills training.

These modifications are aligned with the prior research on early childhood aggression and bullying behaviors as well as developmental characteristics of young children. Antisocial and aggressive behaviors usually take place in groups and children are more likely to continue to exhibit these behaviors when they belong to a group (Rutter et al., 1998). Similarities in antisocial and aggressive behavior are hallmarks that define childhood peer groups (Cairns & Cairns, 1991). Classmates often dislike children who belong to peer groups that engage in aggressive/bullying behaviors, however most aggressive children belong to established subgroups of similar children and are even described as "best friends" in this smaller context. Though small in numbers, the bully peer group can be a powerful influence in classroom settings by ridiculing and victimizing other children. Covertly this group is in competition for hegemony in the classroom milieu (Cairns, Cairns, Neckerman, Gest, & Gariepy, 1988). Thus, it is imperative that teachers not only examine their pedagogy for correct standards and objectives, but also for inequities of power (McLaren, 2003).

Inequities of power may be present between and within group and subgroup dynamics in the classroom. Figure 9.1 illustrates the different roles that peers play in the bully/victim interactions (Olweus, 2001). As the figure makes clear, one bully/victim interaction is actually part of the larger peer group dynamic. O'Connell, Pepler, and Craig (1999) found that peers were present in 85% of bullying incidents which took place on playgrounds and in classrooms and many adopted roles similar to those identified by Olweus' (see Figure 9.1). Peers spent nearly 23% of their time actively joining with the bully to abuse the victim in the Followers/Henchmen role. In the Henchmen role, the peers share in the bully's status and power by becoming accomplices. Peers, who take on the role of inciting or reinforcing the bully and may help to prolong the bullying episode, are called Supporters or Passive Bullies. Passive Supporters/Possible Bullies are watchers of the bullying episode, but do not take an active role. The Disengaged Onlookers are outsiders who are inactive and pretend not to see what is happening. Peers, who want to help the victim but are scared to help, are Possible Defenders, and Defenders of the Victim are the peers who step forward to help and try to stop the bullying episode. Salmivalli, Lagerspetz, Bjorkzvist, Osterman, and Kaukiainen (1996) found that roles could be assigned to 87% of students who are present at a bullying episode.

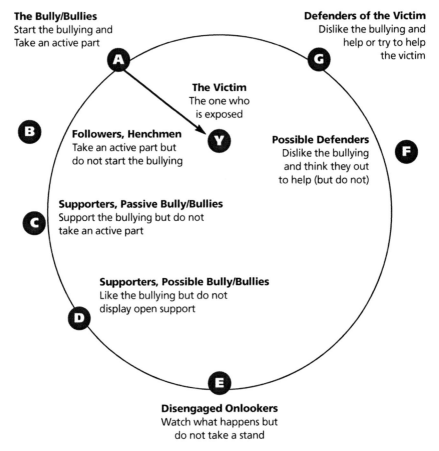

Figure 9.1.   The bullying cycle. Students' modes of reaction/roles in an acute bullying situation (Olweus, 2001).

RELATIONAL AND PHYSICAL BULLYING

Olweus (1993) reports that schools are where most bullying incidents occur and while at school, nearly all bullying happens in the places where there is the least supervision. In Arnold, Homrok, Ortiz, and Stowe's (1999) study on peer rejection and aggression in six childcare center classrooms, they described the classrooms unstructured and unsupervised activities as accounting for the "high rates of [rejection and aggressive] behaviors" (p. 187). They found that the number of peer rejection acts children received was closely connected to their levels of aggressive acts.

The emergence of these behaviors needs to be better understood, but these findings raise the possibility that, at least in young children, rejection acts do not play a primary casual role in the development of aggression, while aggression acts may play a central, casual role in a children's experience of rejection acts. (p. 192)

They suggest that further studies include peer relationships of aggressive children that include prevention and intervention programs.

Relational Aggression

Nelson, Robinson, and Hart (2005) in a landmark study were the first to demonstrate that preschool girls, ages 4 and 5, participated in exclusionary behavior and threats to withdraw friendship as two examples of relational aggression or relational bullying. Relational bullying is not conducted in isolation, but relies on peer support to be effective. This study states that preschoolers establish and maintain social hierarchies much in the same way as adolescents. Nelson (2005) explains further, "We are all aware of girls who secure their social hierarchy through relationship manipulation during adolescence, but it is striking that these aggressive strategies are already apparent and related to increased social centrality in preschool" (¶4). Several of the relational bullying tactics preschool girls employ are:

- Not allowing a specific child (usually another girl) to play with the group.
- Demanding other children, again usually girls, not to play with a specific child.
- Threatening to not play with a child unless certain needs/demands are met.
- Refusing to listen to someone they are mad at (the aggressive children may even cover their ears).

Physical Aggression

Aggression develops early in life and physical aggression in children under the age of 10 is an indicator of future violent behavior (Elliott, Hamburg, & Williams, 1998). Chess and Thomas (1991) found that aggressive children were more active, more irregular, had lower thresholds for tolerating differences, were low on adaptability, and were rated high on intensity, persistence, and distractibility. When compared with normal developing children, aggressive children extract very different responses from both children and adults. In many classrooms, peers reject aggressive children and they are left out of peer playgroups. Thus, creating a pattern of negative social behavior based on constant rejection of their classmates (Asher & Dodge, 1986; Newcomb, Bukowski, & Pattee, 1993; Parker & Asher, 1987).

However, not all aggressive children are rejected by their peers (Cairns et al., 1988). Cairns and Cairns (1994) discovered that smaller subgroups of aggressive peers would form within the classroom. Strayer's (1980) work established that in preschool settings children formed same sex groups based on individual similarities, such as aggression styles. These groups contained elaborate hierarchies that centered on one or a core group of dominant children who were looked up to and imitated more during playtime than the nondominant passive children.

Farver (1996), in a study with 60 four-year-olds, found evidence supporting Cairns and Cairns' (1994) and Strayer's (1990) work that aggressive preschool children formed groups of "aggressive individuals and reciprocated friendships with children similar to themselves" (p. 344). She noted that one child was the bully or nucleus of the group, while other aggressive children acted in more peripheral, secondary, or isolated support roles much in the same way as outlined by Olweus (2001) in Figure 9.1. Farver reported that children closer to the bully conducted more aggressive acts per hour than children further away from the bully in the aggressive group. Her implications stress that instead of targeting a specific child as the bullying instigator; efforts should concentrate on the larger peer group.

> However, it may be more important for the teacher to become aware of how play group dynamics function to promote and maintain children's aggressive behavior. . . . Furthermore, because young children's affiliations are not static, teachers should intervene by helping to reform or realign the composition of children's social cliques. (Farver, p. 347)

Media Influences

Adequate knowledge of an aggressive group is critical information for a teacher. Physical bully groups might be formed and influenced from television watching and the media. It is estimated that children watch more than 28 hours of television each week (Feldman, Coats, & Spielman, 1996). Instead of talking to an adult, playing with siblings or friends, or going to school, children in the United States spend more time watching the television. An average child, before the age of 12, has viewed over 8,000 TV enacted murders. Preschool children are curious and easily influenced, often mimicking and repeating what they see and hear on television without knowledge of right and wrong (Simmons, Stalsworth, & Wentzel, 1999). Children between the ages of 2 and 8 are even more vulnerable to television violence due to their maturational inability to separate what they view from reality (Aidman, 1998). Research on children and television violence illustrates that exposure to televised violence increases aggressive behaviors (Berkowitz, 1962), causes children to be more accepting of aggressive behaviors in others (Noble, 1975), and can be a better predictor of adult aggression than socioeconomic and childrearing factors (Simmons et al.).

Fortis-Diaz (1998) observed her own kindergarten children during free play and noticed aggressive acts of play from a particular group of boys and in "every instance there was a more powerful winner over a weaker, defeated 'victim'" (p. 233). On one hand she struggled with the gender differences she observed in the unstructured free play and did not want to ban one kind of play, but this peer group appeared to be stuck imitating violent media images that she felt were more likely to cause injury than they were to foster development. Therefore, she decided to implement daily discussions about free play with the children, thus allowing her to find out what the children were playing, why they chose those themes (such as cops), and the misconceptions surrounding the themes. Through the daily conversations, the class confronted their misinformation, the teacher brought in guest speakers, and she introduced the concept of changing to more non-aggressive behavior during free play. Fortis-Diaz concluded that children would, when given appropriate instruction, choose for themselves to create safer free play environments.

Rough and Tumble Play

Aggressive play includes the infliction of bodily harm and often includes anger and resentment, which is very different from the type of play known as rough and tumble play (Reed & Brown, 2000). Rough and tumble play consists of running, chasing, fleeing, wrestling, open-hand slapping, pushing, falling, and play fighting. Pellegrini (1995) has established a clear connection between boys rough and tumble play and social problem solving, academic achievement, alternative role taking, negotiating give-and-take, deciding who follows and who leads, and social dominance. Aggressive play accounts for less than 5% of play on playgrounds (Pellegrini, 1988). Reed and Brown analyzed rough and tumble play behaviors of elementary age boys and discovered that rough and tumble play was the means by which they expressed care and intimacy towards each other. However, the type of care expressed in rough and tumble play does not fit into the traditional framework of care and many teachers do not recognize it as such.

Acknowledging Relational and Physical Peer Groups

It is not a secret that bullying is happening in our centers and schools. Shidler (2001) argues that "violence occurs every day within earshot of teachers, ranging from verbal taunts or pushing, shoving and other types of physical contact" (p. 167) and that teachers often do nothing. Thus, damaging the self-esteem and dignity of children and perpetuating the bullying cycle. In relational and physical bullying it is critical to acknowledge the power of the bully and his or her immediate Followers/Henchmen and Supporters/Passive Bullies in the classroom milieu. As educators we need to examine our own classroom spaces to see how we can minimize times when bullying might be taking place. The room might need to be reorganized to increase visibility. Instead of free choice centers, redefine groups or access to the centers for an adequate period of time to help limit bullying. Recruit parental help if possible or cross-grade tutors to help monitor peer interactions.

Close attention should be paid to media influences on play behaviors of peer groups because children's worldviews are cognitively impaired when they over rely on television for entertainment (Kellner, 1990). "Children no longer live in the secret garden of childhood" (Steinberg & Kincheloe, 2004, p. 30). Through television they see and hear adult images and have access to an adult world, which increases their anger, irritability, verbal aggression, fear, anxiety, and desensitizes their threshold towards violence (National Coalition on Television Violence, n.d.). While it is true that aggressive children remain marginalized by many of their classroom peers, the research demonstrates that most children form smaller subgroups of similar aggressive characteristics. Adults must be aware of who the children are in the group that support the bully, ignore the bully, and those who defend themselves against the bullying peer group. With this information, appropriate interventions for each specific group may be developed.

Bullying usually takes place outside of the classroom, before and after school, in the hallways, and on playgrounds (Olweus, 2003). Therefore, an increase in teacher visibility during outside play by having them spread out and walk the playground area would help decrease bullying peer group behavior (Leff, Power, Costigan, & Manz, 2003). The goal of recess or developmental play should be to encourage children's social competence, which will enable them to adapt skillfully to the demands of their school and peer relationships (Pellegrini & Glickman, 1990). Teachers should not police the playground and constrict the only free time children have in their very structured day.

LACK OF VERBAL SCRIPTS AND SOCIAL SKILLS TRAINING

Curriculum and Methods

When examining early childhood curriculum textbooks the focus of the first few chapters are typically on building relationships, getting to know the children, and creating a supportive classroom environment (e.g., Gestwicki, 1999; Jalongo & Isenberg, 2000; Trister Dodge, Jablon, & Bichart, 1994). Early childhood educators understand that building a caring environment is crucial to children's emotional and intellectual development, and only after this environment is firmly in place, can the rest of the curriculum emerge. The specific teaching of anti-bullying verbal scripts should be integrated into the curriculum targeting children in every role in the bully/victim circle (Figure 9.1). Victims and potential victims (Possible Defenders) need scripts to defend themselves. Children who take on the roles of Supporters/Passive Bullies, Passive Supporters/Possible Bullies, and Disengaged Onlookers, need a different set a scripts because bystanding or avoidance leads to desensitization to others' suffering (Safran & Safran, 1985). Many children stay in the Passive or Disengaged roles because they do not know what to do or do not want to do the wrong thing (Cowie, 2000). Providing verbal scripts is one anti-bullying strategy teachers can implement to arm all children against the bully peer group.

Lake (2001) discussed specific strategies to integrate moral elements and behaviors into the classroom curriculum. Children enjoy discussions of issues of right and wrong, fairness, including everyone in a group, name-calling, and tattling. Teachers can create lively and rich dialogue by tapping into what children feel is important to them and by using these situations as topics for conversations or storytelling events. During the discussions, teachers have an opportunity to teach the specific scripts and provide practice and feedback to the children, such as a role-play. Cowie (2000) found that students expressed an increase in self-confidence, responsibility, safety, and a decrease in bullying in their schools when they were trained to use conflict resolution skills by trained peer mediators. These conflict resolution trainings included anti-bullying scripts. "Adults play a significant role in this process by giving young people appropriate skills and by providing a supportive environment in which to practice their skill" (p. 87).

All children are peacemakers and learn peacemaking skills in the cooperative learning framework outlined by Johnson, Johnson, and Holubec (1994). The skills learned are caring, listening, and perspective taking, which then lead to non-violent resolution of conflicts. Skills are taught by role-playing and allowing the children to explain their feelings, responses, and alternatives to each situation. Other strategies include using puppets, books, and asking, "what else could they do in the story?" or "what else could they have said?" Cowie, Smith, Boulton, and Laver's (1994) work has documented that cooperative learning decreases victimization of vulnerable children within classroom settings. Bullies and their Followers/Henchmen often characterize their victims as deserving, being odd, and use language to justify their aggression (Teräsahjo & Salmivalli, 2003). The group work and prosocial skills involved in cooperative learning require children to work together face-to-face, fully attend to each other, collaborate, and develop mini-communities in table or desk groupings (Johnson et al.). Thus, minimizing social cliques within classroom and reducing victimization.

Classroom Management

The most common type of classroom management system in early childhood education is some form of assertive discipline (Kohn, 1993). While effective in maintaining control of children in the short term, this type of management system does nothing to foster social scripts, social behaviors, and actually promotes the idea that children must conform to adult behaviors (Bailey 1997, 2000; Kohn, 1993, 1996). When a child misbehaves, the adult punishes him or her, maybe talks to or at the child; however in only a very small handful of cases does the child practice saying or doing the behavior in the correct way. Discipline approaches that utilize power and control decrease prosocial behaviors in children (Krevans & Gibbs, 1996; Stanhope, Bell, & Parker-Cohen, 1987). Classroom misbehavior can actually provide an ideal opportunity to teach anti-bullying verbal scripts. Practicing scripts via role-playing is a powerful technique as it allows children to apply the language and to be ready with the appropriate response before a bullying incidence occurs.

Curriculum for the Whole Child

Verbal scripts are powerful tools in early childhood bullying prevention. Many children do not have the language skills to say "No," "Stop," "Stay away from her/him," "We don't like that," "Go away," "We don't like it when you call us names," just to name a few specific scripts that are commonly taught. Harrist and Bradley (2003) discuss the need for role-playing to prevent social exclusion in targeted kindergarten classrooms. Their study extends Paley's (1992) work in which she addressed the need for scripting and role-playing as two strategies to increase social awareness and peer group interaction while decreasing social cliques in the classroom. However, with the current emphasis on standards-based education and school readiness, many teachers feel overwhelmed and burdened teaching the stated or mandated curriculum. They state that they do not have the time or the administrative support to focus on verbal scripting, social skills training, or role playing, which they know are crucial skills for children to acquire (Lickona, 1991) in order to confront the bully peer group. A shift in classroom practices needs to occur with more emphasis going to the immediate concerns of the whole child, not just the child's academic needs. "Children must be seen as the richest source of curriculum because by rights, they are the curriculum" (Hauser & Jipson, 1998, p. 157).

RECOMMENDATIONS AND CONCLUSION

This analysis adds to the literature in early childhood by identifying, then adapting, the research on adolescent bullying research to make it applicable to bullying in younger aged children. Olweus (1979) and Loeber and Hay (1997) identified the need to address peers contributions in bullying victimization. The purpose of this chapter was to demonstrate that this is not only an adolescent problem, but an early childhood issue as well. Young children are involved in bullying peer groups that play a significant role in the bullying victimization cycle of violence.

Why do children form bully peer groups? For boys, the research indicates that personality characteristics or typical reaction patterns combined with physical strengths or weaknesses are very important indicators (Olweus, 2003). Additionally, environmental factors such as the "attitudes, behavior, and routines of relevant adults—in particular, teachers and principals—play a crucial role in determining the extent to which bullying problems will manifest themselves in a larger unit, such as a classroom or school" (p. 14). For girls the data is not conclusive. However, it is clear that addressing just the bully or victim and not including the roles that peers play in the bully/victim circle will not help to extend our understanding of the problem and decrease the behaviors.

Two things must change in order for there to be a significant decrease in bullying behaviors in early childhood education: educators must (a) understand the harm bullying can have on all children in their classrooms and actively confront bullying and victim behaviors by implementing a stated anti-bullying curriculum, and (b) address bullying as a peer group construct. As the bully/victim circle of violence illustrates (see Figure 9.1), bullying episodes are not carried out in isolation, because peers are present and can be identified as having a role (Cowie, 2000).

In classroom settings teachers unconsciously treat boys and girls differently; for example, boys being taught independence and girl's dependency (McLaren, 2003). This is known as the hidden curriculum, that is, unintentional outcomes of the classroom or schooling process. Like the stated curriculum, the hidden curriculum includes teaching and learning styles that are emphasized in the classroom as well as tacit ways that knowledge and behavior get constructed outside of the classroom materials and lessons. It is in this hidden landscape that bully peer groups exist and operate. Children are reporting increased levels of victimization—40% of 3rd graders

(Silvernail et al., 2000) and 50% of kindergartners (Kochenderfer & Ladd, 1997)—yet teachers remain unaware of the amount of victimization. Almost half of the bullied children never tell their teachers, or another adult, that they were bullied (Smith & Shu, 1998). The research clearly demonstrates that children are learning about bullying in school. A concern for early childhood educators would be whether we want children to learn about bullying from other children through the hidden curriculum because the teacher is unaware, or do we want them to learn about bullying in a classroom that has taken a proactive stance?

Given that children identified as bullies often continue to engage in aggressive and antisocial behaviors through adolescence and into adulthood (Farrington, 1995; Jessor & Jessor, 1977; Smith, 1995), anti-bullying prevention programs in early childhood would appear to be a more effective strategy than remedial programs. A promising intervention model, peer group restructuring, states that children's natural groups must be identified before their social status can be improved (Rodkin & Hodges, 2003). Peer groups usually have between three and seven members and share similar gender and behavior. Because most teachers do not understand the culture of peer groups within their classrooms, they need to be trained to see the social rank of children operating within different groups. Teachers are encouraged to "understand how the critical social elements of status, peer groups, friendships, and enemy relationships are patterned in their classrooms" (p. 390). Teachers who are successful guide their children toward higher levels of moral reasoning, exhibit caring behaviors in the classroom, and anticipate interpersonal problems by knowing their children's social status, peer groups, friends, and enemies. These teachers also understand that the bully/victim relationship always involves a power imbalance that affects peers (Olweus, 1993) and they are constantly looking for clues within the peer groups for evidence of this imbalance.

Addressing both the school and home, the Olweus Bullying Prevention Program (1993, 2001) has over 25 years of research on the identification of problem behaviors, especially aggressive behaviors, and has identified four key principles needed in order to create a safe environment.

1. Warmth, positive interest, and involvement from adults;
2. Firm limits on unacceptable behavior;
3. Consistent application of nonpunitive, nonphysical sanctions for unacceptable behavior or violations of rules; and
4. Adults who act as authorities and positive role models.

When specifically addressing the needs of a school, the administration, teachers, and parents need to form a bullying prevention coordinating committee, train staff, provide time for discussion groups, and provide effective supervision during recess and lunch periods. At the classroom level, prevention measures include, classroom and school rules specifically addressing bullying, regular classroom meetings that address bullying behaviors, and meetings with students' parents.

Olweus (1993) also recommends that teachers participate in social milieu development programs where problems concerning bullying and victimization are explored and discussed. A common theme of many anti-bullying programs is that teachers need to demonstrate complete intolerance for bullying and get children to do likewise. Passively allowing social cliques and bully peer groups to form can be the death of an overall sense of community in any teacher's classroom (Lickona, 1991). "Universal moral values—such as treating all people justly and respecting their lives, liberty, and equality—bind all persons everywhere because they affirm our fundamental human worth and dignity" (Lickona, p. 38).

> Given the normative nature of bullying, it will be a continual struggle to keep it to within acceptable limits—limits such that suicides caused by bullying, actual physical harm to victims, or life-long depression and feelings of low self-worth in those victimized become rare indeed. (Smith & Brain, 2000, p. 7)

ACKNOWLEDGMENTS

I wish to thank Diana C. Rice and Stephanie Al Otaiba for their support with this chapter.

REFERENCES

Aidman, A. (1998). Television violence: Content, context, and consequences. *The ERIC Review, 7*(1), 8–11.

Arnold, D. H., Homrok, S., Ortiz, C., & Stowe, R. M. (1999). Direct observation of peer rejection acts and their temporal relation with aggressive acts. *Early Childhood Research Quarterly, 14*(2), 183–196.

Asher, S. R., & Dodge, K. (1986). Identifying children who are rejected by their peers. *Developmental Psychology, 22,* 444–449.

Bailey, B. A. (1997). *There's gotta be a better way: Discipline that works!* Oviedo, FL: Loving Guidance.

Bailey, B. A. (2000). *Conscious discipline: 7 basic skills for brain smart classroom management.* Oviedo, FL: Loving Guidance.

Banks, R. (1997). *Bullying in schools.* Office of Educational Research and Improvement. U.S. Department of Education, ERIC: Washington DC: U.S. Government Printing Office.

Berkowitz, L. (1962). *Aggression: A social psychological analysis.* New York: McGraw-Hill.

Cairns, B., & Cairns, R. (1991). Social cognition and social networks: a developmental perspective. In D. J. Pepler & K. H. Rubin (Eds.), *The development and treatment of childhood aggression* (pp. 249–278). Hillsdale, NJ: Erlbaum.

Cairns, R., & Cairns, B. (1994). *Lifelines and risks: Pathways of youth in our times.* Cambridge: Cambridge University Press.

Cairns, R., Cairns, B., Neckerman, H., Gest, S., & Gariepy, J. (1988). Social networks and aggressive behavior: Peer support or peer rejection? *Developmental Psychology, 24,* 815–823.

Casaer, P., de Vries, L., & Marlowe, N. (1991). Prenatal and perinatal risk factors for psychosocial development. In M. Rutter & P. Casaer (Eds.), *Biological risk factors for psychosocial disorders* (pp. 139–174). Hillsdale, NJ: Erlbaum.

Chess, S., & Thomas, A. (1991). Temperament. In M. Lewis (Ed.), *Child and adolescent psychiatry: A comprehensive textbook.* Baltimore: Williams & Wilkins.

Cowie, H. (2000). Bystanding or standing by: Gender issues in coping with bullying in English schools. *Aggressive Behavior, 26,* 85–97.

Cowie, H., Smith, P. K., Boulton, M., & Laver, R. (1994). *Cooperation in a multiethnic classroom.* London: David Fulton.

Elliott, D. S., Hamburg, B., & Williams, K. R. (1998). Violence in American schools: an overview. In D. S. Elliott, B. Hamburg, & K. R. Williams (Eds.), *Violence in American schools* (pp. 3–30). Cambridge: Cambridge University Press.

Ericson, N. (2001). *Addressing the problem of juvenile bullying.* OJJDP Fact Sheet #27. U.S. Department of Justice, Office of Justice Programs, Office of Juvenile Justice and Delinquency Prevention. Washington, DC: U.S. Government Printing Office.

Farrington, D. P. (1995). The challenge of teenage antisocial behavior. In M. Rutter (Ed.), *Psychosocial disturbances in young people: Challenges for prevention* (pp. 83–130). New York: Cambridge University Press.

Farrington, D. P., Loeber, R., & Van Kammen, W. B. (1990). Long-term criminal outcomes of hyperactivity-impulsivity-attention deficit and conduct problems in childhood. In L. Robins & M. Rutter (Eds.), *Straight and devious pathways from childhood to adulthood* (pp. 62–81). New York: Cambridge University Press.

Farver, J. M. (1996). Aggressive behavior in preschoolers' social networks: Do birds of a feather flock together? *Early Childhood Research Quarterly, 11,* 333–350.

Feldman, R. S., Coats, E. J., & Spielman, D. A. (1996). Television exposure and children's decoding of nonverbal behavior. *Journal of Applied Social Psychology, 26*(19), 1718–1733.

Fortis-Diaz, E. (1998). Just who are the "bad guys" anyway? An attempt at redirecting children's aggressive play. *Early Childhood Education Journal, 25*(4), 233–237.

Garbarino, J. (1999). *Lost boys: Why our sons turn violent and how we can save them.* New York: The Free Press.

Gestwicki, C. (1999). *Developmentally appropriate practice: Curriculum and development in early education* (2nd ed.). Albany: Delmar Publishers.

Harrist, A. W., & Bradley, K. D. (2003). "You can't say you can't play": Intervening in the process of social exclusion in the kindergarten classroom. *Early Childhood Research Quarterly, 18,* 185–205.

Hauser, M. E., & Jipson, J. A. (1998). A conversation about curriculum and pedagogy. In M. E. Hauser & J. A. Jipson (Eds.), *Intersections: Feminisms/early child-
hoods* (pp. 149–158). New York: Peter Lang.

Hodgins, S. (Ed.) (1993). *Mental disorder and crime.* Newbury Park, CA: Sage.

Huesmann, L. R., Eron, L. D., Lefkowitz, M. M., & Walder, L. O. (1984). Stability of
aggression over time and generations. *Developmental Psychology, 20,* 1120–1134.

Indicators of School Crime and Safety. (2005). National Center of Educational Statistics. U.S. Department of Education. NCES 2006-001.

Jalongo, M. R., & Isenberg, J. P. (2000). *Exploring your role: A practitioner's introduction
to early childhood education.* New Jersey: Prentice Hall.

Jessor, R., & Jessor, S. L. (1977). *Problem behavior and psychosocial development: A longitudinal study of youth.* New York: Academic Press.

Johnson, D. W., Johnson, R. T., & Holubed, E. J. (1994). *The new circles of learning:
Cooperation in the classroom and school.* Alexandria, VA: Association for Supervision and Curriculum Development.

Junger-Tas, J. (1992). Changes in the family and their impact on delinquency. *European Journal of Criminal Policy and Research, 1,* 27–51.

Kellner, D. (1990). *Television and the crisis of democracy.* Boulder: Westview.

Kochenderfer, B. J., & Ladd, G. W. (1997). Victimized children's responses to
peers' aggression: Behaviors associated with reduced versus continued victimization. *Development and Psychopathology, 9,* 59–73.

Kohn, A. (1993). *Punished by rewards: The trouble with gold stars, incentive plans, A's,
praise, and other bribes.* Boston: Houghton Mifflin.

Kohn, A. (1996). *Beyond discipline: From compliance to community.* Alexandria, VA:
Association for Supervision and Curriculum Development.

Krevans, J., & Gibbs, J. C. (1996). Parents' use of inductive discipline: Relations to
children's empathy and prosocial behavior. *Child Development, 67,* 3263–3277.

Lake, V. E. (2001). Linking literacy and moral education in the primary classroom.
The Reading Teacher, 25, 125–129.

Leff, S. S., Power, T. J., Costigan, T. E., & Manz, P. H. (2003). Assessing the climate
of the playground and lunchroom: Implications for programming. *The School
Psychology Review, 32*(3), 418–430.

Lickona, T. (1991). *Educating for character: How our schools can teach respect and responsibility.* New York: Bantam Books.

Loeber, R., & Hay, D. (1997). Key issues in the development of aggression and violence from childhood to early adulthood. *Annual Review of Psychology, 48,*
371–410.

Loeber, R., & Stouthamer-Loeber, M. (1986). Family factors as correlates and predictors of juvenile conduct problems and delinquency. In N. Morris & M.
Tonry (Eds.), *Crime and justice* (vol. 7, pp. 29–149). Chicago: University of Chicago Press.

McLaren, P. (2003). Critical pedagogy: A look at the major concepts. In. A. Darder
& R. D. Torres (Eds.), *The critical pedagogy reader* (pp. 69–96). New York: Routledge Falmer.

Mednick, S., Moffitt, T., & Stack, S. (Eds.) (1987). *The causes of crime: New biological
approaches.* Cambridge: Cambridge University Press.

National Coalition on Television Violence. (n.d.). Retrieved June 16, 2006, from, http://www.utexas.edu/coc/journalism/ SOURCE/j363/nctv.html

Nelson, D. (2005). *Mean girls start in preschool, BYU study shows.* BYU News. Retrieved February 12, 2007, from, http://byunews.byu.edu/release.aspx?q=mean%20 girls%20start%20 preschool &story=archive05/may/mean

Nelson, D. A., Robinson, C. C., & Hart, C. H. (2005). Relational and physical aggression of preschool-age children: Peer status linkages across informants. *Early Education and Development, 16,* 115–139.

Newcomb, A. F., Bukowski, W. M., & Pattee, L. (1993). Children's peer relations: A meta-analytic review of popular, rejected, neglected, controversial, and average sociometric status. *Psychological Bulletin, 113,* 99–128.

Noble, G. (1975). *Children in front of the small screen.* Thousand Oaks, CA: Sage Publications.

O'Connell, P., Pepler, D., & Craig. W. (1999). Peer involvement in bullying: Insights and challenges for intervention. *Journal of Adolescence, 22,* 437–452.

Olweus, D. (1979). Stability of aggressive reaction patterns in males: A review. *Psychological Bulletin, 86*(4), 852–875.

Olweus, D. (1991). Bully/victim problems among schoolchildren. In D. J. Pepler & K. H. Rubin (Eds.), *The development and treatment of childhood aggression* (pp. 411–449). Hillsdale, NJ: Erlbaum.

Olweus, D. (1993). *Bullying at school: What we know and what we can do.* Cambridge, MA: Blackwell.

Olweus, D. (2001). Peer harassment: A critical analysis and some important issues. In J. Juvonen &. S. Graham (Eds.), *Peer harassment in school* (pp. 3–20). New York: Guilford.

Olweus, D. (2003). A profile of bullying at school. *Educational Leadership, 6*(6), 12–17.

Paley, V. G. (1992). *You can't say you can't play.* Cambridge: Harvard University Press.

Parker, J. G., & Asher, S. R. (1987). Peer relations and later personal adjustment: Are low-accepted children at risk? *Psychological Bulletin, 102,* 357–389.

Patterson, G. R. (1995). Coercion as a basis for early age of onset for arrest. In J. McCord (Ed.), *Coercion and punishment in long-term perspectives* (pp. 81–105). Cambridge: Cambridge University Press.

Pellegrini, A. D. (1988). Elementary school children's rough and tumble play and social competence. *Developmental Psychology, 24*(6), 802–806.

Pellegrini, A. D. (1995). A longitudinal study of boys' rough-and-tumble play and dominance during early adolescence. *Journal of Applied Developmental Psychology, 16,* 77–93.

Pellegrini, A. D., & Glickman, C. D. (1990). Measuring kindergartners' social competence. *Young Children, 45,* 40–44.

Reed, T., & Brown, M. (2000). The expression of care in the rough and tumble play of boys. *Journal of Research in Childhood Education, 15*(1), 104–116.

Rodkin, P. C., & Hodges, V. E. (2003). Bullies and victims in the peer ecology: Four questions for psychology professionals. *The School Psychology Review, 32*(1), 384–400.

Rowe, D. C., & Farrington, D. P. (1997). The familial transmission of criminal convictions. *Criminology, 35,* 177–201.

Rutter, M., & Giller, H. (1983). *Juvenile delinquency: Trends and perspectives*. New York: Guilford.

Rutter, M., Giller, H., & Hagell, A. (1998). *Antisocial behavior by young people*. New York: Cambridge University Press.

Rutter, M., Silberg, J., & Simonoff, E. (1993). Whither behavior genetics? A developmental psychopathology perspective. In. R. Plomin & G. E. McClearn (Eds.), *Nature, nurture and psychology* (pp. 433–456). Washington, DC: American Psychological Association.

Safran, J. S., & Safran, S. P. (1985). A developmental view of children's behavioral tolerance. *Behavioral Disorder, 10,* 87–94.

Salmivalli, C., Lagerspetz, K., Bjorkqvist, K., Osterman, K., & Kaukiainen, A. (1996). Bullying as a group process: participant roles and their relations to social status within the group. *Aggressive Behavior, 22,* 1–15.

Shidler, L. (2001). Teacher-sanctioned violence. *Childhood Education, 77,* 167–187.

Silvernail, D. L., Thompsom, A. M., Yang, Z., & Kopp, H. J. P. (2000). *A survey of bullying behavior among Maine third graders*. Gorham, ME: Maine Center for Educational Policy, Applied Research and Evaluation, University of Southern Maine. Retrieved August 8, 2003, from, http://lincoln.midcoast.com/<wps/against/bullying.html).

Simmons, B. J., Stalsworth, K., & Wentzel, H. (1999). Television violence and its effects on young children. *Early Childhood Education Journal, 26*(3), 149–153.

Smith, D. J. (1995). Youth crime and conduct disorders: Trends, patterns and causal explanations. In M. Rutter & D. J. Smith (Eds.), *Psychosocial disorders in young people: Time trends and their causes* (pp. 389–489). Chichester, UK: Wiley.

Smith, P. K., & Brain, P. (2000). Bullying in schools: Lessons from two decades of research. *Aggressive Behavior, 26,* 1–9.

Smith, P. K., & Shu. S. (1998). *Cross-national study of bullying: Final comparative report for England*. Final Report to the Japanese ministry of Education, Tokyo, Japan.

Steinberg, S. R., & Kincheloe, J. L. (2004). *Kinderculture: The corporate construction of childhood* (2nd ed.). Cambridge, MA: Westview Press.

Stanhope, L., Bell, R. Q., & Parker-Cohen, N. Y. (1987). Temperament and helping behavior in preschool children. *Developmental Psychology, 23*(3), 347–353.

Strayer, F. F. (1980). Child ethology and the study of preschool social relations. In H. C. Foot, A. J. Chapman, & J. R. Smith (Eds.), *Friendship and social relations in children* (pp. 235–265). New York: Wiley.

Strayer, F. F. (1990). *Social interaction and behavioral development during early childhood*. Montreal: La maison d'ethologie de Montreal.

Teräsahjo, T., & Salmivalli, C. (2003). "She is not actually bullied." The discourse of harassment in student groups. *Aggressive Behavior, 29,* 134–154.

Trister Dodge, D., Jablon, J. R., & Bickart, T. S. (1994). *Constructing curriculum in the primary grades*. Washington, DC: Teaching Strategies, Inc.

Underwood, M. K., Galen, B. R., & Paquette, J. A. (2001). Top ten challenges for understanding gender and aggression in children: Why can't we all just get along? *Social Development, 10,* 248–266.

CHAPTER 10

THE DEVELOPMENT
OF ETHNIC PREJUDICE
IN EARLY CHILDHOOD

Theories and Research

Drew Nesdale

Ethnic prejudice has long been a significant social problem in ethnically and racially diverse countries (Brown, 1995). Indeed, contrary to earlier reports that ethnic prejudice (for simplicity, the term *ethnic prejudice* is used to refer to both ethnic and racial prejudice) was systematically declining, recent evidence suggests that it may simply be being expressed in new disguises, and may actually be increasing (e.g., Dovidio & Gaertner, 1991; Pettigrew & Meertens, 1995).

Although the presence of ethnic prejudice (i.e., unjustified feelings of dislike or hatred towards members of ethnic or racial minority groups) is problematic in any sector of a community, the possibility that it may be widespread among children during early and middle childhood is of particular concern. During this period, children acquire social knowledge and attitudes that have the potential to lead to short- and long-term psychological, if not physical, harm to the members of ethnic and racial minority groups. Moreover, there is the possibility that prejudice acquired at this time might endure into adulthood and foster intergroup divisions that are

Contemporary Perspectives on Socialization and Social Development..., pages 213–240
Copyright © 2007 by Information Age Publishing
213

long-lasting (Durkin, 1995). In view of such considerations, it is not surprising that the development of children's ethnic prejudice has been of considerable interest to researchers for more than 75 years.

However, while there has been an extensive amount of research that has addressed the development of ethnic prejudice in young children, and several theories have been proposed to account for the phenomenon, there is currently little agreement on many of the central issues. For example, issues such as the age at which prejudice emerges in children, whether or not there are age-related phases or stages through which prejudice develops, what the psychological processes or mechanisms are which govern the acquisition of ethnic prejudice, and the impact that children's emerging linguistic and cognitive abilities, as well as their increasing social knowledge, have upon their acquisition and retention of ethnic prejudice, remains to be clarified. That said, although the theoretical detail differs, there is certainly agreement among theorists and researchers concerning the importance of the early childhood period to the acquisition process.

The aim of this chapter is to review theory and research on the development of ethnic prejudice in children. Accordingly, the four major theoretical accounts of children's prejudice are described, together with an evaluation of the extent of their research support. The chapter concludes with a brief consideration of the implications of the research findings for educational practice.

There are several points of clarification and qualification concerning the present chapter that are worth noting. First, although the title of the chapter refers to children's "ethnic" prejudice, the theories and research that are the purview of this chapter relate to, or encompass, both racial and ethnic prejudice. Prior to the 1970s, researchers tended to focus on the intergroup attitudes of different racial groups (i.e., groups differentiated by skin pigmentation, hair texture, and facial features, especially Caucasian and Negroid Americans), and used the term *race* in relation to these groups. More recently, and particularly following increases in interracial marriage, as well as immigration by other (not necessarily racial) groups, researchers have also examined the attitudes of different ethnic groups (i.e., groups differentiated by attributes such as: customs, language, social and political mores and conventions, religion, and possibly also race). The result has been that whereas some researchers have continued to use the term race and to focus on *racial prejudice* (e.g., Aboud, 1993; Black-Gutman & Hickson, 1996; Cramer & Anderson, 2003), others, presumably responding to the apparent overlap between race and ethnicity, have used the terms interchangeably, or juxtaposed the terms, or have used ethnic prejudice as the more inclusive term (e.g., Kowalski, 2003; Van Ausdale & Feagin, 1996; Nesdale, 2004). Given that the critical issue is whether children differentiate themselves and others on the basis of some category (e.g., skin color, gender, religion, language), rather than the particular category that they use, the present chapter uses the term ethnic prejudice inclusively so as to encompass both ethnic and racial prejudice.

Second, the particular focus of this chapter is on theories and research relating to dominant or majority group children since it is this group that most commonly expresses prejudice towards members of ethnic minority groups (Verkuyten & Masson, 1995) and it is this group that has received most research attention (Aboud, 1988, Nesdale, 2001a).

Third, whereas researchers have tackled an ever-increasing array of issues related to children's ethnicity, especially in the past two decades, it is simply beyond the scope of the present chapter to address all or most of these issues, certainly in any detail. For example, although the acquisition or construction of children's ethnic identity is certainly relevant to the development of their ethnic prejudice, at least according to some approaches, little attention has been given to this topic due to space limitations (see Adler, 2004; Ramsey, 1997; Sheets, 1999). For the same reason, although increasing attention has been given to issues such as the impact of teachers on children's ethnic identity development (Hollins & Oliver, 1999; Sheets & Hollins, 1999), and the implications of this for the preparation and practice of teachers (Hollins & Guzman, 2005; Sheets, 2004), the discussion of these issues will have to be taken up elsewhere.

Finally, the research cited in this chapter includes work carried out as far back as the 1930s. Although there might be a tendency to think of the older research as being somewhat dated, and perhaps as being uniquely reflective of specific socio-political eras, this appears not to be the case. Rather, despite using different methods and participant samples, the research findings over the decades have displayed a considerable (and depressing) level of consistency in relation to the ethnic attitudes of children who are members of dominant ethnic groups. In contrast, there has been some variation in the ethnic attitudes of members of ethnic minority groups as a function of the socio-political era, especially in relation to their attitudes to their own group. However, as noted above, the attitudes of ethnic minority group members are not a focus of the present chapter.

THEORIES OF CHILDREN'S ETHNIC PREJUDICE

To date, there have been four major approaches to accounting for the development of ethnic prejudice in children, including emotional maladjustment, social reflection, cognitive development, and social identity. Since the first two approaches are currently receiving less emphasis, their treatment here will be somewhat cursory with greater emphasis being placed on the latter two approaches.

Emotional Maladjustment

The emotional maladjustment approach links the acquisition of prejudice in children to the development of a particular personality type, the Authoritarian Personality (Adorno, Frenkel-Brunswick, Levinson, & Sanford, 1950). Much influenced by Freudian thinking, children's prejudice is considered to stem from emotional maladjustment arising from a repressive and harshly disciplined upbringing. Under these circumstances, the child's resulting frustration, anger and hostility towards his/her parents is considered to be displaced away from the parents towards scapegoats who are weaker and lack authority and power, such as members of ethnic minority groups (Nesdale, 2001a).

While a positive feature of this theory is that it provides an explanation for any differences in levels of prejudice that may occur between individuals (Aboud, 1988), it does not account for the uniformity of prejudice across whole groups of people that may occur in particular places and times, nor why some groups are the recipients of prejudice whereas others are not (Brown, 1995). In general, the approach ignores the influence on children's ethnic attitudes of important aspects of their social environment, including the attitudes of significant others, prevailing societal norms, and the relationships between the members of the dominant cultural group and the members of minority groups.

Social Reflection

The social reflection approach takes the latter point as a fundamental premise—children's prejudice is considered to reflect the community's attitudes and values, which are typically transmitted by the child's parents. The most widely accepted version of this approach has been that children simply learn their ethnic attitudes from these sources in the same way that they learn other social attitudes and behaviors (Allport, 1954; Rosenfield & Stephan, 1981). Thus, as Horowitz put it as far back as 1936, "attitudes toward Negroes are now chiefly determined not by contact with Negroes but by contact with the prevalent attitude towards Negroes" (1936, pp. 34–35). Presumably, such learning occurs because the children are rewarded for their imitative behavior and/or want to please their parents.

However, although the importance accorded to parents as the primary source of children's ethnic attitudes has remained largely unchallenged over many years, research support for this approach is actually quite mixed. On the one hand, consistent with it are findings of positive correlations between the ethnic attitudes of children and their parents (e.g., Bird, Monachesi, & Burdick, 1952; Harris, Gough, & Martin, 1950; Horowitz &

Horowitz, 1938; Goodman, 1952; Mosher & Scodel, 1960; Radke & Trager, 1950). In addition, there is evidence of distinct similarities in the statements of parents and their children concerning ethnic minority groups (e.g., Radke-Yarrow, Trager, & Miller, 1952).

On the other hand, however, there have also been reports of either low (e.g., Bird et al., 1952; Frenkel-Brunswick & Havel, 1953) or non-existent correlations (Aboud & Doyle, 1996b) between the ethnic attitudes of children and their parents. Further, still other studies have found that when there is similarity between parents and children in their negative statements towards ethnic minorities, the children frequently explicitly source the negative statements to their parents, declining to take ownership of them (e.g., Horowitz & Horowitz, 1938; Porter, 1971; Radke, Trager, & Davis, 1949). Moreover, although children as young as 4 to 5 years may incorporate trait-like terms or implied dispositions ("bad," "dirty," "ugly") in their verbal descriptions of minority group children (Horowitz & Horowitz, 1938; Porter, 1971; Radke-Yarrow et al., 1952; Teichman, 2006; Van Ausdale & Feagin, 1996), there is often little sense that such terms had trait connotations for them and/or that they were part of a set of beliefs which were shared by their group (i.e., a stereotype). In other words, there is not strong evidence that the attributes or behaviors are perceived to reflect stable characteristics of members of the particular ethnic outgroup which could be expected to be revealed on other occasions (see Nesdale, 2001b, for a review of the relationship between parents, language, and ethnic prejudice in children).

Viewed in this light, the research findings suggest that children's acquisition of ethnic prejudice is a little more complicated than that proposed by the social reflection approach. Consistent with that approach, it seems plausible that, especially prior to school age, parents' verbal utterances and non-verbal behaviors would greatly influence children's ethnic attitudes, at least in terms of what the children say and do in relation to the members of ethnic minority groups. In this sense, during these years, it could be argued that children's ethnic attitudes *reflect* those of their parents—what they say and do primarily comprises a reproduction of what their parents say and do.

However, as they increase in age, and especially as they experience preschool and then elementary school, the likelihood that children's ethnic attitudes merely reflect those of their parents surely diminishes. Both their intellectual capacities and social knowledge dramatically increase during these years and they become ever-more active participants in seeking to understand and control both their cognitive and social worlds (Durkin, 1995). On this basis, it would be incorrect to assume that children should simply be regarded as empty containers into which prevailing societal prejudices are poured, or as sponges that soak up dominant ethnic attitudes (Brown, 1995; Milner, 1996).

Cognitive Development

To a certain extent, the latter view accords with recent accounts of children's prejudice which have emphasized the influence exerted on children's ethnic attitudes by their cognitive development (e.g., Aboud, 1988; Aboud & Doyle, 1996a, 1996b; Bigler, 1995). Aboud and her colleagues, for example, have argued that there is no strong evidence that children's prejudice is influenced by the attitudes of parents or peers. Instead, according to Aboud's (1988) sociocognitive theory (ST), a child's attitude to other groups of children depends upon his/her levels of development in relation to two overlapping sequences of perceptual-cognitive development.

One sequence involves the *process* that dominates a child's experience at a particular time. The child is initially dominated by affective-perceptual processes associated with fear of the unknown and attachment to the familiar. Perceptual processes subsequently dominate with preference for the (similar) ingroup and rejection of the (different) outgroup being determined primarily by physical attributes (e.g., skin color, language, body size). Thereafter, cognitive processes take ascendancy with the advent of the concrete operational stage of cognitive development around 7 years of age and, later, formal operational thinking (Flavell, 1963). The effect of the transition to cognitive processes is that the child is increasingly able to understand the individual rather than the group-based qualities of people.

Overlapping the foregoing sequence is a purported second sequence of development that is concerned with changes in the child's *focus of attention*. Whereas very young children mostly focus on themselves and their preferences and perceptions, older children emphasize categories of people such that individuals are seen as members of these categories or groups. Still later, however, children focus on individuals, who are liked or disliked for their personal rather than group qualities.

Based on these sociocognitive developments, ST argues that ingroup bias and outgroup prejudice increase to a peak between 5–7 years of age, when differences between groups are paramount to them. At this age, *all* children display ethnic prejudice. However, with subsequent increases in the child's cognitive abilities, occasioned by the onset of concrete operational thinking around 7 years of age, ST proposes that there is a systematic decline in group-based biases, which is further enhanced when the child's ever-increasing cognitive abilities allow him/her to attend to the differences between individuals. Consequently, ST predicts that children's attitudes towards ethnic outgroups become more positive beyond 7 years of age whereas their attitudes towards the ingroup become less positive, as the members of the two groups are viewed in an increasingly similar way.

Although ST offers a theoretically consistent account of children's prejudice in terms of their developing perceptual-cognitive processes, it is fair to say that research support for this theory is also currently mixed (Nesdale, 2001a). On the one hand, consistent with ST are many studies in which children from the ethnically dominant group displayed increasing ingroup positivity and/or outgroup negativity up to 6–7 years, followed by a systematic decline (see reviews by Aboud, 1988; Nesdale, 2001a). In addition, research has revealed that children's understanding of conservation, an achievement of the concrete operational stage of cognitive development, is correlated with ethnic attitude flexibility, the understanding that ethnically similar and different individuals can have different and similar attributes, respectively (e.g., Doyle, Beaudet, & Aboud, 1988), and ethnic constancy, the understanding that ethnicity remains the same despite superficial transformations in skin color or clothing (e.g., Aboud, 1984; Semaj, 1980). Research has also revealed that the acquisition of concrete operational thinking, and ethnic attitude flexibility, coincided with a decrease in ingroup bias, and preceded a reduction in outgroup prejudice (e.g., Doyle & Aboud, 1995; Doyle et al., 1988).

On the other hand, however, whereas ST's account might be taken to indicate that ethnic prejudice ceases to be a problem during the elementary school years, or is substantially ameliorated, as a result of children's increasing cognitive abilities, research suggests that this is not the case. For example, in studies that have reported an association between conservation and prejudice, up to 50% of the children who could conserve, still displayed ethnic prejudice (e.g., Doyle & Aboud, 1995).

Further, the actual nature of the pattern of children's responses that ST seeks to explain is not unambiguous. Although there are certainly a number of studies that have reported an unambiguous decrease in ethnic prejudice after 7 years, as ST would predict (e.g., Aboud & Mitchell, 1977; George & Hoppe, 1979; Vaughan, 1964; Williams, Best, & Boswell, 1975), other studies have reported not only that ingroup prejudice remained at the same level from 7 to 12 years (e.g., Asher & Allen, 1969; Banks & Rompf, 1973; Milner, 1973; Teplin, 1976; Weiland & Coughlin, 1979), but that ingroup prejudice actually increased during these years (e.g., Bartel, Bartel, & Grill, 1973; Hraba & Grant, 1970; Vaughan & Thompson, 1961).

However, perhaps of critical importance is the possibility that the main body of findings which ST seeks to explain may actually consist of children's *ingroup preferences* rather than their outgroup *dislike or prejudice* (e.g., Brand, Ruiz, & Padilla, 1974; Cameron, Alvarez, Ruble, & Fuligni, 2001; Katz, 1976; Nesdale, 2001a; Proshansky, 1966; Stephan & Rosenfield, 1979). The basis of this view is that, given the cognitive and linguistic limitations of young children, the main methods used to assess children's ethnic prejudice, certainly up to the late 1990s, rested on children's choice of ethnically-differentiated dolls, photos, or drawings, or the attribution of traits to such stimuli (see Aboud, 1988). The problem with these stimuli is that they might only index children's level of ingroup preference, rather than whether they feel dislike for members of ethnic outgroups.

There are a number of arguments that provide support for this view. For example, the ethnic choice technique calls for a choice response, frequently a forced response between only two alternatives (e.g., a black doll versus a white doll) that does not necessarily imply dislike for, or rejection of, the unchosen stimulus figure (e.g., Brand et al., 1974; Katz, 1976). In addition, preference responses are undiscriminating because they do not provide a sensitive assessment of children's intensity of affect for either the ingroup or the outgroup (Williams et al., 1975). Further, by stripping away all individuating information until only the skin color cue remains as a basis for choice, the technique artificially and unrealistically enhances the salience of the ethnicity category over other socially relevant categories, such as gender and age.

Related to the previous point, race or ethnicity is simply not a salient category to the majority of dominant group children until 6 or 7 years or later. Younger children almost invariably respond to gender before race (Boulton, 1995; Goldstein, Koopman, & Goldstein, 1979; Ramsey, 1991), unless the intergroup situation is one of tension or conflict (Radke et al., 1949; Teichman, 2006). Indeed, Epstein et al. (1976) demonstrated that cleanliness was a more potent determinant of preferences than was race in second to fourth grade children, while Richardson and Royce (1968) reported that physical handicap was a greater deterrent to young children's friendship than race.

Moreover, a number of studies have reported a lack of correspondence between ethnicity and friendship choice (e.g., Boulton & Smith, 1993; Fishbein & Imai, 1993; Hraba & Grant, 1970; Ramsey, 1991) and that if ethnic cleavage does occur, it tends not to be before children are 9 or 10 years of age (e.g., Brand et al., 1974; Proshansky, 1966; but see also Lambert & Taguchi, 1956). Finally, children who are given the opportunity to rate minority group children on bi-polar scales (i.e., like-dislike) tend to express greater liking for the ingroup versus the outgroup, rather than liking for the ingroup and dislike for the outgroup (Aboud & Mitchell, 1977; Nesdale, 2000). Indeed, contrary to Aboud's position, a number of writers have argued that when real ethnic prejudice does emerge in children, signified by, for example, racial cleavage, epithets or tension, it does not actually appear until children are well into middle childhood, around 9 or 10 years of age (Goodman, 1952; Katz, 1976; Milner, 1996; Proshansky, 1966). That said, however, there is evidence that ethnic prejudice can be revealed at an earlier age, especially when the social environment is fractured by long-standing ethnic tension and violence (Teichman, 2006).

On this latter point, it is also important to note that ST offers a developmental account that is largely indifferent to the social context and motivational considerations. For example, it is unlikely that the initiation of prejudice in children is governed simply by the child's affective-perceptual processes associated with fear of the unknown (and attachment to the familiar). On the contrary, some but not all physical differences are associated with prejudice in both children and adults, the physical differences to which young children respond are also those of social significance to adults (Katz, Sohn, & Zalk, 1975), and strong prejudices (e.g., towards particular national groups, religions) can occur even in the absence of physical differences (Tajfel, Jahoda, Nemeth, Rim, & Johnson, 1972). Together, these points emphasize the fact that the differentiation of ethnic and racial cues by young children is not determined solely by their perceptual distinctiveness based on unfamiliarity. Rather, the cues to which even young children respond have a distinctiveness that is socially determined, particularly by the labels and evaluative statements applied to groups by peers and adults (Katz, 1976; Vaughan, 1987).

In sum, although the preceding review of the emotional maladjustment, social reflection, and cognitive development approaches is necessarily abbreviated, it is clear that markedly different theoretical constructions have been built upon the available body of research findings. Although each approach accounts for some of the findings, none provides a comprehensive explanation of the development of children's prejudice, encompassing within it all of the available findings.

However, the review thus far has served to identify a number of central issues that must be taken into account in any comprehensive explanation of the development of children's prejudice. First, the theory must account for the appearance of outgroup dislike and hatred versus ingroup preference. Second, the theory must account for the fact that children's attitudes are not necessarily mere reflections of those of their parents or siblings. Third, the theory must take into account the fact of children's developing perceptual, cognitive and linguistic abilities. Fourth, the theory must give due recognition to social motivational issues. Fifth, the theory must account for the fact that some children develop ethnic prejudice whereas others do not.

Social Identity

Contrary to the preceding perspectives, the social identity approach proposes that children's intergroup attitudes are greatly influenced by social motivational considerations relating to their social group memberships. Central to this focus is the assumption that inclusion and belonging are important to children and motivates them to pursue social contacts, friendships, and social group memberships from an early age (Milner, 1996; Nesdale, 2004; Rubin, Bukowski, & Parker, 1998; Vaughan, 1987). Indeed, according to some writers, such behavior may reflect an inborn, fundamental need to belong and to be accepted (Baumeister & Leary, 1995).

Consistent with this perspective are findings indicating that children as young as 5–6 years tend to like, and see themselves as similar to, ingroup members (Bigler, 1995; Bigler, Jones, & Lobliner, 1997; Nesdale, Durkin, Maass, & Griffiths, 2004, 2005; Nesdale & Flesser, 2001) and to derive at least some of their sense of self-worth from their acceptance by a particular social group (Nesdale & Pelyhe, 2005). In addition, research has shown that, from 5 years onwards, children show less and less liking for ingroup members who do not conform to group norms (Abrams, Rutland, Cameron, & Marques, 2003; Abrams, Rutland, & Cameron, 2003; Nesdale, 2000; Nesdale & Brown, 2004).

Research also indicates that young children spontaneously compare the standing of their group with other groups (Chafel, 1986; Yee & Brown, 1992) and that they prefer to be members of higher rather than lower status groups because they derive social self-esteem from their membership of the former (Nesdale & Flesser, 2001; Nesdale, Durkin, et al., 2005). However, although they prefer the increased status conferred by a higher status group, they still indicate greater liking for their ingroup than a higher status outgroup (Nesdale & Flesser, 2001, Nesdale et al., 2004). Importantly, also, children who are rejected by their peer group display heightened state anxiety, decreased self-esteem, enhanced risk-taking, and a tendency towards greater anti-social behavior, from as young as 6 years of age (Nesdale & Lambert, in press-a, in press-b; Nesdale & Pelyhe, 2005).

In response to such findings, Nesdale (1999, 2004) proposed social identity development theory (SIDT) as an explicitly group-based account of the development of children's ethnic prejudice. SIDT proposes that children who display ethnic prejudice pass through four sequential development phases (undifferentiated, ethnic awareness, ethnic preference, ethnic prejudice). The phases differ in terms of the behaviors that characterize them, and the events that precipitate changes from one phase to the next.

In the *undifferentiated* phase (prior to 2–3 years), racial/ethnic cues are typically not salient to young children—they respond to objects and people in their environment mainly in terms of what catches their attention. Increasingly, however, they become more selective and discriminating and begin to respond differentially to cues such as gender and age.

The *ethnic awareness* phase begins to emerge at around 3 years, especially among those children who reside in multi-racial societies. A number of studies have confirmed that children can accurately identify and distinguish between skin color hues at this age (e.g., Clark & Clark, 1939; Goodman, 1946; Stevenson & Stevenson, 1960). As Katz (1976) has emphasized, it is likely that awareness begins following an adult's identification/labeling of an outgroup member (e.g., "yes, that person has black skin—he is an Afro-American"). It is the perception of such differences, particularly when accompanied by a verbal label, which is likely to facilitate social categorization based on skin color. It is important to note, however, that young children do not appear to construct social categories on an idiosyncratic basis (e.g., "yes, that person has blue shorts/a big nose"). As noted earlier, children enter a social environment in which the key social categories are already specified and the nature of intergroup relations is established. Accordingly, the social categories which children are likely to emphasize are not simply those that are strange and unfamiliar (cf. Aboud, 1988)—they will be those that have social significance in the community (e.g., Vaughan, 1987; Katz, 1976).

Children's awareness of these categories will be sharpened by any negative evaluations communicated by adults, verbally or non-verbally (Milner, 1983). In addition, it is possible that, in relation to the white and black social categories, the evaluative associations will be further enhanced by the positive and negative associations with the colors white and black (e.g., Renninger & Williams, 1966; Williams & Roberson, 1967) and light and dark (e.g., Brown & Johnson, 1971; Katz, 1973), respectively. However, while ethnic awareness may begin to emerge at around 3 years, the further refinement, elaboration and clarification of the child's concept of a racial/ethnic group continues over many years, perhaps even up to 10 to 11 years of age, and appears to comprise a number of age-related phases (see Vaughan, 1963, 1987).

A crucially important and early achievement in this sequence concerns the child's ethnic self-identification—the realization that she or he is a member of a particular group. The evidence suggests that self-identification begins to occur soon after children become aware of ethnic or racial categories. Accurate ethnic self-identification has been reported in dominant group children as young as 3 years (Marsh, 1970) and in virtually all dominant-group children in multi-racial communities by 6 to 7 years (Aboud, 1988). It remains unclear whether awareness of a child's own ethnic identity precedes or follows his/her awareness of another person's ethnicity, although there are reasons to suppose that it is the former (see below). Whatever is the case, ethnic self-identification serves to usher in the next phase in the sequence, ethnic preference, which overlaps the child's ongoing development of ethnic awareness.

The central features of the *ethnic preference* phase are three-fold. First, and most importantly, the child learns that s/he belongs to, or is a member of, a particular ethnic group, and that the members share something together that is different to others. The result is that the child begins to identify with his/her group and commences an ongoing focus on, and preference for their ingroup(s). Second, there is an increasing sense of being different to the members of other ethnic groups who, third, are perceived as being increasingly similar to each other (termed, the outgroup homogeneity effect; Linville, 1998). However, the critically important point to be emphasized here is that SIDT argues that ethnic self-categorization mainly activates a focus on, and accompanying preference for, the *ingroup*. Of course, this preference is enhanced if the ingroup is perceived to be positively distinctive compared with other groups, for it adds to their emerging sense of self-esteem based on their membership of the group.

Thus, the major effect of this new understanding is an early focusing on the ingroup rather than the outgroup, on similarity rather than difference, on relative superiority rather than inferiority. Indeed, research by Katz and her colleagues (e.g., Katz, 1973; Katz & Seavey, 1973; Katz et al., 1975) has revealed that white children as young as three years more readily distinguished faces of their own versus another ethnic group. That is, the effect of ethnic self-identification and the application of group labels was that outgroup faces were actually made less differentiable and/or accessible.

With the passage of time, children are exposed to, and acquire, information that is consistent with, and enhances the positive distinctiveness of their group. Inevitably, at the same time as children acquire positively discriminating information about the ingroup, they begin to hear and acquire information which is (typically) less positive/more negative about comparison ethnic outgroups. Note that while this information may be retained and may form the basis of an eventual outgroup stereotype, it does not appear to be the focal concern of children at this age. As noted earlier, ethnic stereotypes typically do not appear to consolidate until after 6 or 7 years of age. Nevertheless, negative outgroup information may still contribute to their sense of relative ingroup superiority and self-esteem (Milner, 1996).

In short, rather than instigating outgroup prejudice (cf. Aboud, 1988; Tajfel & Turner, 1979), the effect of ethnic self-identification is to instigate a focus on, and bias towards, the ingroup. Consistent with this view is the array of findings that have emerged in the ethnic choice and trait attribution studies described earlier (Nesdale, 2001a). For example, when given a forced or restricted choice between ingroup and outgroup stimulus figures (e.g., dolls, pictures, drawings), dominant group children almost invariably indicate a preference for the ingroup figure. Similarly, if required to make a choice between assigning positive versus negative attributes to ingroup versus outgroup figures, the ingroup figure will be awarded the more positive attributes. While there is an obvious ambiguity in this data, the present position is that these findings reveal children's *preference for the ingroup,* rather than dislike or rejection for the outgroup.

In addition, as noted above, research indicates that friendship and play-mate preferences are unrelated to ethnic choices or trait attribution responses (e.g., Hraba & Grant, 1970; Fishbein & Imai, 1993), that there is no correlation between trait attributions and outgroup bullying (e.g., Boulton, 1995), that the negativity of the trait attributions decreases when the response is open-ended versus forced choice (e.g., Lerner & Buehrig, 1975; Lerner & Schroeder, 1971), and that young children rarely give rejection of the outgroup stimulus figure as a reason for their choice of the ingroup stimulus figure (e.g., Zinser, Rich, & Bailey, 1981).

Further, as noted previously, in the few studies in which young children have given independent responses to ingroup and outgroup stimulus fig-ures, and the responses have been on a bi-polar scale (i.e., like-dislike, pos-itive-negative), the children have almost invariably used only the liking or positive half of the scale. That is, the outgroup stimulus figure has been rated as relatively less likeable or less positive than the ingroup stimulus fig-ure, not as being disliked or negative (e.g., Aboud & Mitchell, 1977; Gene-see, Tucker, & Lambert, 1978; Nesdale, 2000). Interestingly, in contrast to ethnicity, research has revealed that children as young as 4 or 5 years are quite prepared to reveal strong dislike towards opposite versus same gen-der stimulus persons—here, the stimulus figures are unambiguously rated in the disliked half of a bi-polar scale (e.g., Yee & Brown, 1994).

In sum, according to the present analysis, ethnic self-identification and ethnic preference tend to occur in all children, sooner or later. They reflect the child's growing understanding of the social structure in the community, the statuses of the different groups and their inter-relation-ships, and the language used to describe other group members. For domi-nant group children, they prompt a focus on, and commitment to, the ethnic ingroup. (In contrast, minority group children sometimes reject their ingroup in favor of the culturally dominant outgroup; Clark & Clark, 1947; Gregor & McPherson, 1966). However, if ethnic preference is merely that (i.e., preference not prejudice), the question remains as to how ethnic preference turns into a negative attitude or ethnic prejudice.

According to SIDT, the *ethnic prejudice* phase entails an active process of change from a state of mere ethnic preference. Contrary to Aboud's (1988) claim that ethnic prejudice diminishes in children from 7 years onwards as a result of cognitive acquisitions, SIDT contends that it is pre-cisely in this period that prejudice actually crystallizes and emerges in those children who come to hold such attitudes.

SIDT argues that ethnic prejudice requires shifts in focus in each of the child's perceptual, affective, cognitive and behavioral domains. Rather than being focused on the ingroup and its positive differentiation from the outgroup, prejudice implies at least an equal focus on ingroup and outgroup, if not an obsessive focusing on the outgroup. Instead of liking an outgroup member less than an ingroup member, prejudice means that outgroup members are disliked or hated. Rather than knowing and being able to reproduce (negative) 'facts' about ethnic minorities, a prejudiced person holds them as his/her own. Finally, instead of engaging in inter-ethnic play and friendship, prejudice means derogating and discriminating against minority group members, whenever the occasion arises.

Clearly, the transition from having a preference for the ingroup to feeling prejudice towards an ethnic minority group is not inconsiderable. According to SIDT, whether ethnic prejudice actually emerges and crystallizes in children depends upon one or more of at least three factors. First, the emergence of ethnic prejudice depends upon the extent to which the child is identified with his/her group. That is, the more that the child is committed to, involved with, believes in, or is concerned about the welfare of, his/her particular group, the more likely it is that s/he will like the members of the ingroup *and* dislike the members of outgroups. Under high ingroup identification, all other groups are the wrong groups, or bad groups, and should be disliked.

Second, the appearance of ethnic prejudice is also influenced by whether the child's group holds ethnic prejudice as a norm or expectation. Given that the child wants to be a member of the group, if the group has an expectation that members of ethnic minority groups are to be disliked and discriminated against, then the child will conform to the group norm and display ethnic prejudice. Of course, the likelihood of this happening will increase to the extent that the child is identified with the group. The more the child identifies, the greater the likelihood that the child will reveal conformity to the norm of prejudice.

Third, ethnic prejudice will increase to the extent that there is a belief among the ingroup members that their group is threatened in some way by members of the outgroup. As pointed out by Stephan, Ybarra, Martinez, Schwarzwald, and Tur-Kaspa (1998), such threats might include realistic threats (i.e., threats against the status, power, physical or material wellbeing of the ingroup), symbolic threats (i.e., threats against the values, beliefs or standards of the ingroup), or stereotype threats (i.e., threats arising from the ingroup's view of the nature of the outgroup). As outgroup threat is perceived to increase, so ethnic prejudice towards that group will be increased.

Several important implications follow from SIDT. For example, according to SIDT, prejudice does not emerge in all children as a matter of course (cf. Aboud, 1988). SIDT argues that there are conditions under which children may never display ethnic prejudice. These include contexts in which children identify strongly with a group that does not endorse prejudice towards ethnic minority groups and settings in which inter-ethnic relations are harmonious. A context in which some super-ordinate group goal dominates the interest of distinct ethnic groups can also be conducive to the maintenance of positive intergroup relations (see Gaertner, Dovidio, Anastosio, Bachman, & Rust, 1993).

A further implication is that since SIDT is primarily founded upon social motivational rather than perceptual-cognitive considerations, it does not predict that the appearance of ethnic prejudice in children is linked to specific ages, meaning particular cognitive acquisitions (cf. Aboud, 1988). According to SIDT, the emergence of ethnic prejudice in children is dependent upon their unique social situation. At any time, children's attitudes towards members of ethnic outgroups might become more positive, more negative, or remain the same, depending upon the social situation and their prevailing social group identification. Thus, whereas ethnic prejudice is typically not displayed by children before 6 or 7 years, it may be revealed by children at an earlier age in those communities which are riven by long-standing ethnic tension and violence, such as occurs in Northern Ireland between Protestants and Catholics, and in the Middle East between Jews and Palestinians (Teichman, 2006).

That said, given that children's social knowledge does increase as they increase in age, SIDT would anticipate that, in a particular circumstance, a child's lesser liking for the members of a particular ethnic minority outgroup, or even their dislike for an outgroup, might be moderated or reduced. That is, as children increase in age, it is likely that they develop an increasing tendency to regulate the expression of particular attitudes and behavior in accordance with their beliefs about what is generally acceptable in a particular situation (Rutland, Cameron, Milne, & McGeorge, 2003). Consistent with this is evidence that children begin to understand and engage in self-presentational behavior from approximately seven to eight years of age (Aloise-Young, 1993; Banerjee, 2002; Banerjee & Yuill, 1999; Bennett & Yeeles, 1990) and that they become increasingly aware that intergroup prejudice and discrimination are generally considered to be unacceptable and inappropriate (Brown & Bigler, 2004; Greenwald & Banaji, 1995; Killen, Pisacane, Lee-Kin, & Ardila-Rey, 2001; Rutland et al., 2003; Theimer, Killen, & Stangor, 2001).

Research evidence in support of SIDT's predictions is accumulating, especially in studies utilizing more realistic paradigms. Although SIDT provides a good account of the results of the extant ethnic choice and trait attribution studies (see reviews by Aboud, 1988; Nesdale, 2001a), these paradigms, as noted earlier, have distinct limitations, if not outright flaws. In particular, they typically necessitate a choice being made between photos or dolls, and these stimuli supposedly represent single members of different ethnic groups. That is, the children are asked to respond to no more than one (representative) member of an ethnic outgroup. Accordingly, in recent years, researchers have sought to remove the forced choice and to construct situations in which the children's membership in one group is established, prior to examining their attitudes towards the members of an outgroup.

For example, consistent with SIDT's predictions concerning children in the ethnic preference phase, Bigler and colleagues reported that the random assignment of 6- to 11-year-old children to groups (differentiated by the color of their shirts) at a summer camp prompted ingroup favoritism in the children in both groups, and that children with higher levels of self-esteem showed higher levels of intergroup stereotyping (Bigler, 1995; Bigler et al., 1997). Other intergroup studies have also revealed that when social comparisons and competitiveness between groups are emphasized, children's ingroup favoritism increases (Vaughan, Tajfel, & Williams, 1981; Yee & Brown, 1992).

Nesdale and colleagues (Nesdale, Durkin, et al., 2004, 2005; Nesdale & Flesser, 2001; Nesdale, Griffiths, Durkin, & Maass, 2005; Nesdale, Maass, Durkin, & Griffiths, 2005; Nesdale, Maass, Griffiths, & Durkin, 2003) have also carried out a series of studies using a variant of the minimal group paradigm (Tajfel, Flament, Billig, & Bundy, 1971) that have provided further support for SIDT. In these studies, children are randomly assigned membership of a same age, gender, and ethnicity ingroup for an intergroup drawing competition. Their attitudes towards their ingroup are then compared with their attitudes towards a competitor outgroup comprised of same age and gender children who have the same or different ethnicity to the ingroup. Importantly, in these studies, the intensity of children's attitudes towards the ingroup versus the outgroup are assessed via their responses on bi-polar scales, rather than by a forced choice or preference response.

Consistent with SIDT's ethnic preference stage, these studies have shown that young children preferred to be members of high versus low status groups and that, whereas they always liked their ingroup more than the comparison outgroup, the latter group was liked less when it was comprised of children with different rather than the same race or ethnicity as the ingroup (Nesdale et al., 2003; Nesdale, Durkin et al., 2004; Nesdale & Flesser, 2001).

Of critical significance, however, is the fact that, whereas the former results emphasized the impact of group processes on the children's *ethnic preferences,* recent research has also supported SIDT's proposals concerning the factors that turn ethnic preference into *ethnic prejudice.* Thus, Nesdale, Durkin, et al. (2005) and Nesdale, Maass, et al. (2005) demonstrated that young children's decreased liking for an ethnic outgroup, compared with their ingroup, turned to explicit dislike or *prejudice* when the children were highly identified with their ingroup, and/or the ingroup had an explicit norm of outgroup prejudice versus acceptance. In addition, both studies also found that ethnic preference changed to ethnic prejudice when the members of the ingroup believed that the status of the ingroup was threatened by the outgroup.

In sum, as the preceding discussion has revealed, the case for SIDT as an account of the development of children's ethnic prejudice is compelling, thus far. The theory provides a good fit for the findings that have been revealed via ethnic choice and trait attribution studies. In addition, the theory has been tested in newer paradigms that have enabled assessment of children's attitudes towards groups rather than individuals, and in which it has been possible to assess the intensity of children's ethnic attitudes. Significantly, the results of the latter studies have provided consistent support for the main tenets of SIDT.

IMPLICATIONS FOR INTERVENTIONS

The critical issue that remains to be considered concerns the development of techniques or strategies that would minimize or moderate the development of children's ethnic prejudice. Given that a number of intervention strategies from a variety of perspectives have been proposed (e.g., Allport, 1954; Derman-Sparks & Phillips, 1997; Hawkins, 1995; Katz & Zalk, 1978; Weiner & Wright, 1973), a detailed review of these approaches, and the related empirical literature, is beyond the scope of the present chapter (however, see Aboud & Levy, 2000, for such a review).

However, in view of the research support provided for SIDT to date, there appear to be some potentially important implications from that research for the development of an effective intervention program. Five critical elements will be briefly touched upon. The first element is that of *category awareness.* The critical starting point is with children's ethnic self-identification for this provides the platform upon which ethnic prejudice may be constructed in some (but not all) children. As we have seen, the effect of ethnic self-identification is two-fold. When the child identifies with his/her own ethnic group, ethnic minority outgroups are perceived to be different from and, typically, not as good as, the ethnic ingroup, and the members of minority outgroups tend to be seen as similar, if not indistinguishable, a tendency which increases with the acquisition of ethnic stereotypes.

The very real problem here is that the self-categorization process described above appears to be a natural process that underpins people's (i.e., children's, adolescents', and adults') preferences for *any* ingroup of which they are a member, and that it is probably driven by a fundamental human motive to be accepted and to belong (Baumeister & Leary, 1995). Whereas recognition of this fact serves to emphasize the difficulty of the task, it also makes clear that, from an early age, and increasingly thereafter, children need to be made aware of what categories are, how we use them, and with what consequences. In other words, children need to be encouraged to develop a conscious awareness of how we tend to group objects and people, how we emphasize some qualities and minimize others in accomplishing this task, how we assign attributes to the group members, and how this impacts on our interactions with them. As part of this emphasis, there are also good grounds for having children simulate the experience of being a member of a low status category, as has been successfully undertaken by several researchers (Breckheimer & Nelson, 1976; Weiner & Wright, 1973).

Complementing the emphasis on children's category awareness, there is a need to develop their *individual differentiation* abilities. Rather than seeing and responding to children as undifferentiated members of particular ethnic minority groups (or, indeed, any particular social groups), there is a need for children to look beyond the socially endorsed categories and to recognize the attributes, abilities and characteristics that combine to make up an individual child. The importance of this issue has also been recognized by others (Aboud & Levy, 2000; Bowers & Swanson, 1988; Katz et al., 1975), and several studies have demonstrated that interventions designed to strengthen children's abilities to differentiate among members of an ethnic outgroup can reduce prejudice (Aboud & Fenwick, 1999; Katz & Zalk, 1978). In a similar vein, researchers have found that prejudice is reduced in children who can classify using multiple attributes (Bigler & Liben, 1993).

The effect of category awareness and individual differentiation is elaborated and extended by *intercultural contact*. However, although the value of intercultural contact in reducing ethnic prejudice is now generally accepted (Aboud & Levy, 2000; Nesdale & Todd, 2000), research has made clear that positive results are not obtained simply by providing the opportunity for intercultural contact, such as would be present, for example, in an integrated pre-school or elementary school (Patchen, 1983; Schofield, 1982). Instead, for intercultural contact to be successful, contact situations need to be engineered that cut across children's existing social groups and which encompass features that facilitate positive intercultural contact (Allport, 1954). Two such situations include the jigsaw classroom (Aronson, Blaney, Stephan, Sikes, & Snapp, 1978) and cooperative learning groups (Johnson & Johnson, 1975). The success of these approaches is that they are designed to facilitate equal-status and cooperative activity between members of different intercultural groups that allow for the disconfirmation of stereotypic traits and qualities and, instead, the appreciation of children's individual qualities.

The fourth critical element is the development of children's *emotional empathy;* that is, the ability to experience the same feelings as those of another person in response to a particular situation. Although several writers have suggested that enhancing children's empathy is one technique that can be used to increase children's liking for ethnic outgroup members (e.g., Aboud & Levy, 2000; Feshbach & Feshbach, 1998), little research has actually addressed the relationship directly. However, research has shown that children display empathy from an early age, even as early as the preschool years (Eisenberg et al., 1990; Radke-Yarrow, Zahn-Waxler, & Chapman, 1983), and that increasing empathy is associated with increased prosocial or helping behavior (Eisenberg et al., 1990; Krevans & Gibbs, 1996; Litvack-Miller, McDougall, & Romney, 1997; Roberts & Strayer, 1996; Strayer & Roberts, 2004; Warden & Mackinnon, 2003).

On this basis, it is plausible that more empathic children from the dominant ethnic group would display more positive attitudes towards members of ethnic minority groups, than would less empathic children. Consistent with this, Nesdale, Griffiths, et al. (2005) reported that greater empathy was associated with greater liking for the members of an ethnic minority outgroup. However, two points about these findings are worthy of note. First, although the children's liking for the different ethnicity outgroup was significantly correlated with their level of empathy, the children still expressed greater liking for a same ethnicity outgroup. Second, in a follow-up study, the researchers found that the children's empathy exerted no effect when their ingroup had a norm of outgroup prejudice. The latter finding re-affirms the powerful impact of ingroup identity and hence the magnitude of the task involved in minimizing children's tendencies towards ingroup bias and outgroup rejection.

Accordingly, the final element in facilitating positive ethnic attitudes is *coalition building.* In short, it is critical that parents, teachers and peers join together in showing zero tolerance for ethnic prejudice. At present, most of the pro-active efforts appear to be left in the hands of teachers with research showing that comparatively few parents even discuss the issue of ethnic prejudice with their children (Kofkin, Katz, & Downey, 1995), apparently out of fear of making their children prejudiced (Aboud & Fenwick, 1999). However, research shows that when the issue is discussed by parents and children, or by peers with differing attitudes, the outcome tends to be positive (Aboud & Fenwick, 1999; Kofkin et al., 1995)

CONCLUSIONS

Prior to the formulation of SIDT, three main accounts of children's ethnic prejudice had been proposed. These accounts included the view that ethnic prejudice in children is a form of emotional maladjustment arising from a faulty parent–child relationship; that ethnic prejudice emerges in children as a reflection of the views of significant others, especially their parents; and that ethnic prejudice is determined by changes in children's perceptual-cognitive abilities. Although each approach accounts for some of the extant findings, the present review suggests that none provides a comprehensive explanation of the development of children's ethnic prejudice.

In particular, the present analysis argues that the critical issues upon which the preceding approaches fall short concern the need to differentiate ingroup preference from outgroup prejudice, to recognize that children simply do not as a matter of course adopt as their own the ethnic attitudes and behaviors of their parents and peers, to accept that changes in perceptual and cognitive abilities do not straightforwardly determine ethnic attitudes, and to emphasize the importance to children of being members of valued social groups.

Social identity development theory (SIDT) has been designed to take these issues into account. Importantly, SIDT emphasizes the critical significance of social identity processes in the development of children's ethnic attitudes and, in so doing, facilitates a long overdue shift away from the prevailing emphasis in much social developmental research on the predominance of cognitive processes.

As the discussion has revealed, the case for SIDT is compelling, thus far. The theory provides a good fit for the findings that have been revealed via ethnic choice and trait attribution studies. In addition, support for the theory has been strengthened by the results from newer paradigms that have enabled the intensity of children's intergroup attitudes to be assessed. Significantly, the results of the latter studies have provided consistent support for the main tenets of SIDT.

On this basis, five critical elements for an effective approach to reducing or minimizing children's ethnic prejudice have been outlined. These include the elements of category awareness, individual differentiation, intercultural contact, emotional empathy, and coalition building. Although the efficacy of some of these individual elements in reducing children's ethnic prejudice has been explored, others need to be assessed in future research. Given the importance of the issue, this research is sorely needed.

REFERENCES

Aboud, F. (1984). Social and cognitive bases of ethnic identity constancy. *Journal of Genetic Psychology, 184,* 217–230.

Aboud, F. (1988). *Children and prejudice.* Oxford, UK: Blackwell.

Aboud, F. (1993). The developmental psychology of racial prejudice. *Transcultural Psychiatric Review, 30,* 229–242.

Aboud, F., & Doyle, A. (1996a). Does talk of race foster prejudice or tolerance in children? *Canadian Journal of Behavioural Science, 28,* 161–170.

Aboud, F., & Doyle, A. (1996b). Parental and peer influences on children's racial attitudes. *International Journal of Intercultural Relations, 20,* 371–383.

Aboud, F. E., & Fenwick, V. (1999). Exploring and evaluating school-based interventions to reduce prejudice. *Journal of Social Issues, 55,* 767–786.

Aboud, F. E., & Levy, S. R. (2000). Interventions to reduce prejudice and discrimination in children and adolescents. In S. Oskamp (Ed.) *Reducing prejudice and discrimination* (pp. 269–293). Mahwah, NJ: Erlbaum.

Aboud, F. E., & Mitchell, F. G. (1977). Ethnic role taking: The effects of preference and self-identification. *International Journal of Psychology, 12,* 1–17.

Abrams, D., Rutland, A., & Cameron, L. (2003). The development of subjective group dynamics: Children's judgments of normative and deviant in-group and out-group individuals. *Child Development, 74*(6), 1840–1856.

Abrams, D., Rutland, A., Cameron L., & Marques, J. M. (2003). The development of subjective group dynamics: When in-group bias gets specific. *British Journal of Developmental Psychology, 21*(2), 155–176.

Adler, S. M. (2004). Home–school relations and the construction of racial and ethnic identity of Hmong elementary students. *School Community Journal, 14,* 57–75.

Adorno, T. W., Frenkel-Brunswick, E., Levinson, D. J., & Sanford, R. N. (1950). *The authoritarian personality.* New York: Harper and Row.

Allport, G. W. (1954). *The nature of prejudice.* Cambridge, MA: Addison-Wesley.

Aloise-Young, P. A. (1993). The development of self-presentation: Self-promotion in 6- to 10-year-old children. *Social Cognition, 11,* 201–222.

Aronson, E., Blaney, N., Stephan, C., Sikes, J., & Snapp, M. (1978). *The jig-saw classroom.* London: Sage.

Asher, S. R., & Allen, V. L. (1969). Racial preference and social comparison processes. *Journal of Social Issues, 25,* 157–167.

Banks, W. C., & Rompf, W. J. (1973). Evaluative bias and preference behaviour in black and white children. *Child Development, 44,* 776–783.

Banerjee, R. (2002). Audience effects on self-presentation in childhood. *Social Development, 11,* 487–507.

Banerjee, R., & Yuill, N. (1999). Children's explanations for self-presentational behaviour. *European Journal of Social Psychology, 29*(1), 105–111.

Bartel, H. W., Bartel, N. R., & Grill, J. J. (1973). A sociometric view of some integrated open classrooms. *Journal of Social Issues, 29*(4), 159–173.

Baumeister, R. F., & Leary, M. R (1995). The need to belong: Desire for interpersonal attachments as a fundamental human motivation. *Psychological Bulletin, 117*(3), 497–529.

Bennett, M., & Yeeles, C. (1990). Children's understanding of self-presentational strategies of ingratiation and self-promotion. *European Journal of Social Psychology, 20,* 455–461.

Bigler, R. S. (1995). The role of classification skill in moderating environmental influences on children's gender stereotyping: A study of the functional use of gender in the classroom. *Child Development, 66,* 1072–1087.

Bigler, R. S., Jones, L. C., & Lobliner, D. B. (1997). Social categorisation and the formation of intergroup attitudes in children. *Child Development, 68*(3), 530–543.

Bigler, R. S., & Liben, L. S. (1993). A cognitive-developmental approach to racial stereotyping and constructive memory in Euro-American children. *Child Development, 64,* 1507–1518.

Black-Gutman, D. & Hickson, F. (1996). The relationship between racial attitudes and social-cognitive development in children: An Australian study. *Developmental Psychology, 32,* 448–456.

Bird, C., Monachesi, E. D., & Burdick, H. (1952). Infiltration and the attitudes of white and Negro parents and children. *Journal of Abnormal Social Psychology, 47,* 688–689.

Bowers, V. & Swanson, D. (1988). *More than meets the eye.* Vancouver, B.C.: Pacific Educational Press.

Boulton, M. (1995). Patterns of bully/victim problems in mixed race groups of children. *Social Development, 4,* 277–293.

Boulton, M. J., & Smith, P. K. (1993). Ethnic, gender partner, and activity preferences in mixed race schools in the U.K.: Playground observations. In C. Hart (Ed.) *Children on playgrounds: Research perspectives and applications* (pp. 210–238). Albany, NY: State University of New York Press.

Brand, E. S., Ruiz, R. A., & Padilla, A. M. (1974). Ethnic identification and preference: A review. *Psychological Bulletin, 81,* 860–890.

Breckheimer, S. E., & Nelson, R. O. (1976). Group methods for reducing racial prejudice and discrimination. *Psychological Reports, 39,* 1259–1268.

Brown, R. (1995). *Prejudice. Its social psychology.* Oxford, UK: Basil Blackwell.

Brown, C. S., & Bigler, R. S. (2004). Children's perceptions of gender discrimination. *Developmental Psychology, 40*(5), 714–726.

Brown, G., & Johnson, S. P. (1971). The attribution of behavioural connotations to shaded and white figures by caucasion children. *British Journal of Social and Clinical Psychology, 10,* 306–312.

Cameron, J. A., Alvarez, J. M., Ruble, D. N., & Fuligni, A. J. (2001). Children's lay theories about ingroups and outgroup: Reconcpetualizing research on prejudice. *Personality and Social Psychology Review, 5,* 118–128.

Chafel, J. A. (1986). A naturalistic investigation of the use of social comparisons by young children. *Journal of Research and Development in Education, 19*(3), 51–61.

Clark, K. B., & Clark, M. K. (1939). Segregation as a factor in the racial identification of Negro pre-school children: A preliminary report. *Journal of Experimental Psychology, 8*(2), 161–163.

Clark, K. B., & Clark, M. P. (1947). Racial identification and preference in Negro children. In T. M. Newcomb & E. L. Hartley. *Readings in Social Psychology* (pp. 169–178). New York: Henry Holt & Co.

Cramer, P., & Anderson, G. (2003). Ethnic/racial attitudes and self-identification of Black Jamaican and white New England children. *Journal of Cross-Cultural Psychology, 34*(4), 395–416.

Derman-Sparks, L., & Phillips, C. B. (1997). *Teaching/learning anti-racism: A developmental approach.* New York: Teachers College, Columbia University.

Dovidio, J. F., & Gaertner, S. L. (1991). Changes in the expression and assessment of racial prejudice. In H. J. Knopke, R. J. Norrell, & R. W. Rogers (Eds.), *Opening doors: Perspectives on race relations in contemporary America* (pp. 119–148). Tuscaloosa: University of Alabama Press

Doyle, A. B., & Aboud, F. E. (1995). A longitudinal study of white children's racial prejudice as a social-cognitive development. *Merrill-Palmer Quarterly, 41,* 209–228.

Doyle, A. B., Beaudet, J., & Aboud, F. E. (1988). Developmental patterns in the flexibility of children's ethnic attitudes. *Journal of Cross-Cultural Psychology, 19,* 3–18.

Durkin, K. (1995). *Developmental social psychology: From infancy to old age.* Oxford, UK: Blackwell.

Eisenberg, N., Fabes, R. A., Miller, P. A., Shell, R., Shea, C., & May-Plumlee, T. (1990). Preschoolers' vicarious emotional responding and their situational and dispositional prosocial behavior. *Merrill-Palmer Quarterly, 36*(4), 507–529.

Epstein, I. M., Krupat, E., & Obudho, C. (1976). Clean is beautiful: Identification and preference as a function of race and cleanliness. *Journal of Social Issues, 32,* 109–118.

Feshbach, N. D., & Feshbach, S. (1998). Aggression in schools: Towards reducing ethnic conflict and enhancing ethnic understanding. In P. K. Trickett, & C. J. Schellenbach (Eds.), *Violence against children in the family and the community* (pp. 269–286). Washington DC: American Psychological Association.

Fishbein, H. D., & Imai, S. (1993). Preschoolers select playmates on the basis of gender and race. *Journal of Applied Developmental Psychology, 14,* 303–316.

Flavell, J. H. (1963). *The developmental psychology of Jean Piaget.* New York: Litton.

Frenkel-Brunswick, E., & Havel, J. (1953). Prejudice in the interviews of children: Attitudes toward minority groups. *Journal of Genetic Psychology, 82,* 91–136.

Gaertner, S. L., Dovidio, J. F., Anastosio, P. A., Bachman, B. A., & Rust, M. C. (1993). The common ingroup identity model: Recategorization and the reduction of intergroup bias. In W. Stroebe & M. Hewstone (Eds.), *European Review of Social Psychology Vol. 4* (pp. 1–26). Chichester, UK: Wiley.

George, D. M., & Hoppe, R. A. (1979). Racial identification, preference, and self-concept. *Journal of Cross-Cultural Psychology, 10,* 85–100.

Goldstein, C. G., Koopman, E. J., & Goldstein, H. H. (1979). Racial attitudes in young children as a function of interracial contact in the public schools. *American Journal of Orthopsychiatry, 49,* 89–99.

Goodman, M. (1946). Evidence concerning the genesis of interracial attitudes. *American Anthropologist, 48,* 624–630.

Goodman, M. (1952). *Race awareness in young children.* Cambridge, MA: Addison-Wesley.

Greenwald, A. D., & Banaji, M. R. (1995). Implicit social cognition: Attitudes, self-esteem, and stereotypes. *Psychological Review, 102,* 4–27.

Gregor, A. J., & McPherson, D. A. (1966). Racial preference and ego-identity among white and Bantu children in the republic of South Africa. *Genetic Psychology Monographs, 73,* 217–253.

Harris, D., Gough, H., & Martin, W. E. (1950). Children's ethnic attitudes. II: Relationships to parental beliefs concerning child training. *Child Development, 21,* 169–181.

Hawkins, J. A. (1995). Technology for tolerance. *Teaching Tolerance, 4,* 16–21.

Hollins, E. R., & Guzman, M. T. (2005). Research on preparing teachers for diverse populations. In M. Cochran-Smith & K. M. Zeichner (Eds.), *Studying teacher education: The report of the AERA panel on research and teacher education* (pp. 477–548). Mahwah, NJ: Erlbaum.

Hollins, E. R. & Oliver, E. I. (1999). *Pathways to success in school: Culturally responsive teaching.* Mahwah, NJ: Erlbaum.

Horowitz, E. L. (1936). The development of attitude toward the Negro. *Archives of Psychology, 194,* 2–48.

Horowitz, E. L., & Horowitz, R. E. (1938). Development of social attitudes in children. *Sociometry, 1,* 301–338.

Hraba, J., & Grant, G. (1970). Black is beautiful: A reexamination of racial preference and identification. *Journal of Personality and Social Psychology, 16*(3), 398–402.

Johnson, D. W., & Johnson, R. T. (1975). *Learning together and alone.* Engelwood Cliffs, NJ: Prentice-Hall.

Katz, P. A. (1973). Perception of racial cues in preschool children: A new look. *Developmental Psychology, 8*(2), 295–299.

Katz, P. A. (1976). The acquisition of racial attitudes in children. In P. A. Katz (Ed.), *Towards the elimination of racism* (pp. 125–154). New York: Pergamon Press.

Katz, P. A. & Seavey, C. (1973). Labels and children's perception of faces. *Child Development, 44,* 770–775.

Katz, P. A., Sohn, M., & Zalk, S. R. (1975). Perceptual concomitants of racial attitudes in urban grade-school children. *Developmental Psychology, 11,* 135–144.

Katz. P. A. & Zalk, S. R. (1978). Modification of children's racial attitudes. *Developmental Psychology, 11,* 135–144.

Killen, M., Piscane, K., Lee-Kim, J., & Ardila-Rey, A. (2001). Fairness or stereotypes? Young children's priorities when evaluating group exclusion and inclusion. *Developmental Psychology, 37,* 587–596.

Kofkin, J. A., Katz, P. A. & Downey, E. P. (1995). *Family discourse about race and the development of children's race attitudes.* Paper presented at Society for Research in Child Development Meeting, Indianopolis.

Kowalski, K. (2003). The emergence of ethnic and racial attitudes in pre-school aged children. *Journal of Social Psychology, 143,* 677–699.

Krevans, J., & Gibbs, J. C. (1996). Parents' use of inductive discipline: relations to children's empathy and prosocial behavior. *Child Development, 67*(6), 3263–3277.

Lambert, W. E., & Taguchi, Y. (1956). Ethnic cleavage among young children. *Journal of Abnormal Psychology, 53,* 380–382.

Lerner, R. M., & Buehrig, C. J. (1975). The development of racial attitudes in young Black and White Children. *Journal of Genetic Psychology, 127,* 45–54.

Lerner, R. M., & Schroeder, C. (1971). Kindergarten children's active vocabulary about body build. *Developmental Psychology, 5,* 179.

Linville, P. W. (1998). The heterogeneity of homogeneity. In J. M. Darley & J. Cooper (Eds.), *Attribution processes, person perception, and social interactions: The legacy of Edward E. Jones* (pp. 423–487). Washington, DC: American Psychological Association.

Litvack-Miller, W., McDougall, D., & Romney, D. M. (1997). The structure of empathy during middle childhood and its relationship to prosocial behavior. *Genetic, Social, & General Psychology Monographs, 123*(3), 303–324.

Marsh, A. (1970). Awareness of racial differences in West African and British children. *Race, 11,* 289–302.

Milner, D. (1973). Racial identification and preference in "black" British children. *European Journal of Social Psychology, 3*(3), 281–295.

Milner, D. (1983). *Children and race: Ten years on.* London: Ward Lock Educational.

Milner, D. (1996). Children and racism: Beyond the value of the dolls. In W. Peter Robinson. *Social groups and identities: Developing the legacy of Henri Tajfel* (pp. 249–268). Oxfrod, UK: Butterworth-Heinemann.

Mosher, D. L., & Scodel, A. (1960). Relationships between ethnocentrism in children and the ethnocentrism and authoritarian rearing practices of their mothers. *Child Development, 31,* 369–376.

Nesdale, D. (1999). Social identity and ethnic prejudice in children. In P. Martin & W. Noble (Eds.), *Psychology and Society* (pp. 92–110). Brisbane: Australian Academic Press.

Nesdale, D. (2000). Developmental changes in children's ethnic preferences and social cognitions. *Journal of Applied Developmental Psychology, 20,* 501–519.

Nesdale, D. (2001a). Development of prejudice in children. In M. Augoustinos & K. Reynolds (Eds.), *Understanding prejudice, racism, and social conflict* (pp. 57–72). London: Sage.

Nesdale, D. (2001b). Language and the development of children's ethnic prejudice. *Journal of Language and Social Psychology, 20*(1/2), 90–110.

Nesdale, D. (2004). Social identity processes and children's ethnic prejudice. In M. Bennett & F. Sani (Eds.), *The development of the social self* (pp. 219–246). East Sussex: Psychology Press.

Nesdale, D. & Brown, K. (2004). Children's attitudes towards an atypical member of an ethnic in-group. *International Journal of Behavioral Development, 28*(4), 328–335.

Nesdale, D., Durkin, K., Maass, A., & Griffiths, J. (2004). Group status, outgroup ethnicity, and children's ethnic attitudes. *Journal of Applied Developmental Psychology,* 25, 237–251.

Nesdale, D., Durkin, K., & Maass, A., & Griffiths, J. (2005). Threat, group identification, and children's ethnic prejudice. *Social Development, 14,* 189–205.

Nesdale, D., & Flesser, D. (2001). Social identity and the development of children's group attitudes. *Child Development, 72*(9), 506–517.

Nesdale, D., Griffiths, J. Durkin, K., & Maass, A. (2005). Empathy, group norms and children's ethnic attitudes. *Journal of Applied Developmental Psychology, 26,* 623–637.

Nesdale, D. & Lambert, A. (in press-a). Peer group rejection, affect and children's antisocial behavior. *International Journal of Behavioral Development.*

Nesdale, D. & Lambert, A. (in press-b). Peer group rejection and children's risk-taking behavior. *European Journal of Developmental Psychology.*

Nesdale, D., Maass, A., Durkin, K., & Griffiths, J. (2005). Group norms, threat and children's ethnic prejudice. *Child Development, 76,* 1–12.

Nesdale, D., Maass, A., Griffiths, J., & Durkin, K. (2003). Effects of ingroup and out-group ethnicity on children's attitudes towards members of the ingroup and outgroup. *British Journal of Developmental Psychology, 21,* 177–192.

Nesdale, D. & Pelyhe, H. (2005). Effects of peer rejection on children: Affect, self-esteem, and attitudes to the ingroup and outgroup. Griffith University. Australia.

Nesdale, D., & Pelyhe, H. (in press). Effects of experimentally induced peer group rejection on children's anxiety, self-esteem, and ingroup and outgroup attitudes. *European Journal of Developmental Psychology.*

Nesdale, D. & Todd, T. (2000). Effect of contact on intercultural acceptance: A field study. *International Journal of Intercultural Relations, 24,* 341–360.

Patchen, M. (1983). Student's own racial abilities and those of peers of both races, as related to interracial behaviour. *Sociology and Social Research, 68,* 59–77.

Pettigrew, T.F., & Meertens, R.W. (1995). Subtle and blatant prejudice in Western Europe. *European Journal of Social Psychology, 25,* 57–75.

Porter, J. D. R. (1971). *Black child, white child. The development of racial attitudes.* Cambridge MA: Harvard University Press.

Proshansky, H. M. (1966). The development of intergroup attitudes. In L. W. Hoffman & M. L. Hoffman (Eds.), *Review of child development research* (pp. 311–371). New York: Russell Sage.

Radke, M. J., & Trager, H. G. (1950). Children's perceptions of the social roles of Negroes and whites. *Journal of Psychology, 29,* 3–33.

Radke, M. J., Trager, H. G., & Davis, H. (1949). Social perceptions and attitudes of children. *Genetic Psychology Monographs, 40,* 327–447.

Radke-Yarrow, M., Trager, H., & Miller, J. (1952). The role of parents in the development of children's ethnic attitudes. *Child Development, 23,* 13–53.

Radke-Yarrow, M., Zahn-Waxler, C., & Chapman, M. (1983). Prosocial dispositions and behavior. In P. Mussen (Ed.). *Manual of child psychology: Vol 4. Socialization, personality, and social development* (pp. 469–545). New York: Wiley.

Ramsey, P. G. (1991). The salience of race in young children growing up in al all-white community. *Journal of Educational Psychology, 83,* 28–34.

Ramsey, P. G. (1997). Young children's thinking about ethnic differences. In J. Phinney & M. Rotherman (Eds.), *Children's ethnic socialization* (pp. 249–263). Newbury Park, CA: Sage.

Renninger, C. A., & Williams, J. E. (1966). Black–white color connotations and race awareness in pre-school children. *Perceptual and Motor Skills, 22,* 771–785.

Richardson, S. A., & Royce, J. (1968). Race and physical handicap in childrens' preferences for other children. *Child Development, 39,* 467–480.

Roberts, W., & Strayer, J. (1996). Empathy, emotional expressiveness, and prosocial behavior. *Child Development, 67,* 449–470.

Rosenfield, D., & Stephan, W. G. (1981). Intergroup relations among children. In S. S. Brehm & S. Kassin (Eds.), *Developmental social psychology* (pp. 271–297). Oxford, UK: Oxford University Press.

Rubin, K., Bukowski, W., & Parker, J. G. (1998). Peer interactions, relationships and groups. In W. Daemon (Series Ed.) and N. Eisenberg (Vol. Ed.), *Handbook of child psychology: Vol.3, Social emotional and personality development* (5th ed., pp. 619–700). New York: Wiley.

Rutland, A., Cameron, L., Milne, A., & McGeorge, P. (2003, August). *Self-presentation and intergroup attitudes in children*. Paper presented at the XIth European Conference on Developmental Psychology, Milan, Italy.

Schofield, J. W. (1982). *Black and white in school: Trust, tension, or tolerance?* New York: Praeger.

Semaj, L. (1980). The development of racial evaluation and preference: A cognitive approach. *Journal of Black Psychology, 6*, 59–79.

Sheets, R. H. (1999). Human development and ethnic identity. In R. H. Sheets & E. R. Hollins (Eds.), *Racial and ethnic identity in school practices: Aspects of human development* (pp. 99–101). Mahwah, NJ: Erlbaum.

Sheets, R. H. (2004). Preparation and development of teachers of color. *International Journal of Qualitative Studies in Education, 17*, 163–166.

Sheets, R. H., & Hollins, E. R. (1999). *Racial and ethnic identity in school practices: Aspects of human development*. Mahwah, NJ: Erlbaum.

Stephan, W. G., & Rosenfield, D. (1979). Black self-rejection: Another look. *Journal of Educational Psychology, 71*, 708–716.

Stephan, W. G., Ybarra, O., Martinez, C. M., Schwarzwald, J., & Tur-Kaspa, M. (1998). Prejudice toward immigrants to Spain and Israel. *Journal of Cross-Cultural Psychology, 29*(4), 559–576.

Stevenson, H. W., & Stevenson, N. G. (1960). Social interaction in an interracial nursery school. *Genetic Psychology Monographs, 61*, 37–75.

Strayer, J., & Roberts, W. (2004). Children's anger, emotional expressiveness, and empathy: Relations with parents' empathy, emotional expressiveness, and parenting practices. *Social Development, 13*(2), 229–254.

Tajfel, H., Flament, C., Billig, M. G., & Bundy, R. P. (1971). Social categorisation and intergroup behaviour. *European Journal of Social Psychology, 1*, 149–178.

Tajfel, H., Jahoda, G., Nemeth, C., Rim, Y., & Johnson, N. B. (1972). The devaluation by children of their own national and ethnic group: Two case studies. *British Journal of Social and Clinical Psychology, 11*, 235–243.

Tajfel, H., & Turner, J. (1979). An integrative theory of intergroup conflict. In W. G. Austin & S. Worchel (Eds.), *The social psychology of intergroup relations* (pp. 33–47) Monterey: Brooks/Cole Publishing Company.

Teichman, Y. (2006). *Intergroup inclusion and exclusion in a context of an intractable conflict: Developmental perspective*. Paper presented at European Association of Experimental Social Psychology, Medium Sized Meeting: Social developmental perspectives on intergroup inclusion and exclusion, University of Kent, July, 2006.

Teplin, L.A. (1976). A comparison of racial/ethnic preferences among Anglo, Black and Latino children. *American Journal of Orthopsychiatry, 46*(4), 702–709.

Theimer, C. E., Killen, M., & Stangor, C. (2001). Young children's evaluations of exclusion in gender-stereotypic peer contexts. *Developmental Psychology, 37*, 18–37.

Van Ausdale, D., & Feagin, J. R. (1996). Using racial and ethnic concepts: The critical case of very young children. *American Sociological Review, 61*, 779–793.

Vaughan, G. M. (1963). Concept formation and the development of ethnic awareness. *Journal of Genetic Psychology, 103*, 93–103.

Vaughan, G. M., (1964). The development of ethnic attitudes in New Zealand school children. *Genetic Psychology Monographs, 70,* 135–175.

Vaughan, G. M. (1987). A social psychological model of ethnic identity development. In J. S. Phinney & M. J. Rotheram (Eds.), *Children's ethnic socialization: Pluralism and development* (pp. 73–91). Newbury Park, CA: Sage.

Vaughan, G., Tajfel, H., & Williams, J. A. (1981). Bias in reward allocation in an intergroup and an interpersonal context. *Social Psychology Quarterly, 44,* 37–42.

Vaughan, G. M., & Thompson, R. H. T. (1961). New Zealand children's attitudes toward Maoris. *Journal of Abnormal Social Psychology, 62,* 701–704.

Verkuyten, M., & Masson, K. (1995). "New Racism," self esteem, and ethnic relations among minority and majority youth in the Netherlands. *Social Behaviour and Personality, 23*(2), 137–154.

Warden, D., & Mackinnon, S. (2003). Prosocial children, bullies and victims: An investigation of their sociometric status, empathy and social problem-solving strategies. *British Journal of Developmental Psychology, 21*(3), 367–385.

Weiland, A., & Coughlin, R. (1979). Self-identification and preferences. A comparison of white and Mexican-American first and third graders. *Journal of Cross-Cultural Psychology, 10*(3), 356–365.

Weiner, M. J., & Wright, F. E. (1973). Effects of undergoing arbitrary discrimination upon subsequent attitudes toward a minority group. *Journal of Applied Psychology, 3,* 94–102.

Williams, J. E., Best, D. L., & Boswell, D. A. (1975). The measurement of children's racial attitudes in the early school years. *Child Development, 46,* 494–500.

Williams, J. E., & Roberson, J. K. (1967). A method for assessing racial attitudes in preschool children. *Educational and Psychological Measurement, 27,* 671–689.

Yee, M. D., & Brown, R. (1992). Self-evaluations and intergroup attitudes in children aged three to nine. *Child Development, 63,* 619–629.

Yee, M. D., & Brown, R. (1994). The development of gender differentiation in young children. *British Journal of Social Psychology, 33,* 183–196.

Zinser, O., Rich, M. C., & Bailey, R. C. (1981). Sharing behaviour and racial preference in children. *Motivation and Emotion, 5,* 179–187.

CHAPTER 11

SOCIAL LEARNING AND WEIGHT-RELATED PROBLEMS

Moria Golan

INTRODUCTION

The global obesity epidemic is one of today's most pertinent public health issues affecting all major groups in society, including children (James, Rigby, & Leach, 2004). The prevalence of obesity has doubled in children over the past 20 years (Bundred, Kitchiner, & Buchan, 2001; Troiano, Flegal, Kuczmarski, Campbell, & Johnson, 1995). Given the increased risk of an overweight child becoming an obese adult, with extensive implications for morbidity or becoming an eating disorder sufferer, extensive consideration needs to be given to the social-ecological context in which the child is raised.

Multiple factors are related to the high incidence of weight-related problems in childhood. Both genetic (endogenous) and environmental (exogenous) factors contribute to the development of childhood obesity as well as eating disorders (Barsh, Farooqi, & O'Rahilly, 2000). Many authors support a model in which susceptibility to these health problems is determined largely by genetic factors; however, the environment determines individual phenotypic expression (Barsh et al., 2000).

In modern industrialized societies, food and drink are more available and affordable than ever before. Industrialized agro-food systems estab-

Contemporary Perspectives on Socialization and Social Development..., pages 241–266
Copyright © 2007 by Information Age Publishing

lished by global corporations have made cheap calorie-dense foods, fats, and oils widely available across the world and have caused what researchers call a *nutrition transition*. There is a shift in diets towards more fast and pre-packaged foods with high fat and high calorie content (Adair & Popkin, 2005; Sobal, 2001a).

Moreover, fewer people have jobs requiring hard physical labor, car ownership has increased rapidly, and homes have laborsaving devices. There is greater dependence on mechanized transportation as well as loss of safe, open spaces for physical activity (Sobal, 2001b). These days, children are watching more television and playing video games, and doing less physical activity. As they watch, they also may tend to eat more high fat and high calorie snack foods, and they may not stop eating when they are full because of the distraction.

This *obesogenic environment* that encourages sedentary behavior and the consumption of a calorie-dense diet with greater energy than is required, as well as discouraging physical activity, affects how dietary intake patterns are established in early childhood and may ultimately influence the development of obesity (Swinburn, Egger, & Raza, 1999). Paradoxically, the same obesogenic environment also stigmatizes fatness, idealizes thinness, and encourages quick approaches to weight loss (Battle & Brownell, 1996).

Moreover, the change in gender roles and the feminist movement, which have focused on contributions to changes in occupation, to change in power balance and family structure, are associated with change in family functioning, family life, and parenting practices which also influence health behaviors (Hill & Trowbridge, 1998; Zametkin, Zoon, Klein, & Munson, 2004). Loneliness and social isolation, psychosocial/family problems, and preoccupation with food and diets are more common among obese children (Zametkin et al., 2004). Sobal asserted that children and adolescents tend to participate in global culture more rapidly than their parents and may more readily adopt food preferences and recreational activities that could place them at higher risk than adults of becoming overweight (Sobal, 2001b).

Human beings live in a dynamic *social ecology* as well as a physical one. An ecological perspective relates to *multiple levels of influence* (intrapersonal or individual factors, interpersonal factors, institutional or organizational factors, community factors, and public policy factors) and recognizes *reciprocal causation* between individuals and their environments: behavior both influences and is influenced by the social environment in which it occurs. The circle of influence includes those closest to an individual, such as family members, friends, and other peers, but the circle can expand to school, health professionals, and other people one identifies with or admires.

One of the models that best encompasses this concept is the *social learning theory* (SLT), according to which, personal (e.g., self-efficacy), environmental (e.g., social circle), and behavioral (e.g., preventive health practices) factors reinforce each other in a *reciprocal manner.* Adults who are oriented toward healthier lifestyles, for example, create healthy environments that can promote children's dispositions toward health. Similarly, those who possess greater knowledge and self-efficacy are likely to surround themselves with environments that further promote these qualities (Bandura, 1986). SLT assumes that most behaviors are learned responses and can be modified. Thus, learning through observing the behavior of others (i.e., modeling) is important from an SLT perspective (Pandura, 1995).

There are other useful theories of interpersonal influence (social power, interpersonal communication, social networks, and social support) as well as theories and models that attempt to explain health behavior change (the health belief model, the theory of reasoned action, and the trans-theoretical model), but they are not discussed in this monograph because of length constraints.

This chapter will discuss the various elements of the social learning theory as reflected in children's intrapersonal factors, interpersonal factors, social environment, their choice of health behavior, and the risk for weight related problems.

CHILDREN'S INTRAPERSONAL FACTORS

Food Selection and Energy Regulation

Excess calorie intake, relative to energy expenditure, will result in the storage of energy as fat, eventually leading to excessive levels of fat in the body. Children's preferences for energy-dense foods, especially sweets and fats may place children at risk of overweight (Hill & Trowbridge, 1998).

Food selection is a three-stage process. Initially, there are biological tendencies to consume pleasant tasting and familiar foods, and then the physiological and social consequences of eating are learned from the results. This learning process results in the development of beliefs and attitude about food that may dominate adult life. At the start of life, food preferences are at least partially influenced by biologically generated internal cues. There appears to be an innate preference for sweet and salty flavors and for the avoidance of bitter and sour tastes (Benton, 2004). It has been hypothesized that such preferences reflect an evolutionary background where sweetness predicts a source of energy, and bitterness predicts toxicity. Children also eat more of the foods they like best (Anliker, Bartoshuk, Ferris, & Hooks, 1991).

The innate preference for a sweet taste is quickly modified by experience. By 6 months of age infants' preference was associated with dietary experience; only those children routinely fed sweetened water, compared with those who were not, showed a greater preference for sweetness. Birch (1992) found that sweetness and familiarity were the major determinants of the food preferences of young children. Birch's experiments support the social learning theory that emphasizes the importance of exposure and experience in promoting healthy food selection. Children choose to eat foods that are served most often, and prefer what has been available and acceptable in the household.

There is growing evidence of an association between the percentage of energy consumed as fat and being overweight in children (Fischer & Birch, 1995; Nguyen, Larson, Johnson, & Goran, 1996). The preference for fatty foods in children 3- to 5-years-of-age is associated with intake and has been found to predict skin-fold thickness, an index of adiposity in children of this age (Fischer & Birch, 1995). The physiological conditioning (internal reinforcement as described by SLT) of flavor preferences for foods high in energy density may have the greatest effect on children's liking of energy-dense foods among families in which those foods are most available and accessible (Birch & Fisher, 1998). The tendency to learn to prefer energy-dense foods can be seen as having been adaptive at times in our history when food was scarce, particularly for young children requiring energy to grow. Today, when energy-dense foods are readily available, this tendency predisposes to obesity. Thus, an association with high calorie density can create taste preference. Moreover, we tend to like foods that result in satiety, which is also an internal reinforcement when eating high calorie density foods (Benton, 2004).

As a generalization, infants and young children have the ability to adjust their food intake both across and within meals; in this way, they have the potential to maintain a relatively constant intake of energy (Benton, 2004). The ability to regulate caloric intake in preschool children is related to their adiposity. Those less able to regulate caloric intake tend to be heavier.

Emotional Eating and Energy Regulation

The affect regulation model posits that dysphoric individuals eat in an effort to provide comfort (internal reinforcement) or distraction from negative emotions, and therefore eating is a learned process. The child has learned that it serves as a compensatory mechanism, which increases the risk for weight gain (Parsons, Power, Logan, & Summerbell, 1999). Thus, obese children may overeat as a consequence of environmental deprivation or as a result of depression, neglect, somatization, familial abuse, and a generally nonsupportive home environment (Christoffel & Forsyth, 1989; Strauss, 1999). Neglected children are nine times more likely than others to become obese (Lissau & Sorenson, 1994). Satter (2005) suggests that a child learns to eat for emotional reasons, when his parents regularly and consistently use food to deal with feelings—to diffuse, soothe, or entertain. This error in learning generally takes place somewhere in the first 4 years and is most strongly put in place with the toddler. Physiological eating rather than emotional eating is one of the objectives in health education.

Activity Patterns and Energy Regulation

It is frequently postulated that changes in levels of physical activity in the modern society partially explain increases in the prevalence of overweight among children. Physical activity in children is related to developmental stage, is reduced with increasing age, and is shaped by a combination of the child's characteristics and parent and peer activity patterns, which are in turn shaped by broader contextual factors such as the availability of recreational facilities, school physical education programs, as well as programs for prevention of overweight and promotion of health.

Physical activity in children can be planned or incidental—observation would suggest that in a "time poor" society, the emphasis is placed on planned activity for children (Steinbeck, 2001). While there is debate about the immediate health benefits of physical activity for children, there are data that support lower physical activity levels and increased sedentary behaviors as being associated with a higher prevalence of obesity in children (Sallis, Prochaska, & Taylor, 2000).

An increasingly sedentary lifestyle might influence weight regulation in a number of ways. Television and computer games induce stillness that is more still than other nominated sedentary activities such as reading or drawing (Dietz, Bandini, Morelli, Peers, & Ching, 1994). Klesges, Shelton, and Klesges (1993) demonstrated the effectiveness of this medium in instilling stillness, with children having measurably lower resting energy expenditure when watching TV than when just sitting still.

Moreover, for many, television time is snack time, and the diversion of television reduces the capacity to monitor total energy intake. For many families, meals are taken in front of the television. Those watching television will be exposed to more advertising, but it may also encourage the eating of quickly prepared snack foods rather than more elaborate meals (Taras, Sallis, Patterson, Nader, & Nelson, 1989). Parents whose children watch more television tended to choose foods that were easy to prepare because the children ate them without complaining. There was evidence that watching television was associated with eating some foods that were not normally advertised, suggesting that this activity is a marker for parental attitudes to the provision of their children's meals. The frequent watching of television during a meal was associated with 5% more of their energy intake coming in the form of pizza, salty snacks, and soda, and 5% less from fruit, vegetables, and juices (Taras et al., 1989).

Television as a child-minder may reduce access to active playtime. Television has been more extensively investigated than other small screen leisure activities, such as computers, videos, and video games, all of which may be expected to have subtly different impacts on energy expenditure. Trials by Robinson (1999, 2000) have shown that restrictions on TV watching can lead to beneficial effects measured by several different approaches. It appears that gains can be made in obesity prevention through restricting television viewing, although it seems that reduced eating in front of the television is at least as important as decreasing inactivity or increasing activity (Robinson, 1999).

Child Self-Perceptions and Weight-Related Problems

In the social cognitive theory, Bandura (1986) provided a view of human behavior in which the beliefs that people have about themselves are critical elements in the exercise of control and personal agency. Because people's expected outcomes are filtered through a person's expectations or perceptions of being able to perform the behavior in the first place, *self-efficacy*—the confidence in one's ability to make the desired change when it is necessary—is believed to be the single most important characteristic that determines a person's behavior change. A child's *self-esteem* and *self-efficacy* are determinants that influence a child's motivation for change in case of weight related problems. Obese children, more than their nonobese peers, tend to suffer from low self-esteem, low efficacy perception, poor body image, depression, school performance difficulties, and learning problems, and succeed less in weight loss programs (Epstein, Klein, & Wisniewski, 1994; Friedman & Brownell, 1995). It is not known whether these psychosocial problems develop as a consequence of the child's obesity or are factors that increase the child's vulnerability to becoming obese. However, they influence the child's motivation for change. Thus clinicians need to point out strengths; use persuasion and encouragement, and approach behavior change in small steps.

A child who has tried numerous weight-loss diets may feel discouraged until he sees someone who has much the same problem, but who has slimmed down—this may increase his self efficacy and may motivate him to try again—this is one of the premises of the group therapy approach to weight-related problems.

Child's Knowledge about Health

Knowledge about health is an intrapersonal factor that determines behavior change. SLT emphasizes that in order to induce *behavioral capability*, a person needs to know what to do and how to do it. Thus, clear instructions and sometimes training are needed, but still may not be enough. To promote health behavior information and training about action should be provided as along with information about the likely results of the recommended action.

Those with greater knowledge about health enact more healthful behaviors across a variety of domains (Edmundson, Parcel, Feldman, & Elder, 1996). This is the reason why all health promotion programs strive to enhance participant knowledge about health. One of the reasons why knowledge, compared to self-efficacy, is a weaker predictor of behavior is that the relationship between knowledge and behavior seems to have a threshold effect. Although some knowledge about the relationship between health behaviors and outcomes is important in encouraging healthy behaviors, greater knowledge does not necessarily translate into more consistent healthier behaviors, particularly when impediments to behavior change exist (Rimal, 2003).

CHILD'S INTERPERSONAL FACTORS— THE FAMILY ENVIRONMENT

Social learning theory emphasizes that individuals respond to *external stimuli* while actively participating by observing, attending to, retaining, and producing behaviors based on personal and environmental contingencies (operant conditioning—reward and punishment), classical conditioning, and cognitive mediational processes (Bandura, 1977, 1997).

To the extent that children's health behaviors are influenced by adults' health behaviors, it is hypothesized that children's behavioral determinants, including self-efficacy, knowledge, and use of health information, will be affected by behavioral determinants of adults in the household. A primary concept in SLT is *observational learning*, a process through which individuals evaluate and model the behaviors of others (parents, peers, teachers, mass media). To the extent that household adults act as children's socializing agents, children can be expected to model adults' behaviors.

Association between the Eating Habits of Children and Those of Their Parents

Parent and child dietary habits and preferences are likely to reflect genetic and environmental factors. Links among parental adiposity and fat intake, and children's adiposity and fat intake, has been reported (Fisher & Birch, 1995). Children's food preferences were correlated with biological family members as well as pseudo-family members. Associations were significantly greater for biological than pseudo-family pairings, especially when comparing siblings (Faith, 2005).

Oliveria et al. (1992) reported that children whose parents ate diets high in saturated fat also ate diets high in saturated fats themselves. Parents tend to have foods in the home that they like and eat, and with repeated opportunities to eat these foods; young children include many of them in their diets. Consumption of fruits and vegetables were most common in children whose parents routinely consume fruits and vegetables (Benton, 2004). Rimal (2003) found a significant relationship between adults and children's dietary behaviors that could be explained by similarities in food preparation and consumption in the home. However, behaviors that are typically enacted outside the home (e.g., asking cafeterias to serve healthy foods), including food purchase behaviors (reading food labels), as well as adults' and children's food preferences in restaurants, were also similar between parents and their children, indicating a similarity in socialization processes that may underlie the observed relationships between adults' and children's behavioral antecedents, such as their use of health information, knowledge, and self-efficacy.

Association between Children's Activity Pattern and Those of Their Parents

Parental activity is positively related to physical activity among pre-schoolers (Moore et al., 1991). Studies reveal no relationship between parental physical activity and physical activity among elementary school children (McMurray et al., 1993; Sallis et al., 1992), and either no relationship or positive relationships (Sallis, Patterson, McKenzie, & Nader, 1988) with the physical activity of middle school students (grades 5–8). Parental physical activity is positively related to physical activity among older adolescents (Zakarian, Hovell, Hofstetter, Sallis, & Keating, 1994).

Parental Health Promotion Practices

Parents and childcare providers play a major role in determining the foods to which a child is repeatedly exposed. Since children's food preferences are learned through repeated exposure to foods, exposure itself is a major factor in encouraging consumption (Birch, 1992, 1999). Availability and accessibility accounted for 35% of the variability in fruit, juice, and vegetable consumption among elementary school girls, but not in elementary school boys (Johnson & Birch, 1994), and for only 11% of the variability in children's fruit and vegetable consumption among children as a group (Costanzo & Woody, 1985). Parents also control the methods of food preparation and selection of where the family goes out to eat (Cullen, Rittenberry, Olvera, & Baranowski, 2000; Hearn et al., 1998).

Support and direct help from parents, especially if such support is action-oriented (e.g., being active with children, organizing exercise activities, or providing transportation), rather than simply providing prompts to be more active, also increase the availability and probability of children's and adolescents physical activity (Klesges et al., 1984; Klesges, Malcott, Boschee, & Weber, 1986; McKenzie et al., 1991; Sallis, Prochaska, & Taylor, 2000; Zakarian et al., 1994).

Parents as Role Model

The social learning theory emphasizes modeling as an important process in learning behaviors. In order to enhance healthy eating, parents should model healthy eating as well as boundaries in eating foods that are less healthy like sweets or high fat products. Birch (1980) allowed preschool children to observe other children eating the vegetables that the observing children did not like. Older, rather than younger, children were more effective in persuading children to try new foods and mothers were more effective than strangers (Harper & Sanders, 1975). Similarly, observing the mother eating a novel food has been found to make it easier for a child to sample it. Thus, simply offering a vegetable to a role model increased the likelihood that vegetables would be eaten in the future.

There is a readiness to learn to like or dislike foods, depending on the context in which they are eaten and whether they produce a satisfying subjective experience or discomfort. We model our food intake on those around us, particularly those whom we respect. Jansen and Tenney (2001) have shown that a preference for the taste of a higher energy drink was greatest in those drinking it at the same time as the teacher did. It was concluded that a preference for energy-rich foods was most easily established in the presence of an important adult. Benton (2004) suggests that observation of a parent eating and enjoying energy-dense food may enhance preference for these foods.

Parents may also model practices that promote food restriction and disinhibition rather than hunger and satiety sensitivity. The longitudinal nature of The Framingham Children's Study provides a valuable source of data (Hood et al., 2000). They found that those children who have two parents who exhibit high levels of disinhibition, are much more likely to gain excess weight throughout early childhood than are children with fewer parents exhibiting this restraint, but who also report high levels of disinhibition (Westenhoefer, Broeckmann, Munch, & Pudel, 1994). This association may be mediated by direct parental role modeling of unhealthy eating behaviors, or through other indirect, and probably sub-conscious, behavioral consequences such as the suppression of the child's innate regulation of dietary intake.

The family also has an important impact on the child's perception of his body. Birch and Fisher found that mothers' dietary restraint and percep-tions of their daughters' risk of overweight predicted maternal child-feed-ing practices, which in turn predicted the daughters' eating patterns and relative weight (Birch & Fisher, 1998). Others suggested that mothers who are dissatisfied with their own bodies communicate this to their daughters, which may cause the daughter's own body dissatisfaction (Striegel-Moore, 1995). Field et al., (2001) found that both girls and boys who reported that their thinness/lack of fat was important to their father were more likely than their peers to become constant dieters.

Parental Control and Parenting Style

Parents try to foster a healthy lifestyle using various strategies for con-trolling their child's food intake. The impact of parental control on chil-dren's eating habits is an important area for investigation because children's fruit and vegetable consumption is consistently low and parents need to be informed about which feeding strategies are effective and which are counterproductive. Moreover, in response to the obesogenic environ-ment, parents may attempt to limit children's consumption of "junk" or "unhealthy" foods by keeping these foods out of reach or by placing con-straints on when and how much food may be consumed. Experimental studies have shown, however, that restrictive feeding practices increase chil-dren's preferences for restricted foods (Birch, 1980), heighten responsive-ness to the presence of palatable foods, and promote overeating when restricted foods are freely available (Johnson & Birch, 1994).

Johnson and Birch (1994) found that mothers who reported exerting a greater degree of control over their child's food intake had children who demonstrated less ability to internally regulate energy intake. Further-more, children who demonstrated less ability to self-regulate energy intake had higher body fat stores. Thus, external parental control of the child's dietary intake and imposition of stringent parental controls can potentiate preferences for high-fat, energy-dense foods, limit children's acceptance of a variety of foods, and disrupt children's regulation of energy intake by altering children's responsiveness to internal cues of hunger and satiety, indirectly fostering the development of excess adiposity in the child (Birch & Fisher, 1998; Johnson & Birch, 1994). This can occur when well intentioned but concerned parents assume that children need help in determining what, when, and how much to eat, and when parents impose child-feeding practices that provide children with few opportunities for self-control. Thus, parental insensitivity and/or unresponsiveness to feeding cues from the child might be counterproductive to the development of the child's ability to self-regulate and may have adverse consequences for the development of the child's food preferences and intake (Birch & Fisher, 1998).

The child's social environment can also interfere with this self-regulation by instructing a child to finish the food on his plate, a practice that discourages response to bodily cues. Johnson (2000) reported that preschool children who were enrolled in a 6-week role-play exercise to make them aware of internal cues of hunger and satiety improved their self-regulation and ate less lunch after a high calorie drink. Thus, social learning should be utilized to improve children's self-regulation.

Satter (2005) suggests that health care providers and parents should rely on what she refers to as a "trust" paradigm instead of the current "control" paradigm for understanding childhood obesity. She suggests a division of responsibility between parent and child in which it is the parent's responsibility to supply the child with a healthful array of foods and a supportive eating context, and it is the child's responsibility to decide when and how much to eat. In this model, it is assumed that children will eat the amount they need and that it is normal for some children to be overweight. An authoritative feeding style is one in which adults determine which foods are offered, and children determine the amount eaten.

Parenting style may influence the effectiveness of parental child-feeding practices. Parenting style, according to Baumrind (1971, 1991), captures two dimensions that revolve around issues of control. *Parental responsiveness* (the extent to which parents respond to the child's physical and emotional needs, intentionally foster individuality, self-regulation, and self-assertion) and *parental demandingness* (the claims parents make on children). According to Baumrind, authoritative parents provide balanced responsiveness and demandingness—they provide warmth coupled with a reasonable amount of expectations and structure, they are assertive, but not intrusive and restrictive. Authoritarian parents tend to be highly directive and value unquestioning obedience in their exercise of authority over their children, have high expectations. Studies have shown a negative relationship between authoritarian parenting style and children's psychosocial well being and health (Olvera-Ezzell, Power, & Cousins, 1990; Tinsley, 1992).

Permissive parents are more responsive than they are demanding. They essentially allow children to make their own decisions and regulate their own activities. Such parents may avoid setting boundaries and restricting sedentary activity as recommended by the American Academy of Pediatrics Committee (1995). Chen and Kennedy (2004) suggested that a permissive parenting style is associated with greater food intake in Chinese American children. Because such a democratic parenting style may reflect unstructured parenting in the Chinese culture, children in a less structured family environment may not be able to self-regulate their food intake.

Family Functioning

Because most children do not normally think about health issues, adults have to communicate, either directly or indirectly through their behaviors, health-related values if children are to develop healthy lifestyles as adults. For example, greater success can be achieved in getting children to eat well if adults engage children in discussions about food including information about food content, available choices among different foods with similar nutritional content, and the importance of eating well (Rimal & Flora, 1999). Through communication, adults can share their knowledge about health with children, correct children's misconceptions about health issues, encourage children to become critical consumers of health information, provide verbal assurances about children's abilities to enact healthy behaviors, and motivate children through proper incentives (Rimal, 2003).

There are data indicating that poor family functioning, including difficulties with communication and parenting skills, parental distress, and psychopathology, is associated with pediatric obesity (Stunkard & Wadden, 1992; Wilkins, Kendrick, Stitt, Stinett, & Hammarkund, 1998). Complex links have been described between family factors and interactions and children's eating patterns (Birch & Fisher, 1998).

Some studies have found a negative relationship between family functioning and children's weight, and suggest that the better the family functions, the lower the children's weight (Kinston, Loader, Miller, & Rein, 1988; Wilkins et al., 1998). These studies indicate that families with overweight children report poor family functioning compared with families with normal weight children. Yet other studies have found no association between family function and children's weight issues (Stradmeijer, Bosh, Koops, & Seidell, 2000).

Parental Knowledge, Perceptions, and Self-Efficacy

Parental knowledge and perceptions play an important part in childhood weight related problems because knowledge and perceptions shape parental feeding behaviors and attitudes around appearance and health. A focus group study reported that mothers in a Supplemental Nutrition Program for Women, Infants and Children (WIC) frequently perceived that their infants were not satiated which led to the introduction of solids before recommended ages and described situations in which food was used to shape a child's behavior (Baughcum, Burklow, Deeks, Powers, & Whitaker, 1998).

Knowledgeable adults are better able to impart accurate information about health to children, provide answers to common queries about health, and assist children in sorting through conflicting information about health that children are likely to encounter. When health information is readily available in the home, compared to situations when such information is difficult to obtain, children can be expected to use it and benefit from it.

Moreover, use of health information is likely to result in greater knowledge about health, which in turn can lead to greater self-efficacy and positive behaviors (Nader, Sellers, Johnson, & Perry, 1996; Rimal, 2003). These findings highlight the importance of educating mothers and changing their perceptions in order to improve their feeding relationship with their children and preventing weight-related problems.

Social Learning Theory postulates that factors such as self-efficacy and barriers to performing a behavior affect how desired behaviors are modeled and practiced (Bandura, 1986). Low self-efficacy may be a barrier that prevents parents from participating in parent education programs as well as changing problematic feeding practices. Permissive parents with low self-efficacy may avoid setting limits, insist on structured eating, and unconsciously support weight related problems. Hoerr, Utech, and Ruth (2005) asserted that a child's control of mealtime likely had a negative affect on parents' self-efficacy and their ability to positively affect their children's behavior. Parents tended to perceive the child's control as a significant barrier to the quality of mealtime interactions. Chamberlin, Serman, Jain, Powers, and Whitaker (2002) found that mothers felt unable to deal with a demanding child. The health professionals who delivered the nutrition program believed that mothers from a low-income population lacked the knowledge and ability to discipline their children and would therefore give the children anything they desired.

Structure and Family Meals

Structure is an important component in learning self-regulation. Lack of structure stresses children and there is considerable evidence that structure around feeding is eroding. In modern society, working mothers tend to cook less and children tend to eat by themselves and have their own money to buy food—a more democratic atmosphere with the tendency to promote the child's independence; the optimal ratio of control relative to freedom within the family increases (Benton, 2004). Letting young children eat on the run is increasingly the trend, and family meals are decreasing in frequency (Nielsen, Siega-Riz, & Popkin, 2002).

Family meals appear to play an important role in promoting positive dietary intake among children. Whereas in the past, eating for children has generally been within a social context, such as the family meal, in the modern lifestyle, eating alone has become a common event. Unfortunately, the result of this independence is often that unhealthy nutritional patterns abound, including skipping meals and increased consumption of junk food (Graber & Brooks-Gunn, 1996; Tinsley, 1992). Research suggests that when parents provide companionship at mealtime, establish a positive atmosphere, and model appropriate food-related behaviors, their children tend to have improved dietary quality (Stanek, Abbott, & Cramer, 1990). Gillman et al. (2000) reported that those eating more often as a family consumed more fruit and vegetables and less fat. The preference for food eaten in a positive atmosphere tends to increase, whereas preference declines when the atmosphere is negative (Casey & Rozin, 1989). Increased frequency of a family dinner among 9- to 14-year-old children was associated with healthful dietary patterns (Gillman et al., 2000). Longitudinal analyses showed that the frequency of eating a family dinner was inversely associated with overweight prevalence at baseline, but not with the likelihood of becoming overweight (Taveras et al., 2005). Moreover, there are indications that structured mealtime is a valuable component in adopting regular eating habits and preventing eating disorders. When the family environment lacks control, adolescent girls are at higher risk to develop bulimia, hypothesized to be related to the lack of adequate control and self-regulation learned from the family (Agras, Hammer, & McNicholas, 1997).

The Use of Reinforcement Techniques

The social learning theory also emphasizes that a person must value the *outcomes or consequences* that he or she believes will occur as a result of performing a specific behavior or action. These expected outcomes are shaped by reinforcements. Positive reinforcements include consequences and rewards increase the chances that behaviors will be repeated. Negative reinforcements including punishment and lack of response, also affect learning. Most behaviors, including eating and physical activity, are learned and maintained under fairly complex schedules of reinforcement and anticipated future rewards. Some are internal (satiety, comfort, health status, looking and feeling better) and some are external (receiving praise and encouragement). The person's positive expectations for performing the behavior must outweigh the negative expectations.

The social environment often offers sweets, chocolate, and high fat foods in a positive connotation or as a reward; for example, they are given to those we like on special occasions or to say thank you. In this way, the consumption of already pleasurable items is reinforced. If children are given foods as rewards for approved behavior, the preference for those foods is enhanced (Birch, 1980). The use of food as a reward is counter-productive. When mother says, "unless you eat your vegetables you will not have any dessert," the preference for the food used as the reward increases and there is a decrease in the preference for the distasteful food (Newman & Taylor, 1992).

Birch, Marlin, and Rotter (1984) found that when children were rewarded for eating a disliked food, this led to a decline in the preference for that food. Rather than increasing the likelihood an undesirable food would be consumed, the approach had the opposite effect—it became more unlikely that the child would eat the food. It is not helpful to use a food that is initially disliked in a negative context, to gain access to something pleasurable. The use of reinforcement techniques such as parental praise is an important tool to promote health behaviors.

Health promotion programs that provide tangible rewards or praise and encourage self-reward, encourage people to establish positive habits. Extrinsic rewards to help motivate behavior change should be used with caution to avoid developing dependence on external reinforcements. They are often useful as motivators for continued participation but not for sustaining long-term change. Token reward systems and refundable deposits have been used successfully to increase participation rates and reduce attrition in a variety of health promotion programs that involve multiple sessions, such as physical activity, and weight management programs (Elder, Apodaca, John, & Harris, 1999).

CHILD'S INTERPERSONAL FACTORS—PEERS, SCHOOL, MASS MEDIA, AND EDUCATION

Peers

The influence of peers and conformity to peer pressure are often considered hallmarks of adolescents. For children eating and activity typically are social occasions in which peers and other adults play a significant role in shaping eating and activity behaviors via modeling as well as facilitating behaviors. Friends' support for physical activity (Zakarian et al., 1994) is positively related to physical activity among adolescents. Peers can have powerful effects on food selection, especially if they are seen as particularly powerful (Birch, 1980). Peers also have great influence on the development of weight concerns and frequent dieting among preadolescent and adolescent girls and boys. Stice, Presnell, Shaw, and Rohde (2005) reported that adolescents with elevated dietary restraint scores showed an increased risk for obesity onset. Moreover, the use of maladaptive compensatory behaviors for weight control—such as vomiting or laxative abuse—which are often modeled and encouraged by peers, increased the risk for obesity onset.

School Environment

Because children spend such a large proportion of their day in school and have one or two of their meals there each weekday, schools provide an ideal setting to positively influence diet and physical activity (Centers for Disease Control and Prevention, 1996). A wide variety of programs and policies in schools are designed to offer opportunities for students to eat a balanced diet and be physically active. However, there are obstacles in the social and physical environment that press towards unhealthy habits. For example, the unpalatability of healthful food offerings in school cafeterias, easy access to nonnutritious snacks, limited time for lunch period, and weight concerns emerged as significant reasons why students do not eat nutritious meals in school (Bauer, Yang, & Austin, 2004). Bauer et al. suggest designing interventions that tackle environmental influences and are aimed at increasing student physical activity by reducing gender and weight-related harassment and implementing activities that place less emphasis on competition and athletic skills, as well as tackling other components. Physical education teachers play a significant role in the lives of children. They should offer positive, constructive, and immediate feedback without being evaluative, critical, or demanding. To promote self-efficacy and emotional development, children should be taught to be sensitive to their physiological cues and to set their own personal goals in a realistic mode. Students should be taught a health-oriented approach to physical education with an emphasis on health promotion and mastery of skills rather than winning and competition, de-emphasize extrinsic rewards, and emphasize intrinsic values (McWhorter, Wallmann, & Alpert, 2003).

Mass Media

Today, children have become primary consumers. They buy things with their own money, thus they have become the target of millions of dollars in food advertisements which seek to create new customers and encourage existing ones to purchase more. Some of the products advertised fall within the rubric of disease promotion (Crockett & Sims, 1995).

Television is the overwhelmingly favorite venue for these advertisements, and a pervasive purveyor of culture, providing models and messages about food preferences, food selection, and activity patterns to children and adolescents. The largest share of advertisements during children's programming is for food products (Williams, Achterberg, & Sylvester, 1995).

Many researchers in the field of eating disorders discuss the strong role of social pressure exerted through mass media messages and perceptions that induce body dissatisfaction, dieting, and may enhance the development of an eating disorder (Striegel-Moore, Silberstein, & Rodin, 1986). Health promotion programs should use television and other mass media as educational tools, helping children develop healthful habits incorporating educational material that is delivered by appropriate role models. Moreover, parents should teach their children to be a critical audience in order to counteract the media's negative messages.

Education

The central task of health educators is educating and mobilizing individuals, organizations, and communities to promote health. Getting information is often the first step in acting to change health-damaging corporate behavior. Social learning theory is a valuable and effective tool for health educators who want to assist their students in gaining new health supporting skills. Social learning theory can help educators determine why certain learning activities work, and why other activities aren't very effective.

In recent years, there has been a strong push to develop environmental-level health interventions in schools to expand beyond programs that exclusively target individual level behaviors (Centers for Disease Control and Prevention, 1996; Story, Neumark-Sztainer, & French, 2002; U.S. Department of Health and Human Services, 2001). Moreover, there is evidence of the need for interventions to promote healthful dietary and physical activity patterns early in middle school and in elementary school since nutritional and physical activity patterns that had emerged in most adolescents by the 6th grade remained constant throughout high school (Kelder, Perry, Klepp, & Lytle, 1994). However, while people may be aware of nutritional advice, this knowledge is rarely put into practice (Story et al., 2002). Rimal (2003) found that the effect of health information use on behavior was different for adults compared to children. For adults, the contribution of this variable was indirect—it enhanced self-efficacy and knowledge, which in turn enhanced behavior—but its contribution to children's behavior was both direct and indirect (through knowledge). A closer examination of this variable revealed that adults made much greater use of health information than did children.

Davis et al. (2000) reported on a school-based nutrition education effectiveness trial to help fourth- and fifth-grade students eat more fruit, 100% juice, and vegetables. The Gimme Five curriculum was based on social learning theory and targeted at 4th and 5th graders in Georgia schools. Results of the evaluation indicated that the curriculum was effective in increasing fruit consumption, although only half of the curriculum activities were implemented by the teachers. The lowest proportion completed was those most pertinent to behavior change. Eighty-seven percent of parents reported participating in homework activities with their fourth grader, 66% with fifth graders. Sixty-five percent of parents reported viewing a video with their child in both grades. Ten percent attended evening point-of-purchase grocery store activities. The low level of implementation and modest level of participation in family activities suggest that higher levels of behavior change may have occurred if exposure to the intervention had been greater.

Implication for Practice

Children's self-efficacy, knowledge about health, health media use, and dietary behavior are influenced by peers' and adults' self-efficacy, knowledge about health, health media use, and dietary behavior (Rimal, 2003). It seems that campaigns designed to change children's behaviors can significantly increase their impact if they also incorporate strategies aimed at improving adults' knowledge about health and adults' self-efficacy and behavioral determinants. The influence of household adults on children has been extensively documented across a variety of domains, including childhood obesity (Golan & Crow, 2004).

The home environment is undoubtedly the most important setting in relation to shaping children's eating and physical activity behaviors, as well as perceptions, self-esteem and self-efficacy, body image, and future weight-related problems. Wardle, Sanderson, Guthrie, Rapoport, and Plomin (2002) suggest there are four feeding patterns in particular that have been under suspicion as contributing to the development of obesity. Feeding in response to emotional distress (emotional feeding) and using food as a reward (instrumental feeding) are both assumed to encourage the child to associate eating with cues other than hunger, and thereby increase the risk of eating in excess of physiological need. A third feeding practice that has been implicated is excessive prompting or encouragement to eat, deriving either from the parents' enthusiasm to see the child eating food that has been carefully prepared or the belief that a heavier child is a healthier one (Baughcum et al., 1998; Rand & Stunkard, 1978). Finally, there have been suggestions that parental restriction of high-fat foods might be related to an improved quality of children's diets and thereby, perhaps, reduce the likelihood of overweight (De Bourdeandhuij, 1997). Parents should not restrict the amount of food a child eats during meals. Parents should, rather, serve as a source of authority by regulating the quality and pattern of the food environment, by setting limits when appropriate, and by modeling behaviors and attitudes (Faith, 2005).

For physical activity/inactivity, the home environment should restrict childhood sedentary activities (American Academy of Pediatrics, 1995) and establish the "activity ethos" of the family, again with parents as critical role models.

Environment can foster self-esteem by helping children recognize their own worth, cultural food practices, and family tradition; by teaching body satisfaction and a positive body image; and by modeling qualities that facilitate health-promoting behaviors. The best thing that parents can do when acting as role models is to demonstrate that healthy weight management is a reflection of self-care that includes positive food and activity behaviors that come from, and reinforce, a positive self-image (Golan & Crow, 2004).

Designing health promotion interventions to reach entire communities or specific groups-rather than influencing one individual at a time—is a basic goal of public health. The dissemination of health information may be via the classroom, out-of-school settings, radio, television, newspapers, magazines, and the Internet.

According to the social learning theory, interventions for health promotion should ensure the caregivers have appropriate behavioral capability, knowledge, and skills needed to perform the required behavior. Health promotion programs should target improvement of the caregivers' self-efficacy for practicing feeding responsibilities and performing the required actions to promote health behaviors. A key educational method is the use of observational learning through modeling to the caregivers. In addition to helping adults make healthy decisions, information and education are indispensable for socializing the young into health-promoting norms and behaviors and to change unhealthy ones.

The health of communities can be improved through policies such as universal health insurance, programs such as prenatal care visits to poor pregnant women, and a community's own actions such as organizing to demand better health services.

CONCLUSIONS

Bandura's social cognitive theory (1977, 1986) provides a rich explanation of much of the intergenerational socialization processes. Households and communities with efficacious adults promote environments where children's efficacy expectations can flourish. Bandura noted that efficacy expectations influence not only behaviors but also the kinds of social environments that individuals create for themselves. The similarities in adults and children's dietary behaviors are likely similarities in socialization processes. To the extent that children develop healthy dietary behavior habits at home, it is likely that they will continue engaging in similar behaviors outside the home, where adults can typically exert little control.

In order to promote health among all priority populations there is a need to develop, implement, and evaluate programs to address health issues in the full array of multiple settings (e.g., schools, work sites, health care settings, other community sites), during all life stages (gestation; infancy and childhood; adolescence; and early, middle, and late adulthood). Skills teaching needs to replicate the natural processes by which children learn behavior: modeling, observation, and social interaction. Reinforcement is important in learning and shaping behavior. Positive reinforcement is applied for the correct demonstration of behaviors and skills; negative or corrective reinforcement is applied for behaviors or skills that need to be adjusted to build more positive actions.

Teachers and parents, as well as media agents, are important role models, standard setters, and sources of influence that shape health behaviors as well as influence weight-related problems thus should be the target as well as agents of change of health promotion programs.

REFERENCES

Adair, L. S., & Popkin, B. M. (2005). Are child eating patterns being transformed globally? *Obesity Research, 13,* 1281–1299.

Agras, S., Hammer, L., & McNicholas, F. (1997). A prospective study of the influence of eating-disordered mothers on their children. *International Journal of Eating Disorders, 25,* 253–262.

American Academy of Pediatrics. (1995). Committee on Communications. Children, adolescents and television. *Pediatrics, 96,* 786–787.

Anliker, J. A., Bartoshuk, L., Ferris, A. M., & Hooks, L. D. (1991) Children's food preferences and genetic sensitivity to the bitter taste of 6-npropylthioouracil (Prop). *American Journal of Clinical Nutrition, 54,* 316–320.

Bandura, A. (1977). *Social learning theory.* Englewood Cliffs, NJ: Prentice Hall.

Bandura, A. (1986). *Social foundations of thought and action: A social cognitive theory.* Englewood Cliffs, NJ: Prentice-Hall.

Bandura, A. (1997). *Self-efficacy: The exercise of control.* New York: Freeman.

Barsh, G. S., Farooqi, I. S., & O'Rahilly, S. (2000). Genetics of body weight regulation. *Nature, 404,* 644–651.

Battle, E. K., & Brownell, K. D. (1996). Confronting a rising tide of eating disorders and obesity: treatment vs. prevention and policy. *Journal of Addictive Behavior, 21,* 755–765.

Bauer, K. W., Yang, Y. W., & Austin, S. B. (2004). "How can we stay healthy when you're throwing all of this in front of us?" Findings from focus groups and interviews in middle schools on environmental influences on nutrition and physical activity. *Health Education & Behavior, 31*(1), 34–46.

Baughcum, A. E., Burklow K. A., Deeks C. M., Powers S. W., & Whitaker, R. C. (1998). Maternal feeding practices and childhood obesity: a focus group study of low-income mothers. *Archive of Pediatric Adolescent Medicine, 152,* 1010–1014.

Baumrind, D. (1971). Current patterns of parental authority. *Developmental Psychology Monograph, 4,* 101–103.

Baumrind, D. (1991). The influence of parenting style on adolescent competence and substance use. *Journal of Early Adolescence, 11,* 56–95.

Benton, D. (2004). Role of parents in the determination of the food preferences of children and the development of obesity. *International Journal of Obesity, 28,* 858–869.

Birch, L. L. (1980). Effect of peer models' food model choices and eating behaviors on preschoolers' food preferences. *Journal of Child Development, 51,* 489–496.

Birch, L. L. (1992). Children's preferences for high-fat foods. *Nutrition Reviews, 50,* 249–255.

Birch, L. L. (1999). Development of food preferences. *Annals Review Nutrition, 19,* 4162–4165.

Birch, L. L., & Fisher, J. O. (1998). Development of eating behaviors among children and adolescents. *Pediatrics, 101,* 539S–549S.

Birch, L. L., Marlin, D. W., & Rotter, J. (1984). Eating as the "means" activity in a contingency: effects on young children's food preferences. *Child Development, 55,* 432–439.

Bundred, P., Kitchiner, D., & Buchan, I. (2001). Prevalence of overweight and obese children between 1989 and 1998: Population based series of cross sectional studies. *British Medical Journal, 322*(7282), 326–328.

Casey, R., & Rozin, P. (1989). Changing children's food preferences: Parents opinions. *Appetite, 12,* 171–182.

Centers for Disease Control and Prevention. (1996). *Guidelines for school health programs to promote lifelong healthy eating.* Vol. 45. Atlanta, GA: Centers for Disease Control and Prevention.

Chamberlin, L., Sherman, S., Jain, A., Powers, S., & Whitaker, R. (2002). The challenge of preventing and treating obesity in low-income, preschool children. *Archive of Pediatric Adolescent Medicine, 156,* 662–668.

Chen, J. L., & Kennedy, C. (2004). Family functioning, parenting style, and Chinese children's weight status. *Journal of Family Nursing, 10*(2), 262–279.

Christoffel, K. K., & Forsyth, B. W. C. (1989). Mirror image of environmental deprivation: severe childhood obesity of psychosocial origin. *Child Abuse and Neglect, 13,* 249–256.

Costanzo, P. R., & Woody, E. Z. (1985). Domain-specific parenting styles and their impact on the child's development of particular deviance: the example of obesity proneness. *Journal of Social and Clinical Psychology, 3,* 425–445.

Crockett, S. J., & Sims, L. S. (1995). Environmental influences on children's eating. *Journal of Nutrition Education, 27*(5), 235–249.

Cullen, K. W., Rittenberry, L., Olvera, N., & Baranowski, T. (2000). Environmental influences on children's diet: results from focus groups with African-, Euro-, and Mexican-American children and their parents. *Journal of Nutrition Education, 15,* 581–590.

Davis, M., Baranowski, T., Resnicow, K., Baranowski, J., Doyle, C., Smith, M., Wang, D. T., Yaroch, A., & Hebert, D. (2000). Gimme 5 fruit and vegetables for fun and health: Process evaluation. *Health Education & Behavior, 27*(2), 167–176.

De Bourdeandhuij, I. (1997). Family food rules and healthy eating in adolescents. *Journal of Health Psychology, 2,* 45–56.

Dietz, W. H., Bandini, L. G., Morelli, J. A., Peers, K. F., & Ching, P. L. (1994). Effect of sedentary activities on resting metabolic rate. *American Journal of Clinical Nutrition, 59,* 556–559.

Edmundson, E., Parcel, G. S., Feldman, H. A., & Elder, J. (1996). The effects of the child and adolescent trial for cardiovascular health upon psychosocial determinants of diet and physical activity behavior. *Preventive Medicine, 25,* 442–454.

Elder, J. P., Apodaca, G. X., John, P., & Harris, S (1999). Theories and intervention approaches to health behavior change in primary care. *American Journal of Preventive Medicine, 17*(4), 275–284.

Epstein, L. H., Klein, K. R., & Wisniewski, L. (1994). Child and parent factors that influence psychological problems in obese children. *International Journal of Eating Disorders, 15,* 151–157.

Faith, M. S. (2005). Development and modification of child food preferences and eating patterns: behavior genetics strategies. *International Journal of Obesity, 29,* 549–556.

Field, A. E., Camargo, C. A. Jr., Taylor, C. B., Berkey, C. S., Roberts, S. B., & Colditz, G. A. (2001). Peer, parents and media influences on the development of weight concerns and frequent dieting among preadolescents and adolescent girls and boys. *Pediatrics, 107,* 54–60.

Fischer, J. O., & Birch, J. L. (1995). Fat preferences and fat consumption of 3- to 5-year-old children are related to parent adiposity. *Journal of the American Dietetic Association, 95,* 759–776.

Friedman, M. A., & Brownell, K. D. (1995). Psychological correlates of obesity. *Psychological Bulletin, 117,* 3–20.

Gillman, M. W., Rifas-Shiman, S. I., Frazier, A. L., Rockett, H. R., Camargo, C. A., Field, A. E., et al. (2000). Family dinner and diet quality among older children and adolescents. *Archives of Family Medicine, 9,* 235–240.

Golan, M., & Crow, S. (2004). Parents are key players in the prevention and treatment of weight-related Problems. *Nutrition Review, 62*(1), 39–50.

Graber, J. A., & Brooks-Gunn, J. (1996). Prevention of eating problems and disorders: including parents. *Eating Disorders, 4,* 348–363.

Harper, L. W., & Sanders, K. M. (1975). The effect of adults' eating on young children's acceptance of unfamiliar foods. *Journal of Experimental Child Psychology, 20,* 206–214.

Hearn, M., Baranowski, T., Baranowski, J., Doyle, C., Smith, M., Lin, L. S., et al. (1998). Environmental influences on dietary behavior among children: availability and accessibility of fruits and vegetables enable consumption. *Journal of Health Education, 29,* 26–32.

Hill, J. O., & Trowbridge, F. L. (1998). Childhood obesity: Future directions and research priorities. *Pediatrics, 101*(3), 570–574.

Hoerr, S., Utech, A. E., & Ruth E. (2005). Child control of food choices in head start families. *Journal of Nutrition Education Behavior, 37,* 185–190.

Hood, M. Y., Moore, L. L., Sundarajan-Ramamurti, A., Singer, M., Cupples, L. A., & Ellison, R. C. (2000). Parental eating attitudes and the development of obesity in children. The Framingham Children's Study. *International Journal of Obesity, 24,* 1319–1325.

James, P. T., Rigby, N., & Leach, R. (2004) The obesity epidemic, metabolic syndrome and future prevention strategies. *European Journal of Cardiovascular Prevention and Rehabilitation 11*(1), 3–8.

Jansen, A., & Tenney, N. (2001). Seeing mum drinking a "light" product: Is social learning a stronger determinant of taste preference acquisition than caloric conditioning? *European Journal of Clinical Nutrition, 55,* 418–422.

Johnson, S. L. (2000). Improving preschoolers' self-regulation of energy intake. *Pediatrics, 106,* 653–661.

Johnson, S. L., & Birch, L. L. (1994). Parents' and children's adiposity and eating style. *Pediatrics, 94,* 653–661.

Kelder, S. H., Perry, C. L., Klepp, K. I., & Lytle, L. L. (1994). Longitudinal tracking of adolescent smoking, physical activity, and food choice behaviors. *American Journal of Public Health, 84*(7), 1121–1126.

Kinston, W., Loader, P., Miller, L., & Rein, L. (1988). Interaction in families with obese children. *Journal of Psychosomatic Research, 32*(4–5), 513–532.

Klesges, R. C., Coates, T. J., Moldenhauer-Klesges, L. M., Holzer, B., Gustavson, J., Barnes, J. (1984). The fats: An observational system for assessing physical activity in children and associated parent behavior. *Behavioral Assessment, 6,* 333–345.

Klesges, R. C., Malcott, J. M., Boschee, P. F., Weber, J. M. (1986). The effects of parental influences on children's food intake, physical activity, and relative weight. *International Journal of Eating Disorders, 5,* 335–346.

Klesges, R. C., Shelton, M. L., & Klesges, L. M. (1993). Effects of television on metabolic rate: Potential implications for childhood obesity. *Pediatrics, 91,* 281–286.

Lissau, I., & Sorenson, T. I. A. (1994). Parental neglect during childhood and increased risk of obesity in young adulthood. *Lancet, 343,* 324–327.

McKenzie, T. L., Sallis, J. F., Nader. P. R., Patterson, T. L., Elder, J. P., Berry, C. C., et al. (1991). Beaches: an observational system for assessing children's eating and physical activity behavior and associated events. *Journal of Applied Behavior Analysis, 24,* 141–151.

McMurray, R. B., Bradley, C. B., Harrell, J. S., Bernthal, P. R., Frauman, A. C., & Bangdiwala, S. I. (1993). Parental influences on childhood fitness and activity patterns. *Research Quarterly for Exercise and Sport, 64,* 249–255.

McWhorter, J. W., Wallmnn, H. W., & Alpert, P. T. (2003). The obese child: motivation as a tool for exercise. *Journal of Pediatric Health Care, 17*(1), 11–17.

Moore, L. L., Lombardi, D. A., White, M. J., Campbell, J. L., Oliveria, S. A., & Ellison, C. (1991). Influence of parents' physical activity levels on activity levels of young children. *Journal of Pediatrics, 118*, 215–219.

Nader, P. R., Sellers, D. E., Johnson, C. C., & Perry, C. L. (1996). The effect of adult participation in a school-based family intervention to improve children's diet and physical activity: The child and adolescent trial for cardiovascular health. *Preventive Medicine, 25*, 455–464.

Newman, J., & Taylor, A. (1992). Effect of a means-end contingency on young children's food preferences. *Journal of Experimental Child Psychology, 64*, 200–216.

Nguyen, V. T., Larson, D. E., Johnson, R. K., & Goran, M. I. (1996). Fat intake and adiposity in children of lean and obese parents. *American Journal of Clinical Nutrition, 63*, 507–513.

Nielsen, S. J., Siega-Riz, A. M., & Popkin, B. M. (2002). Trends in energy intake in U.S. between 1977 and 1996: Similar shifts seen across age groups. *International Journal of Obesity, 10*, 370–378.

Oliveria, S. A., Ellison, R. C., Moore, L. L., Gillman, M. W., Garrahie, E. J., & Singer, M. R. (1992). Parent–child relationships in nutrient intake: The Framingham children's study. *American Journal of Clinical Nutr*ition, 56, 593–598.

Olvera-Ezzell, N., Power, T. G., & Cousins, J. H. (1990). Maternal socialization of children's eating habits: Strategies used by obese Mexican-American mothers. *Child Development, 61*, 395–400.

Parsons, T. J., Power, C., Logan, S., & Summerbell, C. D. (1999). Childhood predictors of adult obesity: A systemic review. *International Journal of Obesity and Related Metabolic Disorders, 23*(suppl 8), S1–107.

Rand, C., & Stunkard, A. J. Obesity and psychoanalysis (1978). *American Journal of Psychiatry, 135*, 547–551.

Rimal, R. N. (2003). Intergenerational transmission of health: The role of intrapersonal, interpersonal, and communicative factors. *Health Education & Behavior, 30*(1), 10–28.

Rimal, R. N., & Flora, J. A. (1999). Bidirectional familial influences in dietary behavior: Test of a model of campaign influences. *Human Communication Research, 24*, 610–637.

Robinson, T. N. (1999). Reducing children's television viewing to prevent obesity: a randomized controlled trial. *JAMA, 282*, 1561–1567.

Robinson, T. N. (2000). Can a school-based intervention to reduce television use decrease adiposity in children in grades 3 and 4? *The Western Journal of Medicine, 173*, 40.

Sallis, J. F., Alcaraz, J. E., McKenzie, T. L., Hovell, M. F., Kolody, B., & Nader, P. R. (1992). Parental behavior in relation to physical activity and fitness in 9-year-old children. *American Journal of Diseases of Children, 146*, 1383–1388.

Sallis, J. F., Patterson, T. L., McKenzie, T. L., & Nadir, P. R. (1988). Family variables and physical activity in preschool children. *Journal of Developmental and Behavioral Pediatrics, 9*, 57–61.

Sallis, J. F, Prochaska, J. J., & Taylor, W. C. (2000). A review of correlates of physical activity of children and adolescents. *Medicine & Science in Sports & Exercise, 32,* 963–975.

Satter, E, (2005). *Your child's weight, helping without harming* (p. 16). Madison, WI: Kelcy Press.

Sobal, J. (2001a). Social and cultural influences on obesity. In P. Bjorntorp (Ed.), *International textbook of obesity* (pp. 305–322). New York: Wiley.

Sobal, J. (2001b). Commentary: Globalization and the epidemiology of obesity. *International Journal of Epidemiology, 30*(5), 1136–1137.

Stanek, K., Abbott, D., & Cramer, S. (1990). Diet quality and the eating environment. *Journal of American Dietetic Association, 90,* 1582–1584.

Steinbeck, K. S. (2001). The importance of physical activity in the prevention of overweight and obesity in childhood: A review and an opinion. *Obesity Reviews, 2,* 117–130.

Stice E, Presnell K, Shaw H and Rohde P. (2005). Psychological and behavioral risk factors for obesity onset in adolescent girls: A prospective study. *Journal of Consulting and Clinical Psychology, 73*(2), 195–202.

Story, M., Neumark-Sztainer, D., & French, S. (2002). Individual and environmental influences on adolescent eating behaviors. *Journal of American Dietetic Association, 102*(3 suppl.):S40–51.

Stradmeijer, M., Bosh, K., Koops, W., & Seidell, J. (2000). Family functioning and psychosocial adjustment in overweight youngsters. *International Journal of Eating Disorders, 27,* 110–114.

Strauss, R. S. (1999). Childhood obesity. *Current Problems in Pediatric and Adolescent Health Care, 29,* 1–19.

Striegel-Moore, R. H. (1995). Psychological factors in the etiology of binge eating. *Addictive Behavior, 20,* 713–723.

Striegel-Moore, R. H., Silberstein, L. R., & Rodin, J. (1986). Towards an understanding of risk factors for bulimia. *American Psychologist, 41,* 246–263.

Stunkard, A. J., & Wadden, T. A. (1992). Psychological aspects of severe obesity. *American Journal of Clinical Nutrition, 55,* 524–532.

Swinburn, B., Egger, G., & Raza, F. (1999). Dissecting obesogenic environments: The development and application of a framework for identifying and prioritizing environmental interventions for obesity. *Preventive Medicine, 29,* 563–570.

Taras, H. L., Sallis, J. F., Patterson, T. L., Nader, P. R., & Nelson, J. A. (1989). Television's influence on children's diet and physical activity. *Journal of Developmental and Behavioral Pediatrics, 10,* 176–180.

Taveras, E. M., Rifas-Shiman, S. L., Berkey, C. S., Rockett, H. R. H., Field, A. E., Frazier, A. L., et al. (2005). Family dinner and adolescent overweight. *Obesity Research, 13,* 900–906.

Tinsley, B. J. (1992). Multiple influences on the acquisition and socialization of children's health attitudes and behavior: An integrated review. *Child Development, 63,* 1043–1069.

Troiano, R. P., Flegal K. M., Kuczmarski, R. J., Campbell, S. M., & Johnson C. L. (1995). Overweight prevalence and trends for children and adolescents. *Archives of Pediatric Adolescent Medicine, 149,* 1085–1091.

U.S. Department of Health and Human Services. (2001). The Surgeon General's Call to Action to Prevent and Decrease Overweight and Obesity. Rockville, MD: U.S. Department of Health and Human Services, Public Health Service, Office of the Surgeon General.

Wardle, J., Sanderson, S., Guthrie, C. A., Rapoport, L., & Plomin, R. (2002). Parental Feeding Style and the inter-generational transmission of obesity risk. *Obesity Research, 10*(6), 453–462.

Westenhoefer, J., Broeckmann, P., Munch, A. K., & Pudel, V. (1994). Cognitive control of eating behavior and the disinhibition effect. *Appetite, 23,* 27–41.

Wilkins, S. C., Kendrick, O. W., Stitt, K. R., Stinett, N., & Hammarkund, V. A. (1998). Family functioning is related to overweight in children. *Journal American Dietetic Association, 98,* 572–574.

Williams, J. O., Achterberg, C., & Sylvester, G. P. (1995). Targeting marketing of food products to ethnic youth. In C. L. Williams, & S. Y. Kimm (Eds.), *Prevention and treatment of childhood obesity. Annals of the New York Academy of Science 699* (pp. 107–114).

Zakarian, J. M., Hovell, M. F., Hofstetter, C. R., Sallis, J. F., & Keating, K. J. (1994). Correlates of vigorous exercise in a predominantly low SES and minority high school population. *Preventive Medicine, 23,* 314–321.

Zametkin, A. J., Zoon, C., Klein, H. W., & Munson, S. (2004). Psychiatric aspects of child and adolescent obesity: A review of the past 10 years. *Journal of the American Academy of Child Adolescent Psychiatry, 43*(2), 134–150.

CHAPTER 12

MORALITY AND GENDER

Preschool Children's Moral Contracts

Eva Johansson

In Swedish society of today there is a striving for equality between men and women, in the labor market, in politics, in social services and in education. Similar discourse on equity between men and women can be found across Europe and in many other parts of the world. However, the interpretation and implication of values related to gender equality may be different. Moreover, gender differentiation emerges in almost all societies (Ramsey, 2006) and, we know from research, that girls and boys are ascribed different culturally grounded expectations regarding how they should behave towards others from an early age (Davies, 2003).

In Sweden, preschool is included in the national educational system and teachers in early education are, from an international perspective, well educated either at university level (preschool teachers) or within senior high school studies (childcare assistants). The National Curriculum in Sweden (Ministry of Education and Science, 1998) stipulate that teachers should treat boys and girls equally and to counteract against gender barriers and gender discrimination. In this context the value of equal rights, equality between boys and girls is highlighted. Children should be encouraged to learn and develop their abilities regardless of gender expectations (Ministry of Education and Science, 1998). There is however reason to believe that stereotypes of gender and gender barriers continue to impact

Contemporary Perspectives on Socialization and Social Development..., pages 267–300
Copyright © 2007 by Information Age Publishing
All rights of reproduction in any form reserved.

both on teachers' and on children's behavior that do not result in gender equity. It is an extremely complex challenge for teachers to introduce alternative discourses to help children expand their experiences of what it means to be a girl or a boy. Such efforts often end in expanding the children's repertoire of stereotyped practices (Grieshaber & Ryan, 2006) rather than fulfilling the ambition of equity.

The aim of this chapter is to discuss children's morality in relation to gender (i.e., culturally grounded expectations regarding how to behave towards others "as a girl" or "as a boy" in preschool). What is the importance of such expectations for children's morality and what are the implications for teachers' tasks in early childhood education? First, pedagogical research on gender and children's morality, mainly conducted in western societies, will be discussed. This is followed by an analysis of interactions between Swedish preschool children exploring the moral contracts which the children draw up with each other and an examination of the ways gender patterns impact on these contracts. Finally implications for practice and challenges for early childhood teachers are considered.

MORALITY AND MORAL CONTRACTS

In general terms ethics[1] deals with values and norms concerning the good life as well as treatment of others (Frankena, 1978). Here morality is understood as a result of intersubjectivity. Merleau-Ponty (1962) sees human life as intersubjective, and enmeshed in relations with other people, with culture, history and society. We are related to others and we are dependent on each other. According to Løgstrup's theory of ethics (1994) we are given to each other. We are always locked in this relation of dependence and responsibility for the other. But the relation is not built upon rationality and logic. It is a concrete intersubjective relationship out of which moral values and norms of behavior emerge. Morality is understood as children's *lived* experiences of their relations with peers, expressed as values and norms for how to behave towards each other in the everyday life in the context of preschool. The word *lived* emphasizes that morality is not a question of critical reflection or rationality. Furthermore, children's morality is not supposed to become liberated from the context, from their own subjectivity or from the influence from adults and peers.

Moral contracts refer to intersubjective agreements between children on how to behave towards each other (Schutz, 1967; also Hundeide, 2003; Johansson, 1999, 2007). In the research discussed in this chapter, moral contracts mainly concern values and norms for rights and justice and care for others' wellbeing. However, it is important to know that moral contracts can differ since they are related to cultural and contextual interpretations of good or bad. Moral contracts are negotiable and changeable and they are not free from conflicts. The contracts can be more or less tacit or more or less explicit. The agreements are expressed through children's bodily being, through posture, words, emotions and gestures. The contracts relate to children's concrete aims and goals in the specific context, but they are also built on children's previous experiences of moral values and norms. In addition, the contracts are intertwined with children's experiences of previous interactions with specific friends and lived understandings of how interactions in the context of preschool usually are performed. Sometimes these previous experiences of interactions turn into generalizations (constructions) where children label each other as certain types from whom you can expect certain behavior and towards whom you behave in a certain way (Schutz, 1967).

GENDER—WAYS OF BEING A GIRL AND WAYS OF BEING A BOY

In this text, gender is seen as constituting social and cultural definitions of masculinity ("ways of being a boy") and femininity ("ways of being a girl"), which can be construed in a number of inter-human contexts and structures (Paechter, 1998). These definitions of ways of being a boy or a girl structure children's lives and experiences. Davies (2003) writes that children learn to embrace "boyishness" or "girlishness" as if they were constant parts of their personality. Children learn to take this idea of a divided gender order as a given, as a result of the world around them. They take it for granted that children are either boys *or* girls, while at the same time they are clarifying what it means to be a boy or girl, through different discursive practices about how boys and girls, respectively, can and should build their identity. Definitions of masculinity and femininity are related to each other. Men or boys are assigned positions as if they, in fact, had power. Women or girls are assigned positions that indicate vulnerability and their role is to complement and support male power. De Beauvoir (1972) writes that girls in their role as the second sex have passivity (immanence) forced upon them from an early age, while boys are fostered for transcendence.

However, Davies (2003) asserts that gender cannot solely be attributed to structures and conceptions that children accept or into which they are incorporated. Gender is experienced, created and recreated by and between subjects in different concrete social and structural contexts. At the same time, as gender dichotomization is the lens through which we experience the world, people are able to relate to, try to change or dissociate themselves from prevailing gendered conceptions and patterns of action (Davies, 2003). We could thus consider if it is possible for children to experience gender patterns in different ways and if children are able to relate to, challenge, change or and dissociate themselves from a gender and power order. At the same time, girls and boys can be offered *different* opportunities when it comes to experiencing, thinking and living as a girl or a boy in a specific society.

Behaving like a boy or like a girl is also a bodily process (de Beauvoir, 1972; Davies, 2003; Merleau-Ponty, 1962; Young, 1980). A person's gender is inscribed in his or her body by the activities connected with which gender the person has been assigned. Through the lived body, in encounters with others' bodies, children experience and develop knowledge of "boyishness" and "girlishness" and of different ways of acting. Similarly, boys and girls learn what emotions are relevant and desirable for boys and girls, respectively, and in what contexts these emotions should be expressed. In this process, certain relationships with other people and with the surrounding world are encouraged or limited and for children, it is a question of figuring out to which gender they belong and what is normal and accepted.

In this respect, too, it is understandable that children's experiences of being a girl or being a boy can result in different bodily expressions and thus contribute to different experiences of morality. Johansson (1999, 2001, 2003; also Johansson & Johansson, 2003), showed that the body is central in young children's ways of expressing and experiencing morality. In this research, while caring for others was expressed with a gentle tone of voice and protective actions, the defense of rights or condemnation of others could be expressed by a child turning his or her back, a raised arm (averting or in defense) or by silent physical nearness. Cultural expectations of female as motherliness and caring and of manliness as rationality and distancing can thus result in different *ways* of experiencing and shaping morality as well as different expressions and meanings in the experiences of boys and girls (Gilligan & Wiggins, 1988).

RESEARCH ON MORALITY AND GENDER

Research on children's morality is relatively common (see Colnerud & Thornberg, 2003; Johansson, 2006; and Killen & Smetana, 2006 for reviews). It indicates that preschool children experience and uphold moral values and norms, perceive rights and obligations towards each other, and show concern for others' wellbeing. Early in life children are able to differentiate between different social domains and separate moral rules from other social rules (Killen & Smetana, 2006; Turiel & Wainrub, 2000). Early childhood education programs are important arenas in which children's social and moral competence (Berthelsen, 2005; Howes & Sanders, 2006; Johansson, 2006; Johansson & Pramling Samuelsson, 2003) and peer relations (see Ladd, Herald, & Andrews, 2006, for a review) are enacted. There is also a large body of research on gendered patterns of behavior in preschool and school (see Grieshaber & Ryan, 2006, Tallberg Broman, Rubinsten Reich, & Hägerström, 2002 and Öhrn, 2004, for reviews). However, there are relatively few studies that explicitly investigate morality in relation to gender in preschool and school (Killen & Smetana, 2006; Johansson, 2006) even if issues of morality and gender have attracted considerable interest in moral psychology (Walker, 2006). Several researchers in Sweden, as well as internationally, however, agree that the moral ideals in preschool and school are caring for others' wellbeing and that girls learn to represent this ideal better than do boys (Berge, 1999; Davies, 2003; Gannerud, 1999; Grieshaber & Ryan, 2006; Öhrn, 2004). Femininity in preschool and school is often described in more or less stereotyped terms of relating to, taking responsibility for and focusing on others' wellbeing while masculinity is described with words such as individualization, dominance and hierarchization (Davies, 2003; Tallberg Broman et al., 2002). A number of researchers (Davies, 2003; Gannerud, 1999; Johnson, Christie, & Wardle, 2005; Lenz Taguchi, 2003; Nordin Hultman, 2004; Paechter, 1998; Tallberg Broman et al., 2002; Öhrn, 2004) assert that there is a dominance hierarchy between masculinity and femininity, where masculinity is assumed to be superior to femininity.

Gender and Morality a Complex Relationship

In light of the research findings discussed above, being a girl in preschool and school could be expected to focus more on relationships, while being a boy could be expected to focus more on individualism. If we examine the moral theory developed by Gilligan and Wiggins (1988) and Gilligan (1993), we find two orientations in children's development of morality: justice and caring which, according to the researchers, are based on the above-mentioned differences. While principles of justice represent a male attitude, care for others is more a female attribute. Both forms exist and grow in children's early relationships and are based on children's experience of powerlessness and attachments with others. These moral orientations emerge and are organized in different ways in the development of boys and girls. According to Gilligan and Wiggins (1988), they also play an important role in how girls and boys solve and define moral problems. However, research also shows that the relationship between gender and morality is complex rather than direct and that gender stereotypes can be challenged by children. Johnson (2000) writes that even if dichotomizations in terms of gender manifest themselves in children's experiences, the fact is that children sometimes find gender categorizations confusing, contradictory and erratic. Johansson and Johansson (2003) studied moral issues in five schools and observed children in Grades 1–3. They noted caring behaviors among both girls and boys, although the children's own descriptions of caring differed. The girls were described by the children as nice and the boys as "all right," the girls as consoling and the boys as strong. Conceptions of "how it is" and "how it ought to be" affected not only how the children regarded themselves but also their actions. It was easier for girls to be "girlish" and for boys to be "boyish"—something, that could have moral consequences. This means that attributes such as good, considerate and concern for social relations are often ascribed to the world of girls, while attributes such as rational, logical and just are ascribed to the world of boys (Johansson & Johansson 2003; also Reid, 1999; Thornton & Goldstein, 2006; Walkerdine, 1990).

According to Grieshaber and Ryan (2006; see also Browne, 2004; Ärlemalm-Hagsér & Pramling Samuelsson, 2006) teachers and children perform a number of gendered ways of being that depend on the social context and the meanings circulating within a set of social relationships. Research shows that children sometimes challenge gender barriers (Danby & Baker, 1998; Hughes & MacNaughton, 2000). According to Johnson (2000), the tendency of children to use gender categorizations has to do with adults' reactions, actions by children that adults prioritizes, and how adults pay emotional attention to different actions, within or outside, an anticipated gender order. This means that whether or not children challenge or remain within anticipated gender categorizations can also become a moral question.

Studies of children's morality show that power can be an important dimension of their morality (see Johansson, 1999, 2007). Similar results are found in investigations on peer interaction (Danby & Baker, 1998; Ladd et al., 2006; Löfdahl & Hägglund, 2006; see also Ramsey, 2006, for a review). Children use power to both support and violate others, as well as to defend their own and others' rights. Power has also been found to be a feature when children challenge each other's boundaries when it comes to integrity (Dunn, 1987; Johansson, 1999, 2005; Johansson & Johansson, 2003; Nucci, 2001). At the same time, as research indicates that masculinity dominates in relation to femininity, we also know that power can be exercised in different ways. For example, how children acquire varying amounts of space in preschool and school depends on gender (Danby & Baker, 1998; Davies, 2003).

Methodological Ambiguities

The relationship between gender and morality is a complex one and the existing knowledge about this relationship is far from complete. Several researchers point out that it has not been possible to show any simple links between gender and morality (Eisenberg & Fabes, 1998; Johansson, 2006; Turiel, 1998; Walker, 2006). Rather, it is claimed that multidimensional communicative and interactive processes in children's everyday life form the basis of their morality, where gender is one of several dimensions (Turiel & Wainrub, 2000). Children's morality is integrally bound to the social and cultural context, with children's subjective and personal history, and through their interactions with others (adults and peers). Further, researchers (Davies, 2003; Eisenberg & Fabes, 1998; Grieshaber & Ryan, 2006; Johansson, 2006; Turiel, 1998) have pointed to methodological ambiguities where gender differences could be implicit in how the research constructs are operationalized. For example, differences between the prosocial actions of boys and girls could vary not only with the type of act investigated but also by measurement approaches (e.g., sex differences have been found to be greater [favoring girls] in indexes with attributes such as kindness and considerations than for sharing and helping, but were less distinct for instrumental helping [Eisenberg & Fabes, 1998]). Not least, gender differences could vary in relation to what is socially and culturally expected of gender within the cultural context in which the research is conducted and how the constructs are measured.

The Caring Ideal in Preschool and School

From a historical perspective, teaching formerly based on a model of paternity has shifted towards motherhood, not least among teachers working with young children (Florin, 1987). Most teachers are women who base their work primarily on solicitude, which has resulted in preschool and the early years at school coming to be based on a caring ideal (Gannerud, 1999; Hägglund & Öhrn, 1992; Tallberg Broman, et al., 2002; Thornton & Goldstein, 2006). Gannerud (1999) has studied how Swedish female teachers at the junior level of the compulsory school conceive of their profession. She found that there is a caring culture, which is a part of the teachers' pedagogy, and an expansion of the teacher's role with high expectations as regards caring, confirming and solicitude. The teachers themselves emphasize that relationships with, and caring for the students, are the most important parts of their assignment (Gannerud, 1999). According to Jalongo (2002) and Murphy and Leeper (2003), early childhood teachers take the position of caregivers by protecting, offering children affiliation and comfort, by appreciating accomplishments and by meeting children's physical needs. Teachers endeavor to understand young children's unique needs and offer stimulation (Gable, 2002; Turner, 2000). Berge (1999) holds the view that there is a risk of teachers and girls falling into the "caring trap" by taking responsibility and focusing on the needs of others (often the boys). Hägglund and Öhrn (1992) claimed that girls represent the preschool and school's ideal of caring better than do boys, which could give girls a position of power in relation to the boys. In preschool and school, caring acts that "belong" to the sphere of interest of girls and female adults are encouraged. This could mean that boys do not identify caring as something that applies to their gender.

Power

Gendering processes take place from the beginning of life and often result in masculine hegemony (Hatch & Barclay-McLaughlin, 2006). However, this is a complex picture, as evident in this section.

"Boyish" Dominance

At the same time as research on early childhood education show that women have formal control, masculinity nevertheless dominates (Davies, 2003). Odelfors (1996) studied interaction between children aged five to seven years in three Swedish preschool groups in terms of conditions for influence. Odelfors found that the boys were given more space than girls by the teachers, both during circle time, in free activities and at mealtimes. Although the teachers claim that they treat boys and girls equally, their actions show that they focus more on boys than girls (Odelfors, 1996, see also Ramsey, 2006). Girls interact more often with teachers, when it comes to caring and creating order in the everyday life at preschool (Tallberg Broman et al., 2002), while boys are given more time, attention, praise and help by the teachers (Månsson, 2000). Girls are more often interrupted or ignored (Andrésen, 1995) and younger boys are treated as if they were lacking in independence more than the girls (Andenaes, 1992). Teachers claim that boys need more closeness than girls, who are described as being independent (Månsson, 2000). Girls are also described as quiet and less of a challenge to order in the school (Tallberg Broman et al., 2002). According to Ramsey (2006) girls learn to be nurturing, emotionally expressive and skilled at maintaining personal relationships while boys are encouraged to be aggressive, to excel, take physical risks and to hide their emotions.

"Girlish" Power

At the same time as research shows that boys dominate in school, are more visible and integrate with teachers much more than girls, other recent research indicates that girls strive for and achieve influence in the classroom to a greater degree than had previously been assumed (Tallberg Broman et al., 2002; Öhrn, 2004;). Girls try to expand their action space, not only under the pretext of adapting but also by means of explicit confrontations and demands for change (Öhrn, 1998, 2004). While girls' strategies for gaining influence are characterized by normative expressions, boys' strategies are characterized by explicit physical expressions. Girls refer to rules in force while boys use their physical strength to gain influence (Öhrn, 2004).

Through the school system, girls are given the role of support teacher and encouraged to create order (Berge, 1999). However, in the female-dominated preschool and school environment, girls could equally well both take and be given leadership positions and power. Davies (2003) found that while girls' dominance space is the homelike, the inner and the private space, boys have control over the public sphere in preschool. When girls are admitted into the public space, the conditions for this are formulated by the boys and, when boys are admitted into the home space, they are generally forced to enter in a way that confirms the girls' sphere in the use of private space. Girl power in the home sphere can, according to Davies' research, be used for the sole purpose of maintaining the wellbeing of others. Girl power can always be set aside by boy power if the girls make use of the home sphere in a way that challenges traditional gender categorization (Davies, 2003). In contrast, Danby (1998) discovered gender fluidity between feminine and masculine type play in girl's interactions. Danby describes how girls moved between feminine domestic and masculine aggressive play often after being bullied by boy classmates. Hughes and MacNaughton (2000) investigated children's stereotypical gender play with Barbie dolls and action figures. They found that girls easily shifted characters from pretending to be female to pretending to be male. Ängård (2005) investigated children's enactment of gender through stories. She found that girls used both male and female characters in their stories and that they gave their female characters an active position while male characters were given more passive roles. The boys however, used only male characters, which they described as powerful and strong.

In summary, the ideals for being a girl that seem to be created in preschool and during the early school years can be described in terms of motherliness, emotional relations and taking responsibility while it seems that being a boy in early education can be characterized in terms of dominance and physical power. While masculinity may dominate the public space in school and preschool, femininity seems to dominate the more private, homelike sphere. At the same time, other research indicates that traditional power relations and gender categorizations are questioned and sometimes ignored by the children. From teachers' perspectives the moral ideal in early education seems to emphasize caring and relationships. From this position, it follows that there is a risk for girls and teachers to become entangled in the caring trap. Researchers have also pointed to methodological ambiguities where gender stereotypes could be unintentionally embedded in the conduct of the research. There is thus a need for research that investigates children's perspectives on moral issues in relation to the contexts of school and preschool that examines dimensions such as gender and power and that addresses some of the limitations of previous research. It is also essential that we learn more about different educational practices and discourses and how they can contribute or obstruct children's moral understanding. At the same time, it is extremely important to reflect on and examine the bases on which we interpret children's behaviors and intentions in order to be able to uncover our own stereotype expectations, for example, that assume that women and girls are expected to be more focused on the wellbeing of others than men and boys.

CHILDREN'S MORAL CONTRACTS AND GENDER

Let us now study some examples of interaction between preschool children and the way in which gender manifests itself in the children's experiences of morality. The examples are taken from a new study of children's morality (Johansson, 2007). The aim of this research was to study young children's lived experiences of values and norms concerning treatment of and behavior towards each other in everyday life in the context of preschool. The daily interactions of twenty children, ten boys and ten girls, three to six years of age, were video recorded across a period of seven months. The children were part of a day-care group in a small Swedish town. The children's interactions were analyzed with a focus on two main questions: What moral values do children experience and express through their interactions? What norms do the children express and value? The study also focused on children's morality in terms of gender. How do the values experienced and expressed by the children relate to gender?

A primary focus of the analyses reported in this chapter is on the data pertaining to the relationship between morality and gender. Specifically investigated was the nature of the moral agreements children experience and create among themselves and how gender is manifested in these agreements.

The results showed that, irrespective of gender, the children give expression to the similar moral values (Johansson, 2007). Both girls and boys uphold the value of others' wellbeing, defend rights and give expression to justice. At the same time, there are, at times, some differences in the children's moral expressions, in their strategies and the moral contracts they draw up. These differences pertain to the quality of children's peer relationships, the types and goals of play, the emotional involvement in the play, and children's previous and present moral experiences and recognition. In this complex process, gender can influence the character of the play, the identifications of moral values and the strategies to defend moral values that the children use.

In the following analyses, three interactions will be examined and the different moral contracts drawn up between the children involved will be discussed. Two of these interactions have been chosen because they represent, for these children, a typical game involving the boys (The Tower), and a typical game involving the girls (The School). These interactions are built on similar moral values, but differ in the strategies and moral contracts the children draw up within the interactions. The other interaction (The Girl and Boy Sofa) was chosen because the children employ an explicit division of gender, while at the same time, gender barriers are crossed by some of the children. In these examples different moral contracts emerge between the children.

The Tower

In the following interaction, a shared world between the boys is infused with an atmosphere of seriousness in which construction of the project and problem solving is viewed as important. The boys are gathered round a building project, reasoning about it in serious voices. Rights and care for others wellbeing are important components of the moral contract drawn up between the boys.

Per (6:2),[2] Simon (5:7), William (5:5) and Jonas (4:9) are in the hall. On the floor there are small balls and a plastic construction kit, which can be used to build a tower. The parts of the kit are in the form of channels for a ball, which can roll backwards and forwards down onto a round disc. Per is building and Simon is gathering the parts in a pile in front of him.

"They fall down easily." says William and continues: "I mean, it'll collapse soon." William places four modules in front of the structure. Per is building the tower higher and higher. He is silent and concentrating. "Towers like that can collapse at any time," William repeats gravely. He glances at Simon. Simon agrees: "Yeah, well, help, Mattias and the others then," he says gravely and gets up. "They've built a tower this high." Simon shows the size with his hands. Per goes on building. /.../ "It'll collapse soon," says William. Simon grasps the tower. It wobbles. Simon replaces the piece again. Per watches him. "We'll take this one," he says and tries to join the structure to another completed tower. The boys watch Per expectantly who fails to join the towers. The towers seem to be about to collapse. Jonas moves closer.

"I know," says William. "You can put, wait a bit," he adds. "No, you mustn't touch it," objects Per and stands up. William kneels in front of the structures. "If you'd been smart," he says, "You could have taken one of these and put it like this." William shows how another two pieces could be placed on top of the others. He puts the pieces down again and moves. Per stands up and adjusts the tower but does not do what William proposed. Gustav (3:9) comes into the hall. He stands next to the shelf and watches the children. "Where's the ball?" Per asks. William gives Per the ball and he places it in the pipe but it gets stuck. William blows on the ball which picks up speed. The boys watch the ball rolling backwards and forwards between the modules.

In the interaction, one of the children has initiated and is leading the building of a structure. It is Per who has the right to the game. This right appears obvious and is not questioned by the other boys. They participate but they do so only on the periphery of the play and they mainly act as supportive observers. William demonstrates how several pieces could be placed on top of the others but puts the pieces down again and moves. William shows that he respects the fact that it is Per who decides.

The conversation has a serious note. Nobody jokes or laughs. The boys talk in serious voices. An important and difficult project is in progress. The interaction is concerned with stretching and testing the boundaries on whether and how they can succeed in preserving the structure and how the ball can roll. The children know from experience that structures of this type are complex and sensitive and can easily collapse. However when Per realizes that Gustav is present, the situation changes:

Per looks up at Gustav, who is standing beside him and says firmly: "Goddam it, Gustav, if you break this!" Per watches Gustav and then looks at the ball again. At that moment, Gustav stretches out his hand and knocks the structure over. A part of the structure collapses. Gustav puts his hand to his mouth and looks at the boys who all exclaim in accusing voices: "Gustav!" Gustav stretches out his hand once again and pushes. The whole tower collapses. Once again, he puts his hand to his mouth as if he was afraid. Per quickly stands up and pushes Gustav in the chest and at the same time as he yells: "Gustav!" Per has strong lungs. Then he lets go. Gustav shoves Per who sits down with a resigned look on his face.

The children's expectations of Gustav are explicit. He is a danger to the project and could destroy it. Consequently, Per acts very firmly and clearly towards him. It seems as if Gustav is aware of the expectations and lives up to them. When Per has made his threat, Gustav knocks the building down.

/.../ "I'll tell the teacher," says William. "Me too," says Jack. The boys push past Gustav and go into the room to the adults. "Gustav destroys things when they build in there," says William. Gustav is standing in the door opening. He looks at Per who stands up. Gustav then goes in to the adults with Per right behind him. "Yes, he destroyed what I'd built," Per confirms. "When I'd finished it," he continues in an indignant voice.

The children go back into the hall accompanied by the teacher. Per continues to talk agitatedly about what Gustav has done. Simon is still sitting on the floor. "When they'd finished it," says William accusingly. "Yes, Gustav just came and destroyed it," says Per. He sits down in front of the remains of his structure. Gustav is watching them. /.../ Somebody calls out from the toilet. "Oh, has somebody finished," says the teacher and leaves. /.../ Gustav follows the teacher. The four boys are now sitting round the ruined structure and talking agitatedly about what has happened. "Gustav's mean," says Per and starts working on the structure. "If Gustav destroys it again, well, Goddam," he says with emphasis at the same time as he starts to rebuild the structure. /.../ "Then I'll tell the teacher," says Jonas. "Then I'll tell the teacher," he repeats after a short silence. Per agrees, muttering: "Yeah, hell." /.../

The boys are now united in their indignation at what Gustav has done. They become agitated to defend Per's rights. The children's agreement and solidarity with Per are as clearly visible as when they distanced themselves from Gustav and what he has done. Together, they condemn Gustav and, together, they go to the adults and tell them what has happened.

Then Kajsa (3:3) comes in from the toilet: "Did Gustav destroy that?" She sounds surprised. "Ye-es, he tore it down," explains Per. "Aha," says Kajsa and sits down on the floor. "He's mental," says Per. An agitated howl is heard from Gustav in the toilet. A teacher is talking with Gustav about destroying things. "Gustav's mental," says Per again. "I did say, Gustav, if you destroy this." Per turns around and looks in my direction. "Goddam it," he continues, now in a low voice. "And then he just. Then, then he just destroyed it." Per is building at the same time as he is talking. "Gustav's mental," he repeats. "What's that mean?" asks William. "That one is uh. That one is mean," explains Per. "I see," says Jack at the same time as he shakes his head: "He just makes trouble, trouble, trouble and trouble." "He's mean," says Kajsa.

When Kajsa asks if Gustav had destroyed the structure, the story is repeated. Per describes what happened in an indignant voice and Gustav is described in a distancing way as mental. Per clarifies his interpretation when William asks what mental means. Mental means that you are mean, you make trouble and destroy. The children agree with this interpretation.

The boys now get interested in the tower Per is building up again. The boys suggest solutions. Per then combines the towers. The structure has been completed. /.../ Gustav walks in a wide circle when he passes the boys. He looks at them quickly, but does not stop. /.../

What moral contracts were drawn up between the children in this interaction and how was gender involved?

First, there is a hint of a masculine (boyish) ideal of tackling and succeeding in tests, challenging what is difficult and solving complex problems (Davies, 2003). The gendered character of the play probably makes certain values visible for the children. In this interaction, the project of building the structure is important. The boys surround the game with an atmosphere of importance and seriousness; something special and difficult is happening here. The moral contract involves protecting and caring for the project, respecting Per's rights and supporting him in his attempts to complete the structure.

Second, gender and the character of the play is not the only issue here. The value of friendship and caring seems to be as important. Concern for the wellbeing of others is manifested in the form of supportive comments and help, made as constructive suggestions for solving problems. The atmosphere around the project is infused with respect and fellowship and there is a clear hierarchy between the boys, which they all seem to accept. However, when Gustav arrives, the moral contract on supporting Per is disturbed. The taken-for-granted trust that exists between the boys does not seem to include Gustav. Instead, he is regarded as a threat to the project. However, we can also see that the moral contract between the boys is strengthened and becomes more explicit as a result of Gustav's sabotage. Together the boys support and defend Per's rights and his wellbeing. They get help from the teacher. They condemn not only Gustav's actions but also Gustav himself.

Third, previous experiences of interactions influence the current interaction and the moral agreement drawn up between the boys building the tower. It is not only the moral contract surrounding the game that Gustav violates. He is also regarded as someone who repeatedly violates what is valuable to the children in the preschool (i.e., valuing others' rights and wellbeing). Thus, there is a second moral contract operating to support Per by the other boys, which is based on previous experience that justifies the threats against Gustav. Describing Gustav as being mental is a way of stereotyping his behavior and a way of clarifying that he is expected to act in predictable and unmoral ways. We could say that the children typify (Schutz, 1967). Initially Gustav seems to be interested in what is going on in the hall. However, when the threats against him are expressed, then he destroys the construction. It seems as if Gustav is aware of this contract and that he sometimes fulfils those expectations of being a person who destroys. At the same time, we can see that this particular contract does not apply in every situation in relation to Gustav. We will see this in later examples. In other situations with some of the girls, Gustav is sometimes typified as a little person (baby) who does not understand and might therefore need support. In relation to the younger girls, he is a very good friend. In this way, gendering seem to influence the moral contracts children draw up with specific friends. It is however also reasonable to conclude that the age of Gustav in relation to the other boys and also the girls influence the contracts.

Let us briefly look at the teacher's action in this interplay. What is her contribution to the moral contract? The teacher listens to the children, but leaves them very soon since someone else calls for her attention. Later we can hear her mildly talk to Gustav about his behavior and how to act towards others. However, the teacher does not prioritize as a concern the interaction in the hall nor does she prioritize the points of view of all the children. Primarily, the teacher seems to be involved in structuring and organizing the routines and practices as her primary role (Berthelsen, 2005). Thus, the children are left alone in the hall. The contract between Gustav and the others that positions Gustav as being mental remains unchallenged and the moral issues raised by the children remain unanswered by the teacher in this situation. Possibly, the teacher does not recognize the moral interplay occurring between the children or that her own actions have indicated to the children that she has placed a low priority on this moral issue. However, as we can see the dilemma is complex. On one hand it is essential for teachers to become aware of how certain children are positioned and the moral contracts which are manifested between the children in the actual situation. It is also essential for teachers to understand what moral values are of importance for the children within and outside their play and the manner in which these relate to the values that teachers want children to learn. It is crucial for teachers to become aware of their own moral attitudes and how to help children develop a diversity of moral contracts that are in line with the goals of early education. It is easy to understand that this does not make the teachers' responsibility to structure the preschool practice less complex, rather more challenging. Such processes require teachers' sensitivity and a high level of pedagogical skills in actual situations as well as continuing reflection and analysis on how to achieve educational goals through an understanding of children's moral intentions and their moral learning in everyday activities like the situation described in this example.

The School

In the next example, we see how some of the girls establish moral contracts. The children are playing the School Game. The project is led by the older girls and is about what going to school means that includes the roles and positions involved and the demands and rules applying in school. Here, concern for others' wellbeing and rights are important foundations in the moral contract.

Karin (5:8), Hanna (6:5) and Nina (6:0) are playing the School Game in the hall. Nina is the teacher and Hanna is playing the role of support teacher. The girls are kneeling opposite each other, each drawing on a sheet of paper. They are quiet and concentrated. /.../ Linnea (3:4), Oskar (3:6) and Gustav (3:10) come into the hall. "If you want to play, you'll have to fetch a sheet of paper," says Nina. "Yes, yes," says Linnea eagerly. "You have to put your sheet of paper here and there," says Hanna and points at her box. "Then, when it's the break," Nina confirms. "And when we finish, you put your sheets of paper there," Hanna continues. Oskar is sitting on the floor. He is playing by himself, but now and then watches the girls. Soon afterwards, Gustav leaves. /.../

"When you write, maybe I'll draw," says Linnea and puts her head on one side, looking at her playmates. "Yes," says Karin, but Nina objects: "No, we won't. When the teacher tells you to write, then you write," she explains and puts her head on one side, watching Linnea. "We're going to write now," she says. "Now, we're going to write, otherwise you can't be in the school," says Nina. /.../ Oskar looks at Hanna's drawing in silence. /.../

All the children seem to find it natural that the older girls own the right to the game and decide what will happen. There are probably several reasons for this, partly because they started the game, partly because they are the oldest, and partly because they know something about going to school. But the roles in the game also confirm and strengthen rights. The children's roles are well defined. The teacher explains to the pupils how things are done and lays down the conditions for participating in the School Game. If the children want to be in the school, they will have to write. Oskar is interested but he does not take part in the game at this juncture. The girls ignore his presence.

/.../ Nina goes up to Linnea. "Now, you're going to write," she says. "Maybe I don't want to," Linnea objects in a determined tone of voice. Karin who is half lying on the floor opposite Linnea with her chin on her hand, looks at Linnea and says: "Can't you write?" Linnea shakes her head. "We'll pretend that she's writing, then," Nina suggests.

It now becomes clear that Linnea's resistance to writing is due to her not being able to write rather than not wanting to follow the rules for the School Game. Karin understands this without Linnea saying it and she asks her friend whether she is unable to write. This shows that she is sensitive to her friend and supports her so that she can continue to participate in the School Game.

/.../ Linnea goes up to Nina. "I'm never allowed to sit next to the teacher," she says in a complaining voice. "But we're not doing it now," Karin objects. "She sits beside me a little," says Nina and continues: "She only sits beside me a little bit." /.../

The older girls behave in a caring way towards the younger children. They talk in a friendly and supportive way. They also show that the small children need guidance and explanations. When Linnea is dissatisfied because she is not allowed to sit beside the teacher, Hanna takes herself as an example of not being given more favors than her playmates. At the same time, Nina, the teacher, admits that Linnea is partly right and she does so in a friendly and explaining tone of voice. Justice seems to be important to the children.

> /.../ Now Oskar sits down, places paper and felt-tip pens on the floor in front of him and watches Linnea. Nina stands in front of him, hands behind her back: "School is here and the teacher sits here," she says firmly. "Ye-es," Linnea, who is standing beside her, agrees. Nina looks at Oskar, who is still sitting on the floor. Then she moves his drawing with her foot. "No," Oskar shouts in an angry voice and looks at her. "The teacher sat there," says Linnea angrily after which she shouts at Oskar: "You have to write too, you know!" Linnea starts to draw. Oskar is still sitting. He is drawing.
>
> Gustav comes in together with Kajsa (3:4). They sit down on the floor. "Linnea, why does everybody have to draw in here?" says Karin in a dissatisfied voice. /.../ "Well, we'll move." Nina walks around. "We can't play being at school here. It's not possible to play being at school here," she says. The girls gather up everything. "No, it's not possible to play being at school here," Linnea agrees in a firm voice and gets up. /.../ Gustav takes his drawing. "Then I want to play with you," he says and follows the girls to the doll room. "No, no. No boys," says Nina. The girls close the door. Oskar and Gustav are left in the hall.

When there are too many children in the room and the newcomers do not respect how the School Game is played and the teacher's unquestioned position, the girls who "own the right to the School Game" decide to leave. This way of acting is repeated at different times during the study. The girls do not always claim their right to the space; instead, they sometimes leave the room and continue the game somewhere else. In this way, they preserve and retain the right to the game without entering into a conflict about the room. In this case, other conditions are laid down for the School Game and this solves the problem of many children wanting to take part. Boys are not allowed to participate. Gender is now an important condition for being allowed to take part. Let us se what is happening in the next sequence:

> The game continues in the doll room. Oskar appears and stands in the doorway. Hanna, who is sitting near the door, says in a low voice: "No, no you're not allowed to be here." Nina looks at her and says: "Shall we tell ..." "No boys," shouts Linnea. She then puts her head on one side and adds: "But only one is allowed to be in here." She waves the pen. "Only one," she contin-

ues. "Only one boy is allowed to be in here." "Ye-es," say the others and Nina states: "And that's Oskar." Kajsa agrees. "And that's Oskar. I think he's nice," she says with emphasis. Hanna pushes Oskar into the room. "Come on, you can be in here," she says in a friendly voice. Oskar goes into the room and sits down. Linnea looks at Oskar in silence. "I don't think that Gustav, he isn't nice," she says. "No," says Kajsa. Nina agrees: "He's not as nice as Oskar." "He's just stupid and he fights," adds Linnea and waves her pen again. "Yes." Several voices are heard agreeing. /.../ The atmosphere in the room gets agitated.

"There he is," calls Kajsa and points at Gustav, who is passing by in the hall. Linnea, Oskar and Nina look. "There he is," calls Kajsa again. "Ye-es," says Linnea. Gustav says something, he sounds upset: "Otherwise you'll get your butts slapped." The children laugh but soon go back to drawing. /.../ Gustav stands in the doorway and says: "I'm getting angry with you." He sounds sullen. /.../ Gustav leaves.

Once again, the conditions for gaining rights to the School Game are changed. First, there are exceptions to the rule that gender determines whether you have the right to be in the game. The general rule is still that boys are not allowed, but Oskar is allowed to join the game because, according to the children, he is nice. In addition, Oskar is Hanna's brother and Hanna has a respected position in the group. We can, however, note that it is not Hanna who first takes the initiative to propose that Oskar be allowed to join. Linnea confirms the contract, "No boys." but quickly adds an exception: "Only one [boy]." Since the proposal is also supported by Nina, who has the ultimate right to the game, Hanna gives her brother the go-ahead to join the game.

Second, we can see that the gender rule is mainly intended to apply to Gustav and the reasons for this are morally grounded. He fights and does not respect the value of others' wellbeing which Oskar, on the other hand, does. As in the previous situation, the conditions for rights were in part laid down earlier. If you are a person who is typified as someone who destroys, you are not allowed to join the game. Similar to the previous example in which the boys interacted, we recognize these descriptions of Gustav. However, the girls also show that this contract is negotiable and not unequivocal:

/.../ A little later, Gustav comes in with a drawing and shows it to Hanna. "Lovely. A whale. Can't you work a bit more on it," she says in positive, instructing voice. Hanna goes out into the hall with Gustav but soon returns. She is singing softly to herself. The game continues. Gustav appears once again in the doorway. He holds up the drawing and says proudly: "Look!" "That's lovely," says Hanna. "Could I have it?" she asks in a friendly voice. Gustav gives her the drawing. Hanna now turns to the others and asks in a pleading voice: "Couldn't he be allowed to play?" "Ye-es," says Nina and continues, "He can be in the school. He can be a beginner." Hanna takes Gustav by the hand and he scampers into the room. "Beginner," Hanna wonders. "Ye-es," says Nina. "Is he a hamburger,[3] then?" Hanna closes the door. "You can't eat up a person, can you?" Hanna sounds playful when she talks about Gustav as if he were a hamburger. /.../

Gustav shows that he respects not being allowed to be in the game and he stays out in the hall. He does not make any threats or show any tendency to either spoil or join the game. Gustav now sounds happy and he gives a drawing to Hanna. This has an effect. Although Gustav did not express any new wish to join the game, Hanna seems to intuitively understand that he would very much like to join the game. She pleads with her playmates to let him join the game. However, the decision rests with the older children, with Hanna and Nina. Hanna's pleading results in the contract being rene-gotiated and an exception is also made for Gustav. Nina accepts and Gustav is assigned a role in the School Game. He can be a beginner. Perhaps it is because Gustav seems to respect the girls' right to the game that he is allowed to join.

The older girls show that they regard Gustav (as do the younger girls) as a person who needs encouragement and guidance. Maybe this also contrib-utes to the decision to allow Gustav to join the game. We can see that the contract with Gustav is neither absolute nor unequivocal. The children also have experience of Gustav being nice (giving drawings), happy and funny. They laugh at what he says out in the hall. Gustav seems to be eager to change the contract and demonstrates this to the girls.

The game continues, but the children soon begin to show signs of being rest-less. Nina tries to gather them together in the classroom but the children run off. "They don't know how things work in school. We'll teach them," says Nina. /.../

Nina's utterance says something about how she views her and the older girls' task. It is a question of teaching the small children about how things work in school. The younger children lack competence and they do not understand the demands made in school and what is usually done there. The caring trap seems here to be evident as the older girls demonstrate a relational attitude towards their younger peers.

On a general level, the moral contracts drawn up between the children involve values such as rights, justice and others wellbeing. Gendering influ-ences the interactions and the agreements in several ways. In this interac-tion, protecting and respecting the meaning of the specific project related to school is important but the relationships and conditions that are part of the interactions are also important. Being a teacher and a pupil in the school offer children certain identifications of femininity and how to be a girl but also identifications of power and dependence, knowing and not knowing, caring and be cared for. As in the previous example, we can see that one position in the game, the position of teacher, ultimately has the decisive right to the game's content and conditions. However, other positions also give the holders influence, for example, a support teacher and being older. These positions required that the holders cared for the younger children, as well as making allowances for them.

To protect their right to the School Game the children both moved their play and implemented a rule where gender is a precondition for inclusion as well as for exclusion. To be included in this specific game you have to be a girl. This way of acting was repeated at different times during the research when boys or girls used gender to gain and exclude other children from the play. The boys were excluded or given permission to participate in the School Game but it was the girls who decided these conditions. The girls also showed sensitivity to the other children's feelings and situation as well as solicitude. For example, exceptions were made just because their playmates are younger and lack competence. In this way, the value of others' wellbeing is expressed. At the same time caring confirms the girls' position. It also confirms the helplessness and subordinate positions of the younger children. An important basis for the children's actions is the norm in the preschool classroom that you may not hurt others and children who, from experience, are known not to respect this are excluded. At the same time, renegotiations and deviations from this norm take place when children display good moral intentions. The children's interaction and their contracts with others are permeated by their previous experience of interaction with other children and awareness of specific moral values and norms. As was shown in the previous situation peer relationships and friendships are important in these processes.

The Character of Play as the Basis for Moral Contracts

When we compare the interaction in the construction game with the boys and in the game of school played by the girls, we find that the content of the children's games differ and are a significant factor in the moral dimensions which become important to the children. The projects differ in character which means that the children have to deal with varying dilemmas. However, the moral values that the children encounter do not differ other than in the shape they take and their focus. The values the children express seems to be based both on previous experience and the situation in question. In the interaction between the boys in constructing the tower, the children gathered round a risky project to build a tower that forms a track for a ball. The boys know that this is difficult and that it is important for everybody to support and protect the structure. In the interaction around the school, the children have a multifaceted theme of playing the School Game. It is important to do things in the *same* way as they are done in school and to establish and maintain good relations between the teacher and the pupils.

In the School Game, several renegotiations on what should apply in the game take place. In the Tower Game, negotiations seem to be neither necessary nor important. In the School Game, the children encounter several different moral dilemmas, which they have to handle. The greatest dilemma in the Tower Game is related to Gustav and the norm of "not acting to hurt others" was vital. In the boys' interplay, we find different manifestations of the value of others' wellbeing, but these take a different shape and have a different focus compared with those in the School Game. Support for the wellbeing of others is manifested when, for example, the children give helpful suggestions to the builder and show respect for his perspective and when the boys together fetch the teacher. In addition, the children give the builder verbal support when the structure has been destroyed. Solicitude is also manifested in the condemnation of the playmate who sabotages the structure. The boys show that they care for the builder who has the right to the project. In the School Game, concern for the wellbeing of others is directed towards several of the participants, mainly by the teacher and the support teacher towards the pupils but also by the pupils towards playmates not included in the game. Caring is manifested through understanding and special consideration for the different playmates' situation and lack of competence, the wish to participate. In the interaction between the girls, gender is used as a condition for the game and it is the reason for both including and excluding. However, the conditions can be changed, something that seems to be less possible in the interaction between the boys. Inclusion seems to be more important in the girls' interactions.

In the different interactions, typifications, which are generalizations where children label each other as certain types and from whom you could expect certain behaviors (Schutz, 1967), are made of one of the children, Gustav. In the boys' interaction, this results in Gustav not being allowed to join the game at all as he is regarded as a threat, someone who spoils and destroys. This contract remains fixed, neither the boys involved in building the structure nor Gustav seem to want or be able to change it. In the girls' interplay, the children agree that Gustav is mean and that he fights and causes trouble. However, when Gustav makes his positive intentions clear, he is allowed to take part in the game. The contract is changeable and can be interpreted in several different ways. Gustav is treated as a person who lacks competence and needs motherly solicitude and this reinforces the girls' rights rather than threatening them.

What can teachers in early education learn from the situations described? First, it is important to know the variety of dimensions that influence children's morality and the moral contracts they draw up together. Second, it is necessary to learn how gender and power is involved in the children's interaction and how these aspects can be used for moral purposes. Third, it is essential for teachers to look beyond the own gender stereotypes to be able to see the similarities of values that children know and understand in order to help children's moral learning without being trapped by traditional gender stereotypes.

Girl and Boy Sofa

Children sometimes create and emphasize differences which are related to being a boy or a girl. In the previous example, we saw how gender is used as a condition for participating in and being excluded from the game. In the following interaction, the children create a girl and a boy sofa. Such a differentiation marks the boundaries by which relationships are possible (Davies, 2003). However, it is not self-evident that all the children agree at all times with the existing expectations as regards such a gender division. When faced with the choice of adhering to the tacit contract regarding the placement of boys and girls or supporting a friend, one of the girls does not hesitate. She supports her friend despite the gendered nature of children in each group on which the children in each group had agreed. We can conclude that friendship is an important moral value in the perspectives of these children and a higher value is placed on it than that of position ascribed by gender.

The children are going to watch the film, *Doctor Snuggles*, and have eagerly discussed the film during lunch.

> The children begin to sit in the sofas in front of the TV. Several boys are now sitting on one of the sofas. When Oskar (3:8) comes in, Tomas (6:2) calls eagerly: "Oskar, Oskar, Oskar." He hits the sofa vigorously with his hand. Oskar sits down. Anna (4:7) and Kajsa (3:5) sit in the other sofa. "TV, TV, TV," says Fredrik (5:1). He jumps up and down in the sofa. "Boy sofa, boy sofa, boy sofa," says Jonas (5:1). "Boy sofa, boy oh boy," says the teacher. William (5:8) comes in and climbs up onto the sofa where the other boys are sitting. He sits on the arm-rest. "This is the boy, boy sofa," says Jonas rhythmically. Anna and Kajsa are sitting beside each other in the other sofa. "The girls can! The girls can," says Anna. The boys talk with the teacher about not being able to see. /.../

The children create two different spaces that distinguish and mark boundaries. These boundaries are gendered and the spaces are the two sofas—the boy and the girl sofa. They identified conditions for sitting in the different sofas. One of the sofas belongs to the girls' sphere and the other to the boys' sphere.

The children are eager and talk about *Doctor Snuggles.* /.../ Meanwhile, Lisa (6:0) sits down in the sofa beside Anna. /.../ She is followed by Gustav (4:1), who climbs up onto the sofa where the girls are sitting. He lies down on the back of the sofa. "This is the girl sofa," object Anna and Lisa. "This is the girl sofa, but he can sit here if he wants to," says Kajsa who is sitting beside them. "No," Anna objects and leans towards Kajsa. "This is the girl sofa. So then he's a girl." "He isn't," says Kajsa firmly and looks at Anna. Gustav rolls down off the back of the sofa and sits next Kajsa. "Now, now," says the teacher. "This, this is a daycare sofa." Kajsa agrees. "Daycare sofa," she says to Anna. Kajsa stresses daycare sofa and leans forward so her face is close to Anna. "Come here," says Kajsa and puts an arm round Gustav's shoulders. He moves closer to her. She pats his hair a little. He looks at her and says: "I can sit here too." He sounds pleased. Gustav and Kajsa talk in low voices. "I can sit here too," Gustav repeats and she whispers to him and nods to him. "I'll sit here beside Lisa instead," says Anna and moves to a mattress on the floor where Lisa is now sitting. "It's also a girl mattress," she says.

Kajsa and Gustav start talking baby language with each other. Gustav leans close to Kajsa's face. He says in a happy voice: "Gaga, go gog." Gustav stretches out his arm and pretends to hit her. They both laugh.

Gustav is not aware of the distinction created by the children by having girl and boy sofas. When he is about to sit down in the sofa, he is informed that it is a girl sofa. The implication is that he as a boy should not sit there. However, Kajsa defends Gustav. She knows and makes it clear that he is not a girl, irrespective of which sofa he sits in. She invites him to sit beside her and puts her arm round his shoulders. Gustav seems to be unconcerned that he is going against a conception of what boys and girls should do in this situation. Kajsa and Gustav emphasize that Gustav can sit in the girl sofa if he wants. They are in agreement on a moral contract in which freedom of choice is important and their friendship takes precedence over the other playmates' demand for gender division. Caring and shared worlds are important in their contract. Unconcerned about the other children, they create a shared world in the sofa.

Breaking the existing contract stipulating different sofas for boys and girls, Kajsa takes sides with and defends her friend. She shows courage by being alone in acting up to her convictions despite the expectation that she ought to follow the group's decision. Another reason for this could be the support given by the teacher when she defines the sofas as day-care sofas. The teacher perhaps is trying to neutralize the gendering process but as we saw in the Tower Game the teacher seems more focused on organization of practice as described by Berthelsen (2005) than getting involved in the moral contracts that the children draw up.

In this situation, it is clear that expectations as regards gender are involved in the moral contract at the same time that we can see that the two children do not let themselves be dominated by a divided gender order. Their friendship seems to be more valuable than adhering to the conventional contract of dividing the sofas according to gender. They refuse to accept this. At the same time, the other children want to maintain to their contract. Anna shows that she does not agree and moves to where Lisa is sitting keeping to the contract concerning where girls and boys are expected to sit. She emphasizes that the mattress on the floor belongs to the girls' area. From the sofa having previously been a girl sofa, the mattress on the floor now becomes the place for girls. It is, however, not the place in itself that it is important. It is the gendered nature of the place. At the same time it is evident, as we have learnt from previous example, that some of the girls are more likely to accommodate when their rights are threatened. With the exception of Gustav, the boys show no tendency to go against the expected gender division. Nor is the boys' position having the right to the sofa questioned in the same way as the girls' position.

Perhaps this situation is a manifestation of different moral contracts. For the children who have agreed on different sofas for boys and girls, it seems to be important that they keep to the gendered arrangement that they have established. The moral issue is one of being loyal to the common decision. When Kajsa invites Gustav to sit in the sofa, she breaks the contract. However, the two children are friends. The moral issue is not to adhere to the gendered division but to support and preserve their friendship, their shared world.

SAME VALUES BUT DIFFERENT STRATEGIES

Both girls and boys defend rights, justice and the wellbeing of others (Johansson, 2006b) although they sometimes seem to focus on different moral dimensions. The children's interaction is at times framed by different meanings where structures (e.g., the tower) and products seem to be important in the boys' worlds and where the theme of the game and its relations seem to be important in the girls' worlds (e.g., the school). In interactions like these, it might seem that being a boy means that moral contracts are focused on rights and being a girl encourage moral contracts on the wellbeing of others. However, as we have also seen, the children also consider other values in these interactions. Rights are an important basis in the girls' interactions as is solicitude and others' wellbeing in the boys' interactions. It should also be emphasized that the children individually have different experiences and interests when it comes to moral values and norms. The point that I want to make is that being a boy and being a girl sometimes means that different values manifest themselves depending on the children's experiences and the interactions in which they participate.

Different experiences that are concerned with gender identifications are probably of some importance in the children's continued moral discoveries. Building a tower is more of a linear project directed towards a specific goal while playing the School Game is more of a circular process with no specific and final goal. However, as we have seen in this discussion there is an intertwined relationship between several issues such as peer relations, power, positions, and moral recognition that influence children's morality and the moral contracts which they draw up together.

Caring and Power

The analysis indicates that being a boy and being a girl seems to make children acquire different intersubjective and communicative expressions for caring. At one level, it seems that to be a girl means to express and show solicitude as a matter of course when they believe that somebody needs support or help. The girls act in a supportive way towards other children and seem to have developed a spontaneous communication for solicitude where comfort and encouragement are important. The girls also seem to be skilful at perceiving another child's need of solicitude. Here, it is conceivable that the preschool and school caring ideal and the traditions of 'girlishness', where it is very important to relate to others, take responsibility and focus on the wellbeing of others, *supports* dispositions for girls to act in a supportive and caring manner. In the School Game, which belongs to the girls' areas of dominance (Davies, 2003; Hägglund & Öhrn, 1992; Ramsey, 2006), the oldest girls have the power and the rights, although even the somewhat younger girls have a share. The boys, on the other hand, are primarily spectators. When they are given permission to participate, it is in accordance with the conditions created by the girls in the School Game. None of the children questions this. The girls care for their playmates and are skilful at detecting when they might need support. In the School Game, the older girls seem to take the task of teaching and showing solicitude for the young children as a given. This type of caring is part of the play world in demonstrating the teacher's responsibility for the pupils.

Being a boy in the context of preschool means to communicate care for others' wellbeing in a different way. Being a boy means to show concern and give verbal support by condemning, sometimes by means of threats or physical strength. The boys around the tower ask for help from the teacher. They show their support for the victim by talking about and repeating the event, the violation. They gather round the event. They act collectively and firmly. The construction game and problem solving is often referred to the area of boys' competence[4] (Davies, 2003). The boys show in different ways the importance and difficulty of their project, and this makes the sabotage more serious. The ideal of masculinity as involving hierarchical relations, power and dominance, probably supports the boys' specific manifestations of defense in the wellbeing of others. At the same time, such expectations could make it difficult for the boys to conform to the ideal of caring, which preschool and school aim to develop (Davies, 2003; Gannerud, 1999; Hägglund & Öhrn, 1992; Tallberg Broman et al., 2002).

Caring contains complex power dimensions that have to do with competence and dependence. Noddings (1993, 1999) has analyzed the concept of caring and argue that caring represents a moral relationship. It concerns commitment to others, that the other person's needs and experiences affect me. The researcher emphasize that caring is a mutual process which includes both the person offering caring and the other person's response to the solicitude. It is a matter of taking into consideration the other person's perspective on the caring that the giver is willing to offer. The aim of caring is also to help the other person to broaden his competence (Noddings, 1993, 1999). We can find traces of these aspects in both the boys' and the girls' caring for the wellbeing of others. The children make sure that the child they care for is involved and that he or she is supported on his or her own terms, broadens his or her knowledge, and can continue to work on the project. However, caring can also strengthen the power of the children offering it. In Gustav's case, the girls' solicitude seems to be conditional on him taking a subordinate position and following the girls' directives. In this way, they retain their rights and their influence over the conditions for the game.

Rights

Both girls and boys defend their own and others' rights (Johansson, 2007, also Johansson 1999; Johansson & Johansson, 2003). For both boys and girls in the group, it appears to be self-evident that the child who initiates and runs the game also has the right to it. In the examples presented here, the girls express rights by referring to the game and to the fact that they are bigger and know more that their younger friends. The girls negotiate and change the right to participate, but retain their right to make the final decisions on what happens. The boys take it for granted that the builder of the structure has the right to the structure and in their interaction, this does not need to be expressed verbally. But the boys are careful to show that they agree with the builder. They suggest changes and leave it to the builder to accept or reject them. In this way, the builder's absolute right is preserved. This indicates that the children are concerned with rights, irrespective of gender.

At the same time, we see that both boys and girls sometimes use gender and gender identities as a basis for acquiring or being excluded from rights. However, we have also seen that the children sometimes refuse to conform to a divided gender order since other values are important to them. In the boy and girl sofa interaction, two of the children break the expected gender pattern against the wishes of the rest of the group.

Power is constantly present in all relationships and rights do not seem to function without elements of power. It emerged that girls sometimes forgo some rights such as the right to the room where they are playing. On the one hand, the girls retain the right to their game by moving it. On the other, boys are given and take space at the expense of the girls. It is also possible that expectations as regards being a boy or a girl, when girls have traditionally been assigned a subordinate position (Davies, 2003; Gannerud, 1999; Månsson, 2000), is important for the children's interaction and the rights the children maintain. This could mean that girls refrain from asserting their rights. It should, however, be noted that the results of the investigation do not provide any simple explanations. On the contrary, there are many examples of girls asserting their rights and refusing to relinquish them.

Implications for Early Childhood Education

We have established from the research that caring for the wellbeing of others is highly valued by teachers and that caring is an ideal in early childhood education (Gannerud, 1999; Jalongo 2002; Murphy & Leeper 2003). The study however supports the impression from previous investigations that rights in the context of Swedish preschool is highly valued and frequently expressed by the children regardless of gender (cf. Johansson, 1999, 2007). How is this to be understood?

When looking at the Swedish society and at the curriculum it is evident that rights have been highlighted during the last decades and the discourse in society give rights a high position. But beyond this discourse, the value of rights has a lot to do with the collective context of preschool. The practices in preschool are, in the main part, organized around rights, for instance rights to play with things, to share worlds with friends and peers, and rights to be able to create and express meanings (Johansson, 1999, 2007). This is what the activities are all about within children's everyday interactions with friends and teachers in preschool. Therefore, rights are as important for girls as for boys in the context of preschool and can not be seen as a male moral orientation. This does not mean that children always gain rights or that rights are equally shared, rather that the structures of preschool are based on rights and will, of course, influence children's morality.

However, among teachers the ideal to a large extent is still about caring. Maybe this is also an important part of the discourse—a way of talking, as a teacher, about the purposed of early childhood education. It seems that teachers are less aware that the context in preschool and their work is also highly influenced by rights. This highlights the importance for teachers to reflect on the own moral ideals and how these are lived out implicitly and explicitly through the moral contracts that teachers constitute in their interaction with the children. If rights were to dominate the preschool structure and interactions, then it must be important to reflect on how to care for others' wellbeing is also encouraged among the children.

On the other hand, being a girl and a boy in the context of preschool also means showing concern for others' wellbeing, but sometimes in different ways. In this respect the caring ideal intervenes in the children's worlds and gender can be important. In some of the interactions, it is apparent that being a girl means to practice and develop skills in supporting, helping, negotiating and compromising and thus gain influence over one's own and the other children's activities and morality. Adaptation and closeness seem to be important in these contexts. In the interactions we have seen that being a boy in preschool can mean to communicate closeness and solicitude by supporting playmates verbally, gather round the victim and ask for help in order to support the victim. This makes it particularly important for teachers to pay attention to the concern for others' wellbeing shown by boys and girls and to reflect on how to expand children's strategies for caring in preschool and school. Berthelsen (2005) points to the importance of teachers becoming more aware of the moral significance of their actions. There is a morality of schooling because children are exposed to a set of social values to which they are expected to conform.

The suggestion here is that teachers need to become aware of the moral contracts they engage in and live out with the children, the kind of morality they want children to develop, and how this agenda is in congruence with (or even counteracting) the aims of the curriculum. What opportunities are children offered when it comes to experiencing, thinking and living out moral values and contracts?

Morality, Power, and Gender

Morality and gender have bodily dimensions and are manifested in power and closeness, with bodily power tending to be asserted by boys and motherly closeness by girls (Ramsey, 2006). At times, the children seem to be stuck in such female and male gender-typical patterns. Girls and boys sometimes participate in different play worlds where they develop rights on their own terms. Some of the girls, however, are more likely to let other children take over the place where they are playing. At the same time, they do not relinquish their rights as a matter of course; rather, they transfer their play world values and rights to another place. Nevertheless, this points to power relations in which girls forgo parts of the public space (Davies, 2003; Tallberg Broman et al., 2002). The implications for teaching are to consider the role of power, how power can influence the pedagogical practice and children's morality. Power can be used differently, (by children and by teachers) and both for good and bad. For some children this means that their rights and their integrity may not be respected. For other children, power can be used as a tool for gaining rights and for supporting others' wellbeing. It is therefore essential to reflect on how girls and boys assert power and what the consequences for gaining rights and showing care for others wellbeing may be.

Asserting and defending rights is a complicated process and the children in group play sometimes forego these rights. There could be several reasons for this. Possibly, when girls and boys realize that they need more power than they actually have in order to assert their rights, they may give up their rights if they are not confident that they can gain more power in the situation. We have also seen that both boys and girls develop strategies for retaining and asserting rights and that they acquire powerful positions by means of a caring approach or by defending and promoting rights. There is every reason for teachers to consider how and on what terms girls and boys are given space to develop and assert rights as well as on how to help the children to see and respect each others' rights (Johansson, 1999, 2002; see also Covell & Howe, 2001).

In conclusion, are caring and justice related to gender? At the same time as a gender dichotomy permeates children's worlds, we have seen that the children, irrespective of gender, are committed to the same values. Boys and girls experience and express values such as rights and justice but also they care for the wellbeing of others, although sometimes in different ways. Children create meaning in their interactions and certain values become more important for the children than others. Children's morality is interwoven within the social and cultural context, with children's personal history and with interactions with other persons, adults and playmates. As a result, expectations concerning gender are one of several factors that exert an influence on children's morality. It is important to note that conceptions of gender also involve researchers and teachers. Gilligan and Wiggin's theory (1988) is based on ideas about a division of gender where justice is assumed to represent a male moral orientation, while caring is presumed to represent a more female orientation. However, as morality is divided into two dimensions as well as being attributed to gender, we risk not seeing other aspects of children's understanding of morality. Consequently, this theory could also limit our understanding of children's morality. There is a risk that, as researchers and teachers, we become victims of stereotype expectations about children's morality, where girls are expected to be more focused on the wellbeing of others than men and boys. It is thus a question of becoming more aware of what one takes for granted in order to be able to observe the different moral values children express. It is particularly important to pay attention to the concern for others' wellbeing shown by boys and to reflect on and broaden the caring ideal as an aim in preschool and school. Otherwise, there is a great risk that the caring trap (Berge, 1999) will be preserved, that girls will continue to be, as well as perceived as, givers of solicitude and that boys are given little opportunity to be identified as caring persons.

NOTES

1. In Philosophy we can find a distinction between ethics and morality. Andersen (1997) defines ethics as a critical reflection about what is good and right, often expressed in language and as value judgements. Frankena (1978) sees ethics as a philosophical reflection on morality, moral problems and moral judgements. Morality is a societal concern, an instrument that guides and regulates relations between individuals as well as groups. Morality is expressed in general judgements and is a source for individual judgements and behaviors. These definitions relate ethics and morality mainly to a cognitive aspect that is a critical and philosophical reflection about what is good and bad.

2. The child's age is stated in years and months in brackets. Some of the children (Gustav, Kajsa and Jonas) take part in more than one of the three interactions described here. Since the observations were conducted for a period of time, their age differs as the careful reader might notice.

3. The word *nybörjare* in Swedish—"beginner" rhymes with "hamburger" in Swedish.

4. It is however important to note that the School Game also involves construction and problem solving but in a different way. In the Tower, construction is the theme of the play. In the School Game the theme of the play is how to behave in school.

REFERENCES

Andenaes, A. (1992). Vorfor kle seg selv når man kan få mor til å gjøre det? Hjelpeløshet og maskulinitet i små gutters utvikling. NAVE, *Kjønn i kjempers fødeland. Forskeblikk på kultur og identitet* [Gender in fighter's land. A researching look at culture and identity] (pp. 133–141). Oslo, Norway: NAVE.

Andersen, S. (1997). *Som dig själv. En inledning i etik* [As your self. Introduction to ethics]. Nora, Sweden: Nya Doxa.

Andrésen, R. (1995). *Kjønn og kultur. En studie av voksnes deltakelse i barns kjønnsocialisering på grunnlag av et observationsmateriale fra norske barnehager* [Gender and culture. An investigation into adults' participation in children's gender socialisation]. Högskolan i Finnmark, Norway.

de Beauvoir, S. (1972). *The second sex.* Harmondsworth: Penguin.

Berge, B-M. (1999). The material nuturance trap. In G. E. Birkelund, A. K. Broch-Due, & A. Nilsen (Eds.), *Ansvar & protest. Kjønn, klasse og utdanning i senmoderniteten* [Responsibility & protest. Gender, class and education in late modernity]. Bergen, Norway: Sociologisk institutt, Universitetet i Bergen.

Berthelsen, D. (2005). Organisational morality and children's engagement in early childhood programs. In J. Mason & T. Fattore (Eds.), *Children taken seriously: In theory policy and practice* (pp. 317–339). London: Jessica Kingsley Publications.

Browne, N. (2004). *Gender equity in early years.* Maidenhead: Open University Press.

Colnerud, G., & Thornberg, R. (2003). *Värdepedagogik i internationell belysning* [The education of values in an international perspective]. Skolverket, Forskning i fokus 7. Stockholm, Sweden: Fritzes.

Covell, K., & Howe, B. (2001). Moral education through the 3 Rs: Rights, respect and responsibility. *Journal of Moral Education, 30*(1), 29–41.

Danby, S. (1998). The serious work of playful gender: Talk and social order in a preschool classroom. In N. Yelland (Ed.), *Gender in early childhood* (pp. 175–205). New York: Routledge.

Danby, S., & Baker, C. (1998). How to be masculine in the block area. *Childhood, 12*(5), 151–175.

Davies, B. (2003). *Hur pojkar och flickor gör kön* [Frogs and snails and feminist tales—Preschool children and gender]. Stockholm, Sweden: Liber.

Dunn, J. (1987). The beginnings of moral understanding: Development in the second year. In J. Kagan & S. Lamb (Eds.), *The emergence of morality in young children* (pp. 91–111). Chicago: The University of Chicago Press.

Eisenberg, N., & Fabes, R. A. (1998). Prosocial development. In W. Damon (Ed.) and N. Eisenberg (Vol. Ed.), *Handbook of child psychology: Social, emotional and personal development* (Vol. 3, pp. 701–776). New York: Wiley.

Florin, C. (1987). *Kampen om katedern, feminiserings- och professionaliseringsprocessen inom svenska folkskolans lärarkår 1860–1906* [The fight for the teacher's desk]. Stockholm, Sweden: Almquist & Wiksell International.

Frankena, W. (1978). *Etik* [Ethics]. Lund, Sweden: Studentlitteratur.

Gable, S. (2002). Teacher–child relationships throughout the day. *Young Children, 57*(4), 42–46.

Gannerud, E. (1999). *Genusperspektiv på lärargärning: om kvinnliga klasslärares liv och arbete* [Gender perspectives on teaching: female teachers' life and work]. (Goteborg Studies in Educational Sciences, Serial No.137). Göteborg, Sweden: Acta Universitatis Gothoburgensis.

Gilligan, C. (1993). *In a different voice.* Cambridge, MA: Harvard University Press.

Gilligan, C., & Wiggins, G. (1988). The origins of morality in early childhood relationships. In C. Gilligan, J. V. Ward, & J. McLean Taylor (Eds.) (with B. Bardige), *Mapping the moral domain: A contribution of women's thinking to psychological theory and education* (pp. 111–137). Cambridge, MA: Harvard University Press.

Grieshaber, S., & Ryan, S. (2006). Beyond certainties: Postmodern perspectives, research, and the education of young children. In B. Spodek & O. Saracho (Eds.), *Handbook of research on the education of young children* (pp. 533–553). Mahwah, NJ: Erlbaum.

Hatch, A., & Barclay-McLaughlin, G. (2006). Qualitative research: Paradigms and Possibilities. In B. Spodek & O. Saracho (Eds.), *Handbook of research on the education of young children* (pp. 497–514). Mahwah, NJ:Erlbaum.

Howes, C., & Sanders, K. (2006). Childcare for young children. In B. Spodek & O. Saracho (Eds.), *Handbook of research on the education of young children* (pp. 375–391). Mahwah, NJ: Erlbaum.

Hundeide, K. (2003). *Barns livsverden: Sociokulturelle ramer for barns utvikling* [Sociocultural frames for children's development]. Oslo, Norway: Cappelen.

Hughes, P., & MacNaughton, G. (2000). Identity-formation and popular culture. Learning lessons from Barbie. *Journal of Curriculum Theorizing, 16*(3), 57–68.

Hägglund, S., & Öhrn, E. (1992). *Kön, utbildningsmiljöer och prosocial utveckling* [Gender, educational environments and prosocial development]. (Report No. 1992:2). Göteborg, Sweden: Göteborg university, Department of Education.

Jalongo, M. R. (2002)."Who is fit to teach young children?" Editorial: On behalf of the children. *Early Childhood Education Journal, 29*(3), 141–142.

Johansson, E. (1999). *Etik i små barns värld: Om värden och normer bland de yngsta barnen i förskolan* [Ethics in small children's worlds: Values and norms among the youngest children in preschool]. (Goteborg Studies in Educational Sciences, Serial No. 141). Göteborg, Sweden: Acta Universitatis Gothoburgensis.

Johansson, E. (2001). Morality in children's worlds: Rationality of thought or values emanating from relations? *Studies in Philosophy and Education. An International Quarterly, 20*, 345–358.

Johansson, E. (2002). Morality in preschool interaction: Teachers' strategies for working with children's morality. *Early Child Development and Care, 172*, 203–221.

Johansson, E. (2003). Barns erfarenhet av andras väl: Att förstå och gripa in i den andres livsvärld [The child's experience of others' wellbeing: Understanding the other's life-world]. In J. Bengtsson & M. Uljens (Eds.), *Livsvärldsfenomenologi och hermeneutik*, pp. 31–52, (Serial No. 192). Helsingfors, Finland: Helsingfors University, Department of Education.

Johansson, E. (2005). Children's integrity—A marginalised right? *International Journal of Early Childhood, 37*(3), 109–124.

Johansson, E. (2006). Children's morality—Perspectives and research. In B. Spodek & O. Saracho (Eds.), *Handbook of research on the education of young children* (pp. 55–83). Mahwah, NJ: Erlbaum.

Johansson, E. (2007). *Etiska överenskommelser i förskolebarns världar* [Moral agreements in preschool children's worlds]. (Göteborg Studies in Educational Sciences, Serial No. 251) Göteborg, Sweden: Acta Universitatis Gothoburgensis.

Johansson, E., & Johansson B. (2003). *Etiska möten i skolan: Värdefrågor i samspel mellan yngre barn och deras lärare* [Moral encounters in school: Moral issues in interaction between young children and their teachers]. Stockholm, Sweden: Liber.

Johansson, E., & Pramling Samuelsson, I. (2003). *Förskolan-barns första skola* [Preschool-children's first school]. Lund, Sweden: Studentlitteratur.

Johnson, A. (2000). Understanding children's gender beliefs. In A. Fisher & L. Embree (Eds.), *Feminist phenomenology* (pp. 133–151). Dordrecht, Boston, London: Kluwer.

Johnson, J., Christie, J., & Wardle, F. (2005). *Play, development and Early Education.* New York: Pearson.

Killen. M., & Smetana, J. S. (Eds.) (2006). *Handbook of moral development.* Mahwah, NJ: Erlbaum.

Ladd, G. W., Herald, S. I., & Andrews, R. K. (2006). Young children's peer relations and social competence. In B. Spodek & O. Saracho (Eds.), *Handbook of research on the education of young children* (pp. 23–54). Mahwah, NJ: Erlbaum.

Lenz Taguchi, H. (2003). *In på bara benet* [Under the skin]. Stockholm, Sweden: HLS:s förlag.

Löfdahl, A., & Hägglund, S. (2006). Power and participation: Social representations among children in preschool. *Social Psychology of Education, 9*(2), 179–194.

Løgstrup, K. E. (1994). *Det etiska kravet* [The ethical demand]. Göteborg, Sweden: Daidalos.

Merleau-Ponty, M. (1962). *Phenomenology of perception.* New York, London: Routledge.

Ministry of Education and Science. (1998). *Läroplan för förskolan.* Lpfö-98. [Curriculum for preschool education in Sweden]. Stockholm, Sweden: Fritzes.

Murphy, L., & Leeper, E. (2003). *More than a teacher: Caring for children, number two.* Washington, DC: Child Development Services Bureau, EDO82401.

Månsson, A. (2000). *Möten som formar: interaktionsmönster på förskola mellan pedagoger och de yngsta barnen i ett genusperspektiv* [Moulding encounters: interactions between teachers and children in preschool from a gender perspective]. (Studia psychologica et paedagogica. Series altera No. 147). Malmö, Sweden: Malmö university, Department of education.

Noddings, N. (1993). Caring: A feminist perspective. In K. A. Strike & P. Lance Ternasky (Eds.), *Ethics for professionals in education: Perspectives for preparation and practice* (pp. 43–53). New York: Teachers College Press.

Noddings, N. (1999). Care, justice, and equity. In M. S. Katz, N. Noddings, & K. A. Strike (Eds.), *Justice and caring. The search for common ground* (pp. 7–20). New York: Teachers College Press.

Nordin Hultman, E. (2004). *Pedagogiska miljöer och barns subjektsskapande* [Educational contexts and children's identities and subjectivity]. Stockholm, Sweden: Liber.

Nucci, L. P. (2001). *Education in the moral domain.* Cambridge: Cambridge University Press.

Odelfors, B. (1996). *Att göra sig hörd eller sedd.—Om villkoren för flickors och pojkars kommunikation på daghem* [Making oneself heard and seen—on conditions for boys' and girls' communication in the day-care centre]. (Doktorsavhandlingar från pedagogiska institutionen). Stockholm, Sweden: Stockholm university, Department of education.

Paechter, C. (1998). *Educating the other: Gender, power and schooling.* London: The Falmer Press.

Ramsey, P. G. (2006). Early childhood multicultural education. In B. Spodek & O. Saracho (Eds.), *Handbook of research on the education of young children* (pp. 279–301). Mahwah, NJ: Erlbaum.

Reid, J. (1999). Little woman/little men. Gender, violence and embodiment in early childhood classroom. In B. Kamler (Ed.), *Constructing gender and difference. Critical perspectives on early childhood* (pp. 167–189). Creskill, NJ: Hampton Press.

Schutz, A. (1967). *The Phenomenology of the social world.* Illinois: Northwestern University Press.

Tallberg Broman, I., Rubinstein Reich, L., & Hägerström, J. (2002). *Likvärdighet i en skola för alla. Historisk bakgrund och kritisk granskning* [Equity in a school for all. Historical background and critical review]. National Agency for Education, Stockholm, Sweden: Fritzes.

Thornton, C. D., & Goldstein, L. S. (2006). Feminist issues in early childhood scholarship. In B. Spodek & O. Saracho (Eds.), *Handbook of research on the education of young children* (pp. 515–531). Mahwah, NJ: Erlbaum.

Turiel, E. (1998). The development of morality. In W. Damon (Ed.) & N. Eisenberg (Vol. Ed.), *Handbook of child psychology: Social, emotional and personal development* (Vol. 3, pp. 863–932). New York: Wiley.

Turiel, E., & Wainryb, C. (2000). Social life in cultures: Judgments, conflict, and subversion. *Child Development, 71,* 250–256.

Turner, S. (2000). Caretaking of children's souls. Teaching the deep song. *Young Children, 55*(1), 31–33.

Walker, J. (2006). Gender and morality. In M. Killen & J. Smetana (Eds.), *Handbook of moral development* (pp. 93–115). Mahwah, NJ: Erlbaum.

Walkerdine, V. (1990). *Schoolgirl fictions.* London: Verso.

Young, I. M. (1980). Throwing like a girl: A phenomenology of feminine body comportment motility and spatiality. *Human Studies: A Journal for Philosophy and the Social Sciences, 2*(3), 137–156.

Ängård, E. (2005). *Bildskapande—en del av förskolebarns kamratkultur* [Making pictures—a part of preschool children's peer cultures]. Linköping studies in arts and science, Serial No. 315. Linköping, Sweden: Tema barn.

Ärlemalm-Hagsér, E., & Pramling Samuelsson, I. (2006). *Lek och lärande i ett genusperspektiv* [Play and learning from a gender perspective]. Manuscript in preparation.

Öhrn, E. (1998). Gender and power in school: On girls' open resistance. *Social psychology of Education, 1,* 341–357.

Öhrn, E. (2004). *Könsmönster i förändring?—en kunskapsöversikt om unga i skolan* [Changing patterns of gender?—a research overview of young people in school]. Skolverkets monografiserie. Stockholm, Sweden: Fritzes.

CHAPTER 13

DEVELOPMENTAL PERSPECTIVES ON SOCIAL DEVELOPMENT

Olivia N. Saracho and Bernard Spodek

As a result of social development, children generate behavior that is socially expected of them. They acquire the ability to express desirable social behaviors and suppress negative ones across a variety of social contexts. Social development is the children's inborn potential to develop social behavior that meets the standards of a group, and create social competence.

Social Competence

Socially competent children develop both repertoires of socially appropriate behaviors and socially cognitive competencies to become sensitive and responsive to a variety of social situations. Basically, socially competent children get along well with others and avoid negativity and conflict in relationships (Dodge & Murphy, 1984). Indices of social competence include prosocial behaviors, positive attitude toward others, good play skills, ability to solve problems, and controlling emotions, although these vary with gender, development, and contexts. Social competence is a major goal in early childhood education. It involves the behavior and thought processes that result in effective social skills in relation to early childhood programs: situ-

Contemporary Perspectives on Socialization and Social Development..., pages 301–315
Copyright © 2007 by Information Age Publishing
301

ation-specific behavioral repertoires (e.g., actions that build friendships), interpersonal solving, role taking, and verbal self-direction and impulse control (Spodek & Saracho, 1994). The social skills and competencies that children need to be successful in social interactions develop within the context of these relationships. Children may be good playmates at one developmental level but not at another or they may adapt to some contexts better than to others. In social competence, contextual and developmental factors are more important than specific isolated social skills (Stormashak & Welsh, 2005).

CONCEPTUALIZATION OF SOCIAL INTERACTIONS

Many researchers depend on Sullivan's (1953) theory of friendship development to understand the quality of the children's interactions. According to Sullivan (1953), individuals have particular interpersonal needs at different stages in their development. They need certain social skills and competencies for successful social interactions within the context of these relationships. Sullivan (1953) maintains that the individuals' social interaction and social stimulation (e.g., tenderness, companionship, acceptance, intimacy) help them find happiness and psychological welfare; otherwise they will experience distress and maladjustment. When children are able to choose certain peers for more intense social contacts to satisfy their social needs, they have achieved the highest level of social development. These children select peers with characteristics that provide the basis for mutual satisfaction of interpersonal needs. Sometimes mutual relationships are based on children with similar personalities or having a friend with characteristics that they themselves are lacking. Sullivan (1953) stresses that the acceptance by peers is essential in the children's social development. He describes friendship as a collaborative relationship. Friendship relationships emerge as a result of a need for acceptance transformations, which in the elementary school years is a form of peer group interaction. Friends are mutually sensitive to each others' needs and search for mutual satisfaction.

Researchers have challenged Sullivan's theoretical conceptualization by testing his theory through empirical investigations, observing and describing social behavior and relationships from a developmental perspective. Behavioral researchers dispute whether Sullivan's social theory has any concrete informative value or psychological reality. Although Sullivan's theory needs a detailed description of the expected development of social behaviors and competencies, researchers are interested in his concept of analyzing the responsibilities of social situations from a developmental perspective and acknowledging the value of comradeship, peer acceptance, mutual satisfaction, and closeness. They have conducted studies on different populations, cultural groups, and age groups (Stormashak & Welsh, 2005).

The concern for social interest in Sullivan's (1953) theory is similar to the development of social interest in Adlerian theory (Savage & Nicholl, 2003; Seligman, 2006). Alfred Adler, a social constructivist, suggests that it is important to understand social interactions within the context. He assumes that all human beings have the primary expectation and goal to belong and feel important. Adlerians believe that the individuals' beliefs and life style are the bases for their attitudes, behaviors, and personal point of view of self, others, and the world. Their development depends on their early life experiences, the continuous behavior patterns, and the methods that individuals use to belong (Savage & Nicholl, 2003; Seligman, 2006).

STAGES OF SOCIAL BEHAVIORS

Children's social behaviors are developmental and change through infancy, the preschool years, and the school years. They experience an evolution in social development throughout their life. Children first develop the concept of friendship when they begin to differentiate among peers (Gleason & Hohmann, 2006).

Infancy

From birth through age three, the children's social interactions are with caregivers, although parental bonds and attachment in infants are encouraged. In addition, the children usually develop their social-communicative skills by age two. Toddlers develop peer relationships when they engage in play and interact with their peers. Their peer relationships do not actually represented friendships. Infants and toddlers seldom have mutual and stable preferences for specific peers (Furman, 1982). In relation to friendship, they are able to distinguish between familiar and unfamiliar peers.

Preschool Years

Preschool children's peer interaction occurs in their social play. Researchers maintain that play is a key activity where children build their social competence. Peer relationships in the context of play assume an important role in social, communicative, and affective development (Goldstein, Kaczmarek, & English, 2001). Dyer and Moneta (2006) examine the differences in the frequency of social play in British children from two nursery schools. They use Parten's (1932) play categories (parallel, associative, and co-operative play) to assess the social play of children. Their results show that children have a stronger propensity toward associative play. Gottman, Katz, and Hooven (1997) also differentiate among the social requirements related to the different types of play. They show that parallel play demands less of the children's social behavior, but preschool children encounter more social-communicative demands when they initiate nonstereotyped fantasy play.

During fantasy play, children socially coordinate and continually negotiate play roles. In this situation, they may disagree and conflict with each other. To satisfactorily resolve these conflicts, children need to develop more sophisticated social skills. Toward the end of the preschool period, children use their verbal skills, behavioral inhibition, and perspective taking to resolve conflicts. The better preschoolers know each other, the more they engage with one another in fantasy play (Matthews, 1981) and acknowledge one another as friends (Furman & Buhrmester, 1992).

Gleason and Hohmann (2006) identify the friendship concepts of preschool-aged children (ages three to five). They show that reciprocal and imaginary friends are the best sources of social provisions, followed by unilateral friends and non-friends. They conclude (1) that children differentiate between reciprocal and unilateral friends based on the levels of social provisions available in these relationships and (2) that relationship schemas that create the base for relationships with imaginary friends may be related to their reciprocal friends' schemas. Gleason and Hohmann also assume that the children's friendship schemata differ by gender where girls discriminate more than boys between reciprocal and unilateral friends for the social provision of companionship. Sebanc (2003) has identified characteristics of three to five-year-old children's friendships and classifies them under prosocial and aggressive behavior. She showed that (a) friendship positively correlates with prosocial behavior, (b) friendship conflict positively correlates with overt aggression and peer rejection, and (c) friendship exclusivity/intimacy is positively related to aggression but is negatively related to peer acceptance. She concludes that rejection relates to conflict in friendships. Sebanc's results are similar to those found with the school age children's friendship characteristics features and their behavioral correlates.

School Years

Intense friendships for school-age children occur when they are eight-years-old (Furman, 1982). Buhrmester (1996) notes that at this age children focus on developmental issues and concerns that are of interest to them. Children address these concerns through relationships; thus, they develop mutual and exclusive relationships. Since friendship provides a context for addressing issues, the nonoccurrence of friendships may have a negative impact on the children's social adjustment. Other researchers (e.g., Crosnoe, 2001; Dishion, Eddy, Haas, Fuzhong, & Spracklen, 1997; French, 2001; Goldstein et al., 2001) show that those children who have difficulties with peer relationships and fail to develop friendships are at risk of becoming socially maladjusted in later life. The children's social relationships have less egocentrism and a greater sensitivity to others. At this stage children strive for their peers' acceptance (Sullivan, 1953), avoid their rejection, and generate several peer groups that vary in social status.

Peers usually assess children through sophisticated verbal behavior, which usually consists of criticism, negative gossip, and teasing. These schemes help children to identify group attitudes and norms and protect hem from personal exposure (Goldstein et al., 2001). Furman (1996) indicates that school age children have positive social behaviors when they have profound friendships. In contrast, friendship conflict relates to aggressiveness of individual children (Dishion & Andrews, 1995). Negative friendship processes keep antisocial children on a negative pathway (Dishion et al., 1997). Studies with older children have similar results. Berndt, Hawkins, and Jiao (1999) and Crick (1996) support that friendships and positive social behaviors relate to positive outcomes. Stable positive social behaviors and friendships may be of benefit to the children's social development. French (2001) explores the multiple facets of social support provided by mothers, fathers, siblings, and friends of elementary and junior high school students. The results indicate that friends are ranked higher while family members are ranked lower on companionship and satisfaction. In addition, French (2001) reports that friends are considered to be the primary sources of intimacy. Friends offer an outlet for the learning and polishing of socioemotional skills and lasting social relationship models (Crosnoe, 2001).

Friendship experiences promote children's social development. Friendship offers children the opportunities to be proficient in particular social skills. Those without close friends may lack the opportunity (a) to discuss personal thoughts and feelings, (b) to practice and refine their social skills, and (c) to learn from a highly valued peer. In addition, the friends' feedback and interactions contribution to the children's social competence (Buhrmester, 1996). Friends reinforce the children's social skills when friends respond positively; whereas when the children receive negative feedback from friends, their social skill are derailed (Goldstein et al., 2001).

Purposeful developmental research began with Sullivan's (1953) interpersonal theory which considers friendship to be fundamental to socialization. Exciting and interesting concepts concerning the nature, development, and impact of children's friendships are part of his work. Harry Stack Sullivan gives special prominence to the love, intimacy, and cooperation found in the close friendships that children form between 8 to 10 years of age. Follow up studies show that close friendships have both a positive dimension, with characteristics like intimacy, and a negative dimension, with characteristics like rivalry. However, close friendships surface slowly between ages eight to 10 years and the closeness of children's friendships increases gradually during middle childhood and adolescence (Berndt, 2004).

SOCIAL CONTEXTS

Research indicates that characteristics of the children's communities and peer social contexts influence their social development. The children's social development is influenced by a series of group memberships, which begin with the family and continuously expand into the neighborhood, community, and school settings.

Family Environment

Children develop their social skills when they feel safe in their home environment and their family teaches them and models appropriate values and social behaviors. For example, children have effective relationships with their peers when they experience parents who are accepting during infancy. Kahen, Katz, and Gottman (1994) examine the effect of the mothers' and fathers' parenting behavior during parent–child interactions in relation to the children's ability to successfully interact with peers. They show that the fathers' emotional volatility causes the children to play at a low level of engagement with their best friends (e.g., engage in parallel play or monologue). On the other hand, when the mothers and fathers provide affective communication, children play at a higher level of engagement (e.g., establishing common ground activities, exchanging information, self-disclosing personal information or feelings). The children's negativity during peer interaction increases when they have experiences with parents who are intrusive, engage at a low level, and disrespect humor. Results support that both fathers and mothers provide a context for the children's social development, including their ability to participate and sustain interpersonal interactions. In addition, the mothers' parenting contributes to the amount of positive effects that children express during dyadic play. Thus, parents predetermine the children's social development. Other influences include the family, family constellation, peer group, and all of the significant others. Within these relationships, children learn to convey or receive attention and affection. The children's socialization is accelerated with their peer group and significant others when their experiences resemble those with their family and family constellation (Stormashak & Welsh, 2005).

Neighborhood Environment

Since children spend a great portion of their time in their local surroundings, their neighborhood context contributes to their social behavior (Jackson & Mare, 2006). During the last decade researchers have recognized that communities matter in the children's social development and have initiated studies on the context of neighborhoods. Although studies provide constant support of the neighborhood's important impact, researchers are beginning to examine different and multiple pathways that neighborhood transmit their influence on the children's social development. Cantillon (2006) supports how the neighborhood's structural characteristics (i.e., neighborhood stability, income) affect the neighborhood and youths. He shows how accurately perceived neighborhood preference leads to lower neighborhood rates of official delinquency and higher rates of prosocial activity. In contrast, inaccurately perceived neighborhood preference influences more proximal constructs (e.g., community social organization, informal social control, parenting practices, association with delinquent peers). For example, the perceived problems around poverty in the context of neighborhoods contribute to the development of antisocial behavior, whereas detachment from high risk neighborhoods shield some children from the development of behavior problems (Stormashak & Welsh, 2005).

Although various pathways have been found to have significant results across neighborhood children and youth, perceived neighborhood preferences (especially neighborhood stability) are constantly inflicting substantial effects. Therefore, it is important to examine more comprehensive and multilevel preventions efforts (Cantillon, 2006).

Community Environment

The children's social interactions and relationships with their peers can guide them to adopt similar forms of behavior. Also the community can support and reinforce different facets of social behavior. For example, middle class communities typically provide positive recreational outlets; while powerful institutions (such as schools or youth clubs) foster appropriate social behavior. In contrast, deprived communities are typically physically harmful and deficient in resources of positive social support for families and children. These communities may have a violent and stressful environment that can stifle the children's social competence with peers (Attar,

Guerra, & Tolan, 1994) and present critical menace to the children's social adjustment (Scheier, Borvin, & Miller, 1999).

School Environment

The school is a crucial context, which can promote children's social development. The family and community environments contribute to the children's social development and assume an essential role in the children's interactions among peers in the school environment. In addition, the school context influences the development of particular social behaviors (e.g., highly aggressive classrooms), which can be modified through interventions (Stormashak & Welsh, 2005).

INTERVENTIONS

Certain social behaviors can be modified through interventions, which include all social contexts. Interventions that fail to include all contexts develop a "lack of fit" between the children and their environment. Children need to be provided with interventions regarding a social problem solving in all contexts. Thus, the most effective interventions are directed toward improving social competence and focus on home, community, and school contexts. Stormashak and Welsh (2005) identify several research studies on preschool and early childhood interventions that focus on multiple texts of social development such as *Conflict resolution training program* (Stevahn, Johnson, Johnson, Oberle, & Wahl, 2000) and *The Incredible Years* (Webster-Stratton, 2006).

Conflict Resolution Training Program

The *Conflict resolution training program*, which was developed by Stevahn et al. (2000), is a conflict resolution training program has been used with older students and later modified to be used as an early childhood intervention.

Early childhood interventions focus on a prevention model that supports the children's development of prosocial behaviors that might be integrated in the children's environment, which may be more difficult to alter later in the child's life. Stevahn et al. (2000) believe that preschool children should be able to participate in parallel play with other children, ask questions, support peers, and share. Frequently conflicts emerge that require young children to use their social skills in conflicts, including negotiating and managing their emotions within these interactions. At this age interventions that focus on social skills directly have positive effects in improving the children's peer relationships. Stevahn et al. (2000) examined the effectiveness of a conflict resolution training program with kindergarten children. The kindergarten children received nine hours of conflict resolution training that was integrated into a curriculum unit on friendship. Their study indicates that children who learned the social skills through the *conflict resolution training program* became knowledgeable and retained the conflict resolution procedure, had the willingness and ability to use the procedure in conflict situations, and acquired a conceptual understanding of friendship.

The Incredible Years

Social competence interventions in early childhood are based on the environment that includes children, parents, and teachers. Early interventions to promote social outcomes will be defeated if they only focus on one population such as the child or the family. Successful early interventions need to focus on children, their families, and their teachers.

When young children enter a preschool setting, effective interventions need to focus on the children in the preschool context and connect the interventions provided at school with home behavior. Webster-Stratton (1991) originally developed a classroom-based intervention that would help preschoolers receive a social skills intervention that she called, "Dinosaur School." She has revised it, refine it, and developed materials through the years. It has become an extensive curriculum titled, *The Incredible Years* (Webster-Stratton, 2006), with a variety of books and materials for children, teachers, and parents.

For this intervention, children view videotapes of attractive role models using a variety of prosocial skills. Children learn how to solve problems, manage their emotions, and negotiate conflicts. The curriculum consists of a book and videotapes where co-leaders guide the intervention and use puppets to interact with children. The intervention program also includes games and activities to reinforce social skills. It starts with basic social skills (e.g., helping, sharing) and progresses to more complex skills such as solving problems. Both parents and teachers receive training. For example, the component for parents consists of a videotaped on parenting problems. Webster-Stratton (1981) developed this parent training videotape and packaged of visual aids to help therapists with their training. Her parent-training program is based on videotape modeling for parent training. She maintains that these techniques increase the efficiency of training parents and provides a valuable method to meet more of the community's therapeutic needs. Webster-Stratton and Hammond (1997) have used this model and have shown that children who receive social skills training improve their social skills in solving problems, managing conflicts, and interacting with their peers. In addition, parents who received training in parenting and support improve their social skills and can effectively decrease the children's social problems later (Webster-Stratton & Hammond, 1997).

Later Webster-Stratton and her associates (Webster-Stratton, Reid, & Hammond, 2001) tested *The Incredible Years* (Webster-Stratton, 2006)—her intervention model—with parents and teachers of four-year-old Head Start children, parents, and teachers. They show that the intervention program can help mothers reduce their negative parenting behaviors and develop a bond with the teachers. The children had fewer behavior problems at home and school. In addition, children who were considered "highest risk" (high rates of noncompliant and aggressive behavior) had more clinically significant reductions in these behaviors. Teachers also developed better classroom management skills. These effects were still apparent a year later.

Activity-Based Intervention

The intervention program titled, *An activity-based approach to early intervention* (Pretti-Frontczak & Bricker, 2004) was developed for early childhood professionals to use for assessment, developing goals, intervention, and evaluating children from birth to five years of age. It provides a method to assess young children and assist them to achieve their social goals. It includes ready-to-use sample forms and vignettes. It also has a course companion web site that includes links for each chapter, PowerPoint slides, activities, and supplementary embedding schedules, intervention guides, and activity plans. This classroom-based curriculum was developed to promote the children's social behavior and assist teachers through several training workshops and continued guidance. The curriculum has 20 sessions of skill based instruction that help teachers to integrate skill-based learning into everyday activities (Pretti-Frontczak & Bricker, 2004). Classroom lessons concentrate on sharing, problem solving, turn-taking, talking and playing with friends, and learning letters. The intervention also includes parent training and home visits. The parenting intervention helps families implement at home and with siblings the social skills they learn in the parenting groups. Improvements in social competence were maintained over two years. Parenting skills (e.g., positive parenting, parent involvement) also increase, which were maintained into the children's kindergarten year.

CaseQuest

Teachers need to learn how to improve the parents' skills during their teacher education program. Pretti-Frontczak, Brown, Senderak, and Walsh (2005) use an intervention with teacher candidates in an early childhood teacher education program where Pretti-Frontczak et al. (2005) implement a CaseQuest, which includes a hybrid of WebQuests and Case Method Instruction. They use the CaseQuest to develop the early childhood teacher candidates' social competence to work with families of young children and to use technology to conduct the intervention. Pretti-Frontczak et al. use instructional strategies to use with their WebQuests and Case Method Instruction. Although both types of instruction have limitations, their results show that the early childhood teacher candidates' family-guided social skills and work practices increased after the CaseQuest intervention. In addition, their technology skills and knowledge increased after the CaseQuest experience.

The studies cited above support the idea that intervention programs can be used with young children. The preschool children's social competency relates to other developmental areas. Research indicate that interventions need to include all contexts (e.g., home, community, school) and target all individuals involved (e.g., children, parents, teachers) to succeed in the children's social development.

FUTURE PERSPECTIVES IN SOCIAL DEVELOPMENT

Studies suggest that children develop repertoires of socially appropriate behaviors and socially cognitive competencies as they become sensitive and responsive in a variety of social situations that are influenced by their membership in various groups. These groups begin with the family and expand to include peers, neighbors, and school mates. Many researchers have depended on Harry Stack Sullivan's (1953) theory to understand children's social conceptualizations and the quality of children's social interactions. Sullivan indicates that children develop close friendships between eight to 10 years of age. These friendships, which are good predictors of children's success in their peer social world, gradually increase during middle childhood and adolescence (Berndt, 2004). Sullivan's (1953) interpersonal theory of socialization initiated the purposeful social developmental research suggesting that children's social behaviors are developmental and change through infancy, preschool years, and school years.

Researchers have identified several social behaviors that can be altered through interventions, but these interventions must include all social contexts (e.g., home, community, school) and social skills that promote the children's social competence. Social competence undergoes continuous development and, if it is not developed appropriately, may become a risk factor for young children. According to Stormashak and Welsh (2005), interventions that are implemented over long periods of time and have many follow up assessments will be more effective in reducing risk and in enhancing skills. Intervention studies need to consider the importance of implementing quality and challenging support in all authentic life settings such as families, neighborhoods, communities, and schools. Unfortunately, studies on neighborhoods, which are essential environments for the children's development of social competence, have been neglected.

Contemporary research focuses on the effects children's neighborhoods have on the children's social status and on understanding the mechanisms that affect the individual children based on their unique characteristics including age, race, ethnicity, and economic status. Since environmental characteristics rather than genetics or family can be modified, Jackson and Mare (2006) maintain that neighborhoods serve an important role in children's lives. This becomes critical when dealing with young children. The results from these studies can provide an understanding of the impact neighborhoods have on young children's lives and how children can be helped to develop their social skills in this environment, which probably affects the other contexts.

Researchers have added a dimension beyond specific behaviors in the structure of neighborhood and have included social networks as contexts of risk. Their studies indicate that neighborhood peer networks are complex. High risk peers may be central to these networks, and may promote children's development of antisocial behavior. Investigations into peer relationships need to go beyond peer acceptance and rejection and include the repercussions of the children's social network on adjustment. Stormashak and Welsh (2005) suggest mapping the social networks to acquire an understanding of the importance of the characteristics of influential peers and the peer network that may lead to antisocial behavior.

Studies also need to examine the influence of social competence on sibling relationships, since a small number of studies focus on the influence of siblings within the family. Siblings may increase the young children's risk factor or may protect them from deviancy when children who lack social skills are rejected from peers. Therefore, children may be motivated to spend morel time with siblings, while siblings become role models and provide social support. However, the reverse may also occur where siblings can promote the children's deviant behavior and model inappropriate social skills. Intervention research can include siblings to serve as appropriate models and to provide support for appropriate social skills.

Most studies focus on social skills such as situation-specific behavioral repertoires (for example, actions that build friendships), interpersonal solving, role taking, and verbal self-direction and impulse control (Spodek & Saracho, 1994). Children's social skills, interactions, and competencies develop in a variety of contexts (e.g., family, community, school). They may be able to play at one developmental level in one context but not in another or they may conform to some contexts better than in others. Social competence needs to include a variety of contextual and developmental factors and interventions should avoid focusing in specific isolated social skills (Stormashak & Welsh, 2005). Current research indicates close, high-quality friendships are good predictors of the children's success in the peer social world. Berndt (2004) concludes that high-quality friendships can compound the positive or negative influence of friends with positive or negative characteristics, but this hypothesis needs to be evaluated more thoroughly in the future.

Future research may include a variety of studies to redefining the term social development. Its definition may become broadened and incorporate early social skills and competencies in a variety of contexts and social networks to promote academic achievement and reduce the children's risk factors. Interventions can be expanded to promote children's social development in a variety of contexts and include the children's social networks. Interventions can also focus on multiple indicators of the children's adjustment and promote their social competence across developmental contexts (Stormashak & Welsh, 2005).

REFERENCES

Attar, B. K., Guerra, N. G., & Tolan, P. H. (1994). Neighborhood disadvantage, stressful life events, and adjustment in urban elementary-school children. *Journal of Clinical Child Psychology, 23*, 391–400.

Berndt, T. J. (2004). Century in perspectives on their development and their effects. *Merrill Palmer Quarterly, 50*, 206–223.

Berndt, T. J., Hawkins, J. A., & Jiao, Z. (1999). Influences of friends and friendships on adjustment to junior high school. *Merrill Palmer Quarterly, 45*, 13–41.

Buhrmester, D. (1996). Need fulfillment, interpersonal competence, and the development contexts of early adolescent friendship. In W. M. Bukowski, A. F. Newcomb & W. W. Hartup (Eds.), *The company they keep: Friendship in childhood and adolescence* (pp. 158–185). Cambridge, UK: Cambridge University Press.

Cantillon, D. (2006). Community social organization, parents, and peers as mediators of perceived neighborhood block characteristics on delinquent and prosocial activities. *American Journal of Community Psychology, 37*, 111–127.

Crick, N. R. (1996). The role of overt aggression, relational aggression, and prosocial behavior in the prediction of children's future social adjustment. *Child Development, 67*, 2317–2327.

Crosnoe, R. (2001). Friendships in childhood and adolescence: The life course and new directions. *Social Psychology Quarterly, 63*, 377–391.

Dishion, T. J., & Andrews, D. W. (1995). Antisocial boys and their friends in early adolescence: Relationship characteristics, quality, and interactional process. *Child Development, 66*, 139–151.

Dishion, T. J., Eddy, J. M., Haas, E., Fuzhong L., & Spracklen, K. (1997). Friendships and violent behavior during adolescence, *Social Development, 6*, 207–223.

Dodge, K. A., & Murphy, R. R. (1984). The assessment of social competence in adolescents. *Advances in Child Behavior Analysis and Therapy, 3*, 61–96.

Dyer, S., & Moneta, G. B. (2006). Frequency of parallel, associative, and cooperative play in British children of different socioeconomic status. *Social Behavior and Personality: An International Journal, 34*(5), 587–592.

French, D. C. (2001). Social support of Indonesian and U. S. Children and adolescents by family members and friends. *Merrill-Palmer Quarterly, 47*, 377–394.

Furman, W. (1982). Children's friendships. In T. Field, G. Finley, A. Huston, H. Quay, & L. Troll (Eds.), *Review of human development* (pp. 327–342). New York: Wiley.

Furman, W. & Buhrmester, D. (1992). Age and sex differences in perceptions of networks in personal relationships. *Child Development, 63*, 103–115.

Furman, W. (1996). The measurement of friendship perceptions: Conceptual and methodological issues. In W. M. Bukowski, A. F. Newcomb, & W. W. Hartup (Eds.), *The company they keep: Friendship in childhood and adolescence* (pp. 41–65). New York: Cambridge University Press.

Gleason, T. R., & Hohmann, L. M. (2006). Concepts of real and imaginary friendships in early childhood. *Social Development, 15*(1), 128–144.

Goldstein, H., Kaczmarek, L. A., & English, K. M. (Eds.). (2001). *Developmental perspectives of social relationship development.* Baltimore: Paul H. Brookes.

Gottman, J. M., Katz, L. F., & Hooven, C. (1997). *Meta-emotion: How families communicate emotionally.* Mahwah, NJ: Erlbaum.

Jackson, M. I., & Mare, R. (2006). *Cross-sectional and longitudinal measurements of neighborhood experience and their effects on children.* Los Angeles, CA: University of California, California Center for Population Research, On-Line Working Paper Series. Retrieved October 19, 2006, from http://www.ccpr.ucla.edu/isarc28/Final%20Papers/Children's%20Neighborhoods-Jackson-Mare.pdf.

Kahen, V., Katz, L. F., & Gottman, J. M.. (1994). Linkages between parent–child interaction and conversations of friends. *Social Development, 3*, 238–254.

Matthews, W. S. (1981). Sex-role perception, portrayal, and preference in the fantasy play of young children. *Sex Roles, 7*, 979–987.

Parten, M. (1932). Social participation among preschool children. *Journal of Abnormal and Social Psychology, 27*, 242–269.

Pretti-Frontczak, K., & Bricker, D. D. (2004). *An activity-based approach to early intervention.* Baltimore: Paul H. Brookes.

Pretti-Frontczak, K., Brown, T., Senderak, A., & Walsh, J. (2005). A preliminary investigation of the effectiveness of Case quests in preparing family-guided and technologically-competent early childhood interventionists. *Journal of Computing in Teacher Education, 21*, 87–93.

Savage, A. M., & Nicholl, S. W. (2003). *Faith, hope, and charity as character traits in Adler's individual psychology.* Lanham, MD: University Press of America.

Scheier, L. M., Borvin, G. J., & Miller, N. L.(1999). Life events, neighborhood stress, psychosocial functioning, and alcohol use among urban minority youth. *Journal of Child and Adolescent Substance Abuse, 9,* 19–50.

Sebanc, A. M.. (2003). The friendship features of preschool children: Links with prosocial behavior and aggression. *Social Development, 12,* 249–268.

Seligman, L. (2006). *Theories of counseling and psychotherapy: Systems, strategies, and skills.* Upper Saddle River, NJ: Prentice Hall.

Spodek, B., & Saracho, O. N. (1994). *Right from the start: Teaching children ages three to eight.* Boston: Allyn & Bacon.

Stevahn, L., Johnson, D. W., Johnson, R. T., Oberle, K., & Wahl, L. (2000). Effects of conflict revolution training integrated into a kindergarten curriculum. *Child Development, 71,* 772–784.

Stormashak, E. A., & Welsh, J. A. (2005). Enhancing social competence. In D. M. Teti (Ed.), *Handbook of research methods in developmental science* (pp. 271–294). Malden, MA: Blackwell.

Sullivan, H. S. (1953). *The interpersonal theory of psychiatry.* New York: Norton.

Webster-Stratton, C. (1981). Videotape modeling: A method of parent education. *Journal of Clinical Child Psychology, 10,* 93–98.

Webster-Stratton, C. (1991). *Dinosaur social skills and problem solving training manual.* Unpublished manuscript. Seattle, Washington: University of Washington

Webster-Stratton, C. (2006). *The incredible years: A trouble-shooting guide for parents of children aged 2–8 years.* Seattle, Washington: Incredible Years. Materials available on http://www.incredibleyears.com/index.htm and http://www.incredible years.com/programs/teacher.htm.

Webster-Stratton, C., & Hammond, M. (1997). Treating children with early-onset conduct problems: A comparison of child and parent training interventions. *Journal of Consulting and Clinical Psychology, 65,* 93–109.

Webster-Stratton, C., Reid, M. J., & Hammond, M.. (2001). Preventing conduct problems, promoting social competence: A parent and teacher training partnership in Head Start. *Journal of Clinical Child Psychology, 30,* 283–302.

ABOUT THE CONTRIBUTORS

Doris Bergen received her Ph.D. from Michigan State University and has been Professor of Educational Psychology at Miami University, Oxford, Ohio, since 1989. Her research interests have focused on cross-cultural programs for young children, play and humor in early and middle childhood, effects of technology-enhanced toys, adult memories of childhood play, social interactions of children with special needs, effects of early phonological awareness levels on later reading, and gifted children's humor development. She has published seven books, over 40 refereed articles and 25 book chapters. In 2000, she was recognized as a Miami University Distinguished Scholar. She also received a national award as Outstanding Early Childhood Teacher Educator from the National Association of Early Childhood Teacher Educators, and was a National Academy of Science visiting scholar to China. She is co-director of Miami University's Center for Human Development, Learning, and Technology.

Virginia Buysse is a Senior Scientist at the FPG Child Development Institute and Research Associate Professor in the School of Education at the University of North Carolina at Chapel Hill. She has directed multiple federal grant projects focusing on early childhood/early childhood special education. She is Chair of the Research Committee of the Division for Early Childhood. In conjunction with Dr. Goldman, she has conducted a series of studies on friendships in inclusive early childhood settings. She is author of numerous chapters, articles and books, including a co-authored book on consultation in inclusive programs published by Paul H. Brookes and a forthcoming edited volume on the evidence-based practice movement in the early childhood field to be published by Zero To Three.

Gary Creasey is Professor of Psychology at Illinois State University. He received his Ph.D. from Virginia Commonwealth University. His research focuses on attachment and interpersonal relationships.

Contemporary Perspectives on Socialization and Social Development..., pages 317–321
Copyright © 2007 by Information Age Publishing
All rights of reproduction in any form reserved.

Mary Gauvain is a Professor of Psychology at the University of California at Riverside. She is currently an Associate Editor of the *Merrill-Palmer Quarterly* and on the Editorial Board of *Child Development.* She is the author of *The Social Context of Cognitive Development* and co-author of *Readings on the Development of Children* (with Michael Cole). Her research focuses on social and cultural contributions to the development of planning skills and spatial thinking and, most recently, on the ecology of children's everyday lives and how experience in the family and cultural community provide opportunities for the development of cognitive skills. She obtained her M.A. degree in Sociology of Education from Stanford University and her Ph.D. in Developmental Psychology from the University of Utah.

Moria Golan is director of Shahaf, community services for the management of eating disorders. She is a senior researcher and lecturer in the Hebrew University of Jerusalem. Dr. Golan integrates knowledge and skills from various areas: nutrition, family therapy, communication and counseling skills as well as group therapy. She has developed two novel clinical interventions: a unique approach for the prevention and treatment of childhood obesity, with the parents as the sole agents of change, and a unique community-based continuum of care with innovative outreach facilities. Dr. Golan has written numerous articles and chapter in the weight-related problems field, with particular emphasis on parents' role.

Barbara Davis Goldman is a Scientist at the FPG Child Development Institute, Research Associate Professor in the Department of Psychology, and Faculty Mentor for the Center for Developmental Science, all at the University of North Carolina at Chapel Hill. She had also served as the Chair of the Behavioral Institutional Review Board at UNC-Chapel Hill for the past five years. She is a developmental psychologist who conducts research on social and cognitive development in infants and young children with and without disabilities, focusing on early peer interaction and friendships, outcome assessment using standardized measures, alternative assessments of learning and memory, parent–child and teacher–child interaction. She also conducts research in ways to improve the informed consent process for research participants.

Carroll E. Izard is Trustees Distinguished Professor of Psychology at the University of Delaware. He has won the APA G. Stanley Hall award and is a fellow of AAAS, APA, and APS, and has been an NAS visiting fellow with the Russian Academy of Sciences. His research focuses on emotions, emotional development, and on the translation of emotion theory and research into preventive interventions. He is a graduate of Syracuse University.

Patricia Jarvis is Professor of Psychology at Illinois State University. She received her Ph.D. from Virginia Commonwealth University. Her research focuses on stress and coping processes in children and adults.

Eva Johansson is associate professor of education in the Department of Education, Childhood Studies, Göteborg University, Sweden. She is engaged in questions on moral learning in early childhood education, including studies on how children learn and develop morality and how teachers approach such issues in their work. Her research also includes studies on quality aspects in preschool as well as on the relation between play and learning. She has published several books and articles for instance: *Morality in Children's Worlds—Rationality of Thought or Values Emanating from Relations?* (2001), *Children's Integrity—A Marginalised Right* (2005), and *Children's Morality: Perspectives and Research* (2006).

Kurt Kowalski received his Ph.D. in early childhood education from Arizona State University where he studied child development and research methods. He is currently an associate professor in the Department of Educational Psychology and Counseling at California State University, San Bernardino. His research interests include the development of social identity and intergroup behavior in children, teacher beliefs and early education.

Gary W. Ladd is the Cowden Distinguished Professor of Family and Human Development at Arizona State University. Previously, he was a Professor at Purdue University and the University of Illinois at Urbana-Champaign, and a Fellow at the Center for Advanced Studies in the Behavioral Sciences at Stanford. Ladd was Associate Editor for the scientific journals *Child Development* and the *Journal of Social and Personal Relationships*, and currently is Editor of *Merrill-Palmer Quarterly*. He is Director of the Pathways Project, a long-term study of children from kindergarten through high school. Ladd has published books, empirical studies, theoretical articles, and reviews of research on children's social development, and is interested in how socialization experiences with peers, parents, and teachers influence children's early psychological and school adjustment.

Vickie E. Lake is an associate professor of early childhood education at The Florida State University. She earned her B.S. in Teachers of Young Children from Texas Tech University, M.Ed. in Elementary Education from Peabody College for Teachers at Vanderbilt University, and Ph.D. in Curriculum and Instruction from The University of Texas. As a former teacher, staff developer, and early childhood district coordinator, she has worked to further the efforts of social emotional learning for young children. Her primary areas of research interest are moral and character education, development of innovative approaches to the education of young children, and teacher education. She has authored nearly 20 articles on the connection of moral education to preservice teacher education, literacy, and learning environments, and has created several character education curricula.

Ole Fredrik Lillemyr, after completing teacher training, studied music and education and holds the degree of Magister Artium in Education (about eq. to a Ph.D.) He has taught at secondary school, at the university (all levels), and in preschool teacher training (mostly at master level). He was a visiting Professor at the University of Illinois 1980/81. He is Professor of Education at Queen Maud's University College in Trondheim, Norway (formerly Rector at QMUC). He has written and co-authored 12 books and several articles, book chapters, and research reports. Research interests are self-concept, student motivation, curriculum development, play, and sociocultural influences on learning.

Drew Nesdale completed his BA (Honours) at the University of New England (Australia) and MA and PhD at the University of Alberta (Canada). He then worked at the University of Manitoba (Canada) and then at the University of Western Australia. He is the Foundation Professor and Head of the School of Applied Psychology at Griffith University in Queensland (Australia). His main research interests are in intergroup prejudice and stereotypes, peer rejection, and aggression and bullying, in both children and adults.

Olivia N. Saracho is a professor of education in the Department of Curriculum and Instruction at the University of Maryland. Her areas of scholarship include family literacy, cognitive style, play, and teaching and teacher education in early childhood education. She is widely published in the field of early childhood education. Olivia N. Saracho is coeditor, with Bernard Spodek, of the *Handbook of Research on the Education of Young Children*, 2/ed. (2006, Erlbaum). They are also coeditors of the *Contemporary Perspectives in Early Childhood Education* series (Information Age).

Bernard Spodek is Professor Emeritus of Early Childhood Education at the University of Illinois at Urbana-Champaign where he has taught since 1965. He received his doctorate in early childhood education from Teachers College, Columbia University, then joined the faculty of the University of Wisconsin-Milwaukee. He has also taught nursery, kindergarten and elementary classes in New York City. His research and scholarly interests are in the areas of curriculum, teaching and teacher education in early childhood education. Dr. Spodek has lectured extensively in the United States, Australia, Canada, China, England, Greece, Hong Kong, Israel, Japan, Korea, Mexico, Portugal, and Taiwan. From 1976 to 1978 he was President of the National Association for the Education of Young Children, and from

1981 through 1983 he chaired the Early Education and Child Development Special Interest Group of the American Educational Research Association. Currently, he is president of the Pacific Early Childhood Educational Research Association (PECERA). He is widely published in the field of early childhood education.

Christopher J. Trentacosta is an advanced doctoral student in clinical psychology at the University of Delaware. His research interests include early emotional development, prevention and intervention during early childhood, and the relations among school-based mental health services, socioemotional competence, and academic outcomes. He is currently completing his clinical psychology internship at the University of Pittsburgh Medical Center.

Printed in the United States
88835LV00001B/63/A

9 781593 116330